A Practical Guide to Theoretical Frameworks for Social Science Research

This practical book offers a guide to finding, choosing, and applying theoretical frameworks to social sciences research and provides researchers with the scaffolding needed to reflect on their philosophical orientations and better situate their work in the existing landscape of empirical and theoretical knowledge.

Using a multifaceted approach, the book provides clear definitions, primary tenets, historical context, highlights of the challenges and contemporary discussion, and, perhaps more importantly, concrete and successful examples of studies that have drawn on and incorporated each theoretical framework. The authors define and explain the connections among such concepts as ontology, epistemology, paradigm, theory, theoretical frameworks, conceptual frameworks, and research methodology; describe the process of finding and effectively using theoretical and conceptual frameworks in research; and offer brief overviews of particular theories within the following disciplines: Sociology, psychology, education, leadership, public policy, political science, economics, organizational studies, and business. The book also has a dedicated chapter on critical theories, and for each theory, it provides a definition, explores how the theory is useful for researchers, discusses the background and foundations, outlines key terms and concepts, presents examples of theoretical applications, and gives an overview of strengths and limitations.

This book offers a useful starting point for any researcher interested in better situating their work in existing conceptual and theoretical knowledge, but it will be especially useful for graduate students and early career researchers who are looking for clear definitions of complex terms and concepts and for an introduction to useful theories across disciplines.

Dr. Andrea J. Bingham is an Associate Professor of Educational Leadership at California State University Channel Islands in Camarillo, CA, USA. She researches applications of qualitative methodologies, education policy, and school change.

Dr. Robert Mitchell is an Assistant Professor of Leadership, Research, and Foundations at the University of Colorado Colorado Springs, Colorado Springs, CO, USA. He continues to research and teach rural secondary education and education policy.

Daria S. Carter is a doctoral candidate at the University of Colorado Colorado Springs, Colorado Springs, CO, USA. She researches the effects of automation on the workforce with the goal of understanding employee value. She also works in operations at a Fortune 500 technology company.

A Practical Guide to Theoretical Frameworks for Social Science Research

Andrea J. Bingham, Robert Mitchell, and Daria S. Carter

Routledge
Taylor & Francis Group

LONDON AND NEW YORK

First published 2023
by Routledge
4 Park Square, Milton Park, Abingdon, Oxon, OX14 4RN

and by Routledge
605 Third Avenue, New York, NY 10158

Routledge is an imprint of the Taylor & Francis Group, an informa business

© 2023 Andrea J. Bingham, Robert Mitchell, and Daria S. Carter

Library of Congress Cataloging-in-Publication Data
Names: Bingham, Andrea J., author. | Mitchell, Robert (Professor of education), author. | Carter, Daria S., author.
Title: A practical guide to theoretical frameworks for social science research / Andrea J. Bingham, Robert Mitchell, Daria S. Carter.
Description: New York, NY : Routledge, 2023. | Includes bibliographical references and index. |
Identifiers: LCCN 2023041525 | ISBN 9781032199924 (paperback) | ISBN 9781032199894 (hardback) | ISBN 9781003261759 (ebook)
Subjects: LCSH: Social sciences--Research. | Social sciences--Methodology.
Classification: LCC H62 .B5246 2023 | DDC 300.72--dc23/eng/20230914
LC record available at https://lccn.loc.gov/2023041525

ISBN: 978-1-032-19989-4 (hbk)
ISBN: 978-1-032-19992-4 (pbk)
ISBN: 978-1-003-26175-9 (ebk)

DOI: 10.4324/9781003261759

Typeset in Optima
by MPS Limited, Dehradun

Dedication

Andrea J. Bingham
For all my students, present and past, who inspired this work, and for my parents, who gave me countless books so that one day I could write one.

Robert Mitchell
To all students and learners of all ages and types. We hope you find this resource useful.

Daria S. Carter
To my parents, Dave & Meri, who each in their own way taught me the value of an education, and Josh & Genevieve, who supported mine.

Contents

1   Introduction

Introduction

Several years ago, when I was in the midst of completing the coursework for my Ph.D., I experienced what nearly every graduate student dreads – the professor cold call. Our class had been reading up on theory and the use of theory in research. The brilliant, formidable, and often panic-inducing professor turned nonchalantly to me and asked, "So, how would you define theory, Andrea?" My face immediately turned red and I stammered out some long forgotten, and definitely functionally incorrect, answer. The professor simply responded with a thoughtful, but noncommittal, "Hmm."

Although we went on to discuss theory and related difficult concepts like theoretical and conceptual frameworks, I never felt like I obtained a full grasp on what theory was, how to use it, and how it was all related to the process of research. My general feeling of befuddlement didn't ease as we discussed even more complicated concepts, including ontology, axiology, epistemology, and paradigm, and it soon morphed into panic when those discussions turned to the more concrete tasks of developing positionality statements and finding and applying theoretical or conceptual frameworks to actual research. Of course, I eventually got a better handle on these concepts – but even after graduating, I still felt that I couldn't really explain what these concepts meant in simple enough terms.

Of course, being able to simply explain difficult concepts became imperative once I became a professor. It is much harder to hide behind esoteric language when trying to convey genuine understanding to students. And much like I had been, the students in my research methods courses were consistently perplexed by the complex terms that are bandied about so frequently in academia, and for which the explanations generally vary from convoluted to unintelligible. It doesn't help that some terms are often used interchangeably, like epistemology and paradigm, or theoretical, conceptual, and interpretive frameworks. It is from this confusion, which each author has experienced, that we conceived of this book. Our purpose in writing it is to:

1 Clearly define and explain the connections among such concepts as ontology, epistemology, paradigm, theory, theoretical frameworks, conceptual frameworks, and research methodology;
2 Describe the process of finding and effectively using theoretical and conceptual frameworks in research; and
3 Present a brief introduction to some of the more widely used theories, organized by discipline, in order to provide a starting point for researchers looking to better understand theoretical frameworks and use them more effectively in their work.

DOI: 10.4324/9781003261759-1

So why dig into these terms and concepts at all? The easiest answer is: "Because most, if not all, researchers will need to use a theoretical framework to complete their dissertation or to publish their work." That answer, while being technically correct, doesn't get into why those ideas are required at all. Why are they important? Should they be?

In a book on conducting qualitative research in educational settings, Hatch (2002) succinctly outlined why it is critical for researchers to examine the beliefs and philosophical orientations that guide our thinking and decision-making: "Starting with the research questions begins in the middle and ignores the fundamental necessity of taking a deep look at the belief systems that undergird our thinking" (Hatch, 2002, p. 12). In other words, there is work to be done even before developing the questions we wish to answer with our research. Examining our core beliefs about the world and our underlying philosophical orientations forces us to reflect on the knowledge we value and the methods we use to uncover and examine that knowledge. This helps us to make more informed, better-aligned choices in designing, implementing, and interpreting the results of our studies. Additionally, understanding and being able to situate our work in the existing landscape of empirical and theoretical knowledge positions our research to be more impactful and more trustworthy as a whole.

Reflecting on and critically examining our **ontology** – philosophical assumptions about the nature of existence and the structure of reality (Crotty, 1998), our **epistemology** – views about what knowledge is and how we know what we know (Crotty, 1998; Luker, 2008), and our **paradigm** – the belief system that guides how we do research (Alford, 1998; Guba, 1990), makes us better researchers. Our ontological beliefs, epistemological orientations, and paradigmatic assumptions are at the heart of what we choose to research, how we choose to research it, and why. By examining our own ontological, epistemological, and paradigmatic assumptions and orientations, we can critically reflect on the research questions we ask, the research methods we employ to answer those questions, and the lenses through which we understand and make sense of those answers.

These underlying core beliefs drive the theories and methods we gravitate toward in our research, as well as how we use those theories and methods to make sense of the findings of our research and make claims about what those findings mean in the larger context. **Theory** – a systematic set of concepts, categories, and relationships – can be used to provide an explanation for specific phenomena (Kezar, 2006; Tuhiwai Smith, 2016). The **theoretical framework** is the lens, developed from the theory or theories, through which we make sense of and disseminate the results or findings of a research study. As for why theory is important in research, when theory is in dialogue with data, we, as researchers, are inspired to "look at the world around us differently, to see our empirical projects as part of a rigorous and critical ongoing dialogue with others" (Dimitriadis, 2009, p. viii). When we use theory to guide our research, it becomes much easier to move between the abstract and the concrete (Marx, Engels, and Tucker, 1978, p. 38) – to allow the data to tell the world something larger about itself. In short, positioning our work within the larger landscape of knowledge and theory places it in the greater, ongoing conversation. This is what we hope this book will help researchers to do.

To start, in this chapter, we further explore philosophical foundations of research, including ontology, epistemology, research paradigm, and methodology. In Chapter 2, we build on the ideas outlined in this chapter to discuss finding useful theories and concepts, building a theoretical or conceptual framework, and using a framework to support your research design, make sense of your findings, and make a contribution. The remainder of the book is focused on introducing key theories within the following disciplines: sociology, psychology, education, leadership, public policy, political science, economics, organizational and management studies, and business. We also dedicate a chapter to critical theories. For each theory, we provide an overview and a definition, explore how the theory is useful for researchers, discuss the background and foundations, outline key terms and concepts, present examples of theoretical applications, and give an overview of strengths and limitations.

Philosophical Foundations of Research

Part of the reason the concepts we discuss in this book are so difficult is that different scholars define them in different ways, or at least use different terms to refer to the same concepts. Creswell and Poth (2018), for example, refer to ontological and epistemological orientations as "philosophical assumptions" and paradigms as "interpretive frameworks." Crotty (1998) discusses epistemologies as theories of knowledge, and refers to paradigms as theoretical perspectives. Crotty also notes that it is challenging to parse out the differences between ontology and epistemology as they relate to research, and many scholars do not make a clear distinction between the two. Some scholars use paradigm and epistemology to refer to the same general concept (Alford, 1998), while others discuss paradigm as encompassing ontological, epistemological, and methodological viewpoints (Denzin & Lincoln, 2005). Still others see ontology and epistemology as informing paradigm, which in turn informs methodological choices (Hatch, 2002). In this section, we'll briefly explore ontology, epistemology, and paradigm, as those concepts relate to research. Of course, we neither seek to undertake a comprehensive review of these philosophical concepts, nor do we claim that ours is the only, or even the best, way to use these terms. Rather, we aim to provide a general overview. To borrow from Crotty (1998), "this is scaffolding, not an edifice" (p. 2). We aim for the scaffolding provided in this chapter to supply the foundational knowledge needed to engage the rest of the concepts in this book effectively. We do not argue that our definitions are definitive, but we do want to clarify how we are using these terms and whose work we rely on to inform our definitions.

Ontology and Ontological Perspectives

We'll start with ontology as it is the philosophical umbrella under which the other concepts fall. Ontology is the study of the forms and nature of reality (Denzin & Lincoln, 2005; Lincoln & Guba, 1985). As it relates to research, ontology refers to the researcher's underlying philosophical assumptions about what reality is, and how we can come to understand it (Crotty, 1998). Many of the larger metaphysical or philosophical questions about the universe and the nature of being and reality are ontological questions (Hofweber, 2021). Ontological questions include "What does it mean to be?"; "What is the nature of reality?"; "What is true?"; What is real?"; and, perhaps most relevant to research, "Is there one reality or is reality context-bound?" (Denzin & Lincoln, 2005).

Ontological perspectives can generally fall along a continuum from the belief that there is an objective reality (realism) to the belief that reality is fully subjective (relativism) (Figure 1.1). Realism encompasses the belief that there are objective truths, and that reality exists outside of the mind (Crotty, 1998; Guba & Lincoln, 2005). Critical realism refers to the belief that there are objective truths and reality exists outside of the mind, but our understanding of reality will always be imperfect (Guba & Lincoln, 2005). Historical realism, also sometimes referred to as materialist-realism, recognizes the influence of

Ontological Perspectives			
Realism	**Critical Realism**	**Historical Realism**	**Relativism**
Reality exists outside of the mind and can be studied and understood	Reality exists both within and outside of the mind and can mostly be understood, but imperfectly	Reality exists both within and outside of the mind, but it is historically constructed	Multiple realities exist and are localized, and individually and socially constructed

Figure 1.1 Continuum of ontological perspectives. Definitions developed from Crotty (1998) and Guba and Lincoln (2005).

history, race, gender, and class on reality. Relativism assumes that there are multiple realities that are dependent on experience. In a relativist perspective, realities are localized, specific, and co-constructed (Guba & Lincoln, 2005).

A researcher's ontological orientation influences their epistemological orientation. The ontologies mentioned above generally align with how the epistemologies we cover in the next section are situated on a similar continuum.

Epistemology and Epistemological Perspectives

Generally, epistemology refers to our views on what knowledge is and how we come to know what we know (Crotty, 1998; Luker, 2008); in other words, our epistemological perspective is how we think about knowledge. *What* can be known? *How* do we know something? And what is the relationship between a person and knowledge? Your epistemology is the theory of how knowledge is created and discovered to which you ascribe. A researcher's epistemology provides the philosophical foundation for "deciding what kinds of knowledge are possible" and ensuring that the knowledge that is discovered is "adequate and legitimate" (Crotty, 1998, p. 8). Epistemological questions related to research include "What is it possible to know?" and "What is the relationship between research and knowledge?"

As with ontology, there are a variety of epistemologies. We have outlined three general epistemological viewpoints here because we see them as capturing most epistemological orientations, but other scholars parse these out to a greater degree (see Guba & Lincoln, 2005; Denzin & Lincoln, 2005; Heron & Reason, 1997). The epistemologies we discuss here mostly align with the ontologies discussed above, on a similar continuum. Objectivism, which aligns most closely with ontological realism, is the view that truth and knowledge exist independently of human consciousness. As an epistemological orientation in research, objectivism has been criticized as imperialist (Denzin & Lincoln, 2005) – a lens through which "the Other" is studied and categorized. Constructionism refers to the ontological perspective that some knowledge exists outside of the mind, but that meaning can only be made from the engagement between subject and object (Crotty, 1998). Key to a constructionist viewpoint is the emphasis on meaning and how it is constructed and reconstructed across groups and contexts. Finally, subjectivism holds

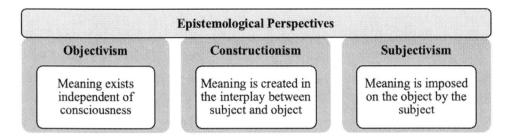

Figure 1.2 Continuum of epistemological perspectives. Definitions adapted from Crotty (1998).

that meaning is subjective; it is imposed on the object by the subject and different subjects can ascribe different meanings. All meaning is held within the mind and multiple meanings and interpretations are possible (Figure 1.2).

Epistemologies are informed by individuals' ontological assumptions and are embedded in and inform paradigms, which in turn influence theoretical and methodological choices.

Research Paradigms

All research – whether the researchers themselves acknowledge it or not – is built on a foundation of the researchers' beliefs, experiences, and underlying philosophical assumptions about the world and how we come to know and understand it – ontology and epistemology. This foundation becomes the researcher's paradigm – "the basic belief system or worldview that guides the investigator, not only in choices of methods, but in ontologically and epistemologically fundamental ways" (Guba & Lincoln, 1994, p. 105). This paradigm represents the researcher's general beliefs about the nature of the world, as well as their theoretical and methodological orientations. Paradigm thus encompasses "the operating rules about the appropriate relationship among theories, methods, and evidence … the combination of theoretical assumptions, methodological procedures, and standards of evidence that are taken for granted in particular works" (Alford, 1998, p. 2). We build our definition of paradigm on Guba and Lincoln's (1994) definition and use the word "paradigm" to refer to these philosophical orientations that researchers bring to their work and through which they define the nature of the world and their relationship to it (Denzin & Lincoln, 2005; Guba & Lincoln, 1994). Ultimately, paradigm is informed by ontological and epistemological orientations, and it drives research choices including theories, questions, methodology, and methods.

The concept of research paradigm was put forth by Kuhn (1970) in *The Structure of Scientific Revolutions*. Kuhn defined paradigm as "the entire constellation of beliefs, values, techniques, and so on shared by the members of a given community" (p. 175). Paradigm can be referred to as a meta-theory (Kezar, 2006), but we find it clearer to differentiate between paradigm and theory as applied to research, so we do not use the term meta-theory at all. As we discuss it, paradigm includes deeper underlying philosophical orientations, while theory reflects accumulated knowledge on a particular subject.

Different scholars refer to different paradigms by many names, encompassing many definitions. We'll outline a few here, but the way we have labeled and categorized paradigms is by no means definitive or comprehensive. Like ontologies and epistemologies,

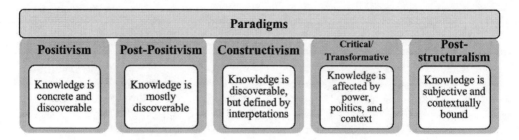

Figure 1.3 Continuum of paradigms. Definitions developed from Crotty (1998).

paradigms can be arranged on a continuum that demonstrates the variation in how people think about knowledge and the process of research (see Figure 1.3).

First, a positivist paradigm holds that science should be objective; there is a concrete reality that can be studied, and universal laws and theories can be developed and applied. A positivist paradigm relies on the idea that objective truth and knowledge can be determined from direct observation through the scientific method (Crotty, 1998). Generally, a positivist paradigm is associated with realist ontology and objectivist epistemological orientations as well as deductive reasoning and statistical analyses. Post-positivism is built on positivist assumptions, but with some caveats and expansions. In a post-positivist paradigm, there is some recognition that objectivity is not always fully possible; however, post-positivists believe that researchers can and should minimize subjectivity through rigorous, prescribed research methodologies and methods. Post-positivism holds that knowledge is mostly discoverable, but truth is not absolute and not everything can be known. As such, post-positivism is more aligned with critical realist ontology and constructionist epistemology.

Further along the continuum, a constructivist paradigm assumes that knowledge and truth exist but are defined by our interpretations. Experience and environment play a role. Meaning is made through our engagement with the world and is not simply waiting to be discovered. In a constructivist paradigm, the meaning-making process is of primary interest (Guba & Lincoln, 2005). A constructivist paradigm can be situated in a critical realist ontology and in a constructionist epistemology. A critical/transformative paradigm is constructivist in that meaning is created from the interactions between people and the world around them; however, the critical/transformative paradigm incorporates the idea that knowledge is influenced by power, politics, and context, including race, gender, and class. This paradigm also assumes that research is meant to be transformative. A critical/transformative paradigm would be situated within a historical realist or relativist ontological perspective and a constructionist or subjectivist epistemology. Finally, in a post-structuralist paradigm, knowledge is fully subjective and context bound. Post-structuralism is a difficult concept because, by its own definition, it can't be defined. The best way we have seen post-structuralism explained is that it is an "antiparadigm" because its tenets can be used to deconstruct all of the other paradigms (Hatch, 2002, p. 17). A post-structural paradigm aligns best with relativist ontology and subjectivist epistemology.

One thing we'd like to draw attention to is how thinking on these concepts has evolved. We do not subscribe to the idea that ontological and epistemological viewpoints, and thus paradigms, are fixed and linear. Rather, we see paradigms as heuristics (Maxwell, 2012). In general, a paradigm is the belief system that guides our actions. It is the researcher's orientation to knowledge generation that is based on and guided by experiences, facts, assumptions, and practices (Burkholder & Burbank, 2019). It is reasonable to conclude then that as experiences, facts, assumptions, and practices are accumulated, constructed, and reconstructed, the belief system that is built upon those things could shift as well. Our paradigms create a holistic view of how we view knowledge, how we see ourselves in relation to this knowledge, and the methodological strategies we use to discover it. As such, your research paradigm is built on the foundation of your ontological and epistemological beliefs as well as your lived experience.

How Is This All Related?

As discussed, ontological viewpoints inform epistemologies and form the basis for paradigm. Figure 1.4 shows the general orientation of ontologies, epistemologies, and paradigms along a continuum that ranges from most "objective" or independent of human consciousness to most "subjective" or dependent on human interpretation.

Where researchers situate themselves on this continuum ontologically and epistemologically, and thus paradigmatically, informs their research interests, methodological choices, and interpretation of findings. An example of this is shown in Figure 1.5.

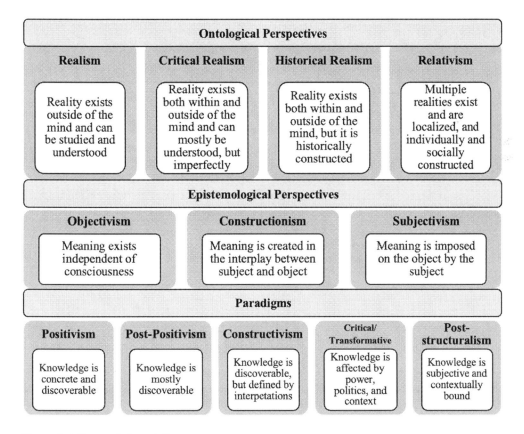

Figure 1.4 Research foundations.

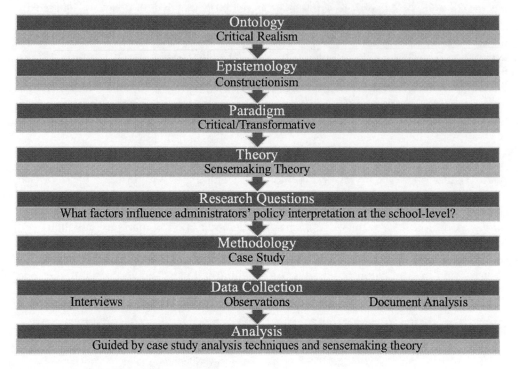

Figure 1.5 Example research flowchart.

Researcher Positionality and Identity

Because of the indelible impact that ontological, epistemological, and paradigmatic viewpoints have on researchers' work, it is critical for researchers to be aware of and to reflect on their own worldviews. Of course, researchers don't always discuss their ontological, epistemological, or paradigmatic assumptions in their research reports. Indeed, this is often the first thing to get cut from a manuscript when a researcher is faced with word/page limits. Regardless of whether it makes it into the actual write-up, reflecting on your underlying beliefs strengthens your research by promoting awareness of potential biases, and supporting better alignment between your research questions, frameworks, and methods. Much like analytic memos that qualitative researchers create during data analysis, written reflections on your philosophical orientations can help shape your decision-making throughout the study and can help you flesh out your understanding of the findings, contributions, and limitations of your work.

In planning a study, it's useful to ask yourself a series of guiding questions, related to your ontological, epistemological, and paradigmatic orientations:

1 What are my beliefs about reality? Do I think it's possible to be objective? How might this influence my research decisions?
2 How is knowledge acquired? What is the best method for understanding our world? Why do I think that is? How might this influence my research decisions?
3 How do I see issues of history, power, and position as affecting knowledge and understanding? How might this influence my research decisions?

4 What kinds of research methodologies and methods do I gravitate toward? Why might that be? How might this influence my research decisions?

A researcher's answers to the above questions can help them better understand their beliefs about the world and be more critical of their approach to their research. Further, this reflection process can help researchers critically examine their relationship to knowledge, to their research interests and study purpose, and to their participants – their **positionality**. Here is an example of a positionality statement in which the researcher discusses their paradigmatic orientation to the research:

> The proposed research is based upon a constructionist epistemological stance. According to Crotty (1998), constructionism holds that truth and meaning are created through social engagement with the world. As Crotty (1998) further explains, "Meaning is not discovered, but constructed" (p. 9); people construct knowledge and make meaning in different ways, even with regard to the same phenomenon. The interaction between subject, or participant, and object, or phenomenon, is what creates meaning. The notion that knowledge is socially constructed and meaning arises from interaction frames the present study and guides my inquiry.
>
> Paradigmatically, and in keeping with constructionism, the current study is guided by symbolic interactionism, which assumes that meaning arises out of social interaction and out of the interaction between subject and object, and that people act according to the meaning they have made from their encounters (Blumer, 1969). These paradigmatic assumptions undergird the application of my chosen methodology: qualitative case study research. In this study, how the participants make sense of and meaning from their interactions is the basis for a qualitative understanding of each participant's reality. As such, I aim for a dialectical engagement with research participants.

The above statement discusses the researcher's basic worldview and emphasizes how this worldview influences the study design decisions that the researcher made. In this example, the discussion focuses on philosophical assumptions about the world, but, of course, positionality statements should also examine the researchers' specific relationship to the study's purpose and context as well. We also advocate for researchers to ask themselves some guiding questions around their relationship to their specific research topic and study:

1 What is my relationship to my research? How might my (informed/uninformed/anecdotal) assumptions impact the research process?
2 How could my prior experiences shape my study design?
3 How could my prior knowledge and experiences shape my understanding of the study context?
4 How could my prior knowledge and experiences shape my interactions with my participants?
5 How do my individual traits (e.g., personality) and identities (e.g., ethnicity, sexuality, religion) influence my interpretations of participant interactions?
6 How could my prior knowledge and experiences shape what I observe in the setting?

The following positionality statement, from this book's first author, is the result of memoing in response to these guiding questions:

> Before I became a professor, I taught high school English to students who were demographically similar to those at [the school under study]. As a result, any time I entered the school, I felt comfortable. There were benefits to this feeling of comfort. Building rapport with teachers, students, and staff came naturally. My connection to and understanding of the world of teaching opened doors and sparked conversations. Being a credentialed teacher allowed me to participate in daily activities rather than simply observe them. I rarely felt like an outsider. However, there were negative aspects to this as well. I struggled with "the invisibility of everyday life" each time I was at the school site (Erickson, 1986, p. 121). The goings-on at the school were reminiscent of what used to be my everyday life, which could have caused me to overlook valuable data about the school and my participants. As such, I always aimed to enter the field and record my impressions as if it were my first day there. I consistently memoed, looking for how the setting was organized, how the participants interacted, and how the happenings in the classroom were related to other actors and environments within the school. I also included a section in my observation protocol for reflections on how my presence affected participants, and aspects of my observations that may have been influenced by my identity as a former teacher. (Bingham, 2021, p. 14)

This positionality statement outlines the benefits and potential pitfalls of the researchers' prior relationship with and understanding of the study context, and how they dealt with these issues.

Finally, we recommend that researchers take racial and cultural considerations into account in conducting their research and reflecting on their positionality. When researchers don't "see color or culture" or if they do not acknowledge that race matters in their research work, they may ignore discriminatory systemic, institutional, or organizational practices or may misrepresent minoritized and/or marginalized populations (Milner, 2007, p. 365). So, it's important for researchers to pose and reflect on racially and culturally grounded questions about themselves, their participants, and their research, which can make them more aware of both known and unanticipated issues, perspectives, and positions. To support researchers in acknowledging and reflecting on racial and cultural influences in research, we like the framework of researcher positionality presented by Milner (2007) because it outlines clear stages and guiding questions, and it emphasizes that this reflective work should be happening throughout the research cycle. These stages include Researching the Self, Researching the Self in Relation to Others, Engaged Reflection and Representation, and Shifting from Self to System. We've added "Reciprocity" to Milner's framework to emphasize the importance of the reciprocal relationship between researchers and communities, even for scholar-practitioners who are part of those communities. See Figure 1.6 for the guiding questions from Milner's framework, with some additional reflective questions around reciprocity.

This reflective work is important for all researchers. The racial and cultural considerations are especially critical when the researcher does not share racial and/or cultural identities with participants.

Researching the Self
• What is my racial and cultural heritage? How do I know?
• In what ways do my racial and cultural backgrounds influence how I experience the world, what I emphasize in my research, and how I evaluate and interpret others and their experiences? How do I know?
• How do I negotiate and balance my racial and cultural selves in society and in my research? How do I know?
• What do I believe about race and culture in society and education, and how do I attend to my own convictions and beliefs about race and culture in my research? Why? How do I know?
• What is the historical landscape of my racial and cultural identity and heritage? How do I know?
• What are and have been the contextual nuances and realities that help shape my racial and cultural ways of knowing, both past and present? How do I know?
• What racialized and cultural experiences have shaped my research decisions, practices, approaches, epistemologies, and agendas?

Researching the Self in Relation to Others
• What are the cultural and racial heritages and the historical landscape of the participants in the study? How do I know?
• In what ways do my research participants' racial and cultural backgrounds influence how they experience the world? How do I know?
• What do my participants believe about race and culture in society and education, and how do they and I attend to the tensions inherent in my and their convictions and beliefs about race and culture in the research process? Why? How do I know?
• How do I negotiate and balance my own interests and research agendas with those of my research participants, which may be inconsistent with or diverge from mine? How do I know?
• What are and have been some social, political, historical, and contextual nuances and realities that have shaped my research participants' racial and cultural ways or systems of knowing, both past and present? How consistent and inconsistent are these realities with mine? How do I know?

Engaged Reflection and Representation
• What is my interpretation of what is happening in the context?
• What are the participants' interpretations?
• Where do these interpretations align? Where do they diverge? Why might that be?

Shifting from Self to System
• What is the contextual nature of race, racism, and culture in this study? In other words, what do race, racism, and culture mean in the community under study and in the broader community? How do I know?
• What is known socially, institutionally, and historically about the community and people under study? In other words, what does the research literature reveal about the community and people under study? And in particular, what do people from the indigenous racial and cultural group write about the community and people under study? Why? How do I know?
• What systemic and organizational barriers and structures shape the community and people's experiences, locally and more broadly? How do I know?

Reciprocity
• What are we taking from communities?
• How are we giving back?
• What do the people in the research context want to know? What is important to them? How does this align with our own agendas as researchers?
• How can we strengthen our partnership?
• How can we provide sustainability in our interactions?

Figure 1.6 Expanded framework of researcher positionality. Adapted from Milner (2007).

How to Use This Book

In the next chapter, we discuss theories, theoretical frameworks, and conceptual frameworks and examine how these concepts connect with philosophical orientation and methodological choices. In the remainder of the book, we present a variety of theories that could be used in research across disciplines. There are myriad ways we could have organized the theories in this book. We could have categorized theories by level focus (individual, organizational, groups, and social) or by theoretical level (grand, meta, middle). However, we have chosen to organize the theories in this book into the disciplines with which they are most closely aligned, in order to support researchers in identifying theories in their own disciplines, as well as to encourage interdisciplinary work. Many of these frameworks can be used across disciplines, and indeed, may be associated with multiple disciplines.

Obviously, no book could include all the various theories used in research around the world. In light of this limitation, painstaking decisions about what to include were common and we are certain that many questions about why one theory was included, and one was excluded will present themselves. To get the best use out of this book, consider it a general guidepost that can lead you toward a theory that is included in this book, or help you find new directions toward something different. There are thousands of different directions your research can take you, and exploring the various linkages to an appropriate theory is a considerable component of the knowledge-building and research process.

References

Alford, R. R. (1998). *The craft of inquiry*. Oxford University Press.

Bingham, A. J. (2021). How distributed leadership facilitates technology integration: A case study of "pilot teachers". *Teachers College Record, 123*(7), 1–34.

Blumer, H. (1969). *Symbolic interactionism: Perspective and method*. Prentice Hall.

Blumer, H. (1986). *Symbolic interactionism: Perspective and method*. University of California Press.

Burkholder, G.J., & Burbank, P.M. (2019). Philosophical foundations and the role of theory in research. In G.J. Burkholder, K.A. Cox, L.M. Crawford, & J.H. Hitchcock (Eds.), *Research design and methods: An Applied guide for the scholar-practitioner*. Sage.

Creswell, J.W., & Poth, C.N. (2018). *Qualitative inquiry and research design: Choosing among five approaches*. Sage.

Crotty, M. (1998). *The foundations of social research: Meaning and perspective in the research process*. Sage.

Denzin, N. K., & Lincoln, Y. S. (2005). Introduction: The discipline and practice of qualitative research. In N. K. Denzin & Y. S. Lincoln (Eds.), *The Sage handbook of qualitative research* (3rd ed., pp. 1–32). Sage.

Dimitriades, G. (2009). Series editor introduction. In J. Anyon (Ed.), *Theory and educational research: Toward critical social explanation* (pp. vii–ix). Routledge.

Erickson, F. (1986). Qualitative methods in research on teaching. In M. Wittrock (Ed.), *Handbook of research on teaching* (pp. 119–161). AERA.

Guba, E.G. (Ed.). (1990). *The paradigm dialog*. Sage Publications.

Guba, E. G., & Lincoln, Y. S. (2005). Paradigmatic controversies. Contradictions, and emerging confluences. In N. K. Denzin & Y. S. Lincoln (Eds.), *The Sage handbook of qualitative research* (3rd ed., pp. 191–215). Sage Publications.

Hatch, J. A. (2002). *Doing qualitative research in education settings*. SUNY Press.

Heron, J., & Reason, P. (1997). A participatory inquiry paradigm. *Qualitative Inquiry, 3*(3), 274–294.

Hofweber, T. (2021). Logic and ontology. In *The Stanford encyclopedia of philosophy*. Retrieved from https://plato.stanford.edu/Archives/Win2012/Entries/logic-ontology/

Kezar, A. (2006). To use or not to use theory: Is that the question? In J. C. Smart (Ed.), *Higher education* (Vol. 21, pp. 283–344). Kluwer Academic Publishers. 10.1007/1-4020-4512-3_6

Kuhn, T. (1970). *The structure of scientific revolutions*. University of Chicago Press.

Lincoln, Y. S., & Guba, E. G. (1985). *Naturalistic inquiry*. Sage.

Luker, K. (2008). *Salsa dancing into the social sciences: Research in an age of info-glut*. Harvard University Press.

Marx, K., Engels, F., & Tucker, R. C. (1978). *The Marx-Engels reader*. New York: Norton.

Maxwell, J. A. (2012). *Qualitative research design: An interactive approach*. Sage.

Milner, H. R. (2007). Race, culture, and researcher positionality: Working through dangers seen, unseen, and unforeseen. *Educational Researcher, 36*(7), 388–400. 10.3102/0013189X07309471

Tuhiwai Smith, L. (2016). *Decolonizing methodologies: Research and indigenous peoples*. Bloomsbury.

2 Understanding and Applying Theoretical and Conceptual Frameworks

Introduction

Just as researchers should reflect on and situate their work in their own underlying philosophical beliefs about the world, they should also use existing knowledge to lay the foundation for and frame their research. This, of course, involves not only a solid grounding in the existing literature, but also an understanding of existing theory. Using theoretical and/or conceptual frameworks can facilitate this work. In this chapter, we explore extant understandings of theory, including what it is, how it works, and how it can be used in research, as well as some of the arguments against theory. After, we explain what a theoretical framework is, as well as the components of a conceptual framework and how it differs from a theoretical framework. We also offer some advice on how to find useful theories and concepts, how to build theoretical and conceptual frameworks, and how to apply frameworks in your research to design and conduct rigorous, trustworthy research.

What Is Theory?

Theory is a critical aspect of academic work, yet it also seems to be one of the most widely misunderstood concepts in research (Kezar, 2006). Merton (1967), for example, argues that "because its referents are so diverse – including everything from minor working hypotheses, through comprehensive but vague and unordered speculations, to axiomatic systems of thought – use of the word often obscures rather than creates understanding" (Merton, 1967, p. 39); in other words, theory as a word and a concept sometimes verges on meaningless. Many scholars over the years have tackled the formidable task of defining theory e.g., (Kezar, 2006; Sutton & Staw, 1995). We do not seek to add a new definition here, but to provide a quick overview of what others have explained, in an effort to offer a general definition of theory as we use it in this book.

Theory involves "constructing abstract interpretations that can be used to explain a wide variety of empirical situations" (Giddens & Griffiths, 2006, p. 9). Developed from rigorous empirical and conceptual work, theory organizes sets of ideas to explain something of interest (Collins & Stockton, 2018). Sutton and Staw (1995) explain that although references, data, lists of variables or constructs, diagrams and figures, and hypotheses or predictions may be important aspects of studies, none of these constitute theory. Rather, theory is the answer to the question "why?" A strong theory offers explanations, connections among phenomena and events, a clear story about why specific acts happen, and is temporally based.

DOI: 10.4324/9781003261759-2

The goal of theory is to "ascend (from both the particular and the abstract) to the concrete" (Marx et al., 1978, p. 38). Theory offers a way to concretize and apply ideas generated from both deductive and inductive processes. In this way, theory can be used to understand or predict events and to make informed assumptions and predictions about the world (Tuhiwai Smith, 2016). It also enables researchers to "deal with contradictions and uncertainties ... [and] gives us space to plan, to strategize, and to take greater control over our resistances. The language of theory can also be used as a way of organizing and determining action" (p. 40). For a theory to be useful in these ways, it should be grounded in existing literature and in the observed phenomena.

There are several levels of theory. Be warned – this can get confusing, as the different levels of theory can refer to other concepts as well, which leads to scholars using the word theory to refer to concepts like epistemology or paradigm, while also using it to refer to specific literature-based frameworks that they are using in their work (Kezar, 2006). Metatheories, for example, refer to a paradigm as we defined it in Chapter 1. Grand theories refer to a "unifying theory that helps us understand a vast area of study" (p. 6). Critical Theory or Feminist Theory, for example, would be grand theories that serve as theoretical umbrellas for a variety of related theories. Grand theories can be and are applied without regard to context. Middle-level theories offer links between grand theories and everyday events, which can allow for more applied theoretical work. Low-level theories are more highly contextualized and derived from analyses of specific phenomena and contexts. Both middle- and low-level theories tend to be more relevant to practitioners.

Similarly, Anfara and Mertz (2014) organize theories into levels aligned with what the theory is concerned with: individual, organizational, group, and social. Individual-level theories are concerned with individual learning, development, behavior, and interactions. Organizational theories are focused on organizations and institutions, including effectiveness, structure, and function. Group theories are concerned with group dynamics, including familial interactions, teams, and networks. Social theories are focused on group behavior, culture, societal development, and markets.

Although theory is established through careful empirical and conceptual work, it can (and should) be revised as new knowledge is generated. It is critical for researchers engaging in theoretically informed work to ask "how much of the empirical realm can it [the theory] handle and how must it be modified and changed as it matures?" (Mills, 1999). This is a key aspect of using theory, understanding theory, and of building theory – a task for which scholars in many disciplines consistently advocate.

Drawing on the existing definitions of theory outlined above, we define "theory" here as a systematic set of concepts, categories, and relationships, developed from empirical and conceptual work, that can be used to provide an explanation for a variety of phenomena (Giddens & Griffiths, 2006; Kezar, 2006; Tuhiwai Smith, 2016). Our definition aligns more with middle- or low-level theories, though we will also discuss grand theories. Theory, as we define it here, can be used to develop the theoretical or conceptual framework for your study.

Theoretical Frameworks

A question that often comes up in graduate level research methods courses is around the difference between a theory and a theoretical framework. As with many of the other terms we've outlined here, theory and theoretical framework are often used interchangeably, though we argue they should not be. As we will use it throughout this book, the theoretical framework is a systematic model of a theory or theories used to study a specific phenomenon (Kezar, 2006, p. 290). The key word in this definition is *systematic*. The theoretical framework should contain an explicit description of theoretical assumptions based on the theory. Additionally, the theoretical framework should consist of the selected theory (or theories) that undergird your thinking with regard to how you understand and plan to research your topic, as well as the concepts and definitions from that theory that are relevant to your topic.

A theoretical framework can be built from one or more theories. For example, I (this book's first author) used a theoretical framework comprised of cultural historical activity theory (CHAT) (see Chapter 6: Education Theories) and sensemaking theory (see Chapter 11: Organizational Theories) in my dissertation study, by integrating some of the core concepts from sensemaking into the CHAT framework. Throughout the course of the study, I drew on CHAT to help me understand cultural-historical context, and how the interactions among components of the organization I was studying drove change. I used sensemaking theory to focus in on how individuals in the study understood those organizational components and on how that understanding shifted based on contradictions that emerged within and among the components of the organization. I utilized the CHAT concept of contradiction to identify underlying causes of challenges and to examine the process of organizational change. I also applied sensemaking concepts such as schema, assimilation, and accommodation to understand how people made sense of those contradictions. See Figure 2.1 for an example of this theoretical framework integrating two theories.

Theoretical frameworks have explanatory properties that support the applicability, transferability, and/or generalizability of the research. The theoretical framework provides "a structure that guides research by relying on a formal theory … constructed by using an established, coherent explanation of certain phenomena and relationships" (Eisenhardt, 1991, p. 205). They can be constructed from a theory or from multiple theories and they

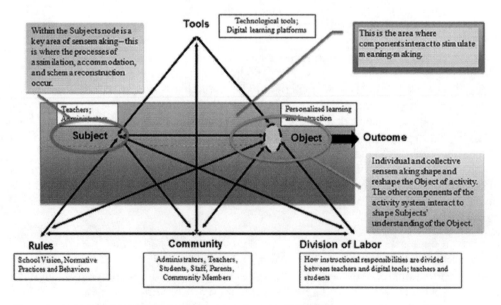

Figure 2.1 Example integrated theoretical framework. Adapted from Bingham (2017b).

exhibit the following properties: (1) they are used to predict action through if-then logic models; (2) they account for variation across contexts; (3) they provide explanations for how and why something might happen in a cause-and-effect model; and (4) they can provide insight and support for recommendations for improvement (Collins & Stockton, 2018; Saldaña & Omasta, 2018, p. 257). Your theoretical framework forms the basis for developing ways to investigate phenomena, as well as for analyzing and understanding that phenomena in the context of the observations and situated in the existing knowledge base (Sutton & Staw, 1995). Ultimately, you can think of a theoretical framework as a set of ideas that guides action, analysis, and interpretation.

Conceptual Frameworks

Although some scholars use theoretical and conceptual frameworks interchangeably, we align ourselves with those who differentiate between theoretical and conceptual frameworks. Conceptual frameworks can be maps that lay out the connections in the literature that apply to a particular study (Collins & Stockton, 2018). Conceptual frameworks can also function as a way to present "the key factors, constructs, or variables" in a study alongside the presumed relationships among them (Miles & Huberman, 1994, p. 440). We define conceptual frameworks here as a web of interconnected concepts that provide a comprehensive understanding of specific phenomena. The interconnected concepts, factors, constructs, and/or variables included in a conceptual framework can be pulled from any existing literature or theories that have informed the work. The conceptual framework can also incorporate the new knowledge generated from the research itself. Maxwell (2012) might have captured it best in sub-titling his chapter on conceptual frameworks as "What Do You Think is Going On?" Indeed, "what you think is going on" captures the essence of what a conceptual framework is – a written or visual depiction of the components of what you're studying and how those components are related (Maxwell, 2012; Miles et al., 2019).

A conceptual framework can integrate paradigm, theory, and existing literature and can also incorporate the findings of the analysis. In developing a conceptual framework, you can incorporate any or all of the following: paradigmatic assumptions, existing theory, and/or themes, findings, and concepts from the existing literature. Conceptual frameworks can also be developed from the findings of your own study and then connected to the existing knowledge base as well to form a framework that encapsulates the existing understanding of the phenomena and how the findings of your study fit within the existing knowledge base.

Often, conceptual frameworks result in visuals, including diagrams and concept maps. Maxwell (2012) explains that concepts maps can be developed as: (1) Abstract frameworks mapping relationships among concepts; (2) A flowchart-like account of events and how you think these are connected; (3) A causal network of variables or influences; (4) A treelike diagram of the meanings of words; or (5) A Venn diagram, representing concepts as overlapping circles. Much like other aspects of a qualitative study, the conceptual framework can be considered emergent. What we mean by that is the framework and any associated figures or visuals may help guide your study but may then be updated and modified as your findings emerge.

Take, for example, the following conceptual framework from Bingham and Burch (2017). This framework was based on Weber's (1978) theory of social action, which identifies four forms of social action: instrumental-rational (bureaucratic, efficiency-based);

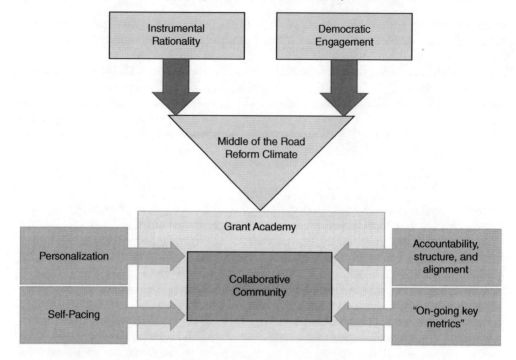

Figure 2.2 Example of conceptual framework (Bingham & Burch, 2017).

traditionalistic (clan-like, based on strong trust and loyalty); affectual (charismatic, committed to a particular leader or group of individuals); and value rational (commitment to shared end-value). However, Bingham and Burch also integrated related concepts in the literature, including the idea of democratic engagement in policy design and decision making. Within the framework, democratic engagement was defined as processes and democratic values (not necessarily end results), and emphasized democratic and localized forms of decision making (Stone, 2011), as well as existing explanatory frameworks concerned with different types of community and how they respond to reforms (Adler et al., 2015). Additionally, they drew on the findings of their study – personalization; self-pacing; accountability, structure, and alignment; and "ongoing key metrics" – to outline how theoretical and conceptual factors interacted in the study's specific context (Grant Academy) (see Figure 2.2).

An important note to remember – a conceptual framework can be considered a theoretical framework, but a theoretical framework is not always a conceptual framework because of the myriad other components that can be included in a conceptual framework.

Why Use a Framework?

Often, students feel like the answer to "why use a theoretical or conceptual framework?" is "because my advisor/professor told me to." Similarly, more established researchers might answer, "because the peer-reviewers told me to." In reality, there are many reasons to use a theoretical or conceptual framework to guide your research. As Anderson and colleagues note, "I don't see how you can do a good piece of work that's atheoretical" (Anderson et al., 2006, p. 154). Indeed, a framework helps to make your study stronger, more rigorous, and ultimately increases the generalizability or transferability of your findings. First, when you state your operating theoretical and conceptual assumptions up front, this allows you to justify your decisions and provides context for the reader to evaluate your reasoning. Second, it situates your work clearly in the existing knowledge base, providing a foundation and justification for your study. Third, using a framework supports moving from the concrete back to the abstract – from describing what's happening in your observations of the phenomenon to explaining what is happening in the phenomenon more generally. Consistent and thoughtful use of a framework also supports moving from the abstract to the concrete – a theory can provide general explanations for the hows and whys of specific events, experiences, and/or phenomena, but your observations may expand on that story and contribute to additional theoretical conceptions. Finally, theory helps predict and explain, which can support the development of clear implications and recommendations.

Finding Useful Theories and Concepts

A major reason that we wrote this book is because finding theories to use in your work – and especially finding the *right* theory – is a common and significant challenge for researchers at every level. There are four major issues to consider in finding and selecting a framework: awareness, appropriateness, usefulness, and applicability.

First, researchers have to actually be aware that a theory or framework exists. This is more difficult than it sounds. There are probably thousands of theories used in research. Certainly, there are hundreds used across the social sciences. It would be extraordinarily difficult for researchers to be aware of and knowledgeable about them all. As a result, researchers are generally most aware of and biased toward theories that are used in the discipline in which they were trained because those are often the theories they see the most in readings or hear about in classes. However, there may often be theories that are more useful or appropriate for your study outside of your discipline. Our aim in this book is to present a variety of theories across disciplines to give researchers a place to begin. However, this only scratches the surface of possible theories in the research universe. So, while our recommendation is that this book is a good place to start, there are also other strategies to find theories and concepts that are most appropriate for your particular research work.

Our first recommendation is to pay attention to and make note of what theories and frameworks are being used when you read/review literature in your area of interest. Keeping an annotated bibliography of theories or tagging particular articles for theoretical frameworks in your chosen reference software can help you keep track of potential theories. Another strategy is to identify foundational or grand theories in your discipline and/or in other relevant disciplines and explore theories and frameworks that are related to any foundational theories that might be useful in your research. As an example, in sociology, there are several grand theories, under which many related theories fall. Structural functionalism, for example, is a grand theory used to understand how societies function. It explains that societies work through the long-term interdependence of social institutions, including education, law, and government (Hier, 2005). Structural functionalism forms the basis for many other sociological theories, including Institutional Theory (see Chapter 4). If you are interested in and conducting a study which concerns societal structures, how societies work, or how societal structures influence individuals or organizations, a theory related to or under the umbrella of structural functionalism might be useful in your work.

It can also be helpful to explore theories and frameworks that take a particular disciplinary lens related to the perspective you're taking in your research. For example, if you are an education researcher, and are interested in individual student learning or behavior, psychology as a discipline might be a good place to start because many psychological theories are focused on individual understanding and behavior (see Chapter 5). If, on the other hand, you are interested in the organizational aspects of education, including how schools as organizations adopt reforms or policies, you might want to examine key theories in organizational and management studies (see Chapter 11). Or, if your interest lies in social and group dynamics and behavior, you might turn to sociology. The key point is that you should look beyond the scholarship on your particular topic or in your particular discipline to identify frameworks that may better support your study.

Researchers should also consider whether a theory is appropriate and whether or not it's useful for their topic and research goals. The theory a researcher chooses to frame their work should address a primary concern of their research (Davis, 2008; Davis, 1986). Effective social theories address concerns that are seen as "'imperative', 'crucial', or 'key' to understanding something that a particular audience holds near and dear," and are "… so pervasive that in order to be successful at all, a theory will simply have to address it" (Davis, 1986, p. 287).

Further, an appropriate theory for your work should be aligned with the topic and level of your analysis. If you are interested in the effectiveness, structure, and function of an organization or set of organizations, and your analysis is occurring at the organizational level, then an organizational theory may be appropriate, but a theory focused on child development would probably not be. Maybe it should go without saying, but any theories you choose must also be useful for your research topic and specific context. To gauge the appropriateness and the usefulness of the theory, ask yourself the following questions:

1 How might this theory be useful in my research?
2 How, if at all, might it better support my understanding of my topic?
3 How, if at all, could it help me design my study?
4 Is this theory aligned with the level of analysis in my study?

It's possible that the answer to these questions might be "sort of," or "mostly." In that case, it might be best to consider drawing on the most useful aspects of the theory, or combining multiple theories into an integrated theoretical framework to engage aspects of each that are most useful for your research.

The final consideration for researchers searching for theories to use in their research is applicability. The critical questions here are:

1 Can this theory support me in conducting applicable research?
2 Will this theory help to situate my work in the existing landscape of knowledge?
3 Can this theory provide the scaffolding necessary to identify the implications of my work and make clear recommendations for practice, policy, and/or future research?

Ultimately, it's important to think about theories and frameworks not as right or wrong, but as useful or not useful for understanding and communicating your research. Frameworks are tools to think with – sometimes they can provide insights, sometimes not. Aim to identify a framework that can help you design your study as well as provide further insight into your analysis and findings.

Applying Theoretical and Conceptual Frameworks

As we've explained, frameworks can be helpful in designing and conducting your study, and in analyzing and reporting the findings of your work. A common issue that we see not only in student work, but also in published research, is the tendency to introduce a theory or framework in the beginning and then never mention it again. Don't do this. The theoretical or conceptual framework should inform not only your methodological decisions and research methods, but also your analysis and your interpretation of findings. The framework you introduce should guide your study throughout, including data collection, protocol design, analysis procedures, and interpretation of findings, and this should be addressed and explained explicitly in the text.

Any framework you use should be a critical aspect of your study design, including data collection procedures and protocol design. Establishing a clear link between your research questions, theoretical framework, and methodology (including data collection and analysis) supports a more rigorous, trustworthy study. Think through this as you plan, and as you conduct your research. See Figure 2.3 for an example of how research questions, theory, and data collection can be aligned.

Research Questions	Aligned Theoretical Concepts	Data Collection (Protocols, Observation Points, Documents)
1. What, if any, are the systemic contradictions that develop around technology-mediated personalization? 2. How do teachers respond to contradictions? How, if at all, do teachers' existing schemas influence how they respond to tensions and contradictions in the system?	CHAT: Activity system CHAT: Tensions and contradictions CHAT: Mediating artifacts CHAT: Expansive learning cycle Sensemaking: Schemas, influence on understanding and response to contradictions	Interview Questions: • What challenges, if any, do you experience in teaching at [SCHOOL]? • How do you respond to those challenges? *Give an example.* • How has your practice changed since last semester? • When you first came to [SCHOOL], I'm sure you had some expectations for what your role would be and what your classroom would be like. How does your experience now compare with those expectations? Observations: • Look for dilemmas, conflicts, critical conflicts, double binds in classrooms, staff meetings, and PDs. Documents: • Comparing strategic plans, charter documents, and other school planning documents over time.

Figure 2.3 Theoretically informed study design.

In the study referenced in Figure 2.3, cultural historical activity theory (CHAT) and sensemaking theory were used to develop the language of the research questions and to create the interview questions, identify points of observation, and identify relevant documents. For example, schemas – individuals' existing knowledge structures, based on their beliefs and experiences (Weick et al., 2005) – a key component of sensemaking, informed the development of the research question: "How, if at all, do teachers' existing schemas influence how they respond to tensions and contradictions in the system?" This then informed the associated interview questions focused on schema, including: "When you first came to [SCHOOL], I'm sure you had some expectations for what your role would be and what your classroom would be like. How does your experience now compare with those expectations?" This particular interview question helped to establish expectations, which is a key aspect of a person's schema that allows them to make predictions about the world, anticipate future events, and interpret information that may be ambiguous or unclear.

The framework should also inform data analysis procedures. Deductive analysis practices, in particular, can help researchers to apply theoretical or conceptual frameworks (Bingham, 2017a; Bingham & Witkowsky, 2022). In a qualitative study, for example, this process generally comes after some inductive analysis of data to identify themes, but you could draw on these strategies at any point in the analysis process. One way the theoretical framework can support the data analysis process is through the development of theory-based codes for the analysis process. By this, we mean creating codes based on the components of the theoretical framework, and then sorting data into those predetermined theory-based categories. Theory-based codes from institutional theory (see Chapter 4), for example, might include "Isomorphism" or "Decoupling." By sorting the data into theoretical categories during analysis, the researcher can get a sense of how the data and the findings fit within the concepts of the theoretical framework, which provides the foundation for a theoretically informed analysis and a robust discussion of the findings (Bingham & Witkowsky, 2022). If there is data that does not fit within concepts of the theoretical framing, then there may be additional theoretical contributions to be made. This is an opportunity for the researcher to connect the findings to the theoretical framing, and to draw on the explanatory properties of the framework to make recommendations. See Figure 2.4 for an example of how theory codes may be applied and used to generate explanations for findings.

The teacher explains that this is how she can see who is doing well and who needs help in real time. [Theory Code: Assimilation] Once the warm-up is over, the teacher says, "Level 6, get your tables together" Some students then leave and others stay, while others come in. "Who is reading?" Students raise their hands. "Who is grading?" Other students raise their hands.

Finding: Real Time Data Analysis Encourages Ability Grouping [Theory Code: Assimilation]

[Theory-Based Explanation of Findings: Teachers made sense of the demands of real time data analysis through a process of assimilation. Rather than reconstructing their existing beliefs about teaching, they used new practices - real time data analysis and data transparency - to facilitate old practices - ability grouping.]

Figure 2.4 Theory-informed data analysis.

The example in this figure is from a study of how teachers use technology to personalize students' learning. The theoretical framework in this study is sensemaking theory. In this example, the theoretical framework has been used to analyze the data, and to provide a theoretically informed explanation for the findings that emerged from the data.

In reporting the findings of a study, the theoretical and/or conceptual framework can help researchers situate their findings in the existing knowledge, as well as provide the foundation necessary to make empirically and theoretically grounded contributions. Much of this work is traditionally done in the discussion and/or implications sections of the research report. The theoretical framework should be applied in the discussion section, and you should discuss how your findings fit with your selected theory, how they diverge from it, and whether the theory was adequate in interpreting your findings. This can also be a place to make theoretical contributions. Here, we've outlined several guiding questions that can support researchers in applying their frameworks to their findings in order to flesh out the larger contributions of their work as well as identify implications and make clear recommendations.

First, there are several guiding questions associated with situating your work in the existing literature, as it may be represented in your conceptual framework:

1 What does my study contribute to the existing body of knowledge?
2 How do my findings support what is found in the existing literature? Where do my findings converge with what we already know?
3 Where do my findings diverge from the existing literature? Why might that be?
4 Based on what my study demonstrated, is there anything that should be added to the existing conceptual framework? How do my findings alter the framework?

Second, a discussion section should also situate the findings in the existing theory and apply your theoretical framework. The following guiding questions can help with that:

1 How do my findings fit within my theoretical framework?
2 Are there any places where my findings do not fit? What does that mean? Why might that be?
3 What, if any, are my theoretical contributions? Based on what my study demonstrated, is there anything that should be added to the existing theoretical framework? How do my findings alter the framework?

Don't be afraid to propose your own theory or modifications to existing theory based on your findings. Indeed, in some methodologies (e.g., grounded theory), this would be expected.

Finally, applying your framework should also support making clear recommendations and should help you explain why your research is important, why people should care about it, and what it all means in the larger context. Recommendations are important! Think in terms of what your study means for research, policy, and practice and be specific – what exactly should be done based on the results of your research, and in relation to the frameworks you've applied?

Here are some associated guiding questions for that analytic work:

1 What should future researchers on this topic study? How should they study it?
2 How, if at all, should existing policy change because of the findings of the study?

3 Should new policy be created? What should it look like?
4 Should existing policy be revised? How?
5 Based on the findings, what should policymakers do?
6 What are some recommendations for practice/practitioners in this area of study?
7 What changes to practice should be made? How should these changes be made? By whom?
8 What questions remain to be answered?

Ultimately, you shouldn't use theory uncritically. In other words, you have to use theory in a way that makes your research more impactful. Further, you must be open to evidence that doesn't fit your chosen framework and be willing to critically examine how and why that might be. This may then result in the addition of other theories, or in an expansion of the existing theory. Think of a theoretical framework as a set of ideas that guides action, analysis, and interpretation, not as a set of hard and fast rules.

Considerations in Using Theoretical and Conceptual Frameworks

There are several considerations for using theory, identifying and building frameworks, and applying them to your research, especially related to equity, diversity, inclusion, and access. First, it's important to remember that, historically, theory has been used as a form of oppression (Smith, 1999) – a way to categorize, generalize about, and denigrate marginalized populations. If theory is applied uncritically, and without any of the reflective work that needs to be done to conduct research that is racially and culturally sensitive and considered (see Chapter 1), theory can be harmful. Researchers, not data, tell the stories of their research and that story is aligned with the researchers' views of the world, including their paradigmatic orientations and their choice of theory and method. If we, as researchers, "begin with a racially biased view of the world, then we will end with a racially biased view of what the data has to say" (Zuberi & Bonilla-Silva, 2008, p. 7). Researchers must commit to the reflective and analytic work needed to confront our own biases and to use theory in a way that helps address and dismantle oppression, not uphold it.

Conclusion

The remainder of this book serves as starting place for getting a sense of existing theories across disciplines. Our hope is that researchers reading this book may find useful theories for their studies, and that they also may find helpful jumping off points for finding additional theories and frameworks that can help them produce more rigorous, trustworthy, applicable research.

References

Adler, P. S., Heckscher, C., McCarthy, J. E., & Rubinstein, S. A. (2015). The mutations of professional responsibility: Toward collaborative community. In D. E. Mitchel & R. K. Ream (Eds.), *Professional responsibility* (pp. 309–326). Springer International Publishing.
Anderson, C., Day, K., & McLaughlin, P. (2006). Mastering the dissertation: Lecturers' representations of the purposes and processes of Master's level dissertation supervision. *Studies in Higher Education, 31*(2), 149–168.
Anfara, V. A., & Mertz, N. T. (2014). *Theoretical frameworks in qualitative research*. Sage Publications, Inc.

Bingham, A. J. (2017a). Personalized learning in high technology charter schools. *Journal of Educational Change, 18*(4), 521–549. https://doi.org/10.1007/s10833-017-9305-0

Bingham, A. J. (2017b). CHAT and sensemaking: An inclusive frame of analysis for investigating educational change. Paper presented in a featured session at the annual meeting of the American Educational Research Association (AERA).

Bingham, A. J. (2023). From data management to actionable findings: A five-phase process of qualitative data analysis. *International Journal of Qualitative Methods, 22*, 1–11. 10.1177/16094069231183620

Bingham, A. J., & Burch, P. (2017). Navigating middle of the road reforms through collaborative community. *Democracy & Education, 25*(2), 10.

Bingham, A. J., & Witkowsky, P. (2022). Deductive and inductive approaches to qualitative data analysis. In C. Vanover, P. Mihas & J. Saldaña (Eds.), *Analyzing and interpreting qualitative research* (pp. 133–148). Sage.

Collins, C. S., & Stockton, C. M. (2018). The central role of theory in qualitative research. *International Journal of Qualitative Methods, 17*(1), 160940691879747. 10.1177/1609406918797475

Davis, K. (2008). Intersectionality as buzzword: A sociology of science perspective on what makes a feminist theory successful. *Feminist Theory, 9*(1), 67–85.

Davis, M. S. (1971). "That's interesting!" Towards a phenomenology of sociology and a sociology of phenomenology. *Philosophy of the Social Sciences, 1*, 309–344.

Davis, M. S. (1986). "That's classic!" The phenomenology and rhetoric of successful social theories. *Philosophy of the Social Sciences, 16*, 285–301.

Eisenhardt, K. M. (1991). Better stories and better constructs: The case for rigor and comparative logic. *Academy of Management Review, 16*(3), 620–627.

Giddens, A., & Griffiths, S. (2006). *Sociology*. Polity.

Hier, S. P. (Ed.). (2005). *Contemporary sociological thought: Themes and theories*. Canadian Scholars' Press.

Kezar, A. (2006). To use or not to use theory: Is that the question? In J. C. Smart (Ed.), *Higher education* (Vol. 21, pp. 283–344). Kluwer Academic Publishers. 10.1007/1-4020-4512-3_6

Marx, K., Engels, F., & Tucker, R. C. (1978). *The Marx-engels reader*. Norton.

Maxwell, J. A. (2012). *Qualitative research design: An interactive approach*. Sage Publications, Inc.

Merton, R.K. (1967). *On theoretical sociology*. Free Press.

Miles, M.B. & Huberman, A.M. (1994). *Qualitative data analysis: An expanded sourcebook*. Sage.

Miles, M. B., Huberman, A. M., & Saldaña, J. (2019). *Qualitative data analysis: A methods sourcebook* (4th ed.). Sage Publications, Inc.

Mills, J. (1999). Improving the 1957 version of dissonance theory. In E. Harmon-Jones & J. Mills (Eds.). *Cognitive dissonance: Progress on a pivotal theory in social psychology*. APA.

Saldaña, J., & Omasta, M. (2018). *Qualitative research: Analyzing life*. Sage Publications, Inc.

Smith, L. (1999). *Decolonizing methodologies: Research on indigenous people*. Dunedin, New Zealand: University of Otago Press.

Stone, D. A. (2011). *Policy paradox: The art of political decision making*. Norton.

Sutton, R. I., & Staw, B. M. (1995). What theory is not. *Administrative Science Quarterly, 40*(3), 371. 10.2307/2393788

Tuhiwai Smith, L. (2016). *Decolonizing methodologies: Research and indigenous peoples*. Bloomsbury.

Weber, M. (1978). *Economy and society: An outline of interpretive sociology*. University of California Press.

Weick, K. E., Sutcliffe, K. M., & Obstfeld, D. (2005). Organizing and the process of sensemaking. *Organization Science, 16*(4), 409–421.

Zuberi, T., & Bonilla-Silva, E. (Eds.). (2008). *White logic, white methods: Racism and methodology*. Rowman & Littlefield Publishers.

3 Critical Theories

Critical Race Theory

Definition and Overview

Critical Race Theory (CRT) is a theoretical perspective positing that race and racism are an inherent and permanent aspect of US society (Bell, 1992). CRT focuses on the interplay of race, power, and law (DeCuir & Dixson, 2004) and CRT scholars across disciplines argue that race should be at the center of any analysis; consequently, CRT foregrounds race and racism in the research process (Solórzano & Yosso, 2002). Central to critical race theory is the idea that "Whiteness" is privileged in the US and that White people's interests and perspectives are dominant (Gillborn, 2015; McIntosh, 2008; Slakoff & Brennan, 2019).

CRT assumes that race is socially constructed, and racial differences are created, maintained, and continually strengthened by society (Gillborn, 2015). Further, racism is:

> complex, subtle, and flexible; it manifests differently in different contexts, and minoritized groups are subject to a range of different (and changing) stereotypes … the majority of racism remains hidden beneath a veneer of normality and it is only the more crude and obvious forms of racism that are seen as problematic by most people.
> (Gillborn, 2015, p. 278)

Racism is thus a taken-for-granted aspect of society – an "ingrained feature of our landscape, it looks ordinary and natural to persons in the culture" (Delgado & Stafancic, 2000, p. xvi). CRT scholarship argues that more formalized approaches, including rules, laws, and policies, can address the more overt forms of inequality and injustice; however, these approaches "can do little about the business-as-usual forms of racism that people of color confront every day" including microaggressions and other more subtle forms of racism (Delgado & Stafancic, 2000, p. xvi).

There are several basic tenets to CRT (DeCuir & Dixson, 2004; Delgado & Stafancic, 2023; Ladson-Billings, 1999; Solórzano, 1997). First, CRT contends that racism is an inherent and permanent part of US society, and this racism is reflected in, and perpetuated by, its laws and its distribution of power (Bell, 1992). Racism is the norm in society, not an anomaly, and because racism is so ingrained in the structures of society, it is difficult to recognize and eradicate (Delgado, 1995). Racism shows up in laws, policies, institutions, and in interpersonal interactions and relations in many forms, including microaggressions – subtle, often unconscious degradations that people of color frequently experience (Solórzano et al., 2000). CRT also holds that race is socially constructed, and that racial categories are

DOI: 10.4324/9781003261759-3

created by societies, and manipulated or set aside when those categories are no longer convenient (Delgado & Stafancic, 2023)

Another important tenet of CRT is interest convergence – the idea that any civil rights gains for people of color have come about because they primarily benefited White people (Bell, 1980). Interest convergence, also sometimes called material determinism, assumes that because White people benefit from racism, there is little incentive to stamp it out (Delgado & Stefancic, 2023). As such, many civil rights gains have only been made because the interests of White people converged with those of people of color. For example, Bell (1980) contended that the decision to desegregate schools did not come from a desire to integrate, improve educational experiences for Black students, and/or adhere to the tenets of the 14th amendment; rather, the goal of desegregation aligned with other goals, like economic and political advances, the improvement of US standing abroad, and further industrialization in the South.

CRT scholars also criticize the three basic components of liberalism: colorblindness, the neutrality of the law, and incremental change (DeCuir & Dixson, 2004). Colorblindness hides the ordinariness of racism and makes it difficult to address because its existence in everyday society is not acknowledged (Delgado & Stefancic, 2023). Additionally, incremental change only allows for change that is "palatable for those in power" and thus furthers the notion of interest convergence (DeCuir & Dixson, 2004, p. 29). Though these aspects of liberalism may appear to support racial equity, the inherent racism that exists in US society makes neutrality impossible.

Another critical aspect of CRT is the emphasis on storytelling as a method of examining the reproduction of social structure and the enmeshment of racism in the American social fabric (Delgado, 1995). CRT emphasizes the centrality of experiential knowledge, and the importance of counternarratives, which can allow for vivid, affective retellings of the experiential knowledge of racism (Delgado, 1995; Yosso et al., 2009). The narratives of dominant groups have long formed the basis of our understanding of societal issues, laws, policies, and reforms, and educational institutions (Cook & Dixson, 2013). As such, the conception of a shared reality presented within these dominant narratives reinforces hegemonic organizational and institutional practices. Collective knowledge is created and maintained in these narratives, thus shaping the general understanding of the experience. Counterstories, or counternarratives, can thus challenge the dominant narratives, and offer an understanding of how marginalized groups may experience the same phenomena in differential ways.

As a theoretical framework, CRT pushed researchers to center race in their work and can help researchers attend to and critically examine issues of race as they arise throughout the analysis (Parker, 1998). Further, it can support researchers in critically interrogating their own methods, particularly around centering the stories of people of color (Delgado, 1995; Yosso et al., 2009) and recognizing the potential for bias and deficit perspectives in quantitative analyses (Gillborn et al., 2018). CRT also offers researchers the vocabulary for discussing and studying racism.

Background and Foundations

CRT is rooted in ideas dating back to W.E.B. DuBois (1903). As a theoretical perspective, CRT emerged in the 1970s, in response to stalled civil rights advances (Delgado & Stefancic, 2001; Taylor et al., 2023). CRT began as part of a movement by legal activists and scholars who were interested in how race, racism, power, and the rule of law intersect (Delgado & Stefancic, 2001). CRT is concerned with many of the same issues discussed in the civil rights or ethnic studies discourse but situates these issues in a broader context.

CRT is built on ideas from radical feminism and Critical Legal Studies (CLS) (Delgado & Stefancic, 2000), and comes from a long line of resistance to racial inequality and injustice (Taylor et al., 2023). In 1978, Freeman critiqued Critical Legal Studies scholarship, explaining that neutrality of law does not exist and that the existing view of race and racism in CLS was rooted in the perspective of the perpetrators of racial oppression, rather than the victims of racial oppression (Brown and Jackson, 2013). Emerging from dissatisfaction with CLS, CRT argued that the emphasis on incrementalism and the reliance on existing legal paradigms to support racial equality was misguided and didn't account for the fact that addressing racism requires sweeping changes (Ladson-Billings, 2023).

Professor Derrick Bell, one of the founders of CRT and the first tenured Black professor at Harvard Law School, developed the idea of interest convergence, which contends that the achievement of "racial equality will be accommodated only when it converges with the interests of whites … remedies, if granted, will secure, advance, or at least not harm societal interests deemed important by middle- and upper-class whites" (Bell, 1980, p. 523). Interest convergence is rooted in the Marxist theoretical assumption that the proletariat is only allowed advances if the bourgeoisie receives even greater benefits from those advances (Taylor, 2023). Interest convergence became a foundational tenet of CRT.

As CRT has developed, intersectionality, which assumes that individuals belong to multiple identity groups, and these identities influence their experiences in intersecting ways, has become a critical component (Crenshaw, 1989). More recently, CRT frameworks have also included the idea of differential racialization as well. Differential racialization refers to the ways in which the dominant group in society racializes minority groups differently at different times to favor one group over another as conditions change (Delgado & Stefancic, 2023, p. 9). Stereotypes, media portrayals, or popular images of marginalized groups may change over time.

In the years since the development of CRT, several other iterations of CRT have emerged as complementary theories that focus more on specific marginalized populations. These other forms of CRT include Asian Critical Race Theory (AsianCrit) (Iftikar & Museus, 2018; Museus & Iftikar, 2013), Disability Critical Race Theory (DisCrit) (Love & Beneke, 2021), Latino Critical Race Theory (LatCrit) (Iglesias, 1997; Solózano & Yosso, 2001), and Tribal Critical Race Theory (TribalCrit) (Brayboy, 2006).

In recent years, CRT has become a flashpoint for manufactured outrage in the US, due to misrepresentation of its concepts in politics and media (Taylor et al., 2023). Indeed, by the end of 2021, 28 US states had passed legislation aiming to ban CRT, in part due to its opponents' fear that CRT classifies all White people as oppressors and all Black people as victims (Ray & Gibbons, 2021). However, CRT as it is actually conceived of and applied by scholars, is, as Taylor et al. (2023) note, "a far cry from the ridiculous, yet dangerous fantasy versions that have been peddled by rightwing think tanks, media outlets, and politicians internationally" (p. i). Rather, CRT offers a framework for critically examining structural racism.

Key Terms and Concepts

Interest Convergence states that progress against racism and oppression only happens when it serves the interests of the dominant group (Bell, 1980).

Microaggressions are "subtle insults (verbal, nonverbal, and/or visual) directed toward people of color, often automatically or unconsciously" (Solórzano et al., 2000, p. 60). They are frequently "subtle, innocuous, preconscious, or unconscious degradations, and putdowns, often kinetic but capable of being verbal and/or kinetic" (Pierce, 1995, p. 281). There are several types of microaggressions, including *microassaults*, which are intentional and explicit verbal or nonverbal attacks; *microinsults*, which are subtle digs at a person's background or racial identity; and *microinvalidations*, which are dismissive remarks about the experiences and histories of people of color (Sue et al., 2007, p. 274; Yosso et al., 2009, p. 662). Microaggressions can include personal microaggressions, institutional microaggressions, and/ or racist jokes (Yosso et al., 2009). Microaggressions have a cumulative impact and have many deleterious mental, physical, and emotional effects for people of color (Pierce, 1995).

Racial realism is the idea that race is a permanent, integral, immutable part of American society (Brown & Jackson, 2013).

Whiteness refers to "a set of assumptions, beliefs, and practices that place the interests and perspectives of White people at the center of what is considered normal and everyday" (Gillborn, 2015, p. 278).

White supremacy, in a CRT framework, refers to "subtle and extensive forces that saturate the everyday mundane actions and policies that shape the world in the interests of White people" (Gillborn, 2015, p. 278). As Taylor (2023) explains, "White supremacy is the background against which other systems are defined" and is itself a political system, which is so omnipresent that even its beneficiaries may not recognize it (p. 5).

In Research

CRT has been used across disciplines including political science, healthcare, women's studies, American studies, ethnic studies, education, and sociology (Delgado & Stefancic, 2001).

One of the disciplines in which CRT has been used most extensively in recent years is education. For years, education researchers argued that race was undertheorized in education (Ladson-Billings & Tate, 1995; Ledesma & Calderón, 2015; Taylor, 2023). In their systematic review of the use of CRT in education, Ledesma and Calderón (2015) found that CRT has been used in K-12 education to explore curriculum and pedagogy, teaching and learning, schooling, and policy/finance and community engagement, as well as in higher education to explore colorblindness, selective admissions policy, and campus racial climate (p. 207). As an example of CRT's application in education, Crowley (2013) used the CRT concepts of interest convergence, the critique of liberalism, and historical revisionism to examine how curriculum is influenced by White supremacy, finding that certain pieces of legislation, like the Voting Rights Act of 1965, are not historically contextualized in curriculum. In another study in education, Anyon et al. (2018), used CRT to investigate racial disparities in school discipline, arguing that "colorblind" disciplinary practices and policies play a role in disciplinary disparities.

CRT has also been used in healthcare to explore health experiences and outcomes for people of color. For example, Adebayo et al. (2022) used a CRT lens to better understand how African American women's maternal healthcare experiences intersected with and were shaped by racial injustice. In this study, Adebayo and colleagues used CRT to uncover racially discriminatory practices and instances of racism that are present in everyday healthcare interactions.

The interdisciplinary nature of CRT makes it a useful framework for exploring a variety of research questions across disciplines.

Strengths and Limitations

As noted above, one of CRT's key strengths is in its interdisciplinarity. Another strength of CRT is in its capacity to support social justice-oriented research and participatory methods. CRT is rooted in activism and promotes a commitment to disrupting the status quo. As Ladson-Billings (1999) noted, "the strategy of those who fight for social justice is one of unmasking and exposing racism in its various permutations" (p. 213). CRT can provide the tools to do so. Further, CRT is committed to intersectionality, recognizing that "oppression and racism are not unidirectional, but rather that oppression and racism can be experienced within and across divergent intersectional planes, such as classism, sexism, ableism, and so on" (Ledesma & Calderón, 2015, p. 207). Finally, CRT provides a lens and a vocabulary through which racism and racist injuries can be examined and named, "victims of racism can find their voice [and] … those injured by racism can discover that they are not alone in their marginality" (Solózano et al., 2000, p. 64).

Although it's not a limitation of the theory so much as a limitation of how it has sometimes been applied, it's also important to note that scholars of CRT have pointed to research that has included CRT as a theoretical lens simply because the participants are people of color or that has included CRT in the introduction of a study, but never revisited it as results are discussed (Lynn & Dixson, 2013).

Key Theorists: Derrick Bell (Originating author); Kimberlé Crenshaw; Richard Delgado; Alan Freeman; Gloria Ladson-Billings; Charles Lawrence; Daniel Solózano

Examples of Use in Research: Adebayo et al. (2022); Anyon et al. (2018); Crowley (2013); Dixon (2018); Yosso et al. (2009)

Intersectionality Theory

Definition and Overview

Intersectionality theory posits that individuals' identities intersect and interact to shape the multiple dimensions of experience (Crenshaw, 1989, 1991). As a theoretical framework, intersectionality highlights how multiple social identities – including sex, gender identity, race, ethnicity, class, and sexual orientation – interact at the individual level of experience to contribute to systems of oppression and privilege (Bowleg, 2012; Crenshaw, 1989, 1995). By acknowledging the existence of multiple intersecting identities, intersectionality offers a framework for understanding the experiential complexities of people who are members of multiple oppressed groups, as well as how multiple systems of privilege and oppression intersect (Bowleg, 2012).

Intersectionality addresses a fundamental concern in social science research; namely, that there are differences in individuals' experiences, which are associated with and dependent on their identities. Specifically, in feminist scholarship, intersectionality addresses longstanding issues of exclusion (Davis, 2008). Intersectionality, like critical race theory and other critical theories, holds that acknowledging experiential differences can be a source of empowerment and justice, not a source of domination (Crenshaw, 1991). An intersectional lens also addresses the larger ideological structures through which subjects, problems, and solutions are framed (Cho et al., 2013, p. 791).

There are three key dimensions of theorizing that define intersectionality in sociological theory, including the inclusion of perspectives from people who are "multiply-marginalized," particularly women of color; "an analytic shift from addition of multiple independent strands of inequality toward a multiplication and thus transformation of their main effects into interactions; and a focus on seeing multiple institutions as overlapping in their co-determination of inequalities" (Choo & Ferree, 2010, p. 131). Research drawing on intersectionality as a theoretical perspective can thus emphasize the perspectives of marginalized people, problematize the relational dynamics of power, and understand inequality as the result of intersecting identities and institutions (Choo & Ferree, 2010).

Intersectionality is a useful theoretical framework for understanding the multiple dimensions of identity and experience. An intersectionality perspective can help researchers to investigate how social inequities are created and sustained (Gillborn, 2015). Ultimately, intersectionality provides a lens through which to understand how forms of oppression and subordination are connected and pushes researchers to, as Matsuda (1991) puts it, "ask the other question:"

> The way I try to understand the interconnection of all forms of subordination is through a method I call 'ask the other question.' When I see something that looks racist, I ask, 'Where is the patriarchy in this?' When I see something that looks sexist, I ask, 'Where is the heterosexism in this?' When I see something that looks homophobic, I ask, 'Where are the class interests in this?' (Matsuda, 1991, p. 1189).

This process of "asking the other question" supports researchers in better understanding the dynamic interrelationships among institutional structures, oppression, and the influence of multiple, overlapping identities.

Background and Foundations

Intersectionality was developed in the late 1980s "as a heuristic term to focus attention on the vexed dynamics of difference and the solidarities of sameness in the context of anti-discrimination and social movement politics" (Cho, Crenshaw, McCall, 2013, p. 787). Intersectionality was introduced as a critique to "single-axis thinking" that undermined legal thinking, disciplinary knowledge, and the struggle for social justice (p. 787).

The term intersectionality has its foundations in Black feminist scholarship and activism and was coined by legal scholar and law professor Kimberlé Crenshaw (1989). The concept of intersectionality emerged from Crenshaw's observation that research, law, policy, and politics frequently overlook or conflate differences within groups (Crenshaw, 1991). As Crenshaw (1991) noted,

> Although racism and sexism readily intersect in the lives of real people, they seldom do in feminist and antiracist practices. And so, when the practices expound identity as woman or person of color as an either/or proposition, they relegate the identity of women to a location that resists telling. (p. 1243)

Crenshaw (1989) argued that anti-discrimination law, feminist theory, and anti-racist politics tended to focus on the experiences of the most privileged members in oppressed groups. Intersectionality was developed specifically in reaction to "the exclusion of Black women from White feminist discourse (which equated women with White) and antiracist discourse (which equated Black with men)" (Bowleg, 2012, p. 1268). Crenshaw's work (1989) examined where race and gender intersect.

Crenshaw explored the concept of intersectionality in her research on Black women's experiences with domestic violence (Crenshaw, 1991), finding that the women in the study suffered the consequences of class-based and gender-based oppression, like poverty and lack of reliable childcare, and that these consequences were compounded by racial discrimination in housing and employment. Through this study, Crenshaw argued that any interventions to address the problems faced by women who were victims of domestic violence must account for the fact that women face different race- and class-based obstacles as well. The use of an intersectional analytic framework helps to "give voice to the particularity of the perspectives and needs of women of color who often remained invisible *as women* even when they were organizing ... and invisible *as blacks* despite their significant leadership in the American civil rights movement" (Choo & Feree, 2010).

The development of intersectionality has been influential in critical race theoretical perspectives (Ledesma & Calderón, 2015). Additionally, it has been heralded as one of the most important developments in feminist theory (Davis, 2008), and has been applied across disciplines to examine how individuals' multiple identities intersect to impact their experiences (Cho et al., 2013). More recently, intersectionality as a theoretical perspective has informed the formation of a field of "intersectional studies," consisting of the investigation of intersectional dynamics, the applications of intersectionality across disciplines, discussion of intersectionality as a methodological and theoretical paradigm, and political interventions drawing on an intersectional lens (Cho et al., 2013, p. 785).

Key Terms and Concepts

Social identities include sex, gender identity, race, ethnicity, class, and sexual orientation, among others.

In Research

Scholars have called for the use of intersectionality in a variety of disciplines and approaches, including policy analysis (Hankivsky & Cormier, 2011), education (Gillborn, 2015), sociology (Choo & Ferree, 2010), and public health (Bowleg, 2012). In the field of psychology, Patil et al. (2018) found 25 studies that drew on intersectionality as a theoretical lens to understand the association between identity intersections and depression, and ultimately argued that an intersectionality framework can be used to identify protective factors and target interventions.

Intersectionality has been used to study issues in public policy and political science as well. Hawkesworth (2003), for example, used an intersectionality framework to understand the marginalization of Congresswomen of color. In drawing on concepts from intersectionality, Hawkesworth puts forth a theory of "racing-gendering," which foregrounds the racialization and gendering in politics. Hawkesworth finds that this process of racing-gendering in Congress serves to silence, exclude, stereotype, render invisible, and diminish the authority of Congresswomen of color. In public policy, scholars have argued that intersectionality has the power to reveal and address the limitations and exclusionary nature of traditional policymaking and implementation (Hankivsky & Cormier, 2011, p. 218).

Strengths and Limitations

The main strength of intersectionality is in its focus on the multiple forms of identity that influence human experience. Intersectionality logically builds on ideas from critical race theory and feminist theory to further flesh out the complexities of experience and the influence of multiple, intersecting identities. Scholars have noted that intersectionality possesses the analytic breadth to appeal to both generalists and specialists and is broad enough to be used across disciplines (Davis, 2008). Another key strength of an intersectionality framework is its roots in activism and resulting focus on disrupting the status quo (Gillborn, 2015).

One limitation that scholars have noted is the possibility for too many sub-divisions of identity. As Delgado (2011) notes, "intersectionality can easily paralyze progressive work and thought because of the realization that whatever unit you choose to work with, someone may come along and point out that you forgot something" (p. 1264). Others have discussed intersectionality as being underutilized in specific disciplines, including sociology, despite its significance for feminist scholars specifically (Choo & Feree, 2010).

Other limitations concern conceptual, methodological, and analytic clarity. As Davis (2008) explains, some feminist scholars have noted that it has sometimes been unclear as to whether intersectionality should be understood

> as a crossroad (Crenshaw, 1991), as 'axes' of difference (Yuval-Davis, 2006) or as a dynamic process (Staunæs, 2003). It is not at all clear whether intersectionality should be limited to understanding individual experiences, theorizing identity, or whether it should be taken as a property of social structures and cultural discourses.
>
> (Davis, 2008, p. 69)

Other scholars have noted that intersectionality does not have a defined methodology (Nash, 2008). Indeed, some scholars have argued that intersectionality may benefit from more conceptual clarity and a more coherent methodology in order to provide the analytic tools to address the complexities it was designed to address (McCall, 2005; Nash, 2008). However, others have noted that the conceptual openness and ambiguity may be exactly why it is useful as a framework (Davis, 2008).

Key Theorists: Kimberlé Crenshaw (Originating author); Mari Matsuda

Examples of Use in Research: Crenshaw (1991); Hawkesworth (2003); Patil et al. (2018)

Feminist Theory

Definition and Overview

Feminist theory examines how gender roles and inequalities are reinforced in society, as well as the role of patriarchy in the oppression of women. An important goal of feminist theory is to examine and confront sexism and oppression and promote equality and justice (hooks, 2000). Key principles of a feminist theoretical framework include gender discrimination, inequality, and oppression; patriarchy; hegemony; and how social, institutional, and political factors influence women's place in society (Grant & Osanloo, 2014). Critical areas of focus in a feminist framework can include discrimination and exclusion, objectification, and gender roles and stereotypes (Nussbaum, 1995; Papadaki, 2007).

Feminist theory is a grand theory, meaning that it is a larger theoretical umbrella under which many other theories can be situated. There are a few basic ideas that form the foundation for feminist theory as a framework. First, feminist theory opposes, or is at least committed to interrogating, the use of dualistic thinking, including embracing binaries like male/female, emotion/reason, gay/straight, etc. (Ferguson, 2017). From a feminist standpoint, dualism is seen as ignoring nuance and generating hierarchies. Feminist thinking also resists essentialism and instead embraces process thinking in order to promote a more analytic assessment of the influence of history and context on the development of gender. Finally, feminist theory is not only intellectual, but also political in nature and is grounded in and committed to freedom, equality, and justice. According to hooks (2000), "feminism is a movement to end sexism, sexist exploitation, and oppression" (p. 80).

One of the key aspects of feminist theory is the importance of narrative storytelling, specifically from the perspective of women. As de Beauvoir (2012[1949]) stated, "men define the world from their own point of view, which they confuse with absolute truth" (p. 62). This highlights the need for stories that counter dominant narratives – a need emphasized in other critical theories as well. The purpose of these stories is to allow women and particularly marginalized women to have a voice, and to present narratives "articulating the world from those women's points of view, identifying the locations from which they speak, and generating both a critique of prevailing conditions and a vision of a better world" (Ferguson, 2017, p. 276). Feminist theorists emphasize that the focus should be on voices who have been historically silenced. Feminist activism and feminist theory are inextricably linked. As Ferguson (2017) notes, "feminist theory is a change-oriented scholarly practice; challenging oppression and working toward justice are not separate applications of a theory made elsewhere but constitutive elements of theory making" (p. 275).

There is not one "feminist theory." Rather, feminist theory takes many forms and different forms of feminist thought have different emphases. Tong (2018), for example, identifies seven types of feminist theory, including liberal, Marxist, radical, psychoanalytic, socialist, existentialist, and postmodern. Others have posited categories of feminist theory that include liberal feminism, cultural feminism, queer feminism, anti-racist feminism, socialist feminism, postmodern feminism, radical feminism, Indigenous feminism, Marxist feminism, postcolonial feminism, and intersectional feminism (Sharma, 2019). Ultimately, feminist theory may be best understood as a family of critical theories, all of which focus on gender, the complexity of experience, and the multidimensional nature of oppression.

As a research framework, feminist theory centers gender as the primary organizing principle of a study (Lather, 1991; Creswell & Poth, 2018). Feminist theory can support researchers in disentangling the patriarchal aspects of social structures at multiple levels, as well as in exploring the experiential knowledge of patriarchy, objectification, hegemony, sexism, and oppression.

Background and Foundations

Feminist theory is grounded in postmodern and poststructuralist viewpoints (Creswell & Poth, 2018; Lather, 1991) and can be roughly divided into four waves (Humm, 1995; 2017; Walker 2001). The first wave refers to early feminist movements, led by Susan B. Anthony and Elizabeth Cady Stanton, and concerned with women's suffrage. The second wave began in the 1960s and focused on reproductive rights, and how women experienced traditional gender roles. Betty Friedan (2010[1962]) is often credited with launching this second wave – what is referred to as reformist feminist theory – in her work describing the dissatisfaction of women in the 1960s and critiquing traditional gender roles and idealized feminine behavior. This version of feminist theory was primarily focused on advancing social equality between women and men. However, Friedan's work was criticized for being exclusively focused on the plight of White, middle-class women (hooks, 1984).

The third wave of feminist theory began in the 1990s and was more inclusive in nature. As feminist theory developed, there was a move toward interdisciplinarity (Hawkesworth, 2012) and toward more inclusive frameworks. In the late 20th century, there was increasing criticism that feminism was primarily concerned with the experiences of predominantly middle-class, White women (Crenshaw, 1991; hooks, 2000). Scholar and theorist bell hooks, for example, argued for new orientations in feminism and feminist theory that would focus not only on ending sexist oppression and exploitation, but also on racist, classist, and imperialist forms of oppression as well (hooks, 1984; Biana, 2020). Each of these forms of subjugation and subordination are interrelated and inseparably connected to each other through what hooks refers to as "interlocking webs of oppression" (hooks, 1984, p. 31). Building on these ideas, the concept of intersectionality developed from Black feminist thought (Bowleg, 2012; Crenshaw, 1989, 1991), as a way to decenter the experiences of White women and emphasize the intersections of race and class with gender. The fourth wave of feminist theory has further drawn on ideas from the third wave and has focused on the intersections of gender, race, and class, and has concentrated on sexual harassment, rape culture, body shaming, sexist imagery, and online misogyny (Rivers, 2017).

Key Terms and Concepts

Patriarchy generally refers to social structures that privilege men and encourage the subordination and subjugation of women (Beechey, 1979). The concept of patriarchy is used in feminist theoretical frameworks to describe and analyze the social structures that oppress women and privilege men (Acker, 1989), with the intention of ultimately dismantling these structures.

Hegemony refers to "the 'spontaneous' consent given by the great masses of the population to the general direction imposed on social life by the dominant fundamental group; this consent is 'historically' caused by the prestige (and consequent confidence) which the dominant group enjoys because of its position and function in the world of production" (Gramsci, 1976, p. 12).

Misogyny refers to hatred of, contempt for, and prejudice against women (Srivastava et al., 2017).

Objectification refers to the portrayal or conception of women as dehumanized sexual things, objects, or commodities (Nussbaum, 1995).

Sexism refers to gender- or sex-based prejudice and/or discrimination.

In Research

Feminist theory, and related theories like feminist standpoint theory and intersectionality, have been used in nearly every discipline, as a way to center gender in the analysis. For example, caring and caregiving has been a common topic for the use of feminist perspectives. Tronto (1987) used a feminist lens to examine the ethic of care. Fisher et al. (1990) discussed a feminist theory of caring. Tronto (1993, 2020) further explored these ideas to examine the gendered nature of morality and the gendered nature of the demands of caregiving, arguing that care-giving is devalued because it is typically taken on by women, and in particular, low-income women of color.

Other studies have used feminist theory to explore misogyny and violence against women across multiple populations and spaces. In one study, Mays (2006) used feminist disability theory to examine violence against women with disabilities. Anderson (2017) drew on feminist theory to explore data from the National Survey of Families and Households in order to examine the connections between structural inequality and family violence. More recently, feminist theory has been used to explore emerging technologies and social media. Shaw (2014), for example, used a feminist lens to investigate sexism and misogyny in online spaces.

Strengths and Limitations

One of the strengths of feminist theory is in its inherent focus on justice and equality, and in its link to activist forms of research. The use of a feminist theoretical framework necessarily places sex and gender at the forefront of the analysis and can support researchers in making substantive impacts toward equality. Another strength is in its conceptual breadth, and capacity to be integrated with other frameworks for more analytic power. Garland-Thomson (2020), for example, advocates for a feminist disability theory that integrates disability studies and feminist theory.

An identified limitation of feminist theory is that its primary focus has been on White women, and particularly, middle- and upper-class White women. Indeed, part of the impetus for the concept of intersectionality (See Chapter 3) was as a response to existing feminist perspectives and the ways in which those perspectives had prioritized the needs and experiences of White women and ignored the particular experiences of women of color and low-income women (Bowleg, 2012; Crenshaw, 1989, 1991).

Key Theorists: Simone de Beauvoir, Kimberlé Crenshaw; Betty Friedan; bell hooks; Mary Wollstonecraft

Examples of Use in Research: Anderson (2017); Fisher et al. (1990); May (2006); Shaw (2014); Tronto (2020)

Queer Theory

Definition and Overview

Queer Theory provides a frame through which to question traditional binary representations of sex, gender, and sexuality, and to critique existing power structures (de Lauretis, 1991; Plummer, 2005). At the core of queer theory are a resistance to heteronormativity, a challenge to the idea of gay and lesbian studies as a monolith, and a focus on how race interacts with sexuality (de Lauretis, 1991). Queer theory is informed by feminist theory and LGBTQI+ studies, which "challenges the normative social ordering of identities and subjectivities along the heterosexual/homosexual binary as well as the privileging of heterosexuality as 'natural' and homosexuality as its deviant and abhorrent 'other'" (Brown & Nash, 2016, p. 5). As Plummer (2005) explains it, "queer theory is really poststructuralism (and postmodernism) applied to sexuality and genders" (p. 365).

Key concepts of queer theory include heteronormativity and the critique of dualistic or binary categorization (Butler, 1999; de Lauretis, 1991). Heteronormativity refers to the idea that society privileges heterosexuality as "normal" and preferred, and heterosexual behaviors are supported, incentivized, and normalized in society (de Lauretis, 1991; Foucault, 1978; Muñoz, 1999; Warner, 1991). This is also related to traditional gendered expectations which are provided by culture and reified in societal structures (Butler, 1990). Queer theory resists dualistic or binary categorizations like heterosexuality/homosexuality, male/female, and gay/lesbian that do not allow for the range of human identity and experience (de Lauretis, 1991; Plummer, 2005). These binaries are eschewed in queer theoretical approaches, not only because they are inaccurate or because they do not encompass the possibilities of identity and experience, but also because they carry with them certain power differentials that are culturally prioritized and reinscribed over time (de Lauretis, 1991; Plummer, 2005).

Plummer (2005) notes several critical themes of queer theory, including resisting homosexual/heterosexual and sex/gender binaries; decentering identity; supporting openness and fluidity in all sexual and gender categories; critiquing mainstream "corporate" homosexuality; challenging normalization and normalizing strategies; embedding power in discourse; allowing for irony in academic work; eliminating the deviance paradigm; exploring and analyzing insider/outsider positions, and engaging interest in fringe sexualities (Plummer, 2005, p. 366).

Queer theory, and specifically the methodological approach of "queering" pushes researchers to ask: "Which aspects of life can exist at the expense of others, existing precisely because others' lives are pushed to margins, seen as expendable, not worthy of living?" (Erol & Cuklanz, 2020, p. 218). This allows research drawing on queer theory to center those on the margins. Further, queer theory reflects the complex, multidimensional, and dynamic intersections of identity, and is characterized by resistance to heteronormative structures.

Queer theory "comes from queered perspectives of the researcher and the researched" (Dilley, 1999, p. 461). Queer theory offers a lens through which to understand the "othering" of groups that do not fit within a heteronormative conceptualization of identity and sexuality. A queer theoretical framework can support researchers in asking transformative questions toward these goals. Namaste (1994), for example, outlines a list of questions that queer theoretical lenses can help researchers interrogate:

How do categories such as "gay," "lesbian," and "queer" emerge?

From what do they differentiate themselves, and what kinds of identities do they exclude?

How are these borders demarcated, and how can they be contested?

What are the relations between the naming of sexuality and political organization it adopts, between identity and community?

Why is a focus on the discursive production of social identities useful?

How do we make sense of the dialectical movement between inside and outside, heterosexuality and homosexuality? (Namaste, 1994, p. 224).

Queer theory is useful in analyses that aim to center the experiences of marginalized populations, particularly those that do not fit into heteronormative categorizations.

Background and Foundations

Queer theory was coined by author and professor Teresa de Lauretis (1991). Queer theory is rooted in poststructuralist and postmodernist thinking, and in the HIV/AIDS activism of the 1970s and 1980s (Brown & Nash, 2016). Foundations of queer theory include the poststructuralist theoretical thinking of Foucault (1978), Derrida (1978), and

Lyotard (1984) (Ades & Kasch, 2007). Poststructural theorists argue that "there are no objective and universal truths, but that particular forms of knowledge, and the ways of being that they engender, become 'naturalized,' in culturally and historically specific ways" (Sullivan, 2003, p. 39). Drawing on these ideas, queer theorists assert that gender and sexuality are socially constructed (Butler, 1990).

Queer theory and queer studies emerged out of that work and was developed in the 1990s as a reaction to and critique of normative approaches to gender and sexuality across disciplines (Erol & Cuklanz, 2020). Queer theory was created to address perceived limitations in related fields, and developed "not only as a corrective to some of the gaps and shortcomings of feminist methods, but also in part as a reaction to the growing field of 'Gay and Lesbian Studies' that left out human experiences that did not fit into those identity categories" (Erol & Cuklanz, 2020, p. 211). Queer theory offered an opportunity to problematize and potentially transcend existing concepts and terms, while not being bound to existing ideologies or discursive norms (de Lauretis, 1991).

While feminist work has often used queer identity as a category of analysis, and queer theory is related to feminist theories, it is not a subset of feminist theory. Although queer theory initially focused exclusively on sexuality, over time, scholars expanded the use of queer theory to include "gender as well as any advocacy, activism, or theorizing about being in the world that takes a counter position to the normativity of a given context" (Erol & Cuklanz, 2020, p. 215).

Key Terms and Concepts

Biopolitics refers to "a set of processes such as the ratio of births to deaths, the rate of reproduction, the fertility of a population, and so on" (Foucault, 2003, p. 243). These processes ultimately result in the control of reproduction, identity, and desire through a normalization of binaries and the incentivization of normative behaviors. For example, the child tax credit incentivizes child-rearing, and certain other tax benefits incentivize marriage.

Deconstruction is a "social analysis of who, why, and what produced a text; an analysis of what is said and – unsaid – through the language, form, structure, and style of a text (a written work, a film, art) (Dilley, 1999, p. 459). Deconstruction in a queer theoretical framework can be expanded to analyze any text, including conversation, life stories, or histories – any kind of qualitative data.

Heteronormativity refers to the idea that heterosexuality is the "normal" and preferred sexual orientation, and that this idea is reinforced in society through institutions and biopolitical initiatives (de Lauretis, 1991; Foucault, 1978).

Liminality describes "a resistance strategy in which elements of heterosexuality and non-heterosexuality are incorporated into one identity that rejects normalized definitions of either heterosexuality or nonheterosexuality" (Abes & Kasch, 2007, p. 621). Liminality facilitates fluidity and is representative of how queer theory resists the idea that identity is stable.

Normativity involves "maintaining interests of state structures, and ultimately, socio-political practices that benefited from distinctions such as normal/abnormal" (Erol & Cuklanz, 2020, p. 216).

Performativity describes "how individuals create genders and sexual identities through everyday behaviors or performatives" (Abes & Kasch, 2007, p. 621; Butler, 1990)

"Queer" is often used in popular culture as a term for LGBTQI+ people more generally. However, in queer theory, the term queer specifically indicates anti-normative and anti-binary with an anti-capitalism emphasis (Erol & Cuklanz, 2020).

"Queering" is to decenter any normative, taken-for-granted assumptions in an academic discipline, a theoretical perspective, or a facet of everyday, human life (Erol & Cuklanz, 2020).

In Research

Queer theory can be considered an interdisciplinary or transdisciplinary perspective (Dilley, 1999). As a framework, it has been used across disciplines to examine texts and literature, and to explore the "lives and experiences of those considered non-heterosexual;" to juxtapose "those lives/experiences with lives/experiences considered 'normal;'" and to examine "how/why those lives and experiences are considered outside of the norm" (p. 462). In literature, Price (2020), for example, drew on queer theory to analyze *Beowulf*, and discuss the "queering" of the monster. In language and communication studies, Leap (1994, 1996) conducted textual analyses of how gay men communicate with each other and how that contrasts with how they communicate with straight people.

Other disciplines, including management and organizational studies, sociology, and education, have engaged queer theory as a framework as well. In education, queer theory has been used to problematize educational curriculum (Sumara & Davis, 1999). Abes and Kasch (2007) used queer theory to better understand how lesbian college students' identities were shaped and reshaped and how they negotiated their sexuality. The researchers also drew on queer theory to push back against heteronormativity in student development theory as a field. In management and organizational studies, Bendl et al. (2009) drew on queer theory to interrogate codes of conduct, finding that although each company in their analysis had advocated inclusion and acceptance, these companies' diversity management practices ultimately reinforced heteronormativity.

Strengths and Limitations

One of the strengths of queer theory is in its resistance to binary categorizations. Another strength is in its interdisciplinary nature. In terms of definitional clarity, scholars have noted that, perhaps because of its roots in poststructuralism and postmodernism, queer theory tends to be "hard to pin down" (Plummer, 2005, p. 365), meaning that there is little prescriptive guidance on what it specifically means and how it should be used. However, this has been noted as both a strength and a limitation of the theory.

One limitation that scholars have noted is that queer theory, while aiming to critique binary categorization, may actually end up creating additional binary categorizations, including "queer" and "normal" (Callis, 2009; Oakes, 1995). Others have also asserted that there is a lack of representation of bisexuality in queer theory (Callis, 2009). Some scholars have critiqued queer theory as focusing too much on the privileged individuals within the category of "queer," specifically arguing that queer theory does not engage enough with the experiences of people of color or with the experiences of other marginalized populations, like homeless LGBT youth, sex workers, and trans-identifying individuals (Johnson, 2001).

Key Theorists: Teresa de Lauretis (Originating author); Judith Butler; Michel Foucault; Eve Sedgewick

Examples of Use in Research: Abes and Kasch (2007); Bendl et al. (2009); Carroll and Gilroy (2001); Green 2007; Leap (1994, 1996); Sumara and Davis (1999)

References

Abes, E. S., & Kasch, D. (2007). Using queer theory to explore lesbian college students' multiple dimensions of identity. *Journal of College Student Development, 48*(6), 619–636.

Acker, J. (1989). The problem with patriarchy. *Sociology, 23*(2), 235–240.

Adebayo, C. T., Parcell, E. S., Mkandawire-Valhmu, L., & Olukotun, O. (2022). African American Women's maternal healthcare experiences: a Critical Race Theory perspective. *Health Communication, 37*(9), 1135–1146.

Anderson, K. L. (2017). Gender, status, and domestic violence: An integration of feminist and family violence approaches. In M. Natarajan (Ed.), *Domestic Violence* (pp. 263–277). Routledge.

Anyon, Y., Lechuga, C., Ortega, D., Downing, B., Greer, E., & Simmons, J. (2018). An exploration of the relationships between student racial background and the school sub-contexts of office discipline referrals: A critical race theory analysis. *Race, Ethnicity, and Education, 21*(3), 390–406.

de Beauvoir, S. (2012). *The second sex.* Knopf Doubleday Publishing Group.

Beechey, V. (1979). On patriarchy. *Feminist Review, 3*(1), 66–82.

Bell, D. A. (1980). Brown v. board of education and the interest-convergence dilemma. *Harvard Law Review, 93*, 518.

Bell, D. A. (1992). *Faces at the bottom of the well: The permanence of racism.* New York: Basic Books.

Bendl, R., Fleischmann, A., & Hofmann, R. (2009). Queer theory and diversity management: Reading codes of conduct from a queer perspective. *Journal of Management & Organization, 15*(5), 625–638.

Biana, H. T. (2020). Extending bell hooks' Feminist Theory. *Journal of International Women's Studies, 21*(1), 13–29.

Bowleg, L. (2012). The problem with the phrase women and minorities: Intersectionality—An important theoretical framework for public health. *American Journal of Public Health, 102*(7), 1267–1273.

Brayboy, B. M. J. (2006). Toward a tribal critical race theory in education. *The Urban Review, 37*, 425–446.

Brown, K., & Jackson, D. D. (2013). The history and conceptual elements of critical race theory. In M. Lynn & A.D. Dixon (Eds.), *Handbook of critical race theory in education* (pp. 29–42). Routledge.

Brown, K., & Nash, C.J. (2016). Introduction. In: Brown, K. & Nash, C. J. (Eds.), *Queer methods and methodologies: Intersecting queer theories and social science research* (pp. 1–23). Routledge.

Butler, J. (1990). *Gender trouble: Feminism and the subversion of identity.* Routledge.

Butler, J. (1999). Revisiting bodies and pleasures. *Theory, Culture & Society, 16*(2), 11–20.

Callis, A. S. (2009). Playing with Butler and Foucault: Bisexuality and queer theory. *Journal of Bisexuality, 9*(3–4), 213–233.

Carroll, L., & Gilroy, P. J. (2001). Teaching "outside the box": Incorporating queer theory in counselor education. *Journal of Humanistic Counseling, Education and Development, 40*, 49–58.

Cho, S., Crenshaw, K. W., & McCall, L. (2013). Toward a field of intersectionality studies: Theory, applications, and praxis. *Signs: Journal of Women in Culture and Society, 38*(4), 785–810.

Choo, H. Y., & Ferree, M. M. (2010). Practicing intersectionality in sociological research: A critical analysis of inclusions, interactions, and institutions in the study of inequalities. *Sociological Theory, 28*(2), 129–149.

Cook, D. A., & Dixson, A. D. (2013). Writing critical race theory and method: A composite counterstory on the experiences of black teachers in New Orleans post-Katrina. *International Journal of Qualitative Studies in Education, 26*(10), 1238–1258. 10.1080/09518398.2012.731531

Crenshaw, K. (1989) Demarginalizing the intersection of race and sex: A Black feminist critique of antidiscrimination doctrine, feminist theory and antiracist politics. *University of Chicago Legal Forum, 1989*(1), Article 8.

Crenshaw, K. W. (1991). Mapping the margins: Intersectionality, identity politics, and violence against women of color. *Stanford Law Review, 43*(6), 1241–1299.

Crenshaw, K. W. (1995). The intersection of race and gender. In K. W. Crenshaw, N. Gotanda, G. Peller, & K. Thomas (Eds.), *Critical race theory: The key writings that formed the movement* (pp. 357–383). The New Press.

Crenshaw, K. (2013). Demarginalizing the intersection of race and sex: A black feminist critique of antidiscrimination doctrine, feminist theory and antiracist politics. In K. Maschke (Ed), *Feminist legal theories* (pp. 23–51). Routledge.

Creswell, J. W., & Poth, C. N. (2018). *Qualitative inquiry and research design: Choosing among five approaches*. Sage publications.

Crowley, R. M. (2013). 'The goddamndest, toughest voting rights bill': Critical Race Theory and the Voting Rights Act of 1965. *Race Ethnicity and Education, 16*(5), 696–724.

Davis, K. (2008). Intersectionality as buzzword: a sociology of science perspective on what makes a feminist theory successful. *Feminist Theory, 9*(1), 67–85.

DeCuir, J. T., & Dixson, A. D. (2004). "So when it comes out, they aren't that surprised that it is there": Using critical race theory as a tool of analysis of race and racism in education. *Educational Researcher, 33*(5), 26–31.

De Lauretis, T. (1991). Queer theory: Lesbian and gay sexualities an introduction. *Differences: A Journal of Feminist Cultural Studies, 3*(2), iii–xviii.

Delgado, R. (Ed.). (1995). *Critical race theory: The cutting edge*. Philadelphia: Temple University Press.

Delgado, R. (2011). Rodrigo's reconsideration: Intersectionality and the future of critical race theory. *Iowa Law Review, 96*, 1247–1288.

Delgado, R., & Stefancic, J. (Eds.). (2000). *Critical race theory: The cutting edge*. Temple University Press.

Delgado, R., & Stefancic, J. (2001). *Critical race theory: An introduction*. New York University Press.

Delgado, R., & Stefancic, J. (2023). *Critical race theory: An introduction*. New York University Press.

Derrida, J. (1978). *Writing and difference*. The University of Chicago press.

Dilley, P. (1999). Queer theory: Under construction. *International Journal of Qualitative Studies in Education, 12*(5), 457–472.

Dixson, A. D. (2018). "What's going on?": A critical race theory perspective on Black Lives Matter and activism in education. *Urban Education, 53*(2), 231–247.

DuBois, W. E. B. (1903). *The souls of black folk: Essays and sketches*. A.C. McClurg.

Erol, A., & Cuklanz, L. (2020). Queer theory and feminist methods: A review. *Investigaciones Feministas, 11*(2).

Ferguson, K. E. (2017). Feminist theory today. *Annual Review of Political Science, 20*, 269–286.

Fisher, B., Tronto, J., Abel, E. K., & Nelson, M. (1990). Toward a feminist theory of caring. In E.K. Abel & M.K. Nelson (Eds.), *Circles of Care: Work and identity in women's lives* (pp. 29–42).

Foucault, M. (1978). *The history of sexuality: Volume 1, an introduction*. Vantage Books.

Foucault, M. (2003). *Society must be defended: Lectures in college de France 1975–1976*. New York, NY: Picador.

Freeman, A. D. (1978). Legitimizing racial discrimination through antidiscrimination law: a critical review of supreme court doctrine. *Minnesota Law Review, 62*(6), 1049–1119.

Friedan, B. (2010[1963]). *The feminine mystique.* WW Norton & Company.

Garland-Thomson, R. (2020). Integrating disability, transforming feminist theory. In C. McCann & S.K. Kim (Eds.), *Feminist theory reader* (pp. 181–191). Routledge.

Gillborn, D. (2015). Intersectionality, critical race theory, and the primacy of racism: Race, class, gender, and disability in education. *Qualitative Inquiry, 21*(3), 277–287.

Gillborn, D., Warmington, P., & Demack, S. (2018). QuantCrit: Education, policy, 'Big Data' and principles for a critical race theory of statistics. *Race, Ethnicity, and Education, 21*(2), 158–179.

Gramsci, A. (1976). *Selections from the prison notebooks.* Lawrence and Wishart.

Grant, C. & Osanloo, A. (2014).Understanding, selecting, and integrating a theoretical framework in dissertation research: Creating the blueprint for house. *Administrative Issues Journal: Connecting Education, Practice and Research*, 12–22

Green, A. I. (2007). Queer theory and sociology: Locating the subject and the self in sexuality studies. *Sociological Theory, 25*(1), 26–45.

Hankivsky, O., & Cormier, R. (2011). Intersectionality and public policy: Some lessons from existing models. *Political Research Quarterly, 64*(1), 217–229.

Hawkesworth, M. (2003). Congressional enactments of race–gender: Toward a theory of raced–gendered institutions. *American Political Science Review, 97*(4), 529–550.

Hawkesworth, M. (2012). Western feminist theories: Trajectories of change. *Gender and Politics: The State of the Discipline*, 199–220.

hooks, b. (2000). *Feminist theory: From margin to center.* Pluto Press.

Humm M. (1995). *The dictionary of feminist theory.* Ohio State University Press.

Humm, M. (2017). The Women's March on London: Virginia Woolf, John Berger, Judith Butler and inter-sectionality. *Przegląd Kulturoznawczy, 34*, 587-592.

Iglesias, E. (1997). Forward: International law, human rights, and LatCrit theory. *University of Miami Inter-American Law Review, 28*, 177–213.

Iftikar, J. S., & Museus, S. D. (2018). On the utility of Asian critical (AsianCrit) theory in the field of education. *International Journal of Qualitative Studies in Education, 31*(10), 935–949.

Johnson, E. P. (2001). "Quare" studies, or (almost) everything I know about queer studies I learned from my grandmother. *Text and Performance Quarterly, 21*(1), 1–25

de Lauretis, T. (1991). Queer Theory: Lesbian and Gay Sexualities An Introduction. *Differences, 3*, iii–xviii.

Ladson-Billings, G., & Tate, W. F. (1995). Toward a critical race theory of education. *Teachers College Record, 97*(1), 47–68.

Ladson-Billings, G. J. (1999). Preparing teachers for diverse student populations: A critical race theory perspective. *Review of Educational Research, 24*, 211–247.

Ladson-Billings, G. J. (2023). Just what is critical race theory and what's it doing in a *nice* field like education? In E. Taylor, D. Gillborn, & G. Ladson-Billings (Eds.), *Foundations of critical race theory in education.* Taylor & Francis.

Lather, P. (1991). *Getting smart: Feminist research and pedagogy with/in the postmodern.* Psychology Press.

Leap, W. L. (1994). Learning gay culture in "a desert of nothing:" Language as a resource in gender socialization. *High School Journal, 77*(1&2), 122–132.

Leap, W. L. (1996). *Word's out: Gay men's English.* University of Minnesota Press.

Ledesma, M. C., & Calderón, D. (2015). Critical race theory in education: A review of past literature and a look to the future. *Qualitative Inquiry, 21*(3), 206–222.

Love, H. R., & Beneke, M. R. (2021). Pursuing justice-driven inclusive education research: Disability critical race theory (DisCrit) in early childhood. *Topics in Early Childhood Special Education, 41*(1), 31–44.

Lynn, M., & Dixson, A. D. (Eds.). (2013). *Handbook of critical race theory in education.* Routledge.

Lyotard, J.F. (1984). *The postmodern condition: A report on knowledge.* University of Minnesota Press.

Matsuda, M. J. (1991). Beside my sister, facing the enemy: Legal theory out of coalition. *Stanford Law Review, 43*(6), 1183–1192.

Mays, J. M. (2006). Feminist disability theory: Domestic violence against women with a disability. *Disability & Society, 21*(2), 147–158.

McCall, L. (2005). The complexity of intersectionality. *Signs, 30*(3), 1771–1800.

McIntosh, P. (2008). White privilege: Unpacking the invisible knapsack. In   P. Rothenberg   (Ed.), *White privilege: Essential readings on the other side of racism* (pp. 123–127). New York: Worth.

Muñoz, J. E. (1999). *Disidentifications: Queers of color and the performance of politics*. University of Minnesota Press.

Museus, S. D., & Iftikar, J. (2013). An Asian critical theory (AsianCrit) framework. *Asian American Students in Higher Education, 31*(10), 18–29.

Nash, J. C. (2008). Re-thinking intersectionality. *Feminist Review, 89*(1), 1–15.

Namaste, K. (1994). The politics of inside/out: Queer theory, poststructuralism, and a sociological approach to sexuality. *Sociological Theory, 12*, 220.

Nussbaum, M. C. (1995). Objectification. *Philosophy & Public Affairs, 24*(4), 249–291.

Oakes, G. (1995). Straight thinking about queer theory. *International Journal of Politics, Culture, and Society, 8*(3), 379–388.

Papadaki, F. (2007) Sexual objectification: From Kant to contemporary feminism. *Contemporary Political Theory, 6*, 330–348.

Parker, L. (1998). 'Race is race ain't': An exploration of the utility of critical race theory in qualitative research in education. *International Journal of Qualitative Studies in Education, 11*(1), 43–55.

Patil, P. A., Porche, M. V., Shippen, N. A., Dallenbach, N. T., & Fortuna, L. R. (2018). Which girls, which boys? The intersectional risk for depression by race and ethnicity, and gender in the US. *Clinical Psychology Review, 66*, 51–68.

Pierce, C.M. (1995). Stress analogs of racism and sexism: Terrorism, torture, and disaster. In C. V. Willie, P. P. Rieker B. M. Kramer, & B. S. Brown (Eds.), *Mental health, racism, and sexism* (277–293). University of Pittsburgh Press.

Price, B. A. (2020). Potentiality and possibility: An overview of Beowulf and Queer Theory. *Neophilologus, 104*, 401–419.

Plummer K. (2005). Critical humanism and queer theory: Living with the tensions. In Denzin N., Lincoln Y. (Eds.), *Handbook of qualitative research* (3rd ed., pp. 357–373). Sage.

Ray, R. & Gibbons, A. (2021). *Why are states banning critical race theory?* Brookings Institute.

Rivers, N. (2017). *Postfeminism(s) and the arrival of the fourth wave*. Palgrave Macmillan.

Shaw, A. (2014). The Internet is full of jerks, because the world is full of jerks: What feminist theory teaches us about the Internet. *Communication and Critical/Cultural Studies, 11*(3), 273–277.

Sharma, M. (2019). Applying feminist theory to medical education. *The Lancet, 393*, 570–578.

Solórzano, D. G. (1997). Images and words that wound: Critical race theory, racial stereo-typing, and teacher education. *Teacher Education Quarterly, 24*(3), 5–19.

Solórzano, D. G., & Yosso, T. J. (2001). Critical race and LatCrit theory and method: Counter-storytelling. *International Journal of Qualitative Studies in Education, 14*(4), 471–495.

Solórzano, D. G., & Yosso, T. J. (2002). Critical race methodology: Counter-storytelling as an analytical framework for education research. *Qualitative Inquiry, 8*, 23–44.

Solorzano, D., Ceja, M., & Yosso, T. (2000). Critical race theory, racial microaggressions, and campus racial climate: The experiences of African American college students. *Journal of Negro Education, 69*(1), 60–73.

Slakoff, D. C., & Brennan, P. K. (2019). The differential representation of Latina and black female victims in front-page news stories: A qualitative document analysis. *Feminist Criminology, 14*, 488–516.

Srivastava, K., Chaudhury, S., Bhat, P. S., & Sahu, S. (2017). Misogyny, feminism, and sexual harassment. *Industrial Psychiatry Journal, 26*(2), 111.

Staunæs, D. (2003). Where have all the subjects gone? Bringing together the concepts of inter-sectionality and subjectification, *Nora1*, *1*(2), 101–110.

Sue, D. W., Capodilupo, C. M., Torino, G. C., Bucceri, J. M., Holder, A. M. B., Nadal, K. L., & Esquilin, M. (2007). Racial microaggressions in everyday life: Implications for clinical practice. *American Psychologist*, *62*(4), 271–286.

Sullivan, N. (2003). *A Critical Introduction to Queer Theory*. New York University Press.

Sumara, D., & Davis, B. (1999). Interrupting heteronormativity: Toward a queer curriculum theory. *Curriculum Inquiry*, *29*(2), 191–208.

Taylor, E. (2023). Introduction. In E. Taylor, D. Gillborn, & G. Ladson-Billings (Eds.), *Foundations of critical race theory in education*. Taylor & Francis.

Taylor, E., Gillborn, D., & Ladson-Billings, G. (Eds.). (2023). *Foundations of critical race theory in education*. Taylor & Francis.

Tong, R. (2018). *Feminist thought, student economy edition: A More Comprehensive Introduction*. Routledge.

Tronto, J. C. (1987). Beyond gender difference to a theory of care. *Signs: Journal of Women in Culture and Society*, *12*(4), 644–663.

Tronto, J. (1993). *Moral boundaries: A political argument for an ethic of care*. Routledge.

Tronto, J. (2020). *Moral boundaries: A political argument for an ethic of care*. Routledge.

Walker, R. (2001). Becoming the third wave. *Identity Politics in the Women's Movement*, *3*(13), 78–80.

Warner, M. (1991). Introduction: Fear of a queer planet. *Social Text*, *29*, 3–17.

Yosso, T., Smith, W., Ceja, M., & Solórzano, D. (2009). Critical race theory, racial microaggressions, and campus racial climate for Latina/o undergraduates. *Harvard Educational Review*, *79*, 659–691.

Yuval-Davis, N. (2006). Intersectionality and feminist politics. *European Journal of Women's Studies*, *13*(3), 193–210.

4 Sociology

Cultural and Social Capital Theories

Definition and Overview

Cultural capital theory posits that the internalization of particular cultural ideals and traditions that are valued by dominant cultural groups in society, and which are typically passed on by individuals' families, can be used as a form of "capital" to achieve social mobility and garner social benefits in an economically divided society (Bourdieu, 1986). Cultural capital, as a form of capital, refers specifically to traits that are rewarded in contexts like education, and which can lead to social mobility (Davies & Rizk, 2018). The objective of human activity is to accumulate and leverage different kinds of capital (DiMaggio, 1979).

There are three primary types of cultural capital: embodied, objectified, and institutionalized (Bourdieu, 1986). Embodied cultural capital consists of both consciously developed and more passively inherited attributes of self. Embodied cultural capital becomes a part of a person's "habitus" – their character and patterns of thinking. Through this process, a person's habitus becomes more susceptible to similar influences. Objectified cultural capital refers to actual physical objects, like works of art, that can symbolically convey cultural capital, and/or can be exchanged for economic capital. Although anyone can possess objectified cultural capital, it conveys the most benefits through the understanding of its cultural meaning and significance. Finally, institutionalized cultural capital refers to academic credentials or qualifications that can signal institutional recognition.

Cultural capital results in what Durkheim calls "the conservation of a culture inherited from the past" (as cited in Bourdieu, 1973, p. 72). In other words, cultural capital is the means by which the dominant class maintains dominance; it's a class-based form of capital, with more privileged classes able to use these internalized resources and knowledge to acquire social profits (Bourdieu, 1986). Cultural capital is acquired over periods of time, and exists in individuals' attitudes and beliefs, personal style, linguistic competence, and knowledge about school, all set and valued by the dominant culture (Lamont & Lareau, 1988). Cultural capital can also be institutionalized as credentials and qualifications that can be used for influence and economic gain. Cultural capital theory holds that cultural capital (or a perceived lack of cultural capital) is how social inequality and class structure are perpetuated.

Social capital theory explains that individuals can use social networks and connections as resources to gain benefits, and that this is one way that socioeconomic stratification is maintained by the dominant class in society (Bourdieu, 1986; Coleman, 1988). As a form

DOI: 10.4324/9781003261759-4

of capital, social capital can be defined as the aggregate resources that individuals wield as a result of their social networks and institutional connections (Bourdieu, 1986; Coleman, 1988). Social capital centers on the idea of trust; it is the scaffolding that makes trust possible. To be considered social capital, these connections among and within social networks must be mutually beneficial, foster trust, and must be able to be used productively to achieve desired outcomes and garner benefits (Coleman, 1990). Bourdieu (1986) emphasizes that the importance of social capital lies in the quality of the connections.

Social capital is cumulative, produces real-world profits or benefits, can be converted into other forms of capital, and can be reproduced and expanded over time (Bourdieu, 1986; Stanton-Salazar, 1997). Social capital theory posits that for individuals born into high-income, high-status families, social capital is a way to increase status and economic capital. However, social capital becomes a form of oppression, not mobility, for low-income, low-status individuals because their social networks are not valued by the dominant group (Bourdieu, 1973). A lack of social capital makes it more difficult for people to gain economic capital or human capital.

Social capital can be expressed through social relationships that provide access to the resources of others in a social network as well as the amount and the quality of those resources (Portes, 1998). There are three forms of social capital: obligations and expectations, information channels, and social norms (Coleman, 1988). Obligations refer to the idea that people in social networks are "always doing things for each other" (Coleman, 1988, p. 102). The degree of trustworthiness in the social structure determines how useful these obligations are as a form of social capital. Information channels are a form a social capital referring to the information that social networks can hold and pass around to members. Social norms, as a form of social capital, are the expectations and norms that are set within a social network. The structure of social relations helps to institute obligations between individuals in the social network, establish trustworthiness, and set norms and expectations for behaviors (Coleman, 1988).

There are three basic functions of social capital: as a source of social control, as a source of family support, and as a source of benefits through extrafamilial networks (Portes, 1998). Social capital allows people to acquire economic capital and resources, embodied cultural capital, and institutionalized cultural capital. However, social capital is not tangible and exists only in social relations (Bourdieu, 1986, Coleman, 1988). There are negative consequences to social capital as well, including the exclusion of outsiders, excess claims on group members, demands for conformity, and downward-leveling norms (Portes, 1998).

Cultural and social capital theories can be useful for researchers trying to understand social stratification and mobility, as well as those researchers interested in economic inequality and the relationships between socioeconomic status, background, and educational achievement. Cultural capital theory can help researchers attend to the influences of individuals' experiences and backgrounds, while social capital theory can support researchers in mapping the social structures and networks that influence achievement and social mobility.

Background and Foundations

Cultural and social capital theories were developed by French sociologist Pierre Bourdieu in the 1960s and 1970s. Bourdieu (1973) was aiming to understand how culture and class is reproduced in the educational system, and specifically, the impact of parental knowledge, education, and other traits on students' educational performance and mobility. Bourdieu sought to develop a theory to explain the symbolic domination and control by which the existing social order is maintained.

Bourdieu (1986) argued that the social world is accumulated history and can be described in terms of "capital" (1986). Toward this goal, he described and examined social mobility and social and cultural reproduction by describing the accumulation and use of cultural and social capital, and how these forms of capital become economic capital. According to Bourdieu (1973), social inequality and class structure is perpetuated most efficiently through the educational system.

In developing ideas of cultural and social capital theories, Bourdieu aimed to combine early sociological ideas put forth by Marx and Durkheim (DiMaggio, 1979). Social capital can be seen as emerging from Marx's ideas of class consciousness and the concepts of a class for itself versus a class in itself. Durkheim discussed something like social capital as "group life" – a possible way to address anomie, a state in which there is a collapse of agreed-upon morals, values, and standards, due to the breakdown of shared goals and increased alienation in a society (Durkheim, 1984). Coleman (1988, 1990) built on Bourdieu's conceptions of social capital to explore the disparities in educational achievement between high-income and low-income students. However, Coleman's work on social capital differs slightly from Bourdieu's. While Bourdieu emphasizes that social capital promotes unequal access, Coleman stresses the positive familial consequences of social capital (Dika & Singh, 2002).

Since the advent of cultural and social capital theories, other scholars have applied more critical lenses to these theories and have developed related theories that focus on the types of capital that students and communities of color bring to schooling. For example, Community Cultural Wealth (CCW), which is grounded in a critical race perspective (see Chapter 3), developed as a response to what is seen as the deficit-framing of cultural capital (Sablan, 2019; Yosso, 2005). Forms of capital in a CCW framework include aspirational capital, which refers to the "ability to maintain hopes and dreams for the future;" familial capital, which includes "connections to and knowledge of family and kinship networks;" navigational capital, which refers to the "ability to navigate through schooling institutions that were not designed with communities of color in mind;" and resistant capital, which is the "knowledge of and motivation to transform oppressive structures" (Sablan, 2018, p. 1987; Yosso, 2005).

Key Terms and Concepts

Correspondence Theory refers to the idea that there is a close relationship between social status and the educational system (Bowles & Gintis, 2002). The correspondence principle is based on the idea that schools socialize students to certain beliefs and values, rather than supporting students' ability to judge their own interests.

Cultural Reproduction refers to how existing cultural norms, behaviors, and practices are reproduced across generations through the socializing influence of institutions and other mechanisms (Bourdieu, 1973).

Doxa is the idea that the world as it appears is self-evident, reinforcing the notion that inequality produces inequality. Doxa explains that social stratification exists because it exists.

Field refers to the social arena in which people maneuver and struggle in pursuit of desirable resources (Bourdieu, 1973, 2018; DiMaggio, 1979). Field is a critical metaphor in cultural capital theory that refers to all the actors and organizations in a social arena and the relationships among them (DiMaggio, 1979). Conflict is inherent in any field.

Habitus is the embodied experience of a person's social interactions, and suggests that a person's familial environment results in natural acquisition of the surrounding cultural capital and natural inclusion in the surrounding social networks (Bourdieu, 1973).

Institutional Agents refer to those individuals that can communicate or transmit institutional opportunities or resources (Stanton-Salazar, 1991).

Symbolic Violence refers to the idea that categories of thought and perception are imposed upon those not in the dominant societal group, who then see the existing social order as desirable (Bourdieu and Wacquant, 2013).

In Research

Cultural and social capital theories have been used broadly in sociology and education to examine and explain achievement disparities. Lareau and Calarco (2012), for example, used a cultural capital framework and found that cultural capital manifests not only in how students interact with educators and with each other, but also in how parents interact with schools and educators; often, parents with high levels of cultural capital feel empowered to ask for exceptions, and they may use their knowledge and resources to secure educational advantages for their children. Students who know how to act in school, according to primarily White, middle-class norms, are then better able to operate within that system (Lareau, 2002; Lareau & Calarco, 2012). Scholars applying theories of cultural capital have also found that middle- and upper-class parents pass on notions of social class that provide advantages and encourage entitlement (Lareau, 2002). Other researchers have used cultural capital as a framework to understand how cultural capital is related to student outcomes, finding that students' advantages and the entitlement created by parents' cultural capital may ultimately influence student performance (DiMaggio & Mohr, 1985).

Other researchers have drawn on cultural capital theory to frame their work, while also critiquing its analytic capacity, specifically for understanding culture, identity, and achievement among nondominant or marginalized racial and ethnic groups (e.g., Carter, 2005). Carter (2005) used cultural capital as a framework to understand how low-income Black and Latino youth perceive, react to, and negotiate the dominant cultural narratives and expectations in educational settings. Carter ultimately argues that educators must embrace multiple forms of cultural capital to stop perpetuating the status quo and causing some students to disengage.

Social capital theory has been used to understand aspects of achievement disparities as well. Croninger and Lee (2001), for example, used a social capital framework to understand whether social capital predicts student dropout. They used social capital as a variable in their quantitative analysis. Using NELS data and measuring social capital as student-teacher relations and student-teacher talks, they specifically focused on whether teachers provide students with valuable forms of social capital and found that teacher-based forms of social capital can reduce the probability of dropping out. Similarly, Sandefur et al. (2006), find that variables associated with parents' social capital are related to increased post-secondary enrollment.

Strengths and Limitations

Both cultural and social capital theories are seen by many researchers as providing a comprehensive framework to better understand cultural and social selection, and social reproduction (Lamont & Lareau, 1988). Further, these concepts can improve the understanding of how social stratification systems are created and maintained. Scholars have argued that social capital theory can offer some concrete guidance for increasing achievement and social mobility. For example, analyses using social capital theory can focus on providing greater agency to students (Croninger & Lee, 2001) and can give insight into what family resources that parents and adolescents can more easily change (Sandefur et al., 2006). Whether or not these theories provide any concrete solutions is up for debate, however, with some scholars arguing that social capital structures can be formally organized to address inequities (Coleman, 1988), and others arguing that social capital theory offers no prescriptive solutions (Portes, 1998). Some have characterized cultural capital, in particular, as "gloomy," and as portraying social reproduction as something that can't be overcome (DiMaggio, 1979).

As far as limitations go, first, as is the case with many theoretical concepts, cultural and social capital and related concepts and terms, have been criticized as too vaguely defined (Davies & Rizk, 2018; DiMaggio, 1979). Some researchers have argued that cultural capital and social capital are not empirically grounded concepts and that their conceptualization describes rather than explains and is too vague to be testable (Dika & Singh, 2002). Further, some researchers have argued that cultural and social capital frameworks, and others like them, treat marginalized groups as a monolith (e.g., Carter, 2005), and could potentially promote a deficit perspective (Dika & Singh, 2002). Indeed, neither cultural nor social capital frameworks as they were originally conceptualized take racial and ethnic differences into account in a meaningful way. Frameworks like Community Cultural Wealth (Yosso, 2005) have been developed in response to this. Finally, researchers have asserted that social capital theory restates the problems but does not provide any guidance for solving them (Portes, 1998). Cultural and social capital can thus provide a theoretical foundation for studies of class and the reproductive nature of education; however, these theories may not offer solutions or suggestions for the education of diverse populations, which presents an opportunity for more concrete contributions in research using cultural and/or social capital as theoretical frames.

Key Theorists: Pierre Bourdieu (Originating author); James Coleman

Examples of Use in Research: Lareau and Calarco (2012); Sandefur et al. (2006)

Institutional Theory

Definition and Overview

Institutional Theory (IT) provides a framework for understanding how institutions operate, how they change (or do not change), and, particularly, how they impact organizations and actors within organizations. IT is specifically concerned with how and why organizational structures persist (Burch, 2007). An institutional perspective holds that organizations will tend to resemble each other because they ultimately conform to institutions (Meyer & Rowan, 1977) – societal rules that are organized and established, and which represent social patterns that demonstrate a process of replication. In other words, institutions are "general societal rules that take the form of cultural theories, ideologies, or taken-for-granted scripts" (Ogawa et al., 2008, p. 84).

There are three main assumptions to institutional theory (Immergut, 1998). First, individuals' expressed institutional preferences and interests don't always represent true preferences. Second, any attempts to aggregate individuals' preferences may ultimately distort those preferences. Finally, institutional arrangements can privilege the interests of certain individuals or groups over others (Immergut, 1998, p. 8). Within the confines of these assumptions, IT focuses on non-local context, including how the environment affects organizations, and the way the environment shapes how the actors within an organization view the world, as well as the structure, action, and thought which occurs within the organization (Immergut, 1998, p. 13). In an institutional framework, organizational forms and the structures and rules within them are institutionalized.

As a research perspective, institutional theory outlines several key concepts and terms – including institutional isomorphism, institutional myths, and institutional logics, as well the logic of confidence (Bingham, 2018; Burch et al., 2020) – that can help researchers make sense of how organizations and individuals within organizations operate and in response to what pressures. Institutional isomorphism – the idea that organizations tend to resemble each other, due to external pressures – represents one of the most central ideas of institutional theory. The homogenization of organizations happens because individuals within the organization attempt to deal with uncertainty in a rational manner. Institutional isomorphism can be categorized in three ways: coercive, in which power dynamics play a role and the organization is coerced by law or politics; mimetic, in which organizations imitate others to reduce uncertainty; and normative, in which organizations emulate other organizations in pursuit of legitimacy (DiMaggio & Powell, 1983, 1991).

Further, an institutional theoretical perspective holds that organizations often adhere to institutional myths – shared ideals or normative pressures of the institutional environment that offer a rational perspective for how organizations should operate – instead of the actual demands of daily work activities (Hallett, 2010; Meyer & Rowan, 1977; 1991). This leads to a gap between formalized organizational structures and general daily work activities in that organization. These institutionalized myths can include professions (occupations controlled by inspection and social rules), programs (ideologies defining appropriate functions), and technologies (accepted technical procedures). These institutional myths become ceremonial for organizations. By adhering to institutionalized myths, organizations demonstrate legitimacy, rationality, and collective values, while also increasing their sustainability in the institutional landscape. However, in conforming to institutionalized myths, organizations may sacrifice efficiency. To account for this, organizations may decouple formal structures and institutionalized rules, which affords the opportunity to resolve conflict between rules and efficiency.

Also central to institutional theory are the concepts of decoupling and loose coupling. As Meyer and Rowan (1991) note, "organizations in an industry tend to be similar in formal structure – reflecting their common institutional origins – but may show much diversity in actual practice" (p. 58). Organizations may thus present a front that is in alignment with institutional norms and expectations, but may not be operationalized in everyday practice (Bingham, 2018). Referred to as the "logic of confidence," this helps organizations maintain legitimacy, while practices of loose coupling and decoupling allow them to respond to internal pressures. Loose coupling describes a process in which an organization deals with conflicting pressures by creating a degree of flexibility between internal and external realities (Burch et al., 2020; Weick, 1976). Decoupling, which is a form of loose coupling, describes gaps between formal policies to which an organization ascribes and the actual day-to-day organizational practices (Meyer & Rowan, 1977). Structural and procedural changes are symbolic rather than operationalized, which provides a buffer between environmental pressures and day-to-day practice (Burch, 2007; Coburn, 2004). These processes of loose coupling and of decoupling allow organizations to maintain their legitimacy while also encouraging flexibility at the organizational level. For example, because schools are often subject to multiple conflicting pressures, they may decouple organizational practices from classroom practices to manage contradictory or inconsistent demands (Burch 2007; Coburn, 2004). As concepts, loose coupling and decoupling have been used to explain why policies and reforms may not have an impact on practice (Coburn, 2004).

Institutional theory provides the tools for understanding organizations and organizational change. As a theoretical framework, IT can help researchers better understand how institutions operate and influence organizations, and how organizations come to resemble each other, as well as the recursive role of institutions in shaping organizations and society.

Background and Foundations

Institutional theory as it is currently understood in sociology emerged from more functionalist perspectives on institutions and as a reaction to rational perspectives of organizational theory. As a precursor to current institutional frameworks, this original version of institutional theory is referred to as "old institutionalism." Old institutionalism focused on how informal interactions "deviated from and constrained aspects of formal structure" and subverted "the organization's intended, rational mission" (DiMaggio & Powell, 1991, p. 13). This perspective emphasized the criticality of local communities and face-to-face interaction in organizational behavior. In an old institutional framework, the institutional context was not seen as playing a large role in organizational behavior or in influencing individual actions in the organization. Instead, organizations were seen as shaping themselves to conform to institutional pressures and the individual actors within organizations could support and/or hinder the institutional structure (Bingham, 2018).

As a sociological perspective concerned with organizations, "new institutionalism" comprises a

> rejection of rational-actor models, an interest in institutions as independent variables, a turn toward cognitive and cultural explanations, and an interest in properties of supraindividual units of analysis that cannot be reduced to aggregations or direct consequences of individuals' attributes or motives. (DiMaggio & Powell, 1991, p. 8)

Critical to an institutional perspective in sociology is the idea that individuals' choices, preferences, and decisions can't be fully understood outside of cultural and historical context (DiMaggio & Powell, 1991, p. 10). Environments "penetrate the organization, creating the lens through which actors view the world and the very categories of structure, action, and thought" (p. 13).

In contrast with the old institutionalism, new institutionalism stresses the taken-for-granted, routine nature of human action, and sees individuals as "constituted by institutions," rather than the other way around. New institutionalism varies by discipline; however, the approach to understanding how institutions and organizations functioned was a response to simpler accounts of social processes. Institutional theory across disciplines is united by the assumption that how institutions are arranged and the social processes within institutions matter (DiMaggio & Powell, 1991, p. 3).

Recently, IT has focused less on identifying and examining larger institutional similarities and more on how actors and agency are embedded or operating within this environment (Burch et al., 2020). Alongside the influence of environmental pressures, institutional theory emphasizes "people in the organization, how they interacted in relation to the environment, and how those interactions shaped organizations" (Burch et al., 2020, p. 410). In other words, IT sees individuals as managing environmental pressures, rather than being paralyzed by them. Scholars working with new institutionalist ideas conceive of processes of institutionalization as a two-way street. Institutionalization evolved through the reproduction of social norms (through processes like isomorphism and diffusion), but rather than making agency within these processes unseen, institutional scholars have theorized how actors in organizations may respond to institutional pressures and have sought to explain those actions through constructs such as organizational fields, legitimacy, institutional logics, and sensemaking.

Key Terms and Concepts

An **Institution** can be broadly defined as "an organized, established, procedure" (Jepperson, 1991, p. 143), which represents "a social order or pattern that has attained a certain state or property ... that reveals a particular reproduction process" (p. 145).

Institutional Myths refer to larger accepted, prevailing standards and procedures that organizations accept in order to garner or maintain legitimacy and stability (Meyer & Rowan, 1977).

Institutional Logics are the orienting practices and symbols that guide organizational behavior.

Isomorphism refers to the idea that organizations influenced by the same institutional pressures ultimately end up looking functionally and organizationally similar (Beckert, 2010; P. J. DiMaggio & Powell, 1983).

Organizational Fields are related organizations. DiMaggio and Powell (1983) describe organizational fields as "sets of organizations that, in the aggregate, constitute a recognized area of institutional life; key suppliers, resource and product consumers, regulatory agencies, and other organizations that produce similar services or products ... the totality of relevant actors" (p. 148).

In Research

Institutional theory has been used extensively in research across a variety of disciplines, including sociology, education, organizations and management studies, and public policy. In education, for example, Coburn (2004) used IT, and specifically the concept of decoupling, to examine how teachers implemented a particular form of reading instruction, and how they responded to institutional pressures. Coburn found that while there was evidence of decoupling, it didn't account for the range of teachers' responses, ultimately arguing that other sensemaking processes, including accommodation and assimilation, led to incremental changes. Institutional theory has been used in other disciplines as well. Jeyaraj and Zadeh (2020), for example, drew on the concept of isomorphism to understand what types of institutional pressures influence cybersecurity responses. They found evidence of all three types of isomorphic pressures, and discovered that mimetic pressures happened over time, while coercive pressures were more significant in the short term and normative pressures were more significant in the long term.

Strengths and Limitations

Institutional theory has been one of the most influential sociological theories in recent decades (Aksom & Tymchenko, 2020; Beckert, 2010). Indeed, IT is one of the most prevalent organizational theories and has been used to great effect to explore how and why organizations change (or do not change). The concepts of isomorphism and decoupling, in particular, have helped to explain common processes in organizations and policy implementation.

Still, there have been significant critiques of various aspects of institutional theory. Some scholars have argued that the term "institution" has become an all-encompassing "umbrella term," making it nearly meaningless (Haveman & David, 2008, p. 588). Other scholars have argued that isomorphism, in particular, has been given too much analytic weight in research drawing on institutional perspectives (Mizruchi & Fein, 1999). However, others have said the opposite, claiming that IT has lost some of its analytic power due to a drift toward a focus on agency and change, rather than maintaining focus on isomorphism (Aksom & Tymchenko, 2020).

Additionally, some researchers have asserted that IT does not fully account for multiple levels of analysis. In response to that critique, several researchers have recommended combining institutional theory with other existing frameworks, in order to better account for issues at other levels of analysis. For example, Ogawa et al. (2008) recommend incorporating Cultural Historical Activity Theory (see Chapter 6) into an IT framework in order to account for learning processes in organizational contexts. Similarly, Bingham (2018) argues that IT can be conceptually integrated with dramaturgy to examine the interplay between institutional pressures and individual actions. Other researchers have argued for more critical forms of IT. For example, Coates et al. (2023) present an updated IT framework that integrates Indigenous Standpoint Theory to form Indigenous Institutional Theory, a theoretical framework and methodological tool that can be used to examine organizations and how they function, with an eye toward understanding discriminatory (e.g., gendered and racialized) structures.

Key Theorists: John W. Meyer; Brian Rowan; Paul DiMaggio; Walter W. Powell

Examples of Use in Research: Burch (2007); Coburn (2004)

Dramaturgical Theory

Definition and Overview

Dramaturgical theory, also often referred to as dramaturgical analysis or dramaturgy, is focused on understanding how people engage in various social actions and how and why they present themselves as they do (Goffman, 1959). As a framework, this theory relies heavily on the theater as a metaphor for categorizing and explaining human behavior.

A dramaturgical framework assumes that every action is a social performance, and that these performances change depending on the social norms of the situation, the audience, and the impression the individual wishes to convey. This performance is designed not only to achieve the goals of the given action, but also to manage the impression the actor gives to others in the interaction. This idea of impression management guides much of Goffman's work on dramaturgy. Impression management theory, which explores the conscious and subconscious ways individuals attempt to shape others' perceptions (Schneider, 1981; Gardner & Martinko, 1988), has been engaged as a standalone theory in sociological research (e.g., Rosenfeld et al., 1994).

Goffman's (1959) theory employs the language of theater and the perspective of social activity as a theatrical performance to explore and explain social action and behavior. In applying a dramaturgical framework, social action is situated in a metaphorical theater, where individuals' performances and activities take place in and are categorized by regions and scenes. A Region is a place, bounded by perception, in which performances of social action happen. Examples could include a workplace or a cocktail party. Regions, or stages, are defined by the actors' position in relation to the audience.

Regions are divided into front regions and back regions. The front region is where performances occur – where the individual seeks to give the impression of maintaining and embodying specific standards. On the front stage, individuals are trying to present and maintain a particular impression. The back region is where performances are developed and where the performance may be knowingly contradicted (Goffman, 1959). On the back stage, people may undermine the impressions they conveyed on the front stage. Off stage, individuals curate impressions that are distinct for different audiences. Image or impression management occurs through each categorized region. For Goffman, all insincere behavior is staged, but not all staged behavior is insincere (Goffman, 1959; Tseëlon, 1992).

Goffman outlines two groups of standards that influence how individuals behave (their "performances") in different regions. First, there is how the actor interacts with and treats the audience (Goffman, 1959, p. 110). Goffman refers to this as "politeness." The second group of standards has to do with how the actor behaves in front of an audience, while not necessarily interacting with them. Goffman categorizes this behavior as "decorum," and subdivides these into moral standards and instrumental standards. Moral standards are ends in and of themselves, while instrumental standards generally have to do with what employers expect of employees and the like. "Make-work" – giving off the impression that one is hard at work at any moment – is part of this idea.

A central idea of dramaturgical theory is Impression Management – the idea that people consciously and subconsciously adjust their activities to convey specific impressions to others (Goffman, 1959). Impression management as a concept can be extended to how people try to shape others' impressions of other people, objects, or ideas. When people attempt to control (consciously or subconsciously) how others perceive them (as opposed to how others perceive objects or ideas), it is referred to as self-presentation.

In a dramaturgical analysis, there are two distinct communication forms: impressions we give – the impressions people purposely convey – and impressions we give off – non-verbal communication conveyed during a social interaction (Goffman, 1959). The key difference between the two forms of communication is intention. Impressions we give are intentional. Impressions we give off may not be intentional. When the impressions we give and the impressions we give off are aligned, symmetry occurs. When verbal and non-verbal communications convey different expressions, asymmetry occurs.

Another central concept is the front. A front is the image presented by individuals to bound and define the social action or situation for the audience. The parameters for the situation are also provided by the others present in the situation, in reaction to the projected front. In defining a situation and presenting the front, individuals acknowledge the audience for the interaction, and adapt their actions accordingly. Fronts are closely related to the idea of idealization, which is a process of outwardly demonstrating ideal standards, while concealing any actions or processes that do not align with those ideal standards. This can apply not only to individuals, but also to organizations. As Goffman (1959) notes,

> Often we find that if the principal ideal aims of an organization are to be achieved, then it will be necessary at times to by-pass momentarily other ideals of the organization, while maintaining the impression that the other ideals are still in force. In such cases, a sacrifice is made not for the most visible ideal but rather for the most legitimately important one. (Goffman, 1959, p. 54)

Dramaturgical theory is useful as a framework for identifying and classifying behaviors, and for analyzing microsocial interactions within defined contexts. Specifically, this framework can support researchers in better analyzing and understanding how people express themselves in everyday situations (including social media) to influence the impressions they make on others in the course of social interactions. As a subset of dramaturgical theory, impression management theory can support researchers in understanding and explaining the impressions people project in a given situation and how those impressions may differ by context. Both dramaturgy and impression management can be used to understand individual, group, and organizational behavior.

Background and Foundations

Developed by Erving Goffman and outlined in his pivotal 1959 text *The Presentation of Self in Everyday Life*, dramaturgical theory emerged as an alternative to functionalist perspectives that dominated sociology in the early and mid-20th century (Denzin, 2002), and as a critique of classical and contemporary macro sociological theory, which was seen as too deterministic (Adler et al., 1987). Dramaturgy is emblematic of the larger movement toward microsociological perspectives and analyzing microsocial interactions.

A dramaturgical perspective is part of a larger sociological framework of symbolic interactionism, a paradigmatic orientation which focuses on how people engage social symbols and assumes that meaning arises out of social interaction and out of the interaction between subject and object. A symbolic interactionist orientation posits that people act according to the meaning they have made from their encounters (Blumer, 1969). Many aspects of dramaturgy, including the central idea of impression management, is rooted in the symbolic interactionist concept of the reflexive self, which identifies the self as capable of "thinking as a subject (I) about the self as an object (me)" (Tseëlon, 1992, p. 503).

Dramaturgical theory forms the basis for impression management theory, which has been adopted across several disciplines, including organizational and management studies and social psychology. Dramaturgical analysis is also the foundation for a paradigmatic and methodological focus on the microsocial interactions present in everyday life. Ethnomethodology, for example, overlaps with and builds on the microsocial focus of dramaturgy to examine how individuals construct, negotiate, and agree upon social order in the microprocesses of social interaction (Garfinkel, 1967). Dramaturgy can also serve as the foundation for many related theories and ideas, including code-switching.

Key Terms and Concepts

Front is the façade that actors present in social situations in order to define the situation for the audience.

Impression Management refers to how people consciously and subconsciously attempt to control or sway others' impressions of them.

The **Region** is where the performance takes place. This is a place where the audience sees the performance, bounded by time and the location of audience in relation to the actor. Regions are divided into the frontstage – where the managed performance takes place – and the backstage – where the performance is prepared and may be knowingly contradicted.

In Research

Dramaturgical theory is useful for what can be referred to as "everyday life" sociology. It is a micro-perspective that can be used to study and draw conclusions about everyday social interaction (Adler et al., 1987). Dramaturgical theory has been applied extensively in sociological analyses of collective meaning production. More specifically, researchers have used this theory to study organizations and behavior, and individual and organizational identity negotiation. In one example, researchers studied collaborative teaching in a sociology class, using dramaturgical concepts to analyze the sociology classroom as a performance space (Preves & Stephenson, 2009). This study specifically drew on the idea of impression management to understand how identities are negotiated in a collaborative teaching environment and how front and back regions may blur in a collaborative teaching situation.

Other researchers have used dramaturgy in studies of politics, governance, and business practices. For example, in one study, an ethnographer used dramaturgical theory to examine micro-level processes of interactions between citizens and officials and attempt to better understand civic participation and decision making (Futrell, 1999). Other researchers have used a form of dramaturgy – critical dramaturgy, informed by critical theory and postmodern theory – to explore issues of corporate responsibility (Boje et al., 2004).

Researchers have also turned the dramaturgical lens on themselves in more recent studies. For example, Gengler and Ezzell (2018) expanded on Goffman's original ideas to develop what they call "methodological impression management" – the "conscious and intentional attempts researchers make to influence participants' perceptions of a research project, their perceptions of the researcher(s) involved, and their relationship with its eventual results" (p. 808).

Finally, and perhaps most saliently in the current era, researchers have recently used dramaturgical theory to examine the presentation of self in social media (Hogan, 2010). Hogan (2010), for instance, engages dramaturgical theory, including the concepts of the presentation of self and impression management, and the notions of front and back stage, and applies those concepts to aspects of social media. Hogan finds that individuals' self-presentation can be categorized as "performances" taking place in synchronous "situations" and as "artifacts," taking place in asynchronous "exhibitions."

Strengths and Limitations

Dramaturgical theory provides a comprehensive analytical framework for examining microsocial interactions and motivations. The idea of impression management, in particular, is useful in examining a wide variety of organizational and individual actions and decisions.

One of the most common critiques of dramaturgical theory is that it is too universal and apolitical. Specifically, scholars have argued that dramaturgical theory neglects issues of class, gender, race, and social injustice (Denzin, 2002). Still, dramaturgy has been used to examine these issues, even if they are not specifically included in the theory itself. For example, researchers have used the concept of impression management specifically, to uncover differential treatment of women in the workplace (Greener, 2007). Further, concepts and theories that explore the implications of gender, or race and ethnicity, such as code-switching, build on ideas from dramaturgy to allow for more comprehensive and inclusive analyses.

Another critique of dramaturgical theory, and specifically, the idea of impression management, is that while Goffman regards impression management as being a catchall for both sincere and insincere behaviors, other sociologists and social psychologists see managed impressions as naturally insincere, while spontaneous behaviors are naturally sincere (Jones & Pittman, 1986; Tseëlon, 1992). Finally, scholars have argued that dramaturgical theory focuses on microsocial interactions without attending to macro-social contexts; in other words, it does not fully attend to the role of organizations and institutions in social activity (Bingham, 2018). However, a dramaturgical perspective can be integrated into other frameworks, such as institutional theory, that *do* focus on larger situational factors.

Key Theorists: Erving Goffman (Originating author)

Examples of Use in Research: Boje et al. (2004); Hogan (2010); Preves and Stephenson (2009)

References

Adler, P. A., Adler, P., & Fontana, A. (1987). Everyday life sociology. *Annual Review of Sociology*, *13*, 217–235.

Aksom, H., & Tymchenko, I. (2020). How institutional theories explain and fail to explain organizations. *Journal of Organizational Change Management*, *33*(7), 1223–1252. 10.1108/JOCM-05-2019-0130

Beckert, J. (2010). Institutional isomorphism revisited: Convergence and divergence in institutional change. *Sociological Theory*, *28*(2), 150–166. 10.1111/j.1467-9558.2010.01369.x

Bingham, A. J. (2018). New institutionalism in everyday life. *International Journal of Sociology of Education*, *7*(3), 237. 10.17583/rise.2018.3532

Blumer, H. (1969). *Symbolic interactionism: Perspective and method*. Prentice Hall.

Boje, D. M., Rosile, G. A., Durant, R. A., & Luhman, J. T. (2004). Enron spectacles: A critical dramaturgical analysis. *Organization Studies*, *25*(5), 751–774. 10.1177/0170840604042413

Bourdieu, P. (1973). Cultural reproduction and social reproduction. In R. Brown (Ed.), *Knowledge, education, and cultural change: Papers in the sociology of education* (pp. 71–112). London: Tavistock Publications Limited.

Bourdieu, P. (1986). The forms of capital. In J. G. Richardson (Ed.), *Handbook of theory and research for the sociology of education* (pp. 241–258). New York: Greenwood Press.

Bourdieu, P. (2018). The forms of capital. In M. Granovetter & R. Swedberg (Eds.), *The sociology of economic life* (pp. 78–92). Routledge.

Bourdieu, P., & Wacquant, L. (2013). Symbolic capital and social classes. *Journal of Classical Sociology*, *13*, 292–302.

Bowles, S., & Gintis, H. (2002). Schooling in capitalist America revisited. *Sociology of Education,* *75*(1), 1–18.

Burch, P. (2007). Educational policy and practice from the perspective of institutional theory: Crafting a wider lens. *Educational Researcher, 36*(2), 84–95.

Burch, P., Bingham, A. J., & Miglani, N. (2020). Combining institutional and distributed frameworks in studies of school leadership. *Peabody Journal of Education, 95,* 408–422.

Carter, P. L. (2005). *Keepin'it real: School success beyond Black and White.* Oxford University Press.

Coates, S. K., Trudgett, M., & Page, S. (2023). Indigenous institutional theory: A new theoretical framework and methodological tool. *The Australian Educational Researcher, 50*(3), 903–920. 10.1007/s13384-022-00533-4

Coburn, C. E. (2004). Beyond decoupling: Rethinking the relationship between the institutional environment and the classroom. *Sociology of Education, 77*(3), 211–244.

Coleman, J. S. (1988). Social capital in the creation of human capital. *American Journal of Sociology, 94,* S95–S120.

Coleman, J. S. (1990). Commentary: Social institutions and social theory. *American Sociological Review, 55*(3), 333–339.

Croninger, R. G., & Lee, V. E. (2001). Social capital and dropping out of high school: Benefits to at-risk students of teachers' support and guidance. *Teachers College Record, 103*(4), 548–581.

Davies, S., & Rizk, J. (2018). The three generations of cultural capital research: A narrative review. *Review of Educational Research, 88,* 331–365.

Denzin, N. K. (2002). Much ado about Goffman. *The American Sociologist, 33*(2), 105–117. 10.1 007/s12108-002-1005-3

Dika, S. L., & Singh, K. (2002). Applications of social capital in educational literature: A critical synthesis. *Review of Educational Research, 72*(1), 31–60.

DiMaggio, P. (1979). On Pierre Bourdieu. *American Journal of Sociology, 84*(6), 1460–1474.

DiMaggio, P., & Mohr, J. (1985). Cultural capital, educational attainment, and marital selection. *American Journal of Sociology, 90,* 1231–1261.

DiMaggio, P. J., & Powell, W. W. (1983). The iron cage revisited: Institutional isomorphism and collective rationality in organizational fields. *American Sociological Review, 48*(2), 147. 10.2307/ 2095101

DiMaggio, P. J., & Powell, W. W. (Eds.). (1991). *The new institutionalism in organizational analysis.* Chicago: University of Chicago Press.

Durkheim, E. (1984). *The division of labor in society.* The Free Press.

Futrell, R. (1999). Performative governance: Impression management, teamwork, and conflict containment in city commission proceedings. *Journal of Contemporary Ethnography, 27*(4), 494–529.

Garfinkel, H. (1967). *Studies in ethnomethodology.* Wiley.

Gardner, W. L., & Martinko, M. J. (1988). Impression management in organizations. *Journal of Management, 14,* 321–338.

Gengler, A. M., & Ezzell, M. B. (2018). Methodological impression management in ethnographic research. *Journal of Contemporary Ethnography, 47*(6), 807–833. 10.1177/0891241617744861

Giddens, A., & Griffiths, S. (2006). *Sociology.* Polity.

Goffman, E. (1959). *The presentation of self in everyday life.* Penguin Books.

Greener, I. (2007). The politics of gender in the NHS: impression management and getting things done? *Gender, Work & Organization, 14*(3), 281–299. 10.1111/j.1468-0432.2007.00343.x

Hallett, T. (2010). The myth incarnate: Recoupling processes, turmoil, and inhabited institutions in an urban elementary school. *American Sociological Review, 75,* 52–74.

Hogan, B. (2010). The presentation of self in the age of social media: Distinguishing performances and exhibitions online. *Bulletin of Science, Technology & Society, 30*(6), 377–386. 10.1177/ 0270467610385893

Immergut, E. M. (1998). The theoretical core of the new institutionalism. *Politics & Society, 26,* 5–34.

Jepperson, R. L. (1991). Institutions, institutional effects and institutionalism. In W. W. Powell & P. J. DiMaggio (Eds.), *The new institutionalism in organizational analysis* (pp. 41–62). Chicago: The University of Chicago Press.

Jeyaraj, A., & Zadeh, A. (2020). Institutional isomorphism in organizational cybersecurity: A text analytics approach. *Journal of Organizational Computing and Electronic Commerce, 30*(4), 361–380. 10.1080/10919392.2020.1776033

Jones, E. E., & Pittman, T. S. (1986). Toward a general theory of strategic self-presentation. In J. Suls (Ed.), *Psychological perspectives on the self* (pp. 231–262). Erlbaum.

Lareau, A. (2002). Invisible inequality: Social class and childrearing in Black Families and White Families. *American Sociological Review, 67,* 747.

Lareau, A. & Calarco, J. M. (2012). Class, cultural capital, and institutions: The ca se of families and schools. In Fiske S.T. & Markus H.R. (Eds.), *Facing social class: How societal rank influences interaction* (pp. 61–86). Russell Sage Foundation.

Lamont, M., & Lareau, A. (1988). Cultural capital: Allusions, gaps and glissandos in recent theoretical developments. *Sociological Theory, 6*(2), 153–168.

Meyer, J. W., & Rowan, B. (1977). Institutionalized organizations: Formal structure as myth and ceremony. *American Journal of Sociology, 83,* 340–363.

Meyer, J. W., & Rowan, B. (1991). Institutionalized organizations: Formal structure as myth and ceremony. In W. W. Powell & P. J. DiMaggio (Eds.), *The new institutionalism in organizational analysis* (pp. 41–62). Chicago: The University of Chicago Press.

Ogawa, R. T., Crain, R., Loomis, M., & Ball, T. (2008). CHAT-IT: Toward conceptualizing learning in the context of formal organizations. *Educational Researcher, 37,* 83–95.

Mizruchi, M. S., & Fein, L. C. (1999). The social construction of organizational knowledge: A study of the uses of coercive, mimetic, and normative isomorphism. *Administrative Science Quarterly, 44,* 653–683.

Preves, S., & Stephenson, D. (2009). The classroom as stage: impression management in collaborative teaching. *Teaching Sociology, 37*(3), 245–256. 10.1177/0092055X0903700303

Portes, A. (1998). Social capital: Its origins and applications in modern sociology. *Annual Review of Sociology, 24,* 1–24.

Rosenfeld, P., Giacalone, R. A., & Riordan, C. A. (1994). Impression management theory and diversity. *American Behavioral Scientist, 37,* 601–604.

Sablan, J. R. (2019). Can you really measure that? Combining critical race theory and quantitative methods. *American Educational Research Journal, 56*(1), 178–203.

Schneider, D. (1981). Tactical self-presentations: Toward a broader conception. In J. T. Tedeschi (Ed.), *Impression management theory and social psychological research* (pp. 23–40). New York: Academic Press.

Sandefur, G. D., Meier, A. M., & Campbell, M. E. (2006). Family resources, social capital, and college attendance. *Social Science Research, 35*(2), 525–553.

Stanton-Salazar, R. (1997). A social capital framework for understanding the socialization of racial minority children and youths. *Harvard Educational Review, 67*(1), 1–41.

Tseëlon, E. (1992). Self presentation through appearance: a manipulative vs. a dramaturgical approach. *Symbolic Interaction, 15*(4), 501–514. 10.1525/si.1992.15.4.501

Weick, Karl E. (1976). Educational organizations as loosely coupled systems. *Administrative Science Quarterly, 21,* 1.

Yosso, T. J. (2005). Whose culture has capital? A critical race theory discussion of community cultural wealth. *Race, Ethnicity, and Education, 8,* 69–91.

5   Psychology

Cognitive Dissonance Theory

Definition and Overview

Cognitive Dissonance Theory (CDT) is concerned with mental inconsistency and involves the interplay of three areas: cognition, psychology, and motivation (Harmon-Jones & Mills, 2019). CDT is a three-step process that holds that a percieved "cognitive inconsistency leads to a motivational state that promotes regulation, which comes mainly through a change of opinions or behaviors" (Vaidis & Bran, 2019, p. 1). In other words, perception, negative impact, then regulation or reduction strategies (Vaidis & Bran, 2018). CDT applies to a situation when what people believe to be true contradicts or clashes with newly acquired information or with how they act; in this situation, a cognitive dissonant state (CDS) is created (Elliot & Devine, 1994; Glatz et al., 2012; Cheng & Chen, 2022). Most CDT theorists agree that this dissonance can vary in magnitude (Harmon-Jones & Mills, 2019). CDT has been a major and well-respected theory in psychology for many decades (Vaidis & Bran, 2019).).

CDT posits that individuals' minds work to resolve the dissonance by changing their attitudes or beliefs, adjusting behavior, changing the environment, varying or filtering exposure to conflicting information, or deploying justification logic, depending on which is easier (Festinger & Carlsmith, 1959; Festinger, 1962a, 1962b; Hinojosa et al., 2017; Cheng & Chen, 2022). The larger or more important the conflict, the more motivated individuals are to resolve it. Alternatively, instead of resolving the inconsistency, one might choose to find ways to cope with the dissonant state, such as justification, ignoring the situation, or finding a compromise (Elliot & Devine, 1994; Vaidis & Bran, 2019). For a hypothetical illustration of CDT, see Figure 5.1.

Cognitive dissonance is a useful theoretical framework for exploring how and why individuals can hold multiple conflicting ideas and/or assumptions in their minds, and for better understanding why individuals' behaviors and actions may not match their espoused beliefs. Researchers studying political beliefs and actions, as well as any disconnect between individual beliefs and actions, can benefit from a CDT framework.

Background and Foundations

Social psychologist Leon Festinger was the first to publish research on the concept of cognitive dissonance theory (CDT) in 1957. Festinger is often considered to be to social psychology what Freud is to clinical psychology (Zajonc, 1990; Harmon-Jones & Mills, 2019). Festinger is not only known for his creation of and contribution to CDT, but also

DOI: 10.4324/9781003261759-5

Cognitive Dissonance Hypothetical Example: You are a new mom

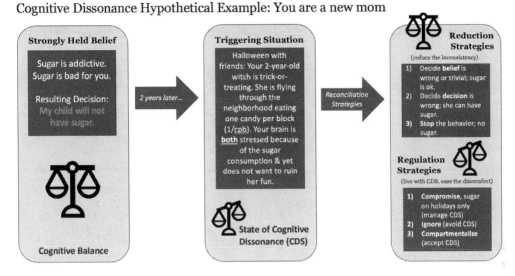

Figure 5.1 Example of cognitive dissonance. Adapted from Vaidis and Bran (2019).

for opening up "a style of research and theory in the social sciences that is now the common property of all creative workers in the field" (Zajonc, 1990, p. 661; Harmon-Jones & Mills, 2019). Over the years, CDT has generated hundreds of research studies in fields such as neuroscience, psychology, and sociology to learn about the origins of human values, attitudes, beliefs, and motivations and their consequences (Harmon-Jones & Mills, 2019).

Due to the maturity of the theory, many researchers have had the opportunity over time to experiment and expound on CDT. For example, Harmon-Jones developed an action-based model of cognitive dissonance (ABM) to explain the underlying reasons behind processes to reduce CDS (Harmon-Jones & Harmon-Jones, 2002). Additionally, several experimental paradigms, which influence the design of experiments to explore and test aspects of CDT have been recently utilized to understand human dissonance processes (Harmon-Jones & Mills, 2019). The first is the free-choice paradigm, which focuses on how individuals process information after a decision is made (freely); or what they think of each option after making a decision, particularly if the decision between two options was a difficult one. People have a tendency to spread the alternatives by applying more positive sentiments to the choices made and applying negative thoughts to the choices not made (Harmon-Jones & Mills, 2019).

A second CDT paradigm is the belief-disconfirmation paradigm (Harmon-Jones & Mills, 2019), describing how individuals work to bolster their beliefs when they receive information that contradicts, or creates dissonance surrounding existing beliefs. When people receive information countering what they believe, they may act to find those who agree, including actively working to persuade others. People may also misinterpret the new conflicting information (Gawronski et al., 2014).

Two additional research paradigms associated with CDT are effort-justification and induced-compliance (Harmon-Jones & Mills, 2019). Induced compliance targets perceived choice (e.g., high or low choice) in actions that are dissonant with beliefs. When people are induced to perform or say something against their beliefs, they can justify compliance and CDS is reduced (Cooper & Fazio, 1984). Similar experimental models to the induced-compliance paradigm include the forbidden-toy paradigm (Harmon-Jones & Mills, 2019), which focuses on the threat of punishment instead of incentives.

Finally, the effort-justification paradigm is also used in dissonance process research (Harmon-Jones et al., 2015; Zentall, 2016). This paradigm holds that the more dissonant the effort required to obtain a desired outcome, the more people will justify the value of that outcome (Harmon-Jones & Mills, 2019). By exaggerating the importance or desirability of the ends, individuals can decrease the dissonance required to achieve the outcome. These four paradigms described here are but a few that can be deployed in CDT research experiment designs.

Key Terms and Concepts

Cognitive Inconsistency or Discrepancy, also sometimes known as a triggering situation or inconsistency, is the circumstance that causes inconsistency between beliefs, attitudes, or actions (Harmon-Jones, 2017; Harmon-Jones & Mills, 2019).

State of Cognitive Dissonance (CDS) is the negative psychological state caused by a contradiction between a belief or attitude and an action. This state generally causes discomfort, but reactions can be as extreme as psychological distress (Festinger, 1957; Harmon-Jones & Mills; 2019; Anderton et al., 2011). Furthermore, CDS can evolve into a fear, or phobia of the dissonance (Festinger, 1962b; Anderton et al., 2011). Typically, this state motivates individuals to seek resolution or return to consistency between thought and action.

Dissonance Ratio refers to the magnitude of dissonance based on the number of dissonant cognitions divided by the number of consonant cognitions plus the number of dissonant cognitions (Harmon-Jones & Mills, 2019; Joule, 1986; Krause, 1972). Consonant cognitions are two aligned ideas (e.g., sugar is addictive; addiction is bad, therefore, sugar is bad). Dissonant cognitions are two obverse ideas (e.g., sugar is addictive; addiction is bad. Sugar is good.). See Figure 5.2.

Regulation Strategies are coping actions, thoughts, or decisions designed to ease the emotional discomfort or tension resulting from CDS (Harmon-Jones & Mills, 2019). These strategies are more about changing attitudes and beliefs Vaidis 2018by downplaying risks, manipulating exposure to information causing the dissonance, or asking others for reassurance (Vaidis & Bran, 2018).

Festinger's Dissonance Ratio

C = Consonance, that which we believe, or supports what we believe
D = Dissonance, that which is the opposite of what we believe

Total Dissonance = D/(D+C)

Figure 5.2 Dissonance ratio. Adapted from Festinger (1957).

Reduction Strategies are used to reduce or eliminate inconsistency by changing thoughts or behaviors (Vaidis & Bran, 2019). Examples of this include fixing the problem to align beliefs with actions, self-affirmation positive behaviors in other contexts even if in a specific context there is dissonance, or by trivializing the conflict. The definition was proposed by Vaidis and Bran (2019) in an attempt to clarify confusion between the two strategy types in resolving CDS. Reduction strategies have historically been the primary focus of research (Vaidis & Bran, 2019).

In Research

CDT is known for being one of the most well-developed, widely studied, and empirically based psychological theories (Vaidis & Bran, 2019). It is widely researched due to its abstract and general definition, as well as its application in a variety of topics (Harmon-Jones & Mills, 2019). As Harmon-Jones's noted, "the explanatory, predictive, and generative power of the theory results from its concern with the dynamic interplay of cognition, emotion, and motivation" (2002, p. 711). A cognitive dissonance framework can be used to describe and analyze the interaction of cognition, emotion, and motivation across disciplines, and has become particularly relevant in recent years in political science and public policy to explore why people may vote against their own interests and why people favor policies that may hinder or slow progress toward goals they support. For example, Bølstad et al. (2013) used a cognitive dissonance theory framework to understand strategic voting along political party lines. CDT has also been used for topics as diverse as emotional dissonance in employees (Pugh et al., 2011) and parents' reactions to youths' drinking and intoxication (Glatz et al., 2012).

Strengths and Limitations

CDT's strengths include its longevity and permanency in the field of social psychology. CDT is "one of the rare social psychology theories that propose a general pattern characterizing the human psyche and construction of reality ... CDT is a very important theory for the field" (Vaidis & Bran, 2019, p. 2). CDT research is mature and well-developed, presenting a large field of research to carry forward.

A limitation of CDT is the lack of consistent instruments to measure states of cognitive dissonance. The most popular scale was designed by Elliot and Devine (1994); however, it is limited in its breadth of measuring different descriptions of discomfort, restricting research only to *uncomfortable, uneasy*, and *bothered*, excluding other powerful states of discomfort such as guilt (Vaidis & Bran, 2019).

An issue with the research around CDT is the inconsistent use of the terminology (Vaidis & Bran, 2019). This originated with Festinger himself in his 1957 publication, *A Theory of Cognitive Dissonance,* when he used the term dissonance to refer to three different concepts: the theory, the state, and the triggering situation. The inconsistent use of the term in research persists today (Vaidis & Bran, 2019). Vaidis and Bran (2019) suggest referring to the theory by its full name: Cognitive dissonance theory (CDT), the triggering situation as the cognitive discrepancy or inconsistency, and the state the inconsistency causes as the CDS, or cognitive dissonance state. Consistent use of the terminology ensures alignment, reliability, and progress of research in the same direction.

Key Theorists: Lyon Festinger (Originating author); Eddie & Cindy Harmon-Jones (Theory development leaders); David Vaidis & Alexandre Bran

Examples in Research: Anderton et al. (2011); Bølstad et al. (2013); Glatz et al. (2012); Pugh et al. (2011)

Attachment Theory

Definition and Overview

Attachment Theory (AT) is a psychological interpersonal model that focuses on how and why human beings connect with their initial caregivers and how that experience shapes self-esteem, self-concept, and future relationships and connections to others. AT holds that the experiences and resulting internal relational models are played out in adult relationships as people replay the experiences as they know them from childhood (Kahn & Kram, 1994). Foundational to the concept of AT is the idea that humans are born with an innate desire to connect with others, specifically with our initial and primary caregivers (Bowlby, 1969.Positive, consistent experiences with initial caregivers lead to the beliefs that others are trustworthy and a strong sense of self-worth. Negative or neglectful caregiver experiences lead children to develop attachment insecurity, or distrust in others, and lack of belief in oneself (Bowlby, 1969).

There are four stages of attachment development known as ABC+D (Bowlby, 1969; Bakermans-Kranenburg & van IJzendoorn, 2009). The "A" is affective interactions, or the initial exchanges between an infant and caregiver such as smiling. The "B" is building attachment, or the infant seeking comfort and safety from the caregiver. The "C" is consolidation of attachment experiences where the infant gains confidence in the relationship and allows for separation without experiencing anxiety. According to AT, our early experiences profoundly impact later relationships, self-esteem, and our sense of security (Cassidy & Shaver, 2016). Therefore, the "+D" is equal to the Internal Working Model (IWM) from which this person will draw and apply to relationships throughout their life (Bowlby, 1969). IWMs are the mental models individuals build around sense of self, others, and the interactions and relationships between the two (Pace & Zavattini, 2011). IWMs are sub-conscious and stable unless disrupted by a negative significant event or ongoing adverse experiences such as abuse, neglect, or rejection from their main guardians (Pace & Zavattini, 2011).

Originally, there were three or four typologies in AT (Bartholomew & Horowitz, 1991). "Secure attachment" individuals described a positive initial experience with caregivers and a positive self-esteem. Alternatively, "anxious attachment" individuals described a negative or non-existent primary caregiver experience and an avoidant view of themselves.

Currently, AT research focuses on two dimensions: attachment-related anxiety and attachment-related avoidance (Brennan et al., 1998). As such, there are two important categories in AT research: Attachment-related anxiety reflecting a low self-worth and attachment-related avoidance reflected in behaviors that demonstrate low trust in relationships resulting in low intimacy and emotional expression (Brennan et al., 1998). Attachment anxiety tends to predispose people to relationship fears, including strong anticipation of abandonment or rejection and hyper-seeking of intimacy and support in relationships (Byrne et al., 2017). Ultimately, how people view themselves and others in relation to their original experiences with attachment impacts how they will interpret and behave in social situations or close relationships in the future.

AT is a useful theory for exploring the processes and behavior tendencies in relationship dynamics (Kahn & Kram, 1994). Dimensions of measurement useful in AT research include avoidance and anxiety, leading to attachment security or insecurity (Byrne et al., 2017). AT is most often associated with early childhood attachment; however, it is also appropriate for understanding internal qualities of security and their impact on relationships of any type in in any context, including romantic re-lationships, friendships, organizations, pets, and at work. Dimensions feeding AT include psychological safety and availability leading to security or insecurity (Byrne et al., 2017).

Background and Foundations

AT was originally developed by John Bowlby, and advanced in collaboration with Mary Ainsworth (Byrne et al., 2017). AT is considered a major theory in personality and psychology research (Brennan et al., 1998). In a study published in 2016, there were over 30,000 studies relating to the concept of attachment (Cassidy & Shaver). Forerunners to Bowlby's AT include Swiss researcher Eugen Bleuler in the late 1800s, a follower of Freud, who recognized the value of attachment (Bleuler, 1911). White, Sullivan, and Thompson in the 1930s and Fairbairn and Winnicott in the 1940s also developed con-cepts focused on relationships, attachment, and sense of self as foundational to problems of neuroses (Schwartz, 2015).

Bowlby started developing the etiology of AT during World War II in his 1944 research relating to the effects of extended separation from mother-figures on young boys (Crittenden, 2017). The seed of the idea was that negative early events could have long-lasting negative ramifications. Later, Bowlby studied the impact of family dynamics on the development of children – specifically, the attachment of children to their parents, or more directly, their mother (Bowlby, 1949).

Meanwhile, AT gained the attention of Mary Ainsworth. Ainsworth and Bowlby met during WWII and the two began collaborating, debating, and otherwise fleshing out AT (Crittenden, 2017). Ainsworth's research methods tended to be anthropological and longitudinal in nature, studying families where they lived (See Ainsworth, 1967). While Bowlby focused on theory development, Ainsworth focused on gathering the data to support the theory (Crittenden, 2017). Ainsworth's emphasis and legacy was on unique differences among individuals regarding AT (Ainsworth et al., 1978).

Ainsworth originated the "21-minute Strange Situation" experiment, allowing re-searchers to understand a child's attachment disposition quickly (Crittenden, 2017). Out of this laboratory test came patterns, or what came to be known as the ABS attachment strategies for infants to elicit comfort and safety from caregivers (Ainsworth et al., 1978). The strange situation procedure became the Separation-Reunion Procedure (SRP) over time and is still used today (Pace & Zavattini, 2011).

Key Terms and Concepts

Attachment-related anxiety can be seen in person with an extreme negative affect rooted in a poor self-image, fear of rejection, hyper-awareness of other's social and emotional cues, and an unnecessarily demanding and inflexible relationship style (Berry et al., 2008; Richards & Schat, 2011).

Attachment-related avoidance can be seen in someone who holds a negative view of *others*, demonstrating social withdrawal and/or hostility, behaving in intense and uncompromising ways (Bartholomew & Horowitz, 1991; Berry et al., 2008). Those who experience attachment avoidance tend to minimize the necessity of relationships as a defensive mechanism to being hurt (Richards & Schat, 2011).

Human attachment can be defined as "the innate propensity of humans to form protective and comforting relationships" and the "individual differences in the quality of attachment relationships" (Crittenden, 2017, p. 438).

In Research

Attachment theory (AT) is useful in interpersonal research and in understanding the impact of relationships in human development, organizations, and success and failure in any context (Byrne et al., 2017). Researchers have used AT to understand the impact of IWMs from early childhood development and their impact on any number of relationships and outcomes throughout life in the context of any field that involves people, including education, work, marriage, parenthood, and organizations. AT research also seeks to understand how to restore positive IWMs that have been damaged from negative experiences. AT is used frequently in the field of psychology to advance understanding of causes, effects, and cures for various mental health issues or interpersonal challenges (Berry et al., 2008).

AT has been used to study a variety of relationships and the impact of those relationships on mental health. For example, Beck and Madresh (2008) used an attachment theory framework to understand people's attachment to their pets and what that means for their mental health. Other scholars have used AT in business contexts to explore employees' relationships to employers and career management (Crawshaw & Game, 2015) and to examine customer engagement (Hinson et al., 2019).

There are several research tools and measures that have developed around AT as well. First, Bowlby's ABC+D of attachment strategies (Crittenden, 2017). Second, Ainsworth famous Strange Situation laboratory experiment that evolved into SRP (Ainsworth et al., 1978; Hesse, 2008). Additionally, Crittenden's Parents Interview and Mary Main's 20-question Adult Attachment Interview (AAI), which are used to assess attachment styles in adulthood remain important tools in AT research (Crittenden, 1982; Hesse, 2008; Pace & Zavattini, 2011; Berry et al., 2008). Another common tool is the Manchester Child Attachment Story Task (MCAST) vignette for young children (Goldwyn et al., 2000).

Strengths and Limitations

A strength of AT is its longevity and durability in the field of psychology. AT research is plentiful and well-developed, with many strong measures and instruments available for use including the MCAST, SRP, AAI, and more.

One common criticism AT receives is its applicability across cultures. AT claims universality (Keller, 2018); however, Henrich and colleagues (2010) identified an issue common in psychology scholarship – the research is often conducted in the context of Western, educated, industrialized, rich, and democratic contexts (Henrich et al., 2010). Keller (2018) references Henrich's work to argue that attachment as a theory was designed in a Western culture with values and norms and therefore it cannot be applied universally. Another related criticism of AT is the focus on the parents and mother-figures (Lamb, 2004; Keller, 2018). In other societies, the fathers, grandparents, siblings, or nannies may assume the primary caregiver role, and it is the culturally accepted norm.

Key Theorists: John Bowlby (Originating author); Mary Ainsworth (Co-leader in theory development); Patricia Crittenden

Examples in Research: Beck and Madresh (2008); Crawshaw and Game (2015); Hinson et al. (2019). Richards and Schat (2011)

Self-Determination Theory

Definition and Overview

Self-Determination Theory (SDT) explains the phenomenon of motivations, or the forces that move people to take action (Ryan & Deci, 2017). Those forces can be perceived values, satisfactions, and rewards, or negative pressure such as costs and cons. The intention of SDT is to understand human motivation for the purpose of predicting or guiding future behavior.

SDT is a humanistic personality and behavior research theory within the motivation theory family (Ryan & Deci, 2017). As a psychological and motivation theory, SDT stands out due to its focus on the effects of different types of motivation within human behavior. According to the SDT perspective, the types of motivation are located along a continuum running from externally controlled behavior to autonomous action (Ryan & Deci, 2017; Teixeira et al., 2012). A primary conclusion of SDT studies is that autonomously-driven activities have the strongest, or most successful outcomes (Vansteenkiste et al., 2018). This macro motivation theory targets understanding the self-actualization of needs and the achievement of an individual's full potential (Deci & Ryan, 2000).

Further, the SDT framework is concerned with the social context in which the human behavior and motivations take place (Ryan & Deci, 2017). Human potential can be dismissed, or at a minimum moderated, or potential can be enhanced and encouraged by those around them, or the situation in which they are in, such as winning a race. For example, enduring an abusive parent or boss can negatively impact potential and motivation and people can become passive and disengaged (Ryan & Deci, 2017). Alternatively, having a strong mentor or champion at work or in sports can grow a person's possibilities. According to Ryan and Deci (2017), it is important to acknowledge that while the social context is external to the person, it is their psychological perception of the external influence that impacts motivation.

SDT posits that there are two types of motivation, intrinsic and extrinsic, as well as the internal psychological needs for competence, autonomy, and relatedness or connection with others (Ryan & Deci, 2017). Intrinsic motivation means doing an activity because it has inherent satisfaction for the individual, such as a sense of accomplishment. Conversely, extrinsic motivation is defined as performing an action for a non-personal reason, such as through applied leadership pressure, a means to an end, or to please another person (Deci, 1975). Externally motivated activities can be assimilated and internalized and become intrinsic in the future. For example, a child might be motivated to learn to read by external rewards at school, such as stars on a chart for all to see. However, over time, the child develops a genuine love for reading and would do so regardless of any public reward.

SDT mediators include incentives and goal contents, both intrinsic and extrinsic (Gilal et al., 2019) as well as dispositional tendencies, or causality orientations (Deci & Ryan, 1985; Teixara et al., 2012). Causality orientations are how humans orient themselves within an environment that goes on to influence their motivations and behaviors. They can behave with internal motivations, external cues, or be passive in a situation. For example, with diets and exercise, causal orientations will influence whether someone will behave with discipline and according to the plan, behave if there are rewards or goals, or not behave any way at all (i.e., doing nothing).

SDT also relies on the concept of perceived self-relevance, or personal significance or meaning (Vansteenkiste, et al., 2018). One's personal desire and interest can power the completion of tasks (Deci & Ryan, 2000). However, internalization, a motivational ideal, exists along a continuum, but does not necessarily demonstrate evolution. A common misconception is that leadership can first apply external pressure and naturally students, employees, or children will adopt "volitionally sustained habits," or sustained behavior without the external motivation to encourage (Vansteenkiste, et al., 2018, p. 34). Studies have proven otherwise, however (Deci & Ryan, 1985). Indeed, externally applied pressure to motivate can backfire and produce opposing results.

Beyond intrinsic and extrinsic motivations, psychological needs also must be met when it comes to motivation. These needs are "nutrients that are essential for growth, integrity, and well-being" (Ryan & Deci, 2017, p. 10). Psychological needs relevant to SDT are autonomy, relatedness to others, and competence in the activity under consideration. These universal human needs, when satisfied, support positive growth and well-being; if thwarted and frustrated, they can result in defensive, reactive, or possibly destructive behaviors (Ryan & Deci, 2017). Regarding SDT goal contents, otherwise known as motives in the theory vernacular, they can also be intrinsic or extrinsic (Deci & Ryan, 2000). Intrinsic goals achieve personal satisfaction, whereas extrinsic goals are about gaining power, wealth, or other external benefits (Kasser & Ryan, 1996).

Causality orientations, or dispositional tendencies in SDT describe how one orients within environments such as political, cultural, biological, or social (Deci & Ryan, 2000; Ryan & Deci, 2017). SDT studies how causal orientations influence motives, actions, and outcomes. Conversely, SDT also considers environmental impact on motivation as there are "certain universals in the social and cultural nutrients required to support healthy psychological and behavioral functioning" (Ryan & Deci, 2017, p. 4).

SDT is a useful framework for studying motivation across a multitude of topics and contexts, including education – how individuals learn; business and organizational studies – how people behave in organizational contexts and how they can be trained and incentivized; and in policy, including what can be used to motivate people to behave in particular ways.

Background and Foundations

Motivation theories speak to what gives people energy to act and the direction in which they head (Ryan & Deci, 2017). SDT can be traced back to 1908 and Yerke and Dodson's research on human performance. Hull carried the motivation "torch" forward in the 1940s, focusing on the drive, or "drive state" behind motivation (Ryan & Deci, 2017, p. 13). In the 1960s, Vroom's expectancy-valence theory and Porter and Lawler's intrinsic/extrinsic work motivation theory, along with Bandura's research shifted studies toward cognitive theories of motivation (Gagné & Deci, 2005; Ryan & Deci, 2017).

SDT is founded in a rich history of human psychological theories and research. It was initially developed by Edward Deci in 1975. Richard Ryan later collaborated with Deci as a research leader on the SDT framework. SDT differentiates itself from other motivational theories in its focus on the type and source, as well as the impact on behavior and actions (Ryan & Deci, 2017).

As is often true with mature theoretical frameworks in the context of ongoing research, SDT has evolved and can be considered a macro-theory (Deci & Ryan, 2008). Within the larger framework of SDT, SDT has been further developed into six mini-theories over time (Ryan & Deci, 2017). See Figure 5.3 for the list of SDT mini-theories, in order of development.

See Figure 5.4 for a visual simplifying basic concepts of SDT mini-theories for ease of understanding, as adapted from Gilal et al. (2019).

Key Terms and Concepts

Autonomy is defined as the independence and volition people employ in their actions. This need is associated with freedom of choice and the ability to act independently. Autonomous behavior can lead to higher satisfaction and successful outcomes (Ryan & Deci, 2017). Within the SDT framework, there exists an autonomy-control continuum from dependance on others to independent control and freedom of choice (Gagné & Deci, 2005). SDT is the only motivation theory with a focus on autonomy and its support leading to regulation of behavior (Ng et al., 2012). In other words, if others support a person's autonomy, they are more likely to achieve high self-regulation in situations that require high self-control such as smoking cessation.

SDT Mini-theories	Description
Cognitive Evaluation Theory (CET)	The process by which social situations and extrinsic motivators such as surveillance, praise, pay, performance evaluations, and deadlines influence intrinsic motivation, sometimes negatively (Gagné & Deci, 2005). Additionally, foundational to CET is the idea that autonomy and competence are critical ingredients for intrinsic motivation.
Organismic integration theory (OIT)	The development of extrinsic motivation into autonomous adoption through internalization.
Causality orientations theory (COT)	The individual persistent characteristic differences that lead to specific outcomes that can be used to predict future results. There are three "orientations" developed by Ryan & Deci, they include autonomy, control, and impersonal or amotivational orientation (Gilal et al., 2019).
Basic psychological needs theory (BPNT)	How basic needs interact and are satisfied (or not), and the impact on human wellbeing, including physical and mental health. The basic needs are autonomy, competence, and relatedness (Gilal et al., 2019)
Goal contents theory (GCT)	Goals, or human aspirations, can be intrinsic (direct, personal satisfaction) or extrinsic (achievement results in other needs being met such as attaining wealth, degrees, titles, and material goods). Whether goals are intrinsic or extrinsic can impact motivation and well-being (Gilal et al., 2019).
Relationship motivation theory (RMT)	Strong and high-quality relationships one-on-one or in a larger social setting impact one's ability to understand "positivity or regard, but also respect for autonomy" (Ryan & Deci, 2017, p. 21). Relationships are essential for human well-being and optimal functioning (Gilal et al., 2019).

Figure 5.3 Mini-theories derived from SDT. Adapted from Ryan and Deci (2017).

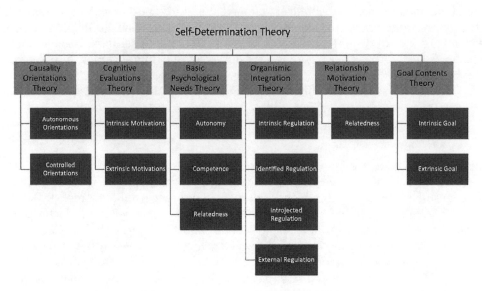

Figure 5.4 Simplified visual of SDT mini-theories. Adapted from Gilal et al. (2019).

Competence is the foundational sense that one can successfully perform or master a task or activity. Competence can provide energy to an activity; however, it is susceptible to depletion or destruction through failure or negative feedback from others (Ryan & Deci, 2017).

Internalization is the transition of an externally-sourced command, demand, or extrinsic motivator to an internally-valued activity or philosophy with personal meaning and ownership (Vansteenkiste, et al., 2018).

Relatedness refers to the need to relate to others and belong as an important member to a social group. Specifically, relationships demonstrate care to and from another, a social coherence otherwise known as homonomy (Deci & Ryan, 2000; Ryan & Deci, 2017).

In Research

SDT is a complex and rich theory containing sub-components which can be used as standalone frameworks. SDT's components and propositions have been widely researched, refined, and supported with empirical evidence (Ryan & Deci, 2017). Research domains where SDT can be easily applied are in education, work, healthcare, virtual environments, and exercise (Deci, 1975; Ryan & Deci, 2017). SDT can also be used to study human nature, capacities, and achievements. SDT is a flexible theory fitting into many research designs, including experiments or observation of natural events, longitudinal or point-in-time cross-sectional, and descriptive (Teixeira, et al., 2012; Ryan & Deci, 2017). SDT serves as a practical, functional, and critical tool within psychological and motivational research.

Gilal et al. (2019) conducted a meta-analysis of SDT use in marketing, attempting to understand how SDT is the best motivational theory to understand and solve marketing problems. Gilal and colleagues found that while other motivational theories are regularly utilized in the marketing research, SDT is a better predictor of consumer behavior (Gigal et al., 2019). In another study, Wehmeyer (2020) drew on SDT to understand the experiences of those living with intellectual disability. Wehmeyer connected SDT with quality-of-life theories for those with developmental disabilities to enable these individuals to control their own lives. In another example, Teixeira et al. (2012) applied SDT to understand exercise motivation and the achievement of healthy, sustained outcomes. This study aimed to understand the relationship between the key SDT constructs and exercise outcomes, and found that intrinsic motivation is a predictor of long-term exercise behaviors and the results are mixed regarding specific constructs and exercise.

Strengths and Limitations

SDT has a well-developed structure, allowing it to be clearly used by researchers. The SDT framework was founded in empirical research as a core element with the intention of supporting evidence-based interventions (Ryan & Deci, 2017). Another strength of SDT is its applicability across domains of research from business, to health, to education, to sports – motivation applies to all domains where there are people involved (Deci, 1975; Ryan & Deci, 2017).

A limitation is the concern around the cultural generalizability of SDT. Still, some research has supported generalizability in cultures with different behaviors and norms from the US (Jang et al., 2009).

Key Theorists: Edward Deci (Originating author); Richard Ryan (Co-leader in theory development); Tim Kasser

Examples in Research: Donald et al. (2020); Gilal et al. (2019); Teixeira et al. (2012); Wehmeyer (2020)

Code-Switching Theory

Definition and Overview

Code-switching (CS) originated in linguistics and was originally focused on how people utilize multiple languages in the same verbal or written communication (Weinreich, 1953; Weston & Gardner-Chloros, 2015). Code-switching could be as minimal as the use of a single foreign word, to using more than one language in a single sentence, and even alternating complete sentences in different languages. Code-switching can also serve to fill a lexical gap in the original language. For example, the German term *schadenfreude* (i.e., delight at the misfortune of another), has no English equivalent, and so, *schadenfreude* is the word typically used to describe this phenomenon even when speaking English. Finally, code-switching can also represent how people use the primary accepted language in a specific field or social setting when required but choose to use their native languages when otherwise able (Kaplan, 2001; Poplavskaya & Choumanskaya, 2022).

The behavior of code-switching functions as a form of communicating identity (Anicich & Hirsh, 2017). It extends beyond language to accent, tone, word-choice, dialect, cultural norms, norms of social interactions, and behaviors as well. More recently, code-switching has evolved to incorporate linguistic and behavioral shifts in differing contexts. CS has more specifically been applied to examine how the preferences and expectations of the dominant culture (typically White and male) and the myth of meritocracy interact to drive expectations that do not account for or incorporate non-dominant cultures and experiences (Carter, 2008; Carter, 2005). For example, several studies have examined how students from minoritized backgrounds may code-switch – navigate between dominant linguistic, behavioral, and cultural norms in school settings, and non-dominant linguistic norms at home – to negotiate cultural codes at school (Carter, 2005; Carter 2008). This allows them to achieve in environments that are often hostile to non-dominant groups and cultures, while also maintaining cultural connections at home.

The term code-switching can also refer to how people manage impressions according to the social context, such as work, home, activities, or time with friends. Generally, socially invoked code-switching is a common concept in today's culture (Krasas, 2018). For example, there is a popular US-based news source, National Public Radio (NPR), that has an ongoing podcast on the topic, *Code switch: Race. In your face* (Drummond, 2013–2023). This is a multi-generational, multi-racial group of journalists who lead a humorous and touching discussion the subject of race and its impact on society through a podcast.

The impact and importance of code-switching varies by person. Discrimination against and profiling of minoritized individuals and non-dominant groups has real and profound impacts on opportunities for employment, educational achievement, and housing, among other things (Moss & Tilly, 1996; Krasas, 2018). As such, for some, code-switching becomes a necessity in discriminatory contexts. However, there is also increasing resistance to the pressure to codeswitch, with the aim of turning the attention away from assimilation and toward cultural relevance and cultural responsiveness.

Code-switching, especially in social contexts, is controversial. For example, in the business world where English is the dominant language, employment has come to prioritize specific behavior coined "soft-skills," which targets personality, behavior, dress, accent, and attitude norms and abilities over technical knowledge (Moss & Tilly, 1996; Krasas, 2018; Chau, 2021). These standards and norms are idiosyncratic and socially constructed and, unsurprisingly, "reflect the practices and preferences of dominant groups such as white, middle-class sociability" (Krasas, 2018, p. 196; DeCelles et al., 2019). This creates bias or prejudice in the employment arena (Roscigno et al., 2012). While code-switching can serve as a technique to give interviewees a better chance at receiving an offer, that code-switching is required at all serves to maintain the White, heteronormative, patriarchal constructs that currently define "professionalism" (Feagin & O'Brien, 2003).

Related to the use of code-switching as a technique to overcome bias and prejudice is also the homogenization of language in writing and filmmaking, called "homogenizing convention" whereby all communication is in English, despite things taking place in non-English speaking contexts (Sternberg, 1981). This is considered "anti-historic Englishing" (Sternberg, 1981, p. 224). Yet again, code-switching becomes necessary for the audience to absorb the writing or movie (Weston & Garner-Chloros, 2015) and it again reflects the preferences of a White, middle-class audience.

Code-switching as a theory and framework is useful in the analysis and prediction of how people move between languages and how they present themselves and their linguistic and cultural identities across different situations. It can also provide the language and framing to help researchers better understand, analyze, and communicate the myths of meritocracy, and how certain cultural groups or minoritized individuals are penalized for not assimilating into dominant cultural narratives.

Background and Foundations

Code-switching, also known as code-mixing, is a classical linguistics theory focused on situations where people speak or otherwise communicate in two or more languages. The term "code" was adopted from communication engineering work on acoustic sciences (Elkins & Hanke, 2018). Code-switching was originally considered the "juxtaposition of two languages within the same sentence or conversation" (Weston & Gardner-Chloros, 2015, p. 196).

Gumperz (1982) is also cited as originating the concept of code-switching (Chau & Lee, 2021), defining it as the "juxtaposition within the same speech exchange of passages of speech belonging to two different grammatical systems or subsystems" (p. 59). Code-switching is rooted in the concept of language contact – the contact between two languages generating crossovers in grammar, words, and pronunciations over time (Weinreich, 1953). Exchanges begin with code-switching, then language changing, and can then become complete language shifts such as developing bilingual skills (Gardner-Chloros & Hickey 2020).

Specific to linguistic code-switching, there are two types: Inter-sentential (varying languages with each sentence but in complete sentences) and intra-sentential (switching languages mid-sentence) (Weston & Gardner-Chloros, 2015). Further, code-switching can be used within drama and literature as a useful technique for both reaching the audience in a language they can understand and conveying the social context of the writing, film, or dramatic performance. See Figure 5.5 for the different code-switching techniques utilized in these situations.

Type	Summary
Referential Restriction	The entirety of the story is purposefully mono-lingual and fully understandable by the audience (Sternberg, 1981). Jane Austen novels follow this strategy by using English with a British accent tone and exchange the entire film (Weston & Garner-Chloros, 2015).
Homogenizing convention	The works includes bilingual settings, conversation, and characters. However, all is communicated in a single language (Weston & Garner-Chloros, 2015). A good example is the movie *Seven Years in Tibet* where there are many languages, cultural settings, and locations, yet all is communicated in English (Pitt et al., 1998). Meir Sternberg describes this as "anti-historic Englishing" (1981, p. 224).
	There exists a continuum within homogenizing convention (Sternberg, 1981; Weston & Gardner-Chloros, 2015). These include
	- Selective reproduction: Minor use of code-switching to hint of larger linguistic code-switching.
	- Verbal transposition: Use of poor grammar to indicate the presence of another language.
	- Conceptual reflection: No linguistic code-switching, yet the use of sociocultural norms
	- Explicit attribution: Use of a second language and narration (or sub-titling) to explain
Vehicular matching	The language, written or spoken, is unabashedly multilingual or multi-dialetic (Sternberg, 1981). The Apple TV series *Tehran* is a prime example of the application of vehicular matching code-switching (Zonder et al., 2020). The main characters are Israeli spies living in Tehran, Iran. Much of the show is in Hebrew, Farsi, or English language with subtitling. However, this is a popular US show where many viewers are unlikely to understand the language of the show and must follow along through the words on the screen.

Figure 5.5 Strategies for literature, drama, poetry, and film-making linguistic code-switching. Adapted from Sternberg (1981). Also referenced, Pitt et al., 1998 and Zonder et al., 2020.

More recently, code-switching has been used in the fields of psychology, sociology, and cultural studies, where code-switching has been applied beyond language to attitudes, behaviors, appearance, and social norms (Krasas, 2018). The application of code-switching in social interactions can be related to impression management and relationship building (Myers-Scotton, 1993; Krasas, 2018; Chau & Lee, 2021), or to the development of multiple forms of cultural and social capital (Carter, 2005). By the 1970s, code-switching was expanded beyond multiple languages to conveying more practical meanings, such as identity (Elkins & Hanke, 2018). Scholars then began to expand code-switching into Bourdieu's "capital" theories: symbolic, economic, and social and power relations (Heller, 1992; Pavlenko & Blackledge, 2006).

Today, the phrase "code-switching" is used more broadly in the larger vernacular of society to mean adjusting to the expectations of others or to the audience for a variety of reasons (Molinsky, 2007; Elkins & Hanke, 2018; DeCelles et al., 2019). Alvarez Cáccamo (2002) suggested that code-switching be re-defined as a more universal way for humans to communicate and connect, utilizing every resource available.

Key Terms and Concepts

Intra-sentential code-switching, in bilingual verbal or written code-switching, means switching languages within sentences (e.g., a sentence has both English and Spanish words within it). This is common among bilingual speakers with high confidence or experience with both languages (Weston & Gardner-Chloros, 2015).

Inter-sentential code-switching is switching languages between sentences (e.g., one sentence is English and one is Spanish) (Hamed et al., 2022). This is common among bilingual speakers with low confidence or experience with the second language (Weston & Gardner-Chloros, 2015).

Nonce borrowing, loanwords, or borrowing refers to single-word borrowing from one language to the spoken language, often nouns, that are easily understood by the listener who has nominal second-language skills (Poplack & Meechan, 1998). This can be a one-off use. However, it can also make its way into the social corpora (Gardner-Chloros & Hickey, 2020). The use of *siesta* (Spanish for afternoon nap) or *agenda* (Latin for plan) in common English language are examples.

Extra-sentential code-switching refers to situations in which a loanword is borrowed from a second language (Hamed et al., 2022).

In Research

Code-switching can be used in a variety of disciplinary work, including linguistics research, psychological research, and behavioral, educational, or social research. As a framework, it can be used to analyze a variety of data including interviews, conversations, speech, documents, media (e.g., film, radio, podcasts, books, magazines, blogs), or other content. Code-switching theory can help researchers to understand not only the evolution of language and the development of languages, but also the communication of self-identities and social connections.

Examples of the uses of code-switching in research include Brunner and Deimer's (2018) study on the use of code-switching as a communication strategy in a multi-lingual Skype setting where participants are learning English. They deploy code-switching as a way to assist when they secondary language expertise cannot conjure the correct wording. Additionally, Hamed et al. (2022) performed linguistics code-switching research on automated speech recognition systems (ASR), focusing on the use of inter-sentential, extra-sentential, and intra-sentential in multi-lingual speech recognition.

Isbell and Stanley (2018) studied the use of musical and social code-switching for musicians as they moved between formal school settings, rock bands, and ethnic musical settings. The researchers focused on the perceptions, experiences, skill with code-switching and comfort. As another example, Vigier and Spencer-Oatey (2017) used an ethnographic case study deploying observation and interview methods to study how teams establish microprocesses and practices for their interactions within an international project team.

Strengths and Limitations

From a linguistics perspective, code-switching is a useful theory in researching the evolution of languages from contact to switching to full bilingual shift. In the more common, broader use of code-switching, it is a tool that allows one to communicate a social identity and connect with those around them (Myers-Scotton, 1993; Elkins & Hanke, 2018).

In social science, code-switching has been found to be useful in examining identity-setting, relationship-building, and aiding in communications where the speaker or listener is not fully fluent in English (Gardner-Chloros, 2020). However, one of the potential limitations of a code-switching lens is the potential to put the focus on how minoritized individuals and non-dominant groups can navigate spaces that do not account for racial or cultural variation, rather than focusing attention on dismantling systemic and institutional discriminatory practices. Encouraging code-switching in these contexts may ultimately increase marginalization (Bicker, 2018).

Other limitations of code-switching are that it can cause confusion among the listeners if the second language, or dialect spoken is unfamiliar to them (Myers-Scotton, 1993). Additionally, in educational setting, code-switching might be necessary if an English-language learner deploys it due to inability to find the correct dominant language words. This code-switching can lead to negative stereotypes (Grosjean, 1982).

Key theorists: Ulrich Weinreich (Foundational theorist); John Gumperz (Originating author); Penelope Gardner-Chloros; Carol Myers-Scotton; Shana Poplock

Examples in Research: Brunner and Diemer (2018); Hamed et al. (2022); Isbell and Stanley (2018) Vigier and Spencer-Oatey (2017)

Groupthink Theory

Definition and Overview

Groupthink Theory (GT) explains dysfunctional decision-making by groups where cohesiveness and a desire for harmony is high and there exists a "concurrence-seeking tendency" (Janis, 1991, p. 237). Groupthink is a "mode of thinking that people engage in when they are deeply involved in a cohesive in-group, when the members' strivings for unanimity override their motivation to realistically appraise alternative courses of action" (Janis, 1972, p. 9). In groupthink situations, members of the group may disagree or have information supporting a different decision. However, they refuse to voice concerns or disagreement to maintain peace (Janis, 1972). This wish to avoid controversy increases the chances that biases and pressures will inappropriately influence decisions. Groupthink represents flawed group decision-making and reduces the effectiveness and problem-solving capability of the whole (Schmidt, 2016). Further, once a decision is made, groupthink often results in irrational commitment to the decision, and in refusing alterations (Joffe, 2021).

Groupthink theory is concerned with group dynamics and their impact on decision-making, specifically poor decisions leading to impactful fiascos (Janis, 1973). Groupthink counteracts the generally accepted idea that "two heads are better than one" (American Psychological Association, 2014; Barber et al., 2014). In theory, multiple people can counteract the restrictions of a single thinker (Janis, 1973). Additionally, research suggests that high-cohesive groups are more likely to achieve objectives than low-cohesion groups (Janus, 1991). However, a group is made of flawed individuals, and therefore, capable of producing decisions leading to sometimes catastrophic failures. This dynamic and process of failed, and commonly premature conclusions, particularly the qualities of consensus-seeking behavior and driving cohesiveness, is known as groupthink (Mayo-Wilson et al., 2013).

There are several factors that contribute to groupthink including high in-group loyalty, fear of expressing dissenting opinions, an over-bearing leader, and lack of processes to gather information from multiple sources or debate pros and cons of current thought (Janis 1983). To remedy groupthink, it is important for groups to foster open communication, deploy critical and purposeful oppositional thinking, (e.g., 'devil's advocate'), engage external groups in examining and proposing solutions, and encourage diverse thinking and debate (Turner & Pratkanis, 1998; Pol et al., 2022).

There are common historic examples of groupthink. For example, the US Bay of Pigs invasion, the space shuttle Challenger launch, the US Iran hostage military rescue, Watergate, and the US government's failure to anticipate the Japanese attack on Pearl Harbor, all represent poor decision-making emerging from groupthink (Janis, 1972; 1983; Esser 1998).

Groupthink Theory contends that there are antecedent conditions to this behavior, including group cohesion, structural faults, and specific factors of the situation (Park, 2000). Examples of structural faults are: insulation in input; leader agenda; lack of processes to avoid groupthink such as a "critical assessment of proposals lest they be adopted for reasons other than merit," or establishing a mindguard who is the keeper of objectivity for the group; and homogeneity of membership (Janis 1991, p. 244; Janis, 1973). Examples of specific factors that contribute to groupthink are external pressure, high stress, low group regard based on previous failed experiences or significant challenges.

There are eight symptoms of groupthink (Janis, 1983), including mistaken perceptions of group invulnerability and moral superiority; lack of input due to stereotyping non-group members and group rationalization; self-imposed censorship; time-based pressure; pressure to agree from truth guardians; and direct pressure on those who disagree to conform (Janis 1983). See Figure 5.6.

Groupthink theory posits that to avoid groupthink, organizations or groups should seek outside input, invite debate, and remove the time pressures which encourage poor decision making (Janis, 1973; 1983). Other specific recommendations include, engaging impartial leadership; assigning an internal "designated dissenter;" dividing the group to debate potential decisions; purposefully seeking external input; and allowing extra time for debate.

Background and Foundations

Groupthink Theory is often attributed to Yale psychologist Irving Janis who popularized the concept in his 1972 book *Victims of Groupthink*. However, the term "groupthink"

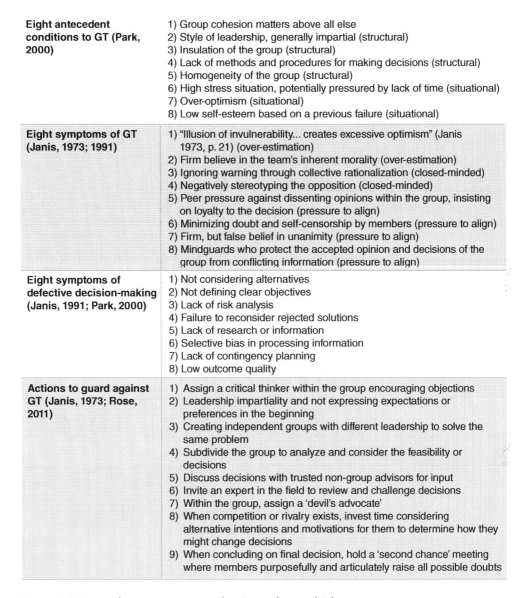

Eight antecedent conditions to GT (Park, 2000)	1) Group cohesion matters above all else 2) Style of leadership, generally impartial (structural) 3) Insulation of the group (structural) 4) Lack of methods and procedures for making decisions (structural) 5) Homogeneity of the group (structural) 6) High stress situation, potentially pressured by lack of time (situational) 7) Over-optimism (situational) 8) Low self-esteem based on a previous failure (situational)
Eight symptoms of GT (Janis, 1973; 1991)	1) "Illusion of invulnerability... creates excessive optimism" (Janis 1973, p. 21) (over-estimation) 2) Firm believe in the team's inherent morality (over-estimation) 3) Ignoring warning through collective rationalization (closed-minded) 4) Negatively stereotyping the opposition (closed-minded) 5) Peer pressure against dissenting opinions within the group, insisting on loyalty to the decision (pressure to align) 6) Minimizing doubt and self-censorship by members (pressure to align) 7) Firm, but false belief in unanimity (pressure to align) 8) Mindguards who protect the accepted opinion and decisions of the group from conflicting information (pressure to align)
Eight symptoms of defective decision-making (Janis, 1991; Park, 2000)	1) Not considering alternatives 2) Not defining clear objectives 3) Lack of risk analysis 4) Failure to reconsider rejected solutions 5) Lack of research or information 6) Selective bias in processing information 7) Lack of contingency planning 8) Low outcome quality
Actions to guard against GT (Janis, 1973; Rose, 2011)	1) Assign a critical thinker within the group encouraging objections 2) Leadership impartiality and not expressing expectations or preferences in the beginning 3) Creating independent groups with different leadership to solve the same problem 4) Subdivide the group to analyze and consider the feasibility or decisions 5) Discuss decisions with trusted non-group advisors for input 6) Invite an expert in the field to review and challenge decisions 7) Within the group, assign a 'devil's advocate' 8) When competition or rivalry exists, invest time considering alternative intentions and motivations for them to determine how they might change decisions 9) When concluding on final decision, hold a 'second chance' meeting where members purposefully and articulately raise all possible doubts

Figure 5.6 Antecedents, symptoms, and actions of groupthink.

was originally coined and defined by William H. Whyte in a 1950s management text (Whyte, 1952; Pol et al., 2022). The original definition leaned more toward the positive in group thinking within the business context – group conclusions were seen as better than individual thinking (Whyte, 1952; Pol et al., 2022). Over time, management texts began to prefer Janis over Whyte, as Whyte moved onto other research topics while Janis marketed the theory, redefined the terms, and carried GT forward to the meaning and framework used today (Pol et al., 2022). Theories similar to GT are Surowiecki's (2004) wisdom of crowds theory, Festinger's (1954) Social Comparison Theory, Moscovici and

Zavalloni's (1969) Group Polarization Theory, Weldon and Bellinger's (1997), Collaborative Inhibition Effect, and Leibenstein's (1950) Bandwagon Effect.

Key Terms and Concepts

Mindguard refers to members of the group who unofficially maintain the consensus (Janis, 1973; Pol et al., 2022).

In Research

Groupthink theory is found in wide interdisciplinary fields such a political science, decision sciences, communication, social psychology, business, policy analysis, and organization research (Turner & Pratkanis, 1998; Esser, 1998; Schmidt, 2016). For example, Breger (2010) conducted research on the culture of family court and applied groupthink theory to examine whether the stronger group of participants (lawyers, judges, and court administrators) over-powered and over-influenced outcomes for families, thus inappropriately impacting due process, justice, fairness, and dignity. Another example is DiPierro et al.'s (2022) research on how to improve team reasoning and decision-making in patient care. Their study sought to understand groupthink decisions and mitigations in the unique context of clinical healthcare. Lastly, Klein and Stern (2009) drew on groupthink theory in academic ideology. Klein and Stern used groupthink theory to understand whether and how higher education social sciences and humanities ideology consensus can have an outsized influence on departmental decisions, and potentially, on research outcomes. They also explored how groupthink can have a persistent quality resistant to challenge and change in this setting.

Groupthink Theory research is well suited to experimental, content analysis, and historic case studies, or a mix of these forms (Park, 2000). Case studies and content analyses have tended to better support Janis's groupthink theory model and have helped to develop the theory and illustrate how it works in various contexts and situations (Esser, 1998). Lab experiments have also helped to test pieces of GT's complex design, measuring and postulating antecedents, symptoms, structures, and situations. Still, there exists only a small amount of GT survey instruments, including one management training questionnaire designed for heuristic needs (Glaser, 1993). Additionally, Park (2000) developed a 146-item survey instrument was developed from Janis's texts and related theory instruments.

Strengths and Limitations

Strengths of GT include theoretical maturity and widespread understanding. Indeed, GT is well-known even outside research circles. Another strength of GT is the organizational understanding and awareness of this theory, serving as a useful warning and encouraging leadership to look for symptoms and avoid negative outcomes. In practice, the concept of groupthink continues to have strong "heuristic value" (Esser, 1998, p. 116).

One of the primary limitations of GT is its lack of empirical evidence (Esser, 1998; Park, 2000). Additionally, this framework lacks research consensus on validity (Park, 2000). As of 2000, of the 30 major studies on GT, five showed no support, 15 demonstrated partial support, and eight concluded in support of GT (Park, 2000). There is limited empirical research in support of GT antecedents and symptoms (Pol et al., 2022). Another limitation is the complex design and high quantity of variables to test (Turner & Pratkanis, 1998). There are 24 variables to test with GT, including eight antecedents, eight symptoms, and eight symptoms of defective decision-making (Park, 2000). The high volume of variables "inflates the power requirements of controlled experimental research" (p. 107). Finally, the aspects of GT are not universally defined across various studies (Rose, 2011).

Due to its commonsense popularity, the concept of groupthink is at "risk of casually characterizing poor group decisions as groupthink, without careful and thorough analysis" and indeed, groupthink could become "a convenient label with little explanatory or predictive power" (Hart 1991; Esser, 1998, p. 126). Furthermore, groupthink requires that everyone agrees in hindsight that a decision was faulty (Klein & Stern, 2009).

Key Theorists: William H Whyte (Foundational theorist); Irving Janis (Originating author); Paul 't Hart

Examples in Research: Ahlfinger & Esser, (2001); Breger (2010); DiPierro et al. (2022); Klein and Stern (2009)

References

Ahlfinger, N. R., & Esser, J. K. (2001). Testing the groupthink model: Effects of promotional leadership and conformity predisposition. *Social Behavior and Personality, 29*(1), 31–41. 10.2224/sbp.2001.29.1.31.

Ainsworth, M. A. (1967). *Infancy in Uganda: Infant care and growth of love.* Johns Hopkins University Press.

Ainsworth, M. A., Blehar, M., Waters, E., & Wall, S. (1978). *Patterns of attachment: A psychological study of the strange situation.* Erlbaum.

Alvarez Cáccamo, C. (2002). Introduction: Class and ideology in code-switching research. Paper presented at *2nd University of Vigo International Symposium on Bilingualism*, Vigo, Spain.

American Psychological Association. (2014, December 18). *Two (or More) Heads Are Better Than One for Reasoning and Perceptual Decision-Making.* https://www.apa.org/pubs/highlights/peeps/issue-36

Anderton, C. L., Pender, D. A., & Asner-Self, K. K. (2011). A review of the religious Identity/Sexual orientation identity conflict literature: Revisiting Festinger's cognitive dissonance theory. *Journal of LGBT Issues in Counseling, 5*(3–4), 259–281. 10.1080/15538605.2011.632745

Anicich, E. M., & Hirsh, J. B. (2017). The psychology of middle power: Vertical code-switching, role conflict, and behavioral inhibition. *The Academy of Management Review, 42*(4), 659–682. 10.5465/amr.2016.0002

Bakermans-Kranenburg, M. J., & van IJzendoorn, M. H. (2009). The first 10,000 adult attachment interviews: Distributions of adult attachment representations in clinical and non-clinical groups. *Attachment & Human Development, 11*(3), 223–263. 10.1080/14616730902814762

Barber, S. J., Harris, C. B., & Rajaram, S. (2014). Why two heads apart are better than two heads together: Multiple mechanisms underlie the collaborative inhibition effect in memory. *Journal of Experimental Psychology. Learning, Memory, and Cognition, 41*(2), 559–566. 10.1037/xlm0000037

Bartholomew, K., & Horowitz, L. M. (1991). Attachment styles among young adults: A test of the four-category model. *Journal of Personality and Social Psychology, 61*(2), 226–244. 10.1037/0022-3514.61.2.226

Beck, L., & Madresh, E. A. (2008). Romantic partners and four-legged friends: An extension of attachment theory to relationships with pets. *Anthrozoös, 21*(1), 43–56. 10.2752/089279308X274056

Berry, K., Barrowclough, C., & Wearden, A. (2008). Attachment theory: A framework for understanding symptoms and interpersonal relationships in psychosis. *Behaviour Research and Therapy, 46*(12), 1275–1282. 10.1016/j.brat.2008.08.009

Bicker, J. (2018). Teacher-led codeswitching: Adorno, race, contradiction, and the nature of autonomy. *Ethics and Education, 13*(1), 73–85. 10.1080/17449642.2018.1430934

Bleuler, E. (1911). *Dementia praecox of the group of schizophrenias.* International Universities Press.

Bølstad, J., Dinas, E., & Riera, P. (2013). Tactical voting and party preferences: A test of cognitive dissonance theory. *Political Behavior, 35*(3), 429–452. 10.1007/s11109-012-9205-1

Bowlby, J. (1949). The study and reduction of group tensions in the family. *Human Relations (New York)*, *2*(2), 123–128. 10.1177/001872674900200203

Bowlby, J. (1969). *Attachment and loss: Attachment*. Basic Books.

Breger, M. L. (2010). Making waves or keeping the calm? Analyzing the institutionl culture of family courts through the lens of social psychology groupthink theory. *Law & Psychology Review*, *34*, 55. https://go.exlibris.link/gqx9pZxl

Brennan, K. A., Clark, C. L., & Shaver, P. R. (1998). Self-report measurement of adult attachment: An integrative overview. In Simpson, J. A. & Rholes, W. S. (Eds.), *Attachment theory and close relationships* (pp. 46-76). Guilford Press.

Brunner, M., & Diemer, S. (2018). "You are struggling forwards, and you don't know, and then you … you do code-switching … " – code-switching in ELF Skype conversations. *Journal of English as a Lingua Franca*, *7*(1), 59–88. 10.1515/jelf-2018-0003

Byrne, Z., Albert, L., Manning, S., & Desir, R. (2017). Relational models and engagement: An attachment theory perspective. *Journal of Managerial Psychology*, *32*(1), 30–44. 10.1108/JMP-01-2016-0006

Carter, P. L. (2005). *Keepin' it real: School success beyond Black and White*. Oxford University Press. 10.1093/acprof:oso/9780195168624.001.0001

Carter, D. (2008). Achievement as resistance: The development of a critical race achievement ideology among Black achievers. *Harvard Educational Review*, *78*(3), 466–497. 10.17763/haer.78.3.83138829847hw844

Cassidy, J., & Shaver, P. R. (2016). *Handbook of attachment: Theory, research, and clinical applications* (3rd ed.). The Guilford Press.

Chau, D. (2021). Spreading language ideologies through social media: Enregistering the 'fake ABC' variety in Hong Kong. *Journal of Sociolinguistics*, *25*(4), 596–616. 10.1111/josl.12486

Chau, D., & Lee, C. (2021). "See you soon! ADD OIL AR!": Code-switching for face-work in edu-social Facebook groups. *Journal of Pragmatics*, *184*, 18–28. 10.1016/j.pragma.2021.07.019

Cheng, H., & Chen, C., (2022). Why people lurk in theme-oriented virtual communities: Integrating achievement goal theory and cognitive dissonance theory. *Information Research*, *27*(1). 10.47989/irpaper923

Cooper, J., & Fazio, R. H. (1984). A new look at dissonance theory. In L. Berkowitz (Ed.), *Advances in experimental social psychology* (pp. 229–266). Elsevier Science & Technology. 10.1016/S0065-2601(08)60121-5

Crawshaw, J. R., & Game, A. (2015). The role of line managers in employee career management: An attachment theory perspective. *International Journal of Human Resource Management*, *26*(9), 1182–1203. 10.1080/09585192.2014.934886

Crittenden, P. M. (1982). *Parents' interview*. University of Virginia.

Crittenden, P. M. (2017). Gifts from Mary Ainsworth and John Bowlby. *Clinical Child Psychology and Psychiatry*, *22*(3), 436–442. 10.1177/1359104517716214

DeCelles, K. A., Leslie, L. M., & Shaw, J. D. (2019). From the editors-Disciplinary code switching at AMJ: The tale of goldilocks and the three journals. *Academy of Management Journal*, *62*(3), 635–640. 10.5465/amj.2019.4003

Deci, E. L. (1975). *Intrinsic motivation*. Plenum Press.

Deci, E. L., & Ryan, R. M. (1985). *Intrinsic motivation and self-determination in human behavior*. Plenum Press.

Deci, E. L., & Ryan, R. M. (2000). The "what" and "why" of goal pursuits: Human needs and the self-determination of behavior. *Psychological Inquiry*, *11*(4), 227–268. 10.1207/S15327965PLI1104_01

Deci, E. L., & Ryan, R. M. (2008). Self-determination theory: A macrotheory of human motivation, development, and health. *Canadian Psychology = Psychologie Canadienne*, *49*(3), 182–185. 10.1037/a0012801

DiPierro, K., Lee, H., Pain, K. J., Durning, S. J., & Choi, J. J. (2022). Groupthink among health professional teams in patient care: A scoping review. *Medical Teacher, 44*(3), 309–318. 10.1 080/0142159X.2021.1987404

Donald, J. N., Bradshaw, E. L., Ryan, R. M., Basarkod, G., Ciarrochi, J., Duineveld, J. J., Guo, J., & Sahdra, B. K. (2020). Mindfulness and its association with varied types of motivation: A systematic review and meta-analysis using self-determination theory. *Personality & Social Psychology Bulletin, 46*(7), 1121–1138. 10.1177/0146167219896136

Drummond S. (Producer). (2013-2023). *Code switch: Race. In your face* [Audio podcast]. National Public Radio (NPR). https://www.npr.org/podcasts/510312/codeswitch

Elkins, B., & Hanke, E. (2018). Code-switching to navigate social class in higher education and student affairs: Code-switching to navigate social class in higher education. *New Directions for Student Services, 2018*(162), 35–47. 10.1002/ss.20260

Elliot, A. J., & Devine, P. G. (1994). On the motivational nature of cognitive dissonance: Dissonance as psychological discomfort. *Journal of Personality and Social Psychology, 67*(3), 382–394. 10.1037/0022-3514.67.3.382

Esser, J. K. (1998). Alive and well after 25 years: A review of groupthink research. *Organizational Behavior and Human Decision Processes, 73*(2–3), 116–141. 10.1006/obhd.1998.2758

Feagin, J. R., & O'Brien, E. (2003) *White men on race: Power, privilege, and the shaping of cultural consciousness*. Beacon Press.

Festinger, L. (1954). A theory of social comparison processes. *Human Relations 7*(2), 117–140. 10.1177/001872675400700202

Festinger, L. (1957). *A theory of cognitive dissonance*. Stanford University Press.

Festinger, L., & Carlsmith, K., (1959). Cognitive consequences of forces compliance. *Journal of Abnormal Social Psychology, 58*, 203–211. 10.1037/h0041593

Festinger, L. (1962a). Cognitive dissonance. *Scientific American, 207*(4), 93–107. 10.1038/scientificamerican1062-93

Festinger, L. (1962b). *A theory of cognitive dissonance*. Stanford University Press.

Gagné, M., & Deci, E. L. (2005). Self-determination theory and work motivation. *Journal of Organizational Behavior, 26*(4), 331–362. 10.1002/job.322

Gardner-Chloros, P. (2020). Contact and code-switching. In R. Hickey (Ed.), *The handbook of language contact* (pp. 181–199). John Wiley & Sons. 10.1002/9781119485094.ch9

Gawronski, B., Ye, Y., Rydell, R. J., & De Houwer, J. (2014). Formation, representation, and activation of contextualized attitudes. *Journal of Experimental Social Psychology, 54*, 188–203. 10.1016/j.jesp.2014.05.010

Gilal, F. G., Zhang, J., Paul, J., & Gilal, N. G. (2019). The role of self-determination theory in marketing science: An integrative review and agenda for research. *European Management Journal, 37*(1), 29–44. 10.1016/j.emj.2018.10.004

Glaser, R. (1993). *Groupthink index*. Organization Design and Development, Inc.

Glatz, T., Stattin, H., & Kerr, M. (2012). A test of cognitive dissonance theory to explain parents' reactions to youths' alcohol intoxication. *Family Relations, 61*(4), 629–641. 10.1111/j.1741-3729.2012.00723.x

Goldwyn, R., Stanley, C., Smith, V., & Green, J. (2000). The Manchester Child Attachment Story Task: Relationship with parental AAI, SAT and child behaviour. *Attachment & Human Development, 2*(1), 71–84. 10.1080/146167300361327.

Grosjean, F. (1982). *Life with two languages: An introduction to bilingualism*. Harvard University Press.

Gumperz, J. J. (1982). *Discourse strategies*. Cambridge University Press. 10.1017/CBO9780511611834

Hamed, I., Denisov, P., Li, C., Elmahdy, M., Abdennadher, S., & Vu, N. T. (2022). Investigations on speech recognition systems for low-resource dialectal Arabic–English code-switching speech. *Computer Speech & Language, 72*, 101278. 10.1016/j.csl.2021.101278

Harmon-Jones, E. (2017). Clarifying concepts in cognitive dissonance theory. *Animal Sentience, 1*(12). 10.51291/2377-7478.1199

Harmon-Jones, E., & Harmon-Jones, C. (2002). Testing the action-based model of cognitive dissonance: The effect of action orientation on post-decisional attitudes. *Personality & Social Psychology Bulletin, 28*(6), 711–723. 10.1177/0146167202289001

Harmon-Jones, E., & Mills, J. (2019). An introduction to cognitive dissonance theory and an overview of current perspectives on the theory. In Eddie Harmon-Jones (Ed.), *Cognitive dissonance* (2nd ed., pp. 3). American Psychological Association. 10.2307/j.ctv1chs6tk.7

Harmon-Jones, E., Price, T. F., & Harmon-Jones, C. (2015). Supine body posture decreases rationalizations: Testing the action-based model of dissonance. *Journal of Experimental Social Psychology, 56*, 228–234. 10.1016/j.jesp.2014.10.007

Hart, P. 't (1991). Irving L. Janis' Victims of Groupthink. *Political Psychology, 12*(2), 247–278. 10.2307/3791464

Heller, M. (1992). The politics of code-switching and language choice. *Journal of Multilingual and Multicultural Development, 13*(1/2), 123–142. 10.1080/01434632.1992.9994487

Henrich, J., Heine, S. J., & Norenzayan, A. (2010). The weirdest people in the world? *The Behavioral and Brain Sciences, 33*(2–3), 61–83. 10.1017/S0140525X0999152X

Hesse, E. (2008). The adult attachment interview: Protocol, method of analysis, and empirical studies. In J. Cassidy & P. R. Shaver (Eds.), *Handbook of attachment: Theory, research, and clinical applications*(pp. 552–598). The Guilford Press.

Hinojosa, A. S., Gardner, W. L., Walker, H. J., Cogliser, C., & Gullifor, D. (2017). A review of cognitive dissonance theory in management research: Opportunities for further development. *Journal of Management, 43*(1), 170–199. 10.1177/0149206316668236

Hinson, R., Boateng, H., Renner, A., & Kosiba, J. P. B. (2019). Antecedents and consequences of customer engagement on Facebook: An attachment theory perspective. *Journal of Research in Interactive Marketing, 13*(2), 204–226. 10.1108/JRIM-04-2018-0059

Isbell, D. S., & Stanley, A. M. (2018). Code-switching musicians: An exploratory study. *Music Education Research, 20*(2), 145–162. 10.1080/14613808.2016.1238061

Jang, H., Reeve, J., Ryan, R. M., & Kim, A. (2009). Can self-determination theory explain what underlies the productive, satisfying learning experiences of collectivistically oriented Korean students? *Journal of Educational Psychology, 101*(3), 644–661. 10.1037/a0014241

Janis, I. L. (1972). *Victims of groupthink: A psychological study of foreign-policy decisions and fiascoes.* Houghton, Mifflin. https://go.exlibris.link/gQWyNpQc

Janis, I. L. (1973). Groupthink and group dynamics: A social psychological analysis of defective policy decisions. *Policy Studies Journal, 2*(1), 19–25. 10.1111/j.1541-0072.1973.tb00117.x

Janis, I. L. (1983). *Groupthink: Psychological studies of policy decisions and fiascoes* (2nd, rev. ed.). Houghton Mifflin. https://go.exlibris.link/c5Y53Zt6

Janis, I. L. (1991). Groupthink. In E. Griffin (Ed.) *A first look at communication theory* (pp. 235–246). McGraw-Hill.

Joffe, A. R. (2021). COVID-19: Rethinking the lockdown groupthink. *Frontiers in Public Health, 9*, 625778. 10.3389/fpubh.2021.625778

Joule, R. V. (1986). Twenty five on: Yet another version of cognitive dissonance theory? *European Journal of Social Psychology, 16*(1), 65–78. 10.1002/ejsp.2420160111

Kahn, W. A., & Kram, K. E. (1994). Authority at work: Internal models and their organizational consequences. *The Academy of Management Review, 19*, 17–50. 10.2307/258834

Kaplan, R. (2001). English—the accidental language of science. In U. Ammon (Ed.) *The dominance of English as a language of science: Effects on other languages and language communities* (pp. 3–26). De Gruyter Mouton. 10.1515/9783110869484.3

Kasser, T., & Ryan, R. M. (1996). Further examining the American dream: Differential correlates of intrinsic and extrinsic goals. *Personality & Social Psychology Bulletin, 22*(3), 280–287. 10.1177/0146167296223006

Keller, H. (2018). Universality claim of attachment theory: Children's socioemotional development across cultures. *Proceedings of the National Academy of Sciences – PNAS, 115*(45), 11414–11419. 10.1073/pnas.1720325115

Klein, D. B., & Stern, C. (2009). Groupthink in academia: Majoritarian departmental politics and the professional pyramid. *The Independent Review, 13*(4), 585–600. https://go.exlibris.link/XZPBDpZ3

Krasas, J. (2018). The work of code switching. *Religion & Theology, 25*(3-4), 190–207. 10.1163/15 743012-02503004

Krause, M. (1972). An analysis of Festinger's cognitive dissonance theory. *Philosophy of Science, 39*(1), 32–50. 10.1086/288407

Lamb, M. E. (2004). *The role of the father in child development* (4th ed.). Wiley.

Leibenstein, H. (1950). Bandwagon, Snob, and Veblen Effects in the theory of consumers' demand. *The Quarterly Journal of Economics, 64*(2), 183–207. 10.2307/1882692

Mayo-Wilson, C., Zollman, K., & Danks, D. (2013). Wisdom of crowds versus groupthink: Learning in groups and in isolation. *International Journal of Game Theory, 42*(3), 695–723. 10.1007/s001 82-012-0329-7

Molinsky, A. (2007). Cross-cultural code-switching: The psychological challenges of adapting behavior in foreign cultural interactions. *The Academy of Management Review, 32*(2), 622–640. 10.5465/AMR.2007.24351878

Moscovici, S., & Zavalloni, M. (1969). The group as a polarizer of attitudes. *Journal of Personality and Social Psychology, 12*(2), 125–135. 10.1037/h0027568

Moss, P., & Tilly, C. (1996). "Soft" skills and race: An investigation of black men's employment problems. *Work and Occupations, 23*(3), 252–276. 10.1177/0730888496023003002

Myers-Scotton, C. (1993). Common and uncommon ground: Social and structural factors in co-deswitching. *Language in Society, 22*(4), 475–503. 10.1017/S0047404500017449

Ng, J. Y. Y., Ntoumanis, N., Thøgersen-Ntoumani, C., Deci, E. L., Ryan, R. M., Duda, J. L., & Williams, G. C. (2012). Self-determination theory applied to health contexts: A meta-analysis. *Perspectives on Psychological Science, 7*(4), 325–340. 10.1177/1745691612447309

Pace, C. S., & Zavattini, G. C. (2011). 'Adoption and attachment theory' the attachment models of adoptive mothers and the revision of attachment patterns of their late-adopted children. *Child: Care, Health & Development, 37*(1), 82–88. 10.1111/j.1365-2214.2010.01135.x

Park, W. (2000). A comprehensive empirical investigation of the relationships among variables of the groupthink model. *Journal of Organizational Behavior, 21*(8), 873–887. 10.1002/1099-13 79(200012)21:8<873::AID-JOB56>3.0.CO;2-8

Pavlenko, A., & Blackledge, A. (2006) *Negotiation of identities in multilingual contexts*. Cambridge University Press.

Pitt, B., Thewlis, D., Wong, B. D., Mako., Wangchuk, J. J., Tsamchoe, L., Jetsun Pema., Annaud, J., Williams, J. H., Smith, I., Johnston, B., & Harrer, H. (1998). *Seven years in Tibet* [movie]. Columbia TriStar.

Pol, O., Bridgman, T., & Cummings, S. (2022). The forgotten 'immortalizer': Recovering William H Whyte as the founder and future of groupthink research. *Human Relations (New York), 75*(8), 1615–1641. 10.1177/00187267211070680

Poplack, S., & Meechan, M. (1998). Introduction: How languages fit together in codemixing. *The International Journal of Bilingualism: Cross-Disciplinary, Cross-Linguistic Studies of Language Behavior, 2*(2), 127–138. 10.1177/13670069800200201

Poplavskaya, T. V., & Choumanskaya, O. A. (2022). Language code mixing in the discourse of IT companies. *Polylinguality and Transcultural Practices, 19*(1), 98–106. 10.22363/2618-897X-2 022-19-1-98-106

Pugh, S. D., Groth, M., & Hennig-Thurau, T. (2011). Willing and able to fake emotions: A closer examination of the link between emotional dissonance and employee well-being. *Journal of Applied Psychology, 96*(2), 377–390. 10.1037/a0021395

Richards, D. A., & Schat, A. C. H. (2011). Attachment at (not to) work: Applying attachment theory to explain individual behavior in organizations. *Journal of Applied Psychology, 96*(1), 169–182. 10.1037/a0020372

Roscigno, V. J., Williams, L. M., & Byron, R. A. (2012). Workplace racial discrimination and middle class vulnerability. *The American Behavioral Scientist, 56*(5), 696–710. 10.1177/0002764211433805

Rose, J. D. (2011). Diverse perspectives on groupthink theory – a literary review. *Emerging Leadership Journeys, 4*(1), https://www.regent.edu/journal/emerging-leadership-journeys/groupthink-theory/

Ryan, R. M., & Deci, E. L. (2017). *Self-determination theory: Basic psychological needs in motivation, development, and wellness.* Guilford Press.

Schmidt, A. (2016, May 26). Groupthink. *Encyclopedia Britannica.* https://www.britannica.com/science/groupthink

Schwartz, J. (2015). The unacknowledged history of John Bowlby's attachment theory. *British Journal of Psychotherapy, 31*(2), 251–266. 10.1111/bjp.12149

Sternberg, M. (1981). Polylingualism as reality and translation as mimesis. *Poetics Today, 2*(4), 221–239. 10.2307/1772500

Surowiecki, J. (2004). *The wisdom of crowds: Why the many are smarter than the few and how collective wisdom shapes business, economies, societies, and nations* (1st ed.). Doubleday.

Teixeira, P. J., Carraca, E. V., Markland, D., Silva, M. N., & Ryan, R. M. (2012). Exercise, physical activity, and self-determination theory: A systematic review. *The International Journal of Behavioral Nutrition and Physical Activity, 9*(1), 78. 10.1186/1479-5868-9-78

Turner, M. E., & Pratkanis, A. R. (1998). Twenty-five years of groupthink theory and research: Lessons from the evaluation of a theory. *Organizational Behavior and Human Decision Processes, 73*(2–3), 105–115. 10.1006/obhd.1998.2756

Vaidis, D. C., & Bran, A. (2019). Respectable challenges to respectable theory: Cognitive dissonance theory requires conceptualization clarification and operational tools. *Frontiers in Psychology, 10*, 1–11. 10.3389/fpsyg.2019.01189

Vaidis, D. C., & Bran, A. (2018). Some prior considerations about dissonance to understand its reduction: Comment on McGrath (2017). *Social and Personality Psychology Compass, 12*(9), 1–13. 10.1111/spc3.12411

Vansteenkiste, M., Aelterman, N., De Muynck, G., Haerens, L., Patall, E., & Reeve, J. (2018). Fostering personal meaning and self-relevance: A self-determination theory perspective on internalization. *The Journal of Experimental Education, 86*(1), 30–49. 10.1080/00220973.2017.1381067

Vigier, M., & Spencer-Oatey, H. (2017). Code-switching in newly formed multinational project teams: Challenges, strategies and effects. *International Journal of Cross Cultural Management: CCM, 17*(1), 23–37. 10.1177/1470595816684151

Wehmeyer, M. L. (2020). The importance of self-determination to the quality of life of people with intellectual disability: A perspective. *International Journal of Environmental Research and Public Health, 17*(19), 7121. 10.3390/ijerph17197121

Weinreich, U. (1953). *Language in contact.* Mouton Gruyter.

Weldon, M. S., & Bellinger, K. D. (1997). Collective memory: Collaborative and individual processes in remembering. *Journal of Experimental Psychology: Learning, Memory, and Cognition, 23*, 1160–1175. 10.1037/0278-7393.23.5.1160

Weston, D., & Gardner-Chloros, P. (2015). Mind the gap: What code-switching in literature can teach us about code-switching. *Language and Literature, 24*(3), 194–212. 10.1177/0963947015585066

Whyte, W. H. (1952). Groupthink. *Fortune*, 1–15. https://fortune.com/2012/07/22/groupthink-fortune-1952/

Zajonc, R. B. (1990). Obituaries: Leon Festinger (1919–1989). *The American Psychologist, 45*(5), 661. 10.1037/h0091620

Zentall, T. R. (2016). Cognitive dissonance or contrast? *Animal Sentience, 12*(1). 10.51291/2377-7478.1111

Zonder, M. (Creator), Shenhar, O. (Writer), Sykrin, D. (Director), Eden, D., Spiegel, S., Leroux, J., Emerson, P., Aranya, A., Koblenz, E., Michalakis, D. (2020–). *Tehran* [TV Series]. Donna Productions & Apple TV+.

6 Education

Ecological Systems Theory

Definition and Overview

Ecological Systems Theory, sometimes referred to as Bronfenbrenner's Ecological Systems Theory or Bioecological Systems Theory, is a multidimensional systems model for understanding learning and human development. An ecological systems model explains how individuals' learning and development is influenced by the nested environments in which they are situated. These environments are referred to as ecological systems (Bronfenbrenner, 1977). The ecological systems theoretical framework is concerned with the multidirectional influences of individual, community, culture, and society – specifically, how individuals relate to and are impacted by immediate and larger ecological systems, as well as how individuals influence those systems and the reciprocal nature of influence between systems.

Bronfenbrenner's (1994) ecological model is based on two defining ideas. The first is that human development happens through increasingly complex interactions between individuals and their immediate environment. These regular interactions are called proximal processes. The second idea is that the individuals' characteristics affect how the environment influences and is influenced by that individual.

Building on these ideas, the Ecological Systems framework proposes five nested, multidirectional ecological systems in which individuals operate and explains how those systems impact learning, development, and behavior (Bronfenbrenner, 1994). The five systems include the microsystem, the mesosystem, the exosystem, the macrosystem, and the chronosystem. The microsystem refers to the immediate environment of the individual under study, and can include family, school, peers, and/or work settings (Bronfenbrenner, 1994). These relationships may have the most impact on the individual as they are often intimate and consistent. Proximal processes operate within the microsystem. The techno-microsystem, encompasses more micro-level influences of technology, the internet, and social media (Johnson, 2010; Johnson & Puplampu, 2008). The mesosystem is made up of the interactions and connections between the individuals' multiple settings (e.g., home and work or home and school); the mesosystem is a "system of microsystems" (Bronfenbrenner, 1994, p. 40). Much like the mesosystem, the exosystem is made up of the connections between two or more settings; however, the exosystem includes interactions between a more immediate system and a system that the individual is not situated in, but which indirectly influences them. This could include, for example, neighborhood communities and family social networks. The macrosystem in made up of cultural and societal values and norms that influence conditions and processes at the

DOI: 10.4324/9781003261759-6

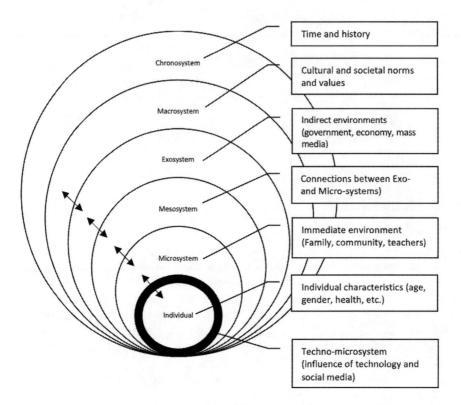

Figure 6.1 The ecological system. Adapted from Bronfenbrenner (1976, 1977, 1979, 1994).

microsystem level. Finally, the chronosystem encompasses change over time, both in the individual and in the environment. Within the chronosystem, there are three levels: microtime – the continuity or discontinuity in ongoing occurrences of proximal process (Bronfenbrenner & Morris, 2006, p. 796), mesotime – the frequency of the episodes/ occurrences of proximal processes, and macrotime – the changes in expectations and events at the societal level, within and across generations. The ecological systems are typically represented by a graphic of nested concentric circles (see Figure 6.1).

Ecological systems theory provides a comprehensive frame of analysis for identifying and understanding the nested, multidirectional levels of influence on how an individual learns and develops. Researchers can use ecological systems theory as a lens to understand the multidimensional influences on learning and development for both children and adults.

Background and Foundations

First introduced in the 1970s by Urie Bronfenbrenner (See Bronfenbrenner, 1976, 1977, 1979), ecological systems theory takes a sociocultural perspective to how environments and interactions shape child development. As the name suggests, ecological systems theory is inspired by ecological sciences – the study of how organisms interact with and relate to one another in the natural world. Building on these ideas from a psychological human development perspective, ecological systems theory was developed with the aim of better understanding the multidirectional nature of child development (Bronfenbrenner, 1994).

Bronfenbrenner (1977) argued that existing theories of child development focused too much on how individuals influenced children's development and not enough on how the environment influences development and how the interactions between children and their environments are multidirectional. Specifically, Bronfenbrenner wanted to move theories of human development away from "the science of the strange behavior of children in strange situations with strange adults for the briefest possible periods of time" (Bronfenbrenner, 1977, p. 513) as in more traditional experiments, in order to focus more on how children learn and behave in their natural environments (Darling, 2007). This represented a transformative shift in the field of child development at the time, moving children from passive objects of study to situating them as active participants in the social world (Elliott & Davis, 2018).

The emphasis on the multidirectional and interactional nature of learner and environment means that ecological systems theory shares many characteristics with other multidimensional theories of learning and development, including social learning theory (Bandura & Walters, 1977) and sociocultural learning theory (Vygotsky & Cole, 1978). However, ecological systems theory moves beyond the more immediate influences on child development (e.g., parents, teachers, community) to also include the constellation of cultural and societal influences and the interrelations between larger environmental influences and those nearer to the individual (Bronfenbrenner, 1977).

Ecological systems theory has evolved since its inception to further focus on the role of the individual and to emphasize process, person, context, and time. In the original conception of ecological systems theory, Bronfenbrenner posited four interconnected environmental systems: (1) the microsystem; (2) the mesosystem; (3) the exosystem; and (4) the macrosystem. Later iterations added the chronosystem as the outermost layer of ecological systems (Bronfenbrenner, 1995b, 1995a), along with the techno-microsystem as an additional layer to the individual level (Johnson, 2010; Johnson & Puplampu, 2008). In 2006, Bronfenbrenner revised the original theory to include more emphasis on the role of the individual (Bronfenbrenner & Morris, 2006; Ettekal & Mahoney, 2017). These revisions precipitated a naming change as well – to bioeco-logical systems theory – though most research drawing on this framework still labels it as ecological systems theory.

Key Terms and Concepts

Microsystem is comprised of the immediate interpersonal relationships experienced by the developing individual (Bronfenbrenner, 1979).

Mesosystem encompasses the interrelations between the environments in which an individual is situated and participates.

Exosystem includes larger systemic events or issues that are not contained in, but which influence the individual's immediate environment.

Macrosystem includes cultural or societal ideologies and belief systems that influence subsystems.

Chronosystem concerns changes in the individual and in the environment over time.

Techno-microsystem encompasses the influence of technology, the internet, and social media on individual development.

Proximal Processes are interactions between individuals and their immediate environments.

In Research

Although initially conceived of as a child development theory, ecological systems theory is used frequently both in PK-12 education and in higher education as well as across disciplines and to understand how individuals at a variety of life stages learn and develop. Given its multilevel, multidirectional nature, ecological systems theory is comprehensive and can be overwhelming to use as a theoretical framework. As such, sometimes researchers may not use all of the nested systems to frame their work, but may choose aspects of the theory to draw on. For example, researchers in higher education have used ecological systems theory, and the concept of the mesosystem in particular, to examine the influence of peer culture in the college experience, specifically around individual and group racial identity (Renn & Arnold, 2003). Other researchers have drawn on this theory to identify neighborhood structural features that affect children's school victimization and to explore interaction effects of school victimization between individual factors and family, school, and neighborhood influences (Foster & Brooks-Gunn, 2013). The holistic nature of ecological systems theory makes it well-suited to multilevel analyses at any level of human development.

Strengths and Limitations

Ecological systems theory is comprehensive, providing a frame for the multilevel, multi-directional, and multidimensional factors that influence learning. It is useful as a framework for quantitative, qualitative, and mixed methods research (Onwuegbuzie et al., 2013). A key strength of this framework is that is offers the tools and language needed to analyze and discuss these factors and how they affect individuals' development and learning in nearly any context. Indeed, ecological systems theory has been used extensively not only in education, but also in social work (Rothery, 2008), public health (Eriksson et al., 2018), and business and management studies (Kline et al., 2013), among other disciplines.

Although some scholars have criticized ecological systems theory as being too broad, the open-ended nature of the theory has also been identified as a strength, with scholars noting that the ecological systems model is open enough to accommodate additions and theoretical evolution (Rothery, 2008). Another critique in recent years has been the lack of specific attention in the framework to social justice. Scholars have noted that ecological systems theory should integrate a social justice lens, in order to better account for environmental realities like oppression, racism, and injustice (Rothery, 2008). Others have argued that the human-centered nature of an ecological systems framework precludes more global societal concerns over sustainability and climate change (Elliott & Davis, 2018).

Key Theorists: Urie Bronfenbrenner (Originating author)

Examples of Use in Research: Foster and Brooks-Gunn (2013); Paat (2013); Renn and Arnold (2003)

Situated Learning Theory and Legitimate Peripheral Participation

Definition and Overview

Situated Learning – also known as Situated Cognition – emphasizes that learning occurs in context; knowledge and learning are relational and meaning is negotiated and developed from context (Brown et al., 1989; Lave & Wenger, 1991). Legitimate Peripheral Participation (LPP) builds on the somewhat nebulous concept of situated learning to explain the more informal processes involved in how people learn new activities, knowledge, and skills as they join and become increasingly more involved in communities of practice (Lave & Wenger, 1991). In this perspective, learning and identity is embedded in the context in which the learner is participating. Legitimate peripheral participation captures how newcomers to a community of practice learn to be full participants *in situ*.

The concept of legitimate peripherality is a complex one. As Lave and Wenger (1991) explain, legitimate peripheral participation is imbued with power relations – peripherality can be empowering when conceived of as a place where a learner moves closer and closer to full participation. However, peripherality can also be disempowering if the learner is kept from full participation by those in power in the community. In other words, legitimate peripherality can be "a source of power or powerlessness, in affording or preventing articulation and interchange among communities of practice" (p. 36). It is also important to note that peripheral participation is a positive concept – it is not meant to imply disconnectedness from the central community of practice, but instead indicates how learners can gain access to better understanding through increased involvement in the community (p. 37).

Learning through legitimate peripheral participation takes place in communities of practice, which are constituted of groups of practitioners with a shared interest, who engage in collective learning efforts (Lave, 1991; Wenger, 1998). In a community of practice, learning is intimately connected to identity. Although discourse in the community of practice is key to legitimate peripheral participation, learning is situated and only occurs in practice, not in how the community discusses practice. The community of practice is the "living curriculum" for community newcomers as they learn (Wenger, 2011, p. 4).

These concepts come together to form a theoretical framework through which to better understand how individuals learn collectively, in practice. Learning is conceived of as social and situated, occurring through legitimate peripheral participation (Lave, 1991). Knowledge and skills are built and identity evolves through individuals' engagement in communities of practice. Mastery can be achieved through full participation in the community of practice.

Researchers can draw on situated learning and legitimate peripheral participation as frameworks to better understand learning in context and to explore how individuals learn in and are integrated into established groups and communities of practice. This framework is applicable not only in educational contexts, but also in any context in which learning, development, and community integration is taking place.

Background and Foundations

Situated learning is philosophically grounded in ideas from cultural and social psychology – specifically, that learning is sociocultural and occurs in social activity (Morell, 2003). Indeed, legitimate peripheral participation is similar to and derived from Vygotsky's "Zone of Proximal Development" (Consalvo et al., 2015), which is described as "the distance between the actual developmental level as determined by independent problem solving and the level of potential development as determined through problem solving under adult guidance or in collaboration with more capable peers" (Vygotsky & Cole, 1978, p. 86). The focus on how people learn through social activities and collaboration is integrally connected to communities of practice.

Situated learning is a bridge between a focus on cognitive processes and a focus on social practice. In their seminal article on situated cognition, Brown at al. (1989) argue that there is no separation between knowing and doing; the activities through which people develop and use knowledge are integral to learning and cognition.

Like most theories in education, situated cognition was developed not just to explain, but to improve teaching and learning. However, Lave and Wenger (1991), the architects of legitimate peripheral participation as a learning theory, argue that learning is not simply situated in daily practices; rather, learning is the primary outcome of social practice. Lave and Wenger determined that the concept of situated learning, as it was, did not go far enough to provide a specific analytic approach to how people learn. As such, the concept of legitimate peripheral participation emerged as a more concrete explanation of how situated learning happens. Lave and Wenger outlined legitimate peripheral participation as an analytical perspective that can help illuminate the specific processes through which learning occurs in social practice. However, Lave and Wenger assert that this perspective is not prescriptive; rather, it draws attention to key aspects of learning within communities of practice.

Lave and Wenger (1991) developed the idea of legitimate peripheral participation to connect ideas of cognitive apprenticeship and situated learning. Legitimate peripheral participation is concerned with communities of knowledge and practice, and specifically, with the relationships between novitiates and existing full participants in communities of practice.

Key Terms and Concepts

Situated Cognition is the idea that the environment, situation, or context in which learning is taking place is critical to understanding how learning occurs and how meaning is made (Spillane et al., 2002).

Situated Learning, often used interchangeably with situated cognition, is the view that all learning is situated in context and as such, individuals learn through engagement in communities and situated activity (Lave, 1991).

Communities of Practice are groups of practitioners with a shared interest, who learn collectively (Wenger, 2011). A community of practice is concerned with a joint enterprise, functions as a result of mutual engagement, and produces a shared repertoire of capabilities that members develop over time (Wenger, 1998).

Legitimate Peripheral Participation is an analytical perspective that outlines how learning and identity shifts occur in the shared activities of communities of practice (Lave & Wenger, 1991). As individuals move from novice participation to full participation in a community of practice, there are opportunities for transformation and mastery.

In Research

Situated cognition and legitimate peripheral participation have been used frequently in education research to better understand how people learn in context, and how newcomers move from the periphery of a community of practice to the core of the community. For example, researchers have used this framework to understand how adult learners transition to higher education by examining how adult students experience higher education as a community of practice and how their experiences were mediated by sense of belonging and identity shifts (O'Donnell & Tobbell, 2007). This framework is also used frequently in teacher education and professional development to understand how new teachers can become experts (Morell, 2003).

Legitimate peripheral participation has also been used to understand community belonging and learning in corporate and other organizational contexts. For example,

Konaposki et al. (2015) and Hamilton (2011) both explored how people engaged in a "family business" are integrated into and learn those businesses. Konopaski et al. (2015) focused on how these businesses maintain continuity through legitimate peripheral participation. Hamilton (2011) conceived of the family and the business as overlapping communities and examined entrepreneurial learning in that context.

Strengths and Limitations

Situated learning on its own is a somewhat vague concept, which limits its usefulness as a theoretical framework. The addition of legitimate peripheral participation and communities of practice helps to concretize the more ambiguous aspects of situated learning. However, there are limitations to a legitimate peripheral participation framework as well. Scholars have argued, for example, that Lave and Wenger dismiss the utility of more formalized teaching and learning practices (Fuller et al., 2005). In addition, legitimate peripheral participation focuses on the identity development of individuals in relation to their participation in communities of practice but does not account for how individuals' outside experiences shape the identity of the community. Other organizational theories, like sensemaking theory or institutional theory may better account for that.

Key Theorists: Jean Lave & Etienne Wenger (Originating authors)

Examples of Use in Research: Davies and Sandiford (2014); Hamilton (2011); Konopaski et al. (2015); Morell (2003); O'Donnell and Tobbell (2007)

Cultural Historical Activity Theory

Definition and Overview

Cultural Historical Activity Theory (CHAT) is focused on the socio-historical, cultural, and contextual factors that influence individual and organizational learning (Engeström, 1999b; Sannino & Engeström, 2018). In a CHAT analysis, learning is shaped by cultural, historical, and social contexts and practice is mediated by the interacting factors of the environment or system in which the actor operates (Roth & Lee, 2007; Sannino et al., 2009). In other words, learning occurs not just in the mind, but in the activities in which people engage with the world, through cultural artifacts such as signs and tools (Sannino & Engeström, 2018). CHAT emphasizes that learning occurs in the interaction between human and environment, and it is critical to look at both in order to understand change.

As a framework, CHAT is useful for understanding individuals' learning processes, the organization within which the individual learns and operates, and the cultural-historical mediators influencing individual and organizational learning (Bertelson & Bødker, 2003; Engeström & Miettinen, 1999). In a CHAT analysis, the organization or environment in which the individual is embedded is referred to as the activity system, and this serves as the overarching unit of analysis. Using the activity system as a lens, researchers can analyze individual learning, while also attending to community issues, organizational factors, the history of localized practices, and the evolution of practices over time (Engeström, 1999a). CHAT also allows for analyses of relationships between activity systems.

A key concept in CHAT is that learning and development is mediated by the interacting components of the activity system in which the individual is situated (Sannino et al., 2009). These mediating factors include the Subjects (the actors in the activity system, whose point-of-view drives the analysis), Tools or mediating artifacts (tools and resources that mediate goals), Rules (norms of the system), Community (others in the system), Division of Labor (division of responsibilities across the system), and the Object (the motive of the activity in the system) (Engeström, 1999a; Engeström & Sannino, 2010; Sannino & Engeström, 2018). The Subjects develop, interpret, and re-interpret the Object. The Object encompasses all the potential actions the Subject or Subjects could take toward a proposed Outcome.

The interacting factors in the activity system create tension and contradiction, which are the drivers of learning and change (Engeström, 1987, 1999a). Contradictions are more than just problems or conflicts (Engeström, 2001); they are "historically accumulating structural tensions within and between activity systems" (p. 137). In other words, contradictions are rooted not only in the individual and the organization within which the individual works, but also in the accumulated history of the system.

Given the many interacting factors of an organization, contradictions within and among components are expected (Engeström, 1987, 1999a). These contradictions prompt cycles of questioning, individual and collective learning, the development of new mediators and organizational arrangements, reconceptualization of the Object of activity, and reflections that feed back into the system to create new knowledge (Virkkunen, 2009). The development and subsequent resolution of contradictions can result in what is referred to in CHAT as expansive learning – concrete changes in how a system or organization operates, including organizational structure, systemic goals, and/or program design (Engeström, 1999b).

There are four primary sources of contradiction in any given activity system. An overarching Primary contradiction in a capitalist society is the contradiction between use-value and exchange-value (Engeström & Sannino, 2010; Sannino & Engeström, 2018). A primary contradiction can also occur within any component of the activity system. Secondary contradictions similarly occur among elements in the system. Tertiary contradictions develop from tensions between new and old elements of activity. Quaternary contradictions occur between central and ancillary activities or between a transformed activity system and other activity systems. Note the distinction between a Primary contradiction (between use-value and exchange-value) and a primary contradiction (a contradiction located within a specific component of an activity system). When Primary is capitalized, it indicates the foundational Primary contradiction in a capitalist society.

In a CHAT analysis, the expansive learning concept is useful for examining how activity systems evolve. The expansive cycle begins with internalization, in which actors in the system socialize neophytes to become competent members of the current system (Engeström, 1999b). Then, as individuals notice contradictions in the system, they attempt to innovate – the process of externalization. As more discordances in the system arise, internalization becomes critical self-reflection, and externalization becomes a search for solutions through which a (re)constructed activity system can emerge (p. 35). If the contradictions are not resolved, expansion does not occur.

CHAT organizes the interacting components of an organization and provides a frame for analyzing how individuals make sense of the conflicting nature of these components and how this produces either successful transformation of the system or regression to traditional practice (Sannino et al., 2009). The activity system and its components are often represented by a triangular heuristic (see Figure 6.2). Sometimes, contradictions are represented by lightning-shaped arrows between components or between activity systems.

On the whole, CHAT offers a roadmap for the analysis of organizational change and evolution in a given activity system, by providing the tools to identify and analyze individual sensemaking, the interacting factors that affect individual and organizational learning and change, and how activity systems relate to and influence each other.

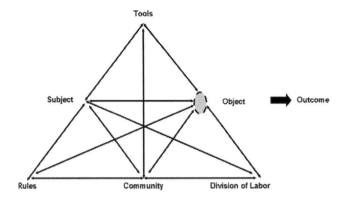

Figure 6.2 The activity system and its components. Adapted from Engeström, Y. (1987).

Background and Foundations

Philosophically, CHAT is rooted in the work of Hegel and Marx (Engeström, 1999a; Lektorsky, 2009; Sannino & Engeström, 2018). Marx et al. (1978[1845]) argued that existing perspectives were missing "the concept of activity that overcomes and transcends the dualism between the individual subject and objective societal circumstances" (p. 3). CHAT emerged as an attempt to focus analysis on human activity, overcome the dichotomy between individual and structure, and encourage a dialectical relationship between levels in order to offer a more complete analysis of individual and organizational learning (Engeström et al., 1999). This grounds CHAT in ideas of revolutionary change (Sannino & Engeström, 2018). From its earliest inceptions, improving the experiences of participants was the agenda and methodological stance of activity theory.

CHAT is grounded in the work of Vygotsky and Leont'ev, founders of the cultural historical school of Russian psychology (Engeström & Miettinen, 1999; Sannino et al., 2009). Originally, activity theorists mainly attended to issues of learning, cognition, and child development. Vygotsky, in particular, studied how children learn in and through social interactions, which became sociocultural learning theory (Vygotsky & Cole, 1978). This attention to interactions as a primary tenet of sociocultural learning theory became foundational to CHAT. Vygotsky developed a simple mediational model that included three components – subjects, tools, and object (Klen-Alves, 2021). In this model, the subject works toward a particular object, using tools or artifacts. Leont'ev (1978) expanded on this, developing a hierarchical model, where activity is divided into three levels – activity (object/motive), action (goal), and operation (conditions). Throughout each level, activity occurs as part of a community, interacting with mediational tools, rules, and a division of labor. Several contemporary scholars (see (Engeström, 1987, 1999a; Sannino et al., 2009) built upon the work of these early theorists to develop more contemporary versions of CHAT that included larger mediational models.

Key Terms and Concepts

Activity is the primary unit of human action, but is not the equivalent of action; rather, it's an attempt to change current reality that is mediated by interacting factors in the activity system.

The **activity system** is the system or organization in which individuals operate.

Mediating Components in the activity system include **subjects** (the participants engaged in the activity), **mediating artifacts** (tools, signs, and language that facilitate achieving specific goals and are a product of history), **rules** (conventions or norms), **community** (others in the system), **division of labor** (continuously negotiated division of responsibilities), and the **object** (evolving purpose) of the activity (Engeström & Miettinen, 1999). The **outcome**, rather than being the goal, is the result of the Object-oriented activity.

Contradictions are disconnections within or between elements of the activity system that are the sources of development and change. Changes in the activity system and in the individuals therein occur through the process of identifying and responding to contradictions in the activity system.

Expansive Learning refers to concrete changes in how the activity system operates, including organizational structure, systemic goals, and/or program design (Engeström, 1999b). Expansive learning involves identifying contradictions in the system, and developing solutions as they arise and evolve, in order to push the system toward transformation.

Internalization is the reproduction of culture within the system, which becomes critical self-reflection as tensions increase in the system (Lektorsky, 2009).

Externalization is the process whereby solutions to problems in the system are sought.

Tensions are disturbances or deviations from what would be considered normal in the system. They are the result of the underlying contradictions in the activity system (Engeström & Sannino, 2011).

In Research

We categorize CHAT as an educational theory because it originates in work on how people learn (See Vygotsky & Cole, 1978). In educational research, CHAT has been used extensively to understand how individuals learn and change, and how the organizations and systems in which they operate evolve alongside and in response to individual learning. For example, researchers have used the CHAT concept of contradictions to examine how educational technology use evolves over time (Murphy & Rodriguez-Manzanares, 2008) or to explore how teachers and leaders make sense of, incorporate, and adopt various educational policies and reforms (Bingham, 2017; Bingham et al., 2018). However, CHAT is applicable not just in schools and educational settings, but in any setting where learning or change occurs. For example, researchers have used CHAT to examine software development and the interplay between development and organizational structure (Adler, 2005). As activity theory has grown in popularity, it is increasingly being applied to issues of innovative organizational change (e.g., Engeström et al., 1995; Engeström, 1999; Engeström, 2009), organizational studies (e.g., Blackler, 2009), and institutional practices (e.g., Makitalo & Saljo, 2009).

Strengths and Limitations

CHAT helps researchers understand learning and change, at both the individual and organizational levels. A CHAT framework supports researchers in attending to individual- and organizational-level mediating factors. A CHAT analysis can also range out from the organization itself to examine constellations of organizations, as well as societal and cultural-historical context (Sannino & Engeström, 2018). Given the complex nature of educational change, instructional reform, implementation, and teacher practice, this makes CHAT a generative frame of analysis in educational research.

However, CHAT is limited in some ways, specifically around zooming in on how the Subjects in the activity system interpret and act on changes in the activity system, how they make sense of the Object of activity, and how external representation of reforms and policies influence those processes. Additionally, Roth (2009) asserts that CHAT scholars have yet to take into account the "agentive dimensions of activity, including identity, emotion, ethics, and morality, or derivative concepts, such as motivation, identification, responsibility, and solidarity – all of which are integral to concrete praxis and its singular nature" (p. 53).

Key Theorists: Lev Vygotsky (Originating author); Michael Cole; Vassily Davydov; Yrjo Engeström; Evald Il'enkov; Aleksei Leont'ev; Alexander Luria; Reijo Miettinen; Raija-Leena Punamäki; Vitaly Rubtsov; Annalisa Sannino; Lisa C. Yamagata-Lynch

Examples of Use in Research: Adler (2005); Anderson and Stillman (2013); Bingham (2016; 2017); Bingham et al. (2018); Murphy and Rodriguez-Manzanares (2008)

Transition Theory

Definition and Overview

Transition theory is concerned with the events and non-events that trigger changes in roles, relationships, and assumptions – life transitions (Chickering & Schlossberg, 1995; Goodman et al., 2006; Schlossberg, 1981). Generally, transition frameworks assert that life events – transitions – are typically experienced by individuals as continuing phenomena which may include multiple difficulties at different points in the transition (Evans et al., 2010; Griffin and Gilbert, 2015; Merriam and Caffarella, 1999).

According to transition theory, there are three types of transitions: anticipated transitions, unanticipated transitions, and non-events (Anderson et al., 2012; Goodman et al., 2006). Anticipated transitions are expected, and often welcomed transitions, like a graduation or a marriage. Unanticipated transitions are unexpected and can include negative events like losing a job, sudden deaths, or accidents, or more positive events like an unexpected promotion. Non-events are transitions that were expected to happen, but never took place, like a move that fell through or not getting into a particular college. Each of these transition types can include very clear transitions, like starting college, or more subtle ones, like getting a haircut. The key is that in order to be considered a transition, the individual to which it is happening has to consider it as such. Generally, although an event or non-event may trigger the transition, the transition itself is something the individual experiences over time (Goodman et al., 2006).

Transitions typically have three phases: "moving in," "moving through," and "moving out" (Chickering & Schlossberg, 1995; Goodman et al., 2006). Moving in refers to how the individual approaches the transition, moving through is how the individual copes with the transition, and moving out is associated with the end of the transition cycle. Take, for example, higher education as a transition. The "moving in" process could refer to a student starting college, while "moving through" could include things like learning to study, making friends, and choosing a major. "Moving out" could include graduating and figuring out what's next – moving on to the next phase or to another transition.

Multiple factors influence an individual's capability to handle transition, including the transition type, process, and context (Anderson et al., 2012; Schlossberg et al., 1995). Individuals' responses to transitions can be affected by the specific characteristics of the transition as well (Schlossberg, 1981). For example, if the transition involves a role change, whether the change is seen as a gain (like getting a new job) or a loss (like getting divorced) can influence how individuals handle that transition (Powers, 2010). The affect, or the feelings the transition provokes, and whether those feelings are positive or negative, is also important to how individuals transition. Additionally, the source of the change and whether it is internal – a conscious choice made by the individual – or external – initiated by other people or by circumstances – has implications for the individual managing the transition. Timing is another key characteristic. Transitions can be seen as "on-time," meaning that the timing of the transition is socially typical, or "off-time," meaning that the timing is out of sync with social norms. The onset of the transition and whether it is gradual or sudden can also affect how well individuals are able to adapt. Having adequate time to prepare for a transition can be critical to successful transitions. Similarly, the duration of the transition and whether it is permanent, temporary, or uncertain can also affect how well individuals deal with the change. Finally, the level of stress associated with the transition can influence adjustment.

Transitions can also be impacted by the availability and utilization of particular resources and assets. These resources and assets are referred to in a Transition Theory framework as the "4 S's:" situation, self, support, and strategies (Goodman et al., 2006). Situation refers to the context in which the transition occurs, and can include the timing and location of the transition. Self refers to the individual's background, beliefs, and prior experiences with similar transitions. Support describes the tools that may help individuals transition and can include financial or social tools. Lastly, strategies are the approaches individuals use to transition successfully. The four S's can be used to help understand the phases of transition (Goodman et al., 2006).

As a framework, transition theory can help researchers describe, analyze, and understand how individuals approach, manage, and make sense of life changes in a variety of circumstances. Further, transition theory offers a framework for identifying the interacting factors that may influence transitions and thus can support researchers in discovering or presenting specific recommendations for supporting transitions across contexts.

Background and Foundations

Transition theory was developed in the field of counseling by Nancy Schlossberg. Schlossberg (1981) advanced the theory from existing work (e.g., Levinson, 1978; Lowenthal and Chiriboga, 1975; Neugarten, 1979), asserting that individuals differ in how they conceptualize and respond to change as well as the recognition that individuals' abilities to manage transitions may vary across their lifetimes, depending on the characteristics of the change. The transition theory model was created to better understand what accounts for differences across individuals as they navigate transitions, as well as the differences that emerge within the same individual at different points in their lives. Additionally, Schlossberg (1981) emphasized that this framework should be used by counselors to help people navigate transitions. Schlossberg ultimately argued that it isn't the transition itself that is the most important, but rather the life stage and situation of the individual navigating the transition. This point endured throughout Schlossberg's work on transitions.

In its original iteration, transition theory put forth the idea that three sets of factors influence transition: (1) The characteristics of the transition; (2) the pre- and post-transition environments; and (3) the characteristics of the individual experiencing the transition (Schlossberg, 1981, p. 5). As transition theory evolved, the moving in, moving through, and moving out phases of transition were fleshed out to better articulate the stages that exist throughout a transition. Additionally, scholars further developed the factors that influence individuals' abilities to handle transition, including the type, process, and context of the transition (Anderson et al., 2012; Schlossberg et al., 1995), as well as the four S's, which affect how individuals manage transitions (Goodman et al., 2006).

Key Terms and Concepts

Transitions are events and non-events that prompt changes in an individual's roles, relationships, and/or assumptions about themselves and the world (Goodman et al., 2006). To be considered a transition as defined in transition theory, the individual to which it's happening must identify it as such.

Situation is the context of the transition, including when and where it happens (Goodman et al., 2006).

Self includes an individual's background, including prior experiences and existing beliefs, specifically around earlier transitions (Goodman et al., 2006).

Support encompasses any tools that an individual could use to help with a transition (Goodman et al., 2006).

Strategies refer to the individual's approach to the transition (Goodman et al., 2006).

In Research

Transition theory is considered an adult development theory and has mainly been applied to understand how adults understand and cope with life transitions. Since its development, transition theory has been used extensively in counseling and higher education. In recent years, there has been a particular emphasis on using transition theory to understand how student veterans, in particular, transition to college (e.g., Griffin & Gilbert, 2015; Jenner, 2017; Robertson and Eschenauer, 2020). For example, Griffin and Gilbert (2015) used transition theory as a lens to examine narratives from veterans, administrators, and student affairs professionals, in order to better understand how higher education institutions can impact and support how veterans' transitions to higher education. Their study is an example of how transition theory can be used not only to investigate how individuals manage transition, but also how organizations and institutions affect individuals' success in managing transitions. Researchers have also used transition theory to examine the transitions of particular sub-groups, including Black male undergraduate students (Goings, 2018), non-traditional students (Gill, 2021; Hunter-Johnson, 2022), international students (Hunter-Johnson, 2022; Witkowsky, 2023), student athletes (Flowers et al., 2014), and commuter students (Jacoby & Garland, 2004).

Strengths and Limitations

A strength of transition theory, stemming from its inception in counseling and its application to higher education and student affairs, is its emphasis on actionable ways to support transitions. As evidenced by recent work (Griffin & Gilber, 2015; Witkowsky, 2023), transition theory can be used to explore the ways in which individuals can strengthen their own responses to transition, as well as how counselors, student affairs professionals, and institutions can support transitions more generally, and for particular groups.

One limitation of transition theory is in its breadth. While it is useful in identifying all of the possible interacting factors that impact how individuals manage transition, it would be difficult for researchers to explore all of these factors in depth. However, it is typical for researchers to draw on aspects of transition theory as a framework, such as the four S's, in order to focus on particular aspects of transition.

Key Theorists: Nancy Schlossberg (Originating author); Mary L. Anderson; Jane Goodman

Examples of Use in Research: Gill (2021); Goings (2018); Griffin and Gilbert (2015); Hunter-Johnson (2022); Jacoby and Garland (2004)

References

Adler, P. S. (2005). The Evolving Object of Software Development. *Organization, 12*(3), 401–435. 10.1177/1350508405051277

Anderson, L., & Stillman, J. (2013). Making learning the object: Using cultural historical activity theory to analyze and organize student teaching in urban high-needs schools. *Teachers College Record, 115*(3), 1–36.

Anderson, M., Goodman, J., & Schlossberg, N. (2012). *Counseling adults in transition: Linking Schlossberg's theory with practice in a diverse world.* Springer.

Bandura, A., & Walters, R. H. (1977). *Social Learning Theory.* Prentice Hall.

Bertelson, O., & Bødker, S. (2003). Activity theory. In J. Carrol (Ed.), *HCI Models, Theories, and Frameworks: Toward a Multidisciplinary Science* (pp. 291–324). Morgan Kaufman.

Bingham, A. J. (2016). Drowning digitally? How disequilibrium shapes practice in a blended learning charter school. *Teachers College Record, 118*(1), 1–30.

Bingham, A. J. (2017). Personalized learning in high technology charter schools. *Journal of Educational Change, 18*(4), 521–549. 10.1007/s10833-017-9305-0

Bingham, A. J., Pane, J. F., Steiner, E. D., & Hamilton, L. S. (2018). Ahead of the Curve: Implementation Challenges in Personalized Learning School Models. *Educational Policy, 32*(3), 454–489. 10.1177/0895904816637688

Blackler, F. (2009). Cultural-historical activity theory and organization studies. In A. Sannino, H. Daniels, & K. Guitierrez (Eds.), *Learning and expanding with activity theory* (pp. 19–38). New York: Cambridge Press.

Bronfenbrenner, U. (1976). *The Experimental Ecology of Education. 5*(9), 5–15.

Bronfenbrenner, U. (1977). Toward an experimental ecology of human development. *American Psychologist.*

Bronfenbrenner, U. (1979). *The Ecology of Human Development: Experiments by Nature and Design.* Harvard University Press.

Bronfenbrenner, U. (1994). Ecological Models of Human Development. In M. Gauvain & M. Cole (Eds.), *Readings on the Development of Children* (2nd ed., pp. 37–43). Freeman.

Bronfenbrenner, U. (1995a). Developmental ecology through space and time: A future perspective. In P. Moen, G. H. Elder, & K. Lüscher (Eds.), *Examining lives in context: Perspectives on the ecology of human development* (pp. 599–618). American Psychological Association.

Bronfenbrenner, U. (1995b). The bioecological model from a life course perspective: Reflections of a participant observer. In P. Moen, G. H. Elder, & K. Lüscher (Eds.), *Examining lives in context: Perseoctives on the ecology of human development* (pp. 599–618). American Psychological Association.

Bronfenbrenner, U., & Morris, P. A. (2006). The Bioecological Model of Human Development. In R. M. Lerner (Ed.), *Handbook of child psychology: Theoretical models of human development* (pp. 793–828). Wiley.

Brown, J. S., Collins, A., & Duguid, P. (1989). Situated Cognition and The Culture of Learning. *Educational Researcher, 18*(1), 32–42. 10.3102/0013189X018001032

Consalvo, A. L., Schallert, D. L., & Elias, E. M. (2015). An examination of the construct of legitimate peripheral participation as a theoretical framework in literacy research. *Educational Research Review*, *16*, 1–18. 10.1016/j.edurev.2015.07.001

Chickering, A. & Schlossberg, N. (1995). *Getting the most out of college*. Needham Heights, MA: Allyn & Bacon.

Darling, N. (2007). Ecological Systems Theory: The Person in the Center of the Circles. *Research in Human Development*, *4*(3–4), 203–217. 10.1080/15427600701663023

Davies, H. M., & Sandiford, P. J. (2014). Legitimate peripheral participation by sandwich year interns in the national health service. *Journal of Vocational Education & Training*, *66*(1), 56–73.

Elliott, S., & Davis, J. M. (2018). Challenging Taken-for-Granted Ideas in Early Childhood Education: A Critique of Bronfenbrenner's Ecological Systems Theory in the Age of Post-humanism. In R. Latiner Raby & E. J. Valeau (Eds.), *Handbook of Comparative Studies on Community Colleges and Global Counterparts* (pp. 1–36). Springer International Publishing. 10.1007/978-3-319-51949-4_60-2

Engeström, Y. (1987). *Learning by Expanding: An Activity-Theoretical Approach to Developmental Research*. Orienta-Konsultit.

Engeström, Y. (1999a). Activity theory and individual and social transformation. In Y. Engeström, R. Miettinen, & R. Punamäki (Eds.), *Perspectives on Activity Theory* (pp. 19–38). Cambridge University Press.

Engeström, Y. (1999b). Innovative learning in work teams: Analyzing cycles of knowledge creation in practice. In Y. Engeström, R. Miettinen, & R. Punamäki (Eds.), *Perspectives on Activity Theory* (pp. 376–406). Cambridge University Press.

Engeström, Y. (2001). Expansive Learning at Work: Toward an activity theoretical reconceptualization. *Journal of Education and Work*, *14*(1), 133–156. 10.1080/13639080020028747

Engeström, Y. (2009). The future of activity theory: A rough draft. In A. Sannino, H. Daniels, & K. Guitierrez (Eds.), *Learning and expanding with activity theory* (pp. 303–327). New York: Cambridge.

Engeström, Y., & Miettinen, R. (1999). Introduction. In Y. Engeström, R. Miettinen, & R. Punamäki (Eds.), *Perspectives on Activity Theory* (pp. 1–18). Cambridge University Press.

Engeström, Y., Engeström, R., & Kärkkäinen, M. (1995). Polycontextuality and boundary crossing in expert cognition: Learning and problem solving in complex work activities. *Learning and Instruction*, *5*, 319–336.

Engeström, Y., Miettinen, R., & Punamäki, R. (1999). *Perspectives on Activity Theory*. Cambridge University Press.

Engeström, Y., & Sannino, A. (2010). Studies of expansive learning: Foundations, findings and future challenges. *Educational Research Review*, *5*(1), 1–24. 10.1016/j.edurev.2009.12.002

Engeström, Y., & Sannino, A. (2011). Discursive manifestations of contradictions in organizational change efforts: A methodological framework. *Journal of Organizational Change Management*, *24*(3), 368–387. 10.1108/09534811111132758

Eriksson, M., Ghazinour, M., & Hammarström, A. (2018). Different uses of Bronfenbrenner's ecological theory in public mental health research: What is their value for guiding public mental health policy and practice? *Social Theory & Health*, *16*(4), 414–433. 10.1057/s41285-018-0065-6

Ettekal, A., & Mahoney, J. L. (2017). Ecological Systems Theory. In K. Peppler (Ed.), *The SAGE Encyclopedia of Out-of-School Learning* (pp. 239–241). SAGE Publications, Inc. 10.4135/9781483385198

Evans, K., Schoon, I., & Weale, M. (2010). Life chances, learning and the dynamics of risk throughout the life course. Centre for Learning and Life Chances in Knowledge Economies and Societies, Institute of Education, University of London.

Flowers, R. D., Luzynski, C., & Zamani-Gallaher, E. M. (2014). Male transfer student athletes and Schlossberg's transition theory. *Journal for the Study of Sports and Athletes in Education*, *8*(2), 99–120.

Foster, H., & Brooks-Gunn, J. (2013). Neighborhood, Family and Individual Influences on School Physical Victimization. *Journal of Youth and Adolescence*, *42*(10), 1596–1610. 10.1007/s10964-012-9890-4

Fuller, A., Hodkinson, H., Hodkinson, P., & Unwin, L. (2005). Learning as peripheral participation in communities of practice: A reassessment of key concepts in workplace learning. *British Educational Research Journal, 31*(1), 49–68. 10.1080/0141192052000310029

Gill, A. J. (2021). Difficulties and support in the transition to higher education for non-traditional students. *Research in Post-Compulsory Education, 26*(4), 410–441.

Goings, R. B. (2018). "Making up for lost time": The transition experiences of nontraditional Black male undergraduates. *Adult Learning, 29*(4), 158–169.

Goodman, J., Schlossberg, N. K., & Anderson, M. (2006). *Counseling adults in transition: Linking practice with theory* (3rd ed.). Springer.

Griffin, K. A., & Gilbert, C. K. (2015). Better Transitions for Troops: An Application of Schlossberg's Transition Framework to Analyses of Barriers and Institutional Support Structures for Student Veterans. *The Journal of Higher Education, 86*(1), 71–97. 10.1080/00221546.2015.11777357

Hamilton, E. (2011). Entrepreneurial learning in family business: A situated learning perspective. *Journal of Small Business and Enterprise Development, 18*(1), 8–26.

Hunter-Johnson, Y. (2022). A leap of academic faith and resilience: Nontraditional international students pursuing higher education in the United States of America. *Journal of International Students, 12*(2).

Jacoby, B., & Garland, J. (2004). Strategies for enhancing commuter student success. *Journal of College Student Retention: Research, Theory & Practice, 6*(1), 61–79.

Jenner, B. M. (2017). Student veterans and the transition to higher education: Integrating existing literatures. *Journal of Veterans Studies, 2*(2), 26–44.

Johnson, G. M. (2010). Internet Use and Child Development: Validation of the Ecological Techno-Subsystem. *Educational Technology & Society, 13*(1), 176–185.

Johnson, G. M., & Puplampu, K. P. (2008). Internet use during childhood and the ecological techno-subsystem. *Canadian Journal of Learning and Technology, 34*(1).

Klen-Alves, V. (2021). The four generations of cultural-historical activity theory. *Brazilian Journal of Socio-Historical-Cultural Theory and Activity Research, 3*(2), 1–21.

Kline, C., Gard McGehee, N., Paterson, S., & Tsao, J. (2013). Using ecological systems theory and density of acquaintance to explore resident perception of entrepreneurial climate. *Journal of Travel Research, 52*, 294–309.

Konopaski, M., Jack, S., & Hamilton, E. (2015). How family business members learn about continuity. *Academy of Management Learning & Education, 14*(3), 347–364.

Lave, J. (1991). Situated Learning in Communities of Practice. In L. B. Resnick, J. M. Levine, & Teasley, Stephanie D. (Eds.), *Perspectives on Socially Shared Cognition* (pp. 63–82). American Psychological Association.

Lave, J., & Wenger, E. (1991). *Situated Learning: Legitimate Peripheral Participation*. Cambridge University Press.

Lektorsky, V. A. (2009). Mediation as a means of collective activity. In A. Sannino, H. Daniels, & K. D. Gutierrez (Eds.), *Learning and Expanding with Activity Theory* (pp. 75–86). Cambridge University Press.

Leont'ev, A. N. (1978). *Activity, Consciousness, and Personality*. Prentice-Hall.

Levinson, D. J., Darrow, C. N., Klien, E. B., Levinson, M. G., & McKee, B. (1978). *The Seasons of a man's life*. Knopf.

Lowenthal, M. F., & Chiriboga, D. (1975). Responses to stress. In M.F. Lowenthal, M. Thurnher, & D. Chiriboga (Eds.) *Four stages of life: A comparative study of women and men facing transitions*. Jossey-Bass.

Marx, K., Engels, F., & Tucker, R. C. (1978). *The Marx-Engels Reader*. Norton.

Makitalo, A. & Saljo, R. (2009). Contextualizing social dilemmas in institutional pra ctices: Negotiating objects of activity in labor market organizations. In A. Sannino, H. Daniels, & Guitierrez K. (Eds.), *Learning and expanding with activity theory* (pp. 129-143). New York: Cambridge Press.

Morell, E. (2003). Legitimate Peripheral Participation as Professional Development: Lessons from a Summer Research Seminar. *Teacher Education Quarterly*, *30*(2), 89–99.

Murphy, E., & Rodriguez-Manzanares, M. A. (2008). Using activity theory and its principle of contradictions to guide research in educational technology. *Australasian Journal of Educational Technology*, *24*(4). 10.14742/ajet.1203

Neugarten, B. L. (1977). Adaptation and the life cycle. In N.K. Schlossberg & A.D. Entine (Eds.), *Counseling adults*. Brooks/Cole.

Neugarten, B. L. (1979). Time, age, and the life cycle. *American Journal of Psychiatry*, *136*, 887–894.

O'Donnell, V. L., & Tobbell, J. (2007). The Transition of Adult Students to Higher Education: Legitimate Peripheral Participation in a Community of Practice? *Adult Education Quarterly*, *57*(4), 312–328. 10.1177/0741713607302686

Onwuegbuzie, A. J., Collins, K. M. T., & Frels, R. K. (2013). Foreword: Using Bronfenbrenner's ecological systems theory to frame quantitative, qualitative, and mixed research. *International Journal of Multiple Research Approaches*, *7*(1), 2–8. 10.5172/mra.2013.7.1.2

Paat, Y.-F. (2013). Working with immigrant children and their families: An Application of Bronfenbrenner's ecological systems theory. *Journal of Human Behavior in the Social Environment*, *23*, 954–966.

Powers, M. S. (2010). Applying Schlossberg's transition theory to nontraditional male drop-outs. [Doctoral dissertation, University of Nebraska - Lincoln]

Renn, K. A., & Arnold, K. D. (2003). Reconceptualizing Research on College Student Peer Culture. *The Journal of Higher Education*, *74*(3), 261–291. 10.1353/jhe.2003.0025

Robertson, H. C., & Eschenauer, R. K. (2020). Student veteran perceptions of college-to-career transition. *College Student Affairs Journal*, *38*(1), 52–64.

Roth, W.-M., & Lee, Y.-J. (2007). "Vygotsky's Neglected Legacy": Cultural-Historical Activity Theory. *Review of Educational Research*, *77*(2), 186–232.

Roth, W.-M. (2009). On the inclusion of emotions, identity, and ethico-moral dimensions of actions. In A. Sannino & H. Daniels (Eds.), *Learning and expanding with activity theory* (pp. 53–74). New York: Cambridge University Press.

Rothery, M. (2008). Critical ecological systems theory. In N. Coady & P. Lehmann (Eds.), *Theoretical Persepctives for Direct Social Work Practice: A Generalist Ecelective Approach* (3rd ed., pp. 89–118). Springer.

Sannino, A., Daniels, H., & Gutierrez, K. D. (2009). Activity theory between historical engagement and future-making practice. In A. Sannino, H. Daniels, & K. D. Gutierrez (Eds.), *Learning and Expanding with Activity Theory* (pp. 1–17). Cambridge University Press.

Sannino, A., & Engeström, Y. (2018). Cultural-historical activity theory: Founding insights and new challenges. *Cultural-Historical Psychology*, *14*(3), 43–56. 10.17759/chp.2018140304

Schlossberg, N. K. (1981). A model for analyzing human adaptation to transition. *The Counseling Psychologist*, *9*(2), 2–18.

Schlossberg, N. K., Waters, E. B., & Goodman, J. (1995). *Counseling adults in transition: Linking practice with theory* (2nd ed.). Springer.

Spillane, J. P., Reiser, B. J., & Reimer, T. (2002). Policy Implementation and Cognition: Reframing and Refocusing Implementation Research. *Review of Educational Research*, *72*(3), 387–431.

Virkkunen, J. (2009). Two theories of organizational knowledge creation. In A. Sannino, H. Daniels, & K. D. Gutierrez (Eds.), *Learning and Expanding with Activity Theory* (pp. 129–143). Cambridge University Press.

Vygotsky, L. S., & Cole, M. (1978). *Mind in Society: Development of Higher Psychological Processes*. Harvard University Press.

Wenger, E. (1998). Communities of practice: Learning as a social system. *Systems Thinker*, *9*(5), 10.

Wenger, E. (2011). Communities of Practice: A Brief Introduction. *Communities of Practice*, *7*.

Witkowsky, P. (2023). Supporting international students through transition. In D. Roberts & R. Ammigan (Eds.), *The role of student affairs in supporting international students at U.S. institutions of higher education*. Palgrave Macmillan.

7 Leadership

Distributed Leadership Theory

Definition and Overview

Distributed Leadership Theory (DL) is a conceptual and practical perspective in which leadership is seen as distributed, or shared, across multiple people, at multiple levels, in formal and informal ways (Fletcher & Käufer, 2003; Gronn, 2000). Defining characteristics of distributed leadership include that leadership stretches across internal teams and levels within the school system, company, or organization (Spillane, 2006). See Figure 7.1 for a visual of how DL is employed in a school and business setting. Ultimately, DL is concerned with the practices of leadership and how those practices lead to organizational improvement and success (Harris & Spillane, 2008). Further, DL is concerned both with task distribution and accomplishment, as well as influence distribution (Harris, 2013).

Conceptually, distributed leadership refers to the idea that leadership is collaborative and dispersed across a variety of members of the organization (Burch et al., 2020). Setting aside the idea of fixed leader-follower dualisms, DL holds that the "flow of influence" comes from many leaders in any organization, expanding the locus of power from a single authority, or one who monopolizes the power and influence (Gronn, 2000, p. 334). DL contrasts with the more traditional idea that leadership stems from a single leader with an "exaggerated sense of agency" (Gronn, 2000, p. 319).

A distributed leadership perspective emphasizes the importance of the organizational setting over the influence of a single leader's individual charisma (Burch et al., 2020). DL thus cannot be disconnected from the organizational setting. From a theoretical perspective, DL focuses on the actors in the organization, how they interact, how they engage in formal and informal leadership roles and actions, and the context in which all of this is situated (Bingham, 2021; Gronn, 2000; Harris & Spillane, 2008). Further, DL emphasizes how the distribution of leadership drives an organization through problems and toward common goals and improvements (Bingham, 2021; Gibb, 1947).

Practically, DL outlines practices that could be useful for organizational improvement and goal attainment by making success a "group project" (Dinham, 2007). For example, a distributed leadership model emphasizes the development of trust and professionalization of actors in the organization, which can foster collaboration, comfort in risk-taking, collective action, and individual and organizational change (Bingham, 2021; Louis et al., 2009). "Boundary spanners" – people who connect one community to another (Wenger, 1998) – are also a key aspect of distributed leadership

DOI: 10.4324/9781003261759-7

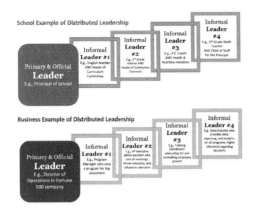

Figure 7.1 Two examples of distributed leadership theory in practice. Adapted from Spillane (2006).

that can facilitate intergroup communication and trust, and can facilitate change. (Bingham, 2021). A distributed leadership perspective also provides a model for how change and improvement can be sustained, even through leadership turnover (Hargreaves & Fink, 2003).

As an organizational model, DL focuses on the many possible leaders who emerge and exert agency and influence according to the circumstances and their skills, taking action as the tasks and goals necessitate (Harris, 2013; Leithwood et al., 2009). The activities, or "collective labor processes" are critical to how leadership is understood (Gronn, 2000, p. 327). In practice, distributed leadership maximizes "sources of information, data, and judgment, and [spreads] the detrimental impact of consequences of miscalculation and risk" (Gronn, 2000, p. 334). A distributed leadership model does not mean that "everyone leads or that everyone is a leader" (Harris, 2013, p. 547); rather, a DL perspective holds that leadership is not hierarchical – it is spread across individuals and levels to great effect. An organization that employs a distributed leadership model is able to draw from a greater pool of resources, intelligence, and feedback.

A distributed leadership perspective is useful both in a practical, normative sense and in a theoretical sense. As a theoretical framework, DL can help researchers understand how specific aims are accomplished (or not, as the case may be) through an analysis of the actions of various forms of leaders (Harris & Spillane, 2008). A DL perspective can provide a framework for categorizing and analyzing specific leadership practices and how they contribute to change. In a practical or normative sense, DL can be used to examine the potential of DL practices for organizational and individual improvement. In many organizations, those not in positions of authority engage in leadership practices alongside those formal leaders. Distributed leadership takes this into account and directs attention to those who practice leadership in organizations despite any formalized hierarchical structures.

Background and Foundations

The roots of DL can be traced to the scholarship of Cecil Gibb in 1940s and 1950s (Thorpe et al., 2011). As Gibb noted,

> Leadership is both a function of the social situation and a function of personality, but it is a function of these two in interaction ... the interaction within the group is very fluid and the momentary group leader is that person who is able to contribute most to progress toward the common goal ... leadership is always relative to the situation. (Gibb, 1947, pp. 268–269)

This idea that leadership can be found in the interactions among organizational actors and that leadership should be collaborative, shared, and ceded at any time to those with the most to contribute to a given aim is the foundation of a distributed leadership perspective.

As a more formalized theory, Distributed leadership's conceptual foundations are grounded in work by Ogawa and Bossert (1995), among others, who posit that leadership is dispersed throughout an organization – not in the leaders themselves, but in the relationships and interactions among organizational actors. Ultimately, leadership potential is already present in organizational actors (Burch et al., 2020). Spillane et al. (2004) further developed distributed leadership as an explanatory frame to pinpoint dimensions of leadership practice and examine relationships among those dimensions toward a goal of enabling leaders to reflect on and analyze their practice (p. 4). Thus, distributed leadership has evolved not only as a theoretical construct in research, but also as a description of the reality of how leadership is exercised in organizational contexts.

Distributed Leadership was further developed by Peter Gronn in 2000. In 2009, Gronn suggested that instead of the phrase "distributed leadership," a more appropriate description to accommodate all of the hybrid versions of DL would be "leadership configurations" (Thorpe et al., 2011; Boldan, 2011). Gronn attempted to shift the conversation from "leaders to leadership" (Thorpe et al., 2011, p. 242).

In Research

Early DL research focused on theory development, how DL is implemented in practice, and how to measure the impacts of DL (Liu & Werblow, 2019). More recent research has turned toward the impact of DL on school outcomes and positive academic correlations such as job satisfaction, teacher knowledge, and student achievement.

Distributed leadership can be used in research in both a theoretical sense and a practical sense. Theoretically, scholars can engage a distributed leadership perspective to examine how decisions and actions are "distributed over leaders, followers and their situation" (Spillane et al., 2004, p. 13). DL provides an explanatory frame through which to better understand how leadership is enacted in each context and how the qualities of leaders impact and influence outcomes and goals (Burch et al., 2020). Additionally, researchers can use DL to make sense of how tasks are accomplished through the interactions of various forms of leaders (Harris & Spillane, 2008).

In a more practical sense, many researchers have studied how distributed leadership practices can be linked to specific outcomes (Leithwood 2009; Thorpe et al., 2011). Bingham (2021) used a DL framework in both a theoretical and a practical sense to understand how a school makes organizational changes to implement technology, and how teachers understand and enact school-level goals of technology use. In that study, a

DL framework was used to first identify and describe a system of distributed leadership in a particular school, and then examine how and why that system supported school- and classroom-level changes. Ultimately, the study showed that organizational practices tied to a DL model facilitated school wide aims (Bingham, 2021).

In another study (Liu & Werblow, 2019), the DL framework was used to understand how leadership is distributed across four important stakeholders at a school: Principals, teachers, the team of managers, and the governing board. After controlling for the context, the researchers sought to understand how DL can impact principal and teacher job satisfaction and commitment. The results suggested that two factors positively influence principal's and teacher's job satisfaction and commitment: Teacher and principal roles in employee development and commitment.

Strengths and Limitations

As a theoretical framework, DL provides the language and tools to parse out aspects of leadership systems and identify how those aspects or the system as a whole influences practice, improvement, and change. As a form of leadership, there are many strengths to a distributed leadership model. DL encourages participation and employee engagement, supports professionalization, trust, and communication (Bingham, 2021), and empowers individuals (Thorpe et al., 2011). Organizationally, DL provides not only those at the top of the hierarchy the opportunity to guide and influence, but also those within the organization, making success a group endeavor. These leadership opportunities give individuals training and growth, while also supporting continued improvement.

Still, there are several limitations or criticisms of DL theory. First, scholars have argued that DL is too nebulous a concept to be truly useful (Tian et al., 2016). Indeed, a singular definition remains elusive (Thorpe et al., 2011). Sometimes DL is differentiated from shared or collaborative leadership (e.g., when there are identified co-leaders), while others see distributed leadership as being the same as shared or collaborative leadership (Harris, 2013; Thorpe et al., 2011). Another common critique of DL is that is simply a distribution of work, a method or design intended to spread the workload amongst those within the organization who are not otherwise compensated for this amount of work or level of authority (Harris, 2013). Additionally, DL can obfuscate what is in reality a traditional hierarchical leadership structure utilizing delegation practices.

As a form of leadership practice, DL has been criticized for not focusing enough on the buy-in from executive leadership. Some scholars have noted that DL is not likely to flourish, much less succeed, without this support (Harris, 2013). Other scholars have argued that formal leadership support is critical in "creating conditions where purposeful and focused leadership distribution is likely to occur" (Harris, 2013, p. 549). Finally, there has been little investigation into how gender, race, and ethnicity influence DL (Lumby, 2019) and/or into how DL may alleviate or perpetuate unfair labor practices, stereotypical divisions of labor, or systems of oppression within an organization.

Key Theorists: Cecil Gibb (Foundational theorist); Rodney Ogawa and Steven Bossert (Originating author); Peter Gronn; James Spillane; Richard Halverson; John Diamond; Alma Harris.

Examples of Use in Research: Bingham (2021); Cheung et al. (2021); Liu and Werblow (2019); Varpanen (2021).

Path-Goal Theory of Leadership

Overview

Path-Goal Theory (PGT) is a leadership theory that outlines three areas leaders need to understand in order for their team to achieve successful outcomes: 1) what *motivates followers*; 2) what team members are *missing* (weaknesses, missing skills, and needs); and 3) the *situational context*, including role, task structure, obstacles, and objective clarity (Côté, 2017; Evans 1970; House & Mitchell, 1975; Northouse, 2016; Wofford & Liska, 1993). Path-Goal Theory is considered a contingency theory of leadership due to the leader adapting their approach according to the characteristics of the environment, employees, and tasks (Côté, 2017; Wofford & Liska, 1993).

A leader implementing Path-Goal methods provides a clear path to goal achievement and removes obstacles along the path (Sujana, 2020). Additionally, leaders understand and provide incentives for members to achieve the goals, purposefully seeking opportunities for member satisfaction (Dugan et al., 2017; House & Mitchell, 1975; Northouse, 2016; Wofford & Liska, 1993). The leader then applies information and resources that complement, supplement, and support the team (Dugan et al., 2017; House & Mitchell, 1975; Indvik, 1986; Northouse, 2016; Sujana, 2020).

Originally, PGT posited four common "pathways" or approaches that should be deployed when leading a team: Directive, supportive, achievement-oriented, and participative (House & Mitchell, 1975). In 1996, House developed an additional four pathways – work facilitation; group-oriented decision process; work-group representation and networking; and value-based leadership – for a total of eight pathways. The best approach depends on the makeup of the team and the situational context (Northouse, 2016, Sujana, 2020) and no leader chooses a single approach across every project and team. Further, more than one approach can be implemented simultaneously for team satisfaction and goal achievement success. A leader selects the most appropriate pathway (or combination of pathways) according to the strengths and needs of the team members (House & Mitchell, 1975; Northouse, 2016). See Figure 7.2 for an organized description of the original four pathways.

Background and Foundations

Although Path-Goal theory was coined in 1957 by Basil Georgopoulous (House, 1971), R.J. House is credited with developing PGT as it's now understood. PGT was inspired by Martin Evans's 1970 research on the "instrumentalities and expectancies" of leadership (House, 1996, p. 324). Evans's theory of leadership asserted that leaders are effective if they have a reward system and provide said rewards when goals are achieved (Evans, 1970; House, 1971; House & Mitchell, 1975). PGT builds on this to take context and task structure into account (House, 1971).

Path-Goal theory is grounded in Expectancy Theory (Vroom, 1964). Expectancy theory, sometimes called motivation theory, focuses on subordinates' perceived value of objectives and rewards and whether individuals believe the outcome and value of their actions will be positive (House, 1971; House & Mitchell, 1975; Northouse, 2016). Expectancy theory also depends on the subordinate's belief that *they* can be successful at performing the task (Northouse, 2016). PGT is the only leadership theory to integrate motivation theory (Côté, 2017; Northouse, 2016).

In 1996, House published a reformulation of PGT expanding the original four approaches to eight and positing that effective leaders "engage in behaviors that compliment

Leadership Behavior	Follower Characteristics	Task Characteristics
Directive *Provides guidance and psychological structure*	Dogmatic Authoritarian	Ambiguous Unclear rules Complex
Supportive Provides *nurturance*	Unsatisfied Need affiliation Need human touch	Repetitive Unchallenging Mundane
Participative *Provides involvement*	Autonomous Need for control Need for clarity	Ambiguous Unclear Unstructured
Achievement-Oriented *Provides challenges*	High expectations Need to excel	Ambiguous Challenging Complex

Figure 7.2 How path-goal theory works utilizing the original four approaches. Adapted from Northouse (2016).

subordinates' environments and abilities in a manner that compensates for deficiencies and is instrumental to subordinate satisfaction and individual and work unit performance" (House, 1996, p. 323). Further, to improve empirical testing for PGT, House developed a framework to improve research testability. This effort attempted to correct flaws in previous research around PGT (House, 1996; Schriesheim et al., 2006). Additionally, House linked PGT with value-based leadership theories, also known as transformational leadership, currently gaining renewed momentum in leadership research (Bass & Avilio, 1993).

Key Terms and Concepts

Directive pathway is an approach in which the leader provides clear objectives, direction, timelines, processes, and policies. This approach is useful when the situation is unclear and/or uncertain. This pathway provides the confidence and clarity the team needs to succeed (House, 1996; Northouse, 2016). This style of leadership is more prescriptive but can have negative associations with authoritarian and dictator-like styles (Barrow & O'Shea, 2020; Phillips & Phillips, 2016).

Supportive pathway is an approach in which the leader focuses on relationships and understanding the team member's needs and desires. Using this knowledge, a leader can steer toward meeting those needs (House, 1996; Northouse, 2016). The assumption is that when a team member has their needs met, they are more engaged, satisfied, and motivated to achieve the necessary organization or business objectives. This approach grows or maintains motivation and high morale through friendly and encouraging support. The context where the supportive approach is most useful is when the project is confusing, challenging, or difficult, as it helps to reduce stress (Famakin & Abisuga, 2016; House, 1996; Northouse, 2016; Sujana, 2020).

Achievement-oriented pathway is an approach in which the leader sets high-performance expectations and challenging objectives for subordinates (House & Mitchell, 1975). This is effective in high-performing and professional environments (House & Mitchell, 1975; Sujana, 2020). Excellence, continuous improvement, and high confidence are characteristic of this type of leadership and work. This approach is also valued in situations where quality and precision matter and the environment is complex. However, when implemented without support or participatory approaches, this approach can become too focused on the goal, and thus results in low team member satisfaction (Sujana, 2020).

Participatory pathway is an inclusive path in which the leader seeks information, agreement, and input from team members on decisions and directions. This approach is useful when followers are highly trained, competent, engaged in their work, and desire some amount of control (Famakin & Abisuga, 2016; House, 1996; Northouse, 2016; Sujana, 2020). This method requires trust, a quality not always available if teams are new and/or temporarily formed to achieve a goal. Team members expect their leader to employ participatory approaches; if they don't, this can lead to dissatisfied or withdrawn team members (Barrow & O'Shea, 2020).

Work facilitation focuses on how leaders set up work – such as planning and organizing the work and scheduling – to allow for team member success (Côté, 2017; House, 1996). This approach is largely tactical and managerial in nature. It includes guiding and mentoring, training and developing subordinates, removing obstacles, and adapting to changes, as needed (House, 1996).

Group-oriented decision process is an approach in which a leader facilitates solutions to problems by engaging the team, ensuring all team members participate and voices are heard, and discussing the pros and cons of various solutions until a group decision is agreed upon (House, 1996). This method can result in higher quality outcomes and team member acceptance (Côté, 2017; House, 1996).

Work-group representation and networking apply in situations where work groups do not hold power, resources, or information, and therefore their legitimacy relies on the perceptions of others (House, 1996). In this situation, the leader's ability to market the team and their accomplishments for the purpose of acquiring necessary resources to achieve objective success for subsequent projects or efforts is critical (Côté, 2017; House, 1996). This requires skilled communication and strong social or professional networks.

Value-based leadership comes from the ability of the leader to communicate strategy, hold the team to high standards, provide positive feedback, display self-confidence, and take personal and organizational risks (Côté, 2017; House, 1996). This type of leader appeals to the morals, values, passions, and "nonconscious motives" of the team members through their vision which guides everyone forward (House, 1996, p. 343). Research shows that value-based leadership has strong effects on subordinate performance and successful outcomes.

In Research

Path-goal theory is useful in research as a framework to study the impact of leadership style on a variety of outcomes and contexts, including government, business, and education. Researchers have used PGT to understand how particular leadership approaches align with the needs and motivations of employees, the task characteristics, and the context of the situation (House, 1996). Research questions could be focused on leadership behaviors and how they impact the goals of the organization and employees, or how they lead to satisfaction and high-quality performance and productivity (Northouse, 2016).

Examples of the application of PGT in research include studies examining the effectiveness of path-goal leadership in schools, hospitals, churches, and businesses, or specific situations such as school leadership during the COVID-19 pandemic (Dare & Saleem, 2022). Researchers have used path-goal theory to compare different types of leadership, including path-goal approaches and transformational leadership (Schriesheim et al., 2006). In comparing styles and techniques, researchers can understand if one leadership type performs better than another in a specific setting. Additionally, PGT can be used to examine the impact of this leadership style across different societies and cultures (Kull et al., 2019).

Strengths and Limitations

Path-goal theory is able to reconcile relevant variables such as task, environment, leader, and followers; it is considered one of the more influential and complete theories regarding leadership (Famakin & Abisuga, 2016). Additionally, it's useful for leaders to understand how best to motivate and support team members toward the goals of the project (Côté, 2017; Northouse, 2016). See Figure 7.3. A path-goal theoretical approach can apply in almost any setting and industry and can be useful to any level of leadership.

Still, there are limitations to PGT. First, PGT doesn't provide prescriptive direction for leaders due to the necessity for all or many paths at once. The weight of any given approach varies by situation and team member needs (Northouse, 2016). An additional limitation is the strong focus on the leaders' behaviors and not on the followers' behaviors (Northouse, 2016). Relatedly, the applicability of PGT also depends on the understanding, assumptions, and biases held by the leader (Dugan, et al., 2017), although thoughtful awareness and self-reflection by the leader can counter biases and assumptions. However, available leaders do not always have the skills and maturity to adjust their leadership style to align with the needs of the followers or the context (Dugan et al., 2017). Finally, in terms of practical application, there is not a significant amount of extant training available for leaders with regard to path-goal leadership strategies (Northouse, 2016).

Figure 7.3 Basic idea behind Path-Goal Theory. Adapted from Northouse (2016).

Path-Goal theory can also complicate research goals, as there are many variables involved and units to measure, including leader and team characteristics, context, incentive, objectives, outcomes, and achievements (House, 1996; Northouse, 2016). For many years after the development of PGT, empirical studies drew on poorly constructed instruments with extraneous variables and/or weak methodology. Thus, the research failed to strongly support the theory (House, 1996; Indvik, 1986; Schriesheim & Schriesheim, 1980; Stinson & Johnson, 1975; Wofford & Liska, 1993). Additionally, several research projects came to contradictory conclusions (Famakin & Abisuga, 2016; Schriesheim et al., 2006). This is due to the complexity of the theory, requiring testing in pieces (Côté, 2017; Evans, 1970; Schriesheim & Schriesheim, 1980). Still, PGT continues to hold a strong place in leadership theory and research (Phillips & Phillips, 2016).

Key Theorists: Martin Evans & Basil Georgopoulous (Foundational theorists); R.J. House (Originating author).

Examples of Use in Research: Dare and Saleem (2022); Karnopp (2019); Kull et al. (2019); Perez (2021).

Servant Leadership Theory

Definition and Overview

Servant Leadership Theory (SL) refers to a leadership style where the primary goal is the serve the needs of the followers (Spears, 1996). As described by Greenleaf (1977),

> The Servant Leader is a servant first … It begins with the natural feeling that one wants to serve, to serve first. The conscious choice brings one to aspire to lead … The best test, and difficult to administer is this: Do those served grow as persons? Do they, while being served, become healthier, wiser, freer, more autonomous, and more like themselves to become servants? (Greenleaf, 1977, p. 7)

Simply put, SL is a theory of leadership that reorients traditional views of leadership by centering the ideas of serving others and supporting their improvement as the most fundamental aspects of leadership.

Use of the term "servant" in the title can mistakenly generate negative associations of leaders being submissive to followers, or take on an "attitude of servility" (van Dierendonck, 2011, p. 1233). Servant leadership, however, is not passivity. Rather, the leader actively focuses on how their leadership can best benefit the others in the organization. Greenleaf (1977) employed the Latin phrase, *primus interpares*, or "first among equals" whereby the leader is responsible to shepherd the followers and organization for the team's benefit instead of for the organization or for the leader's benefit. A leader's power is used in a prosocial way rather than being self-serving (van Dierendonck, 2011).

Servant Leadership is a human-oriented style, as opposed to organization-focused or leader-focused style. A leader with a servant style is focused on the followers, actively seeking opportunities for them and encouraging their growth (van Dierendonck, 2011). The purpose of a servant leadership model is to develop engaged employees who have positive attitudes toward work and are personally growing toward self-actualization (van Dierendonck, 2011). Generating positive outcomes for the followers, rather than for the leader or the organization, is the goal, although the two are not mutually exclusive. Critical outcomes of SL include creating an organizational culture of learning, and fostering an environment of trust and authenticity while also cultivating the unique value of each individual and empowering people to act and lead autonomously. Ultimately, for the context in which SL is taking place, the empowering style encourages team and organizational effectiveness.

Qualities of a servant leader include seeking power for the purpose of helping others, desiring to empower and develop people while also holding them accountable, and focusing attention on the goals of the organization (Spears, 1996). Additional characteristics include strong ethics, being honest and transparent with decisions and interactions, empowering followers to grow and act autonomously, and aiming to transform the organization and followers into a better version of themselves.

Similar leadership styles are often grouped with SL and are referred to as the Newer Generation Leadership forms (NGL) (Fuller et al., 2022). These include Ethical Leadership, Authentic Leadership, Empowering Leadership, Spiritual Leadership, and Transformational Leadership (Fuller et al., 2022; van Dierendonck, 2011). While SL overlaps with these leadership styles, it remains unique in its focus and allegiance to the followers over the organization (Fuller et al., 2022). A recent trend impacting SL theory research and development is a movement to merge the similar prosocial leadership theories into a grand unified theory with a suggested name of "Value Convergent Leadership" (Fuller et al., 2022, p. 12).

As with other leadership theories, SL can be used practically, to outline effective leadership practices, and theoretically, to investigate and understand leadership practices in a variety of organizations and contexts.

Background and Foundations

As mentioned, the concept of servant leadership was first coined by Robert Greenleaf in the 1970s. However, there are similar concepts mentioned as far back as Plato, Aristotle, and the Bible; Jesus Christ, for example, is frequently put forward as an exemplar Servant Leader (Spears, 1996; van Dierendonck, 2011).

This leadership style initially took the form of an idealistic manifesto on Greenleaf's part (van Dierendonck, 2011). Spears (1995) was the initial scholar to translate Greenleaf's declaration into ten practical characteristics of a leader: Listening, empathy, healing, awareness, persuasion, conceptualization, foresight, stewardship, commitment to people growth, and community development. Laub (1999) further developed clusters of six characteristics, including developing people, shared leadership, demonstrating authenticity, understanding and actively valuing followers, developing community, and providing leadership. Laub also developed the first instrument for empirical research on SL (van Dierendonck, 2011).

In the last 20 years, SL has gained momentum as corporations have taken a broader prosocial stance in society, seeking to make a difference beyond profit and gathering shareholders through a positive impact on people, their communities, and the earth (van Dierendonck, 2011). Human capital growth, employee engagement, and well-being are under a growing spotlight and SL is the only leadership theory focused specifically on the *followers* (Avolio et al., 2009; Patterson, 2003).

Key Terms and Concepts

Humane Orientation refers to leadership or organizational culture that is focused on benefiting followers by implementing measures that foster growth, friendship, caring, kindness, authenticity, and generosity (Kabasakal & Bodur, 2004; van Dierendonck, 2011). This philosophy emphasizes the intrinsic value of people.

Power Distance is a part of Geert Hofstede's Cultural Dimensions Theory (Daniels & Greguras, 2014), and refers to the extent followers accept the authority of the leaders – from questioning leadership to blind acceptance (van Dierendonck, 2011). In organizations and cultures with high power distance, followers are obedient and deferential; where there is low power distance, decisions are centralized and leader/follower relationships are more egalitarian.

In Research

Servant leadership, like distributed leadership, transformational leadership, and other leadership theories, can be used both practically and theoretically. Practically, organizations and leaders can use a Servant Leadership perspective to understand current leadership practices and to outline potential best practices of leadership for the organization. As a theoretical framework, SL can support researchers in identifying and categorizing leadership styles and qualities, and in attempting to tie these to particular outcomes or practices. Researchers can compare and contrast competing leadership styles in the same context; examine which characteristics are antecedents, moderators, or mediators; and explore how servant leadership may lead to objective achievement and/or positive outcomes for the followers (van Dierendonck, 2011; Eva et al., 2018). See Figure 7.4 for the various characteristics of SL and how they've been researched over time. van Dierendonck (2011) also developed a conceptual and theoretical framework for SL (see Figure 7.5).

Examples of applying Servant leadership theory in research include studying the main effects on performance outcomes relating to both individuals and teams (Lee et al., 2020). Neubert et al. (2022) studied emic and etic perspectives of SL across the globe.

Scholars	Characteristics Measured
Laub (1999)	Develops people, shares leadership, displays authenticity, values people, provides leadership, & builds community
Wong & Davey (2007)	Serving and developing other, consulting and involving others, humility and selflessness, modeling integrity and authenticity, inspiring and influencing others
Barbuto & Wheeler (2006)	Altruistic calling, emotional healing, persuasive mapping, organizational stewardship, wisdom
Dennis & Bocarnea (2005)	Empowerment, trust, humility, agapao love, vision
Liden, Wayne, Zhao, & Henderson (2008)	Empowering, helping subordinates grow and succeed, putting subordinates first, emotional healing, conceptual skills, creating value for the community, behaving ethically
Sendjaya, Sarros, Santora (2008)	Transforming influence, voluntary subordination, authentic self, transcendental spirituality, covenantal relationship, responsible morality
van Dierendonck & Nuijten (2011)	Empowerment, humility, standing back, authenticity, forgiveness, courage, accountability, stewardship

Figure 7.4 Service leadership measurements and scholars. Adapted from van Dierendonck (2011).

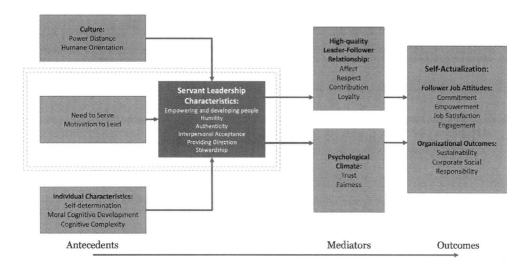

Figure 7.5 Servant leadership antecedents, mediators, and outcomes. Adapted from van Dierendonck (2011).

Additionally, as there is a great deal of research using SL, there have been several meta-analyses or systemic reviews of extant studies (e.g., Eva et al., 2018; Lee et al., 2020). Eva et al. (2018), for example, worked on theory development through a systemic review of the literature, with over 285 articles published in the previous 20 years. They redeveloped van Dierendonck's (2011) conceptual framework, adding moderators.

Strengths and Limitations

A strength of SL is the focus on the followers over the leaders themselves or the organization. No other leadership philosophy or theory focuses so keenly on the followers (van Dierendonck, 2011). An additional strength is the alignment with modern corporate social responsibility and its focus on all of the stakeholders related to a company beyond the shareholders, including employees, the community, the earth, and customers (van Dierendonck, 2011). There is a shift in corporations today toward increasing quality and care for each shareholder, including employees (Spears, 1996).

There are also limitations with SL. First, there has been little consensus around the theory definition (van Dierendonck, 2011). Second, the idealistic prescriptive nature of the leadership style makes it challenging to practically implement and measure. Additionally, the use of the term "servant" can be mistakenly associated with weakness and powerlessness. Further, there is not enough empirical research to solidly prove successful outcomes to the followers and the organization where SL is implemented (van Dierendonck, 2011). More research is needed, and with the advent of recent measures, empirical validation studies should be performed. Lastly, SL is similar to other leadership forms such as ethical, spiritual, authentic, and transformational leadership (Fuller et al., 2022). The overlaps and lack of clear definition for SL can create confusion in research.

Key Theorists: Robert Greenleaf (Originating author); Larry Spears; Dirk van Dierendonck; Max DePree; James Laub.

Examples of Use in Research: Burton et al. (2017); Den Hartog et al. (1999); Li et al. (2021); Newman et al. (2017).

Transformational Leadership

Definition and Overview

Transformational Leadership Theory (TFL) is a traditional, long-standing, and dominant theory that contends that a leader's behavior can "transform and inspire followers to perform beyond expectations while transcending self-interest for the good of the organization" (Avolio et al., 2009, p. 423; Fourie & Höhne, 2019). TFL emphasizes the relationship between the leader and the follower (Price & Weiss, 2013). While TFL is commonly associated with business and firm leadership, it is applicable in any leadership context including sports, church, and education (Kwan, 2020). Indeed, it has been used extensively in educational leadership (Hallinger, 2003).

TFL is rooted in the belief that employees or organizational members are key to a successful future for an organization. This is bolstered by the shift toward a knowledge economy; the value is in the employee's *knowledge*, as opposed to the goods they produce (O'Leary et al., 2002). TFL supports the idea that satisfying employee or member needs, increasing their motivation, and appealing to their aspirations will ultimately increase the success of the organization as a whole (van Dierendonck et al., 2014).

Both TFL and Servant Leadership (SL) focus specifically on the employee. However, TFL's focus is on the employee *for the purpose of improving the organization* or business (Bass, 1985; van Dierendonck et al., 2014). While both SL and TFL can inspire employees, SL centers on the employees, or subordinates, while TFL theory centers on the leader (van Dierendonck et al., 2014).

From a transformational leadership perspective, leaders should understand the goals, mission, vision, and expected performance of an organization, and then use the hierarchical relationship between leader and employee as well as their own charismatic qualities to appeal to employees' aspirations and altruism, and to find ways to influence and inspire employees (or members) to over-achieve goals (Bass, 1985; Avolio, 1999; van Dierendonck et al., 2014). TFL leaders also use their charisma to communicate the future of the organization or company in a positive and inspiring way (Bass & Avolio, 1995).

TFL leaders have long been perceived in leadership circles as more effective than other types of leaders (Judge & Piccolo, 2004). Additionally, they are seen to be equally effective in crisis and stable periods for organizations, giving TFL broad appeal (van Dierendonck et al., 2014). Employees or members learn the norms and values of the organization by identifying with the leader and emulating their philosophies and behaviors (van Dierendonck et al., 2014).

TFL theory holds that there are four primary behaviors: 1) Inspirational Motivation; 2) Idealized Influence; 3) Intellectual Stimulation; and 4) Individualized Consideration (Bass, 1985; Bass & Avolio, 1995; Price & Weiss, 2013). The behaviors are typically known as 4Is. These are described in further detail in the Key Terms and Concepts section below. Rafferty and Griffin (2004) later added a fifth element, personal recognition, which could be considered an extension of Bass's fourth behavior of individualized consideration. Alternatively, other scholars identified six qualities of TFL (Podsakoff et al., 1990). Similar to Bass's four behaviors, they include: 1) casting a vision; 2) encouraging acceptance of group goals; 3) being a role model; 4) setting high standards regarding performance; 5) supporting each member of the team individually; and 6) stimulating intelligent thinking. By demonstrating and developing these leadership behaviors, leaders can influence employees' or members' hearts, minds, and actions (Ma & Jeng, 2018; Peng et al., 2021).

Background and Foundations

While James Downton is associated with coining the phrase "transformational leadership," J.M. Burns used the term and concept in his 1978 book, *Leadership*, where he espoused the virtues of two types of leadership styles: Transformational and transactional (Burns, 1978; Fourie & Höhne, 2019). Burns's conclusions were based on qualitative research on political leaders at the time (Burns, 1978; Andersen, 2015). His conclusions were that transformational leadership was focused on inspiring followers through aspirations and moral endeavors (Fourie & Höhne, 2019).

Burns (1978) argued that leaders were either transformational or transactional, two mutually exclusive leadership styles. Transformational leaders apply inspirational and motivational techniques with employees, appealing to their best selves, their aspirations, and their desires for collective success. Conversely, transactional leaders seek alignment on shared goals and objectives and implement an exchange structure, or transaction-based system to motivate followers (Burns, 1978; Fourie & Höhne, 2019). This exchange structure includes rewards (e.g., promotions, raises, public acknowledgment) or punishments (e.g., demotions) to persuade followers to achieve objectives.

In 1985, Bass carried the TFL concept forward, applying it across contexts and cultures – claiming the theory to be universal (Bass, 1985; Andersen, 2015). Bass developed the concepts behind transformational leadership, spring-boarding the research forward for decades (Fourie & Höhne, 2019), and focusing on the relationship between the leaders and followers and the emphasis on awareness of followers' and organizations' needs (Bass, 1985). It was Bass's work with Avolio that developed the four leadership factors within TFL (4Is) (Fourie & Höhne, 2019).

The influence exerted by leaders ascribing to the TFL philosophy is founded on two influential theories: Bandura's (1977) social learning theory (SLT) and Blau's (1964) social exchange theory (SET) (Peng et al., 2021). TFL leaders apply SLT by serving and acting as examples of what they are asking the employees to do, think, and accomplish. TFL leaders employ SET techniques by caring for the employees, ingratiating themselves with the employees, and building relationships and connections. This leadership behavior is repaid in kind by the employee through commitment, engagement, and loyalty (Peng et al., 2021).

Key Terms and Concepts

Inspirational Motivation refers to situations in which leaders communicate a vision in an inspirational way (van Dierendonck et al., 2014).

Idealized Influence refers to how leaders apply SLT techniques to serve as role models for employees or members to emulate (van Dierendonck et al., 2014).

Intellectual Stimulation is when leaders encourage members or employees to think creatively and innovatively solve problems, as well as to challenge the status quo (Podsakoff et al., 1990; Mittal & Dhar, 2015). This is a key area for a company to maintain a competitive lead.

Individualized Consideration refers to the leadership practice of emphasizing the employee's or member's individual growth and applying SET techniques (van Dierendonck et al., 2014).

Personal Recognition is the leadership practice of recognizing the achievements and skills of the individuals (van Dierendonck et al., 2014).

In Research

As a theory, transformational leadership is known for being one of the more well-developed, widely studied, and empirically-based leadership theories and is associated with many positive outcomes for organizations or businesses (Judge & Piccolo, 2004; van Dierendonck et al., 2014). TFL has been researched over decades, making it an empirically grounded, strong choice as a framework for original research and meta-analyses.

Common research designs that use TFL include longitudinal, cross-sectional (point-in-time across various groups or demographics), and meta-analyses, given that extensive research already exists on the topic (Peng et al., 2021). The survey instrument most tested, updated, and utilized in TFL research is the MLQ-5X – or *Multifactor Leadership Questionnaire: Rater form 5X Short* (Bass & Avolio, 1995; Peng et al., 2021; Price & Weiss, 2013). This survey aligns with the four behaviors (4Is) as documented by Bass and Avolio (1985, 1995). A benefit to utilizing the survey is that it can be used at any level of the organization – from the CEO to a first-line manager to a peer leader on a soccer team (Price & Weiss, 2013). However, caution is advised on research designs that are solely dependent on survey instruments (see Avolio et al., 2009).

TFL theory has been used extensively across disciplines. For example, researchers have examined how TFL practices can increase organizational commitment, or emotional attachment and identification with an organization, as well as how transformational leadership can be a predictor of employee reaction to change and employee engagement (van Dierendonck et al., 2014; Zhu et al., 2016; Peng et al., 2021). Other researchers have found that leaders engaging in transformational leadership practices have been associated with many important organizational metrics such as profitability, productivity, and employee turnover. This effectiveness spans across different cultures, contexts, and organizational levels (Judge & Piccolo, 2004).

Strengths and Limitations

TFL has been empirically tested in many ways since its inception. It is considered to be one of the most researched leadership theories (Avolio, 2005). However, there are detractors who are frustrated with the concept of transformational leadership. First, as the theory posits that a transformational leader is charismatic, those leaders who are considered to be transformational leaders tend to get credit for success simply by virtue of their visibility. This high visibility can cause inappropriate attribution of success to the leader, known as heroic bias (van Dierendonck et al., 2014). Scholars have argued that TFL can bring about an irrational expectation of infallibility, and can encourage narcissism and hubris among leaders, due to the hyperbolic portrayal of transformational leaders as heroes and saviors. The center-stage focus on the leaders themselves supports the tendency to inappropriately give all credit for success to these individuals (Fairhurst, 2007; Tourish, 2008; Fourie & Höhne, 2019). Some researchers have made the argument that if leadership success is about visibility and achievement, even Hitler would be considered a strong example of a transformational leader (Tourish, 2008). In Tourish's words, "Powerless followers create evermore powerful leaders, liberated from all constraints" (2008, p. 527). Transformational leaders are at risk of being idolized and developing personality cults (Fourie & Höhne, 2019). Nevertheless, Bass (1998) attempted to counter this critique through the emphasis on the *goodness of intentions* and *strength in ethics* in TFL behavior.

A second limitation is related to the research methods used to examine transformational leadership. While there is much discussion about TFL theory being "empirically proven," there is also research demonstrating inconsistent results and lack of evidence altogether (e.g., no correlation) (see Santhidran et al., 2013; Seo et al., 2012; Peng et al., 2021). TFL begins with a lack of consensus around "effectiveness" or success, but "success" is not always well-defined or defined consistently (Andersen, 2015). In alignment with research method limitations, many studies employ only survey instruments in their design and these can cause mono-method bias (Avolio et al., 2009; Andersen, 2015). Additionally, "self-reporting may not always produce reliable and accurate responses" (Mittal & Dhar, 2015, p. 894).

Key Theorists: James Downton & J.M. Burns (Foundational theorists); Bernard Bass & B.J. Avilio (Originating author); R. F. Piccolo; Phillip Podsakoff; Gary Yuki.

Examples of Use in Research: Ladkin and Patrick (2022); Crede et al. (2019); Price and Weiss (2013).

References

Andersen, J. A. (2015). Barking up the wrong tree. On the fallacies of the transformational leadership theory. *Leadership & Organization Development Journal*, *36*(6), 765–777. 10.1108/LODJ-12-2013-0168

Avolio, B. J. (1999). *Full leadership development: Building the vital forces in organizations*. Sage.

Avolio, B. J. (2005). *Leadership development in balance: Made/Born*. Erlbaum.

Avolio, B. J., Walumbwa, F. O., & Weber, T. J. (2009). Leadership: Current theories, research, and future directions. *Annual review of psychology* (pp. 421–449). 10.1146/annurev.psych.60.110707.163621

Bandura, A. (1977). *Social learning theory*. Prentice Hall.

Barrow, J., & O'Shea, A. (2020). A case study exploring the impact of valuing practices and emotional labour on the well-being of one senior leader. *Polish Journal of Educational Studies*, *72*(1), 109–124. 10.2478/poljes-2019-0008

Bass, B. M. (1985). Leadership: Good, better, best. *Organizational Dynamics*, *13*(3), 26–40. 10.1016/0090-2616(85)90028-2

Bass, B. J., & Avilio, B. J. (1993). Transformational Leadership: A response to critiques. In M. M. Chemers (Ed.), *Leadership: Theory and research perspectives and directions* (pp. 49–80). Academic Press.

Bass, B. M., & Avolio, B. J. (1995). *Manual for the multifactor leadership questionnaire: Rater form 5X short*. Mind Garden. 10.1037/t03624-000

Bass, B. M. (1998). The ethics of transformational leadership. In J. Cuilla (Ed.), *Ethics: The heart of leadership* (pp. 169–192). Praeger.

Bingham, A. J. (2021). How distributed leadership facilitates technology integration: A case study of "Pilot teachers". *Teachers College Record (1970)*, *123*(7), 1–34. 10.1177/016146812112300704

Blau, P. M. (1964). *Exchange and power in social life*. Transaction Publishers.

Bolden, R. (2011). Distributed leadership in organizations: A review of theory and research: Distributed leadership in organizations. *International Journal of Management Reviews: IJMR*, *13*(3), 251–269. 10.1111/j.1468-2370.2011.00306.x

Burch, P., Bingham, A. J., & Miglani, N. (2020). Combining institutional and distributed frameworks in studies of school leadership. *Peabody Journal of Education, 95*(4), 408–422. 10.1080/0161956X.2020.1800176

Burns, J. M. (1978). *Leadership.* Harper & Row.

Burton, L. J., Welty Peachey, J., & Wells, J. E. (2017). The role of servant leadership in developing an ethical climate in sport organizations. *Journal of Sport Management, 31*(3), 229–240. 10.1123/jsm.2016-0047

Cheung, A. C. K., Xie, C., Zhuang, T., Neitzel, A. J., & Slavin, R. E. (2021). Success for all: A quantitative synthesis of U.S. evaluations. *Journal of Research on Educational Effectiveness, 14*(1), 90–115. 10.1080/19345747.2020.1868031

Côté, R. G. (2017). A comparison of leadership theories in an organizational environment. *International Journal of Business Administration, 8,* 28–35. 10.5430/IJBA.V8N5P28

Crede, M., Jong, J., & Harms, P. (2019). The generalizability of transformational leadership across cultures: A meta-analysis. *Journal of Managerial Psychology, 34*(3), 139–155. 10.1108/JMP-11-2018-0506

Daniels, M. A., & Greguras, G. J. (2014). Exploring the nature of power distance: Implications for micro- and macro-level theories, processes, and outcomes. *Journal of Management, 40*(5), 1202–1229. 10.1177/0149206314527131

Dare, P. S., & Saleem, A. (2022). Toward success while tackling the change in a pandemic age: Path-goal theory leadership as a win-win gadget. *Frontiers in Psychology, 13,* 944145-944145. 10.3389/fpsyg.2022.944145

Den Hartog, D. N., House, R. J., Hanges, P. J., Ruiz-Quintanilla, S. A., Dorfman, P. W., Abdalla, I. A., & Akande, B. E. (1999). Culture specific and cross-culturally generalizable implicit leadership theories: Are attributes of charismatic/ transformational leadership universally endorsed?. *The Leadership Quarterly, 10*(2), 219–256. 10.1016/S1048-9843(99)00018-1

Dinham, S. (2007). How schools get moving and keep improving : Leadership for teacher learning, student success and school renewal. *The Australian Journal of Education, 51*(3), 263-275. 10.1177/000494410705100304

Dugan, J. P., Turman, N. T., & Barnes, A. C. (2017). *Leadership theory: A facilitator's guide for cultivating critical perspectives* (1st ed.). Jossey-Bass.

Eva, N., Robin, M., Sendjaya, S., van Dierendonck, D., & Liden, R. C. (2018). Servant leadership: A systematic review and call for future research. *The Leadership Quarterly, 30,* 111–132. 10.1016/j.leaqua.2018.07.004

Evans, M. G. (1970). The effects of supervisory behavior on the path-goal relationship. *Organizational Behavior and Human Performance, 5*(3), 277–298. 10.1016/0030-5073(70)90021-8

Fairhurst, G., (2007). *Discursive Leadership: In conversation with leadership psychology.* Sage.

Famakin, I. O., & Abisuga, A. O. (2016). Effect of path-goal leadership styles on the commitment of employees on construction projects. *International Journal of Construction Management, 16*(1), 67–76. 10.1080/15623599.2015.1130601

Fourie, W., & Höhne, F. (2019). Thou shalt not fail? using theological impulses to critique the heroic bias in transformational leadership theory. *Leadership (London, England), 15*(1), 44–57. 10.1177/1742715017730453

Fletcher, J.K. & Käufer, K. (2003). Shared leadership: Paradox and possibility. In Pearce C. , & Conger J. (Eds.), *Shared leadership: Reframing the hows and whys of leadership.* (pp. 21). Sage Publications, Inc. 10.4135/9781452229539

Fuller, B., Bajaba, A., & Bajaba, S. (2022). Enhancing and extending the meta-analytic comparison of newer genre leadership forms. *Frontiers in Psychology, 13,* 872568-872568. 10.3389/fpsyg.2022.872568

Gibb, C. A. (1947). The principles and traits of leadership. *Journal of Abnormal and Social Psychology, 42*(3), 267–284. 10.1037/h0056420

Greenleaf, R. K. (1977). *Servant leadership: A journey into the nature of legitimate power and greatness*. Paulist Press.

Gronn, P. (2000). Distributed properties: A new architecture for leadership. *Educational Management Administration & Leadership, 28*, 317–338. 10.1177/0263211X000283006

Hallinger, P. (2003). Leading educational change: Reflections on the practice of instructional and transformational leadership. *Cambridge Journal of Education, 33*(3), 329–352.

Hargreaves, A. & Fink, D. (2003). Sustaining leadership. *Phi Delta Kappan, 84*(9), 693-700.

Harris, A. (2013a). *Distributed leadership matters: Perspectives, practicalities, and potential*. Sage. 10.4135/9781483332574

Harris, A. (2013b). Distributed leadership: Friend or foe? *Educational Management, Administration & Leadership, 41*(5), 545–554. 10.1177/1741143213497635

Harris, A., & Spillane, J. (2008). Distributed leadership through the looking glass. *Management in Education, 22*(1), 31–34. 10.1177/0892020607085623

House, R. J. (1971). A path-goal theory of leader effectiveness. *Administrative Science Quarterly 16*(3), 321–338. 10.2307/2391905

House, R. J., & Mitchell, T. (1975). Path-goal theory of leadership. *National Technical Information Service, 7*(3), 323–352. 10.1016/S1048-9843(96)90024-7

House, R. J. (1996). Path-goal theory of leadership: Lessons legacy, and a reformulated theory. *The Leadership Quarterly, 7*(3), 323–352. 10.1016/S1048-9843(96)90024-7

Indvik, J. (1986). Path-goal theory of leadership: A meta-analysis. *Proceedings of the Academy of Management Meeting, 8*(1), 189–192. 10.5465/AMBPP.1986.4980581

Judge, T. A., & Piccolo, R. F. (2004). Transformational and transactional leadership: A meta-analytic test of their relative validity. *Journal of Applied Psychology, 89*(5), 755–768. 10.1037/0021-9010.89.5.755

Kabasakal, H. & Bodur, M. (2004). Humane orientation in societies, organizations, and leader attributes. *Culture, leadership, and organizations: The GLOBE study of, 62*, 564-601.

Karnopp, J. (2019). Undoing reform: How and why one school leader cleared a shifting path to goal attainment. *Qualitative Report, 24*(11), 2675–2692. https://www.proquest.com/docview/2322631701

Kull, T., Wiengarten, F., Power, D., & Shah, P. (2019). Acting as expected: Global leadership preferences and the pursuit of an integrated supply chain. *The Journal of Supply Chain Management, 55*(3), 24–44. 10.1111/jscm.12208

Kwan, P. (2020). Is transformational leadership theory passé? revisiting the integrative effect of instructional leadership and transformational leadership on student outcomes. *Educational Administration Quarterly, 56*(2), 321–349. 10.1177/0013161X19861137

Ladkin, D., & Patrick, C. B. (2022). Whiteness in leadership theorizing: A critical analysis of race in Bass' transformational leadership theory. *Leadership (London, England), 18*(2), 205–223. 10.1177/17427150211066442

Laub, J. A. (1999). *Assessing the servant organization: Development of the servant organizational leadership assessment (SOLA) instrument* (Order No. 9921922). Available from ProQuest Dissertations & Theses Global; ProQuest One Academic. (304517144). Retrieved from https://www.proquest.com/dissertations-theses/assessing-servant-organization-development/docview/304517144/se-2

Lee, A., Lyubovnikova, J., Tian, A. W., & Knight, C. (2020). Servant leadership: A meta-analytic examination of incremental contribution, moderation, and mediation. *Journal of Occupational and Organizational Psychology, 93*(1), 1–44. 10.1111/joop.12265

Leithwood, K, Mascall, B, & Strauss, T (2009). *Distributed leadership according to the evidence*. Routledge.

Li, P., Sun, J.-M., Taris, T. W., Xing, L., & Peeters, M. C. W. (2021). Country differences in the relationship between leadership and employee engagement: A meta-analysis. *The Leadership Quarterly, 32*(1), 101458. 10.1016/j.leaqua.2020.101458

Liu, Y., & Werblow, J. (2019). The operation of distributed leadership and the relationship with organizational commitment and job satisfaction of principals and teachers: A multi-level model and meta-analysis using the 2013 TALIS data. *International Journal of Educational Research, 96*, 41–55. 10.1016/j.ijer.2019.05.005

Louis, K.S., Mayrowetz, D., Smiley, M., & Murphy, J. (2009). The Role of Sensemaking and Trust in Developing Distributed Leadership. In A. Harris (Ed.), *Distributed Leadership. Studies in Educational Leadership.* Springer. 157-180. 10.1007/978-1-4020-9737-9_9

Lumby, J. (2019). Distributed leadership and bureaucracy. *Educational Management, Administration & Leadership, 47*(1), 5–19. 10.1177/1741143217711190

Ma, X., & Jiang, W. (2018). Transformational leadership, transactional leadership, and employee creativity in entrepreneurial firms. *Journal of Applied Behavioral Science, 54*(3), 302–324. 10.1177/0021886318764346

Mittal, S., & Dhar, R. L. (2015). Transformational leadership and employee creativity mediating role of creative self-efficacy and moderating role of knowledge sharing. *Management Decision, 53*(5), 894–910. 10.1108/MD-07-2014-0464

Neubert, M. J., de Luque, M. S., Quade, M. J., & Hunter, E. M. (2022). Servant leadership across the globe: Assessing universal and culturally contingent relevance in organizational contexts. *Journal of World Business, 57*(2), 1–12. 10.1016/j.jwb.2021.101268

Newman, A., Schwarz, G., Cooper, B., & Sendjaya, S. (2017). How servant leadership influences organizational citizenship behavior: The roles of LMX, empowerment, and proactive personality. *Journal of Business Ethics, 145*(1), 49–62. 10.1007/s10551-015-2827-6

Northouse, P. G. (2016). *Leadership: Theory and practice* (7th ed.). Sage Publications.

Ogawa, R. T., & Bossert, S. T. (1995). Leadership as an organizational quality. *Educational Administration Quarterly, 31*(2), 224–243. 10.1177/0013161X95031002004

O'Leary, B. S., Lindholm, M. L., Whitford, R. A., & Freeman, S. E. (2002). Selecting the best and brightest: Leveraging human capital. *Human Resource Management, 41*(3), 325–340. 10.1002/hrm.10044

Patterson, K. A. (2003). *Servant Leadership: A theoretical model.* Doctoral dissertation, Regent University. No 3082719. https://www.regent.edu/wp-content/uploads/2020/12/patterson_servant_leadership.pdf

Peng, J., Li, M., Wang, Z., & Lin, Y. (2021). Transformational leadership and employees' reactions to organizational change: Evidence from a meta-analysis. *The Journal of Applied Behavioral Science, 57*(3), 369–397. 10.1177/0021886320920366

Perez, J. (2021). Leadership in healthcare: Transitioning from clinical professional to healthcare leader. *Journal of Healthcare Management, 66*(4), 280–302. 10.1097/JHM-D-20-00057

Phillips, A., & Phillips, C. (2016). Behavioral styles of path-goal theory: An exercise for developing leadership skills. *Management Teaching Review, 1*(3), 148–154. 10.1177/2379298116639725

Podsakoff, P. M., MacKenzie, S. B., Moorman, R. H., & Fetter, R. (1990). Transformational leader behaviors and their effects on followers' trust in leader, satisfaction, and organizational citizenship behaviors. *Leadership Quarterly, 1*(2), 107–142. 10.1016/1048-9843(90)90009-7

Price, M. S., & Weiss, M. R. (2013). Relationships among coach leadership, peer leadership, and adolescent athletes' psychosocial and team outcomes: A test of transformational leadership theory. *Journal of Applied Sport Psychology, 25*(2), 265–279. 10.1080/10413200.2012.725703

Rafferty, A. E., & Griffin, M. A. (2004). Dimensions of transformational leadership: Conceptual and empirical extensions. *The Leadership Quarterly, 15*(3), 329–354. 10.1016/j.leaqua.2004.02.009

Santhidran, S., Chandran, V. G. R., & Borromeo, J. (2013). Enabling organizational change: Leadership, commitment to change and the mediating role of change readiness. *Journal of Business Economics & Management, 14*(2), 348–363. 10.3846/16111699.2011.642083

Schriesheim, J. F., & Schriesheim, C. A. (1980). A test of the path-goal theory of leadership and some suggested directions for future research. *Personnel Psychology, 33*(2), 349–370. 10.1111/j.1744-6570.1980.tb02356.x

Schriesheim, C. A., Castro, S. L., Zhou, X., & DeChurch, L. A. (2006). An investigation of path-goal and transformational leadership theory predictions at the individual level of analysis. *The Leadership Quarterly, 17*(1), 21–38. 10.1016/j.leaqua.2005.10.008

Seo, M. G., Taylor, M. S., Hill, N. S., Zhang, X., Tesluk, P. E., & Lorinkova, N. M. (2012). The role of affect and leadership during organizational change. *Personnel Psychology, 65*(1), 121–165. 10.1111/j.1744-6570.2011.01240.x

Spears, L. C. (1995). *Reflections on leadership: How Robert K. Greenleaf's theory of servant leadership influenced today's top management thinkers.* John Wiley & Sons, Inc.

Spears, L. C. (1996). Reflections on Robert K. Greenleaf and servant-leadership. *Leadership & Organization Development Journal, 17*(7), 33–35. 10.1108/01437739610148367

Spillane, J. P., Halverson, R., & Diamond, J. B. (2004). Towards a theory of leadership practice: A distributed perspective. *Journal of Curriculum Studies, 36*(1), 3–34. 10.1080/0022027032000106726

Spillane, J. P. (2006). *Distributed leadership.* John Wiley & Sons.

Stinson, J. E., & Johnson, T. W. (1975). The path-goal theory of leadership: A partial test and suggested refinement. *The Academy of Management Journal, 18*(2), 242–252. https://www.jstor.org/stable/255527

Sujana, C. M. (2020). Contractor project manager leadership style based on path goal theory to support construction sustainability. *IOP Conference Series. Earth and Environmental Science, 426*(1), 12007. 10.1088/1755-1315/426/1/012007

Thorpe, R., Gold, J., & Lawler, J. (2011). Locating distributed leadership. *International Journal of Management Reviews: IJMR, 13*(3), 239–250. 10.1111/j.1468-2370.2011.00303.x

Tian, M., Risku, M., & Collin, K. (2016). A meta-analysis of distributed leadership from 2002 to 2013: Theory development, empirical evidence and future research focus. *Educational Management, Administration & Leadership, 44*(1), 146–164. 10.1177/1741143214558576

Tourish, D. (2008). Challenging the transformational agenda: Leadership theory in transition? *Management Communication Quarterly, 21*(4), 522–528. 10.1177/0893318907313713

van Dierendonck, D. (2011). Servant leadership: A review and synthesis. *Journal of Management, 37*(4), 1228–1261. 10.1177/0149206310380462

van Dierendonck, D., Stam, D., Boersma, P., de Windt, N., & Alkema, J. (2014). Same difference? exploring the differential mechanisms linking servant leadership and transformational leadership to follower outcomes. *The Leadership Quarterly, 25*(3), 544–562. 10.1016/j.leaqua.2013.11.014

Varpanen, J. (2021). Early childhood education leadership in Finland through the lens of structure and agency. *Educational Management, Administration & Leadership, 49*(3), 518–533. 10.1177/1741143220903727

Vroom, V. H. (1964). *Work and motivation.* McGraw Hill.

Wenger, E. (1998). Communities of practice: Learning as a social system. *Systems thinker. 9*(5). 2-3.

Wofford, J. C., & Liska, L. Z. (1993). Path-goal theories of leadership: A meta-analysis. *Journal of Management, 19*(4), 857–876. 10.1016/0149-2063(93)90031-H

Zhu, W., Avolio, B. J., & Walumbwa, F. O. (2016). Moderating role of follower characteristics with transformational leadership and follower work engagement (vol 34, pg 590, 2009). *Group & Organization Management, 41*(3), 407–409. 10.1177/1059601116638774

8 Public Policy

Policy Instruments

Definition and Overview

Policy instruments, also sometimes called policy tools, are the mechanisms through which policy goals are translated into concrete actions (Capano & Howlett, 2020; McDonnell & Elmore, 1987). Policies are how societies regulate themselves and direct human behavior in desired directions (Schneider & Ingram, 1997). Policies work by using resources to achieve political aims (McDonnell & Elmore, 1987). Policy instruments are the means by which the goals of policy are implemented. Through policy instruments, governmental entities are able to secure support for governmental/political actions, laws, and policies, and achieve or prevent social change (Vedung, 1998). The types of tools that policymakers choose to ensure compliance send a clear message about how those policymakers value the targets of the policy (Schneider & Ingram, 1997).

A policy problem ends up on policymakers' agendas through political advocacy, and policymakers typically develop responses to those problems depending on the possible solutions and the resources available to enact those solutions (Kingdon, 2003). A policy instruments framework is concerned with the range of possible avenues available to policymakers in addressing particular problems (McDonnell & Elmore, 1987).

There are four types of policy instruments as outlined by McDonnell and Elmore (1987): Mandates, which are rules intended to exhort compliance by governing individuals' and agencies' actions; Inducements, which exchange money for specific actions; Capacity-building, in which money is given to invest in necessary resources; and System-changing tools, which alter the hierarchies and systems through which public goods and services are delivered. The primary element of mandates is rules, while the expected effect is compliance. The primary element of inducements and capacity-building instruments is money, while the expected effects are production of value and short-term returns, and skills enhancement, competence, and long-term returns, respectively. The primary element of system-changing instruments is authority, while the expected effects are incentives.

Schneider and Ingram (1990, 1997) discuss five categories of policy tools, including authority, incentives, capacity-building, symbolic and hortatory, and learning. Authority tools permit, require, or prohibit actions under certain circumstances and rely on the authority of the government or policymaking body. Incentives influence or encourage action through payoffs for policy-preferred activities, and can be further sub-divided into inducements, charges, sanctions, and force. Capacity instruments enable policy action by providing education, information, training, and/or other resources. Symbolic or hortatory tools attempt to persuade people to engage in particular policy actions by convincing them

DOI: 10.4324/9781003261759-8

that these actions are in line with their beliefs. Finally, learning tools assume that the targets of policy recognize the policy problem, but that there are no clear solutions, and therefore, targets should be given the opportunity to learn about possible solutions.

In deciding what policy instruments will most effectively address a specific issue or problem or achieve a desired aim, policymakers consider the effectiveness of the instrument, the political acceptability, the technical feasibility, the economic impacts, and the long-term consequences (Kraft & Furlong, 2018, p. 108). Policymakers also consider potential unintended effects. There tend to be preferences along political lines for what kinds of policy instruments are most useful (Schneider & Ingram, 1990). Democrats, for example, may engage capacity-building instruments more often or may utilize positive inducements for marginalized groups, while Republicans seem to lean toward these types of instruments for business groups and corporations. Additionally, different historical periods may demonstrate preference for different policy instruments (Schneider & Ingram, 1990).

Policy instruments can be used as a conceptual framework for examining policy design and implementation. This framework can help researchers to identify how policies are designed, what instruments are employed in that design, the mechanisms of in-centivization, how policy targets view and experience different policy instruments in their own lives, as well as explore implementation successes and challenges (McDonnell & Elmore, 1987; Schneider & Ingram, 1990). Additionally, a policy instruments frame-work can support the contextualized study of how and why given policy instruments are applied, and can help researchers investigate the conditions that are necessary for various policy instruments to work as planned (McDonnell & Elmore, 1987). Ultimately, a policy instruments conceptual framework "not only holds the potential for moving beyond static descriptions of the implementation process, but it also embeds key variables such as local response patterns in a larger, theoretically richer context" (McDonnell & Elmore, 1987, p. 135).

Background and Foundations

The classification of policy instruments dates back to the 1950s and 1960s, when various scholars were aiming to distinguish the ways in which policies attempted to influence human behavior and activity (Howlett, 2018). The specific research focus on policy instruments or tools emerged from studies of policy implementation, which identified gaps in how implementation was understood (Schneider & Ingram, 1990). In the early 1980s Salamon (1981), argued that policy implementation researchers should reorient their focus to examining policy tools or instruments and their comparative effectiveness.

Policy instruments, as a framework for understanding policy implementation, emerged from an identified gap in policy implementation research and an effort to systematically identify the relationships among "the policy problems being addressed, the basic design features of a policy, the implementing organization, and the political and organizational context in which policy targets must respond" (McDonnell & Elmore, 1987, p. 134). McDonnell and Elmore (1987) developed the policy instruments framework to concentrate on and categorize the mechanisms by which policy is implemented. McDonnell and Elmore categorized policy instruments as mandates, inducements, capacity, or system-changing. The purpose of the framework was to ultimately help researchers answer the question: "Under what conditions are different instruments most likely to produce their intended effects?" (McDonnell & Elmore, 1987, p. 134). Other policy scholars suggested that policy instruments could be categorized as coercive (mandates, order, rules, etc.), catalytic (incentives), and/or hortatory (cajoling or threatening compliance) (Gormley, 1987). Schneider and Ingram (1990) further built on these ideas to categorize policy tools as authority, incentives, capacity-building, symbolic and hortatory, and learning. More recently, other scholars have argued that individuals have preferences not just for policy problems and goals, but also for the means by which those problems are addressed and those goals are achieved (Vesely, 2021). This idea is referred to as autonomy of policy instrument attitudes (APIA).

Key Terms and Concepts

Capacity-building refers to the transfer of money for investment in future desired outcomes. These desired outcomes may not be tangible or immediately evident.

Inducements refer to transfers of money in return for goods and service (McDonnell & Elmore, 1987, p. 138). These are often accompanied by particular rules about how the money should be used in alignment with the policymakers' intent.

Mandates are the rules that govern actions (McDonnell & Elmore, 1987, p. 138). Mandates require enforcement.

Policy refers to a purposeful "course of action that an individual or group consistently follows in dealing with a problem" (Kraft & Furlong, 2018, p. 6). Policy attempts to get people to do things that they may not have otherwise done (Schneider & Ingram, 1990).

Policy instruments are the mechanisms that translate substantive policy goals into concrete actions (McDonnell & Elmore, 1987, p. 134).

System-changing refers to transfers of authority across individuals or agencies (McDonnell & Elmore, 1987, p. 139). System-changing instruments might aim to increase efficiency or the distribution of funds.

In Research

Policy instruments have been used as a conceptual framework for understanding how policy is designed and implemented at multiple levels of government and in organizations. Williamson (2016), for example, drew on policy instruments to examine emerging "digital policy instruments" through several case studies of new digital data systems. Capano et al. (2020) used Qualitative Comparative Analysis (QCA) to explore the link between policy instruments and good teaching performance. In another study, Jaffe and Stavins (1995) investigated the effects of alternative environmental policy instruments on the diffusion of new technology in concerns about global climate change. Still others have looked at how the selection of policy instruments can influence environmental regulation (Taylor et al., 2012).

Strengths and Limitations

As a conceptual framework, policy instruments have both analytic and practical strengths. Conceptually, a policy instruments framework provides the analytic tools to understand how policies are conceived of and implemented and why policies work or do not work as the case may be. Practically, the identification and analysis of policy instruments can provide policymakers with a better understanding of the options available to them in designing policy (McDonnell & Elmore, 1987). Another major strength of a policy instruments framework is that it can allow for comparative analyses of policy design and implementation (Schneider & Ingram, 1990). As Capano and Howlett (2020) state, a policy instruments framework can "better enlighten the nature of policy dynamics, from a prescriptive point of view, and assist policymakers in taking more effective decisions than can a purely input-based approach" (p. 1).

Some scholars have argued that there are still aspects of policy instruments that are under-researched, including why policymakers choose certain policy instruments over others, how timing and history influence instrument choice, and how ideology is linked to instrument choice (Capano & Howlett, 2020).

Key Theorists: Lorraine M. McDonnell and Richard F. Elmore; Anne Larason Schneider and Helen Ingram.

Examples of Use in Research: Capano et al. (2020); Jaffe & Stavins (1995); Williamson (2016).

Social Construction of Policy Targets

Definition and Overview

Social construction of policy targets is a policy concept explaining that how the targets of public policy are socially constructed can influence the policy agenda, the choice of policy tools, and the rationales that legitimize policy choices (Schneider & Ingram, 1993). Within this framework, policy targets are conceived as being constructed positively or negatively, and with strong or weak political power. The cultural characterizations and popular images of individuals or groups that are targeted or affected by public policy influence and are influenced by what problems end up on the agenda, the design of the policies, and policy perceptions and implementation (Schneider & Ingram, 1993, p. 334). How the targets of policies are conceived of is evident in the rhetoric surrounding the policy, the policy instruments engaged, and the characterization of the targets in the design of the policy itself (Schneider & Ingram, 1993, 1997).

The social construction of policy targets interacts with political power, which can then form a matrix of four different kinds of social constructions (See Figure 8.1): Advantaged, Contenders, Dependents, and Deviants (Schneider & Ingram, 1997, p. 102). The advantaged are politically powerful, and also positively constructed as deserving. Contenders are politically powerful but are negatively constructed as undeserving in some way (greediness, etc.). Dependents are not politically powerful, but they are positively constructed and seen as needing help. Finally, deviants have low or no political power and are negatively socially constructed as undeserving in some way (laziness, violence, stupidity, etc.). These social constructions are so ingrained that they are taken-for-granted as true. Where a group is situated in this matrix of social constructions can influence their experiences with government and their opinions of the usefulness or effectiveness of policy (Schneider & Ingram, 1993).

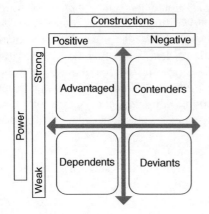

Figure 8.1 Social constructions of policy targets categorizations. Adapted from Schneider and Ingram (1993, 1997).

This idea that policy targets are socially constructed is especially relevant in a degenerative policy-making context, which is a state in which political power is unequally distributed, the "deserving" policy targets are separated from the "undeserving," and communication and political power is characterized by manipulation, and deception (Schneider & Ingram, 1997, p. 103). In a degenerative policy-making context, in which social constructions of policy targets influence policymaking, how target groups are conceived of can change over time (Pierce et al., 2014). For example, while people living with HIV or AIDS were once constructed as "deviants" in public policy, as HIV/AIDS has become more and more destigmatized in society, that group moves into the "contenders" category. As Piece and colleagues (2014) note, this "process of change is both internal and external to target populations, and generally takes multiple decades to occur" (p. 17).

As a conceptual framework, the social construction of policy targets is useful for understanding policy design and agenda-setting in public policy. It can be used as a theoretical framework outlining the process of social construction and can also be used to categorize and problematize those social constructions. Further, this framework supports researchers in interrogating the conscious, subconscious, or unconscious motivations behind policy agenda-setting, design, choice of policy instruments, and implementation.

Background and Foundations

The social construction of policy targets is grounded in a constructivist paradigm and is rooted in the emergence of public policy as a sub-field of political science, which facilitated a focus on specific aspects of the policymaking process, including agenda-setting, problem definition, and implementation (Schneider & Ingram, 1993). The idea of "target population" is derived from the policy design literature and directs research attention to the idea that policies are designed with specific populations in mind and are created to enable or coerce certain behaviors.

Although the idea that policy is aimed at specific sets of people is not a novel one, the idea that these policy targets are socially constructed was new, and shed light on the implementation and effects of policy, as well as on the political process. For example, a policy might be aimed at people living below the poverty line, which is defined and measured in a particular way. However, "social constructions could portray them as disadvantaged people whose poverty is not their fault or as lazy persons who are benefitting from other peoples' hard work" (Schneider & Ingram, 1993, p. 335). In conceiving of public policy in this way, researchers can better identify bidirectional influences and effects, political motivations, and social priorities.

Key Terms and Concepts

Degenerative policy-making contexts are characterized by manipulation and deceit in politics and policymaking, division in the construction of policy targets, and the unequal distribution of political power (Schneider & Ingram, 1997).

Pluralism is the idea that the government's role is to enact public policies that represent the interests of its citizens (Schneider & Ingram, 1997). Policy should be responsive and accountable to the electorate.

Policy tools (instruments) are the mechanisms by which substantive policy goals are translated into concrete actions (McDonnell & Elmore, 1987, p. 134). Policy tools send clear messages about target populations – specifically, about "what kind of people they are, whether they deserve the benefits or burdens that have been assessed, and what their capacities are" (Schneider & Ingram, 1997, p. 96). Policy instruments also demonstrate policymakers' underlying reasoning for policy decisions and send signals to the general population about the characteristics of the target group.

Social Constructions are stereotypes of particular groups put forth in politics, culture, literature, religion, and so on (Schneider & Ingram, 1993). In a social constructions of policy targets framework, social constructions further refer to the cultural characterization of groups that are targeted by specific policies. Social construction, more generally, refers to the understanding of the social world that centers meaning-making (Schneider & Sidney, 2009).

In Research

The concept of socially constructing policy targets has been used as a framework to understand policy and policymaking at the international, national, and state levels, as well as regional and local levels (Pierce et al., 2014). In particular, Schneider and Ingram's (1993, 1997) categorizations of policy targets as advantaged, contenders, dependents, and deviants have been used to explore policy problem definition, design, agenda-setting, and implementation and have also been used to better understand the social construction and representation of various groups in public policy. For example, Hudson and Gonyea (2012) examined how the social construction of elderly people in policymaking has evolved over time, specifically looking at political conceptions and characterizations of the elderly from pre-World War II, when the authors argue they were conceived of as "dependent," to present day, when they are considered "contenders." In another example, Soss (2005) looked at how people respond to the policy designs encountered in security disability insurance and Aid to Families with Dependents policies. Maltby and Kreitzer (2023) examined racialized policy and how perceptions of the targets of social welfare and criminal justice policies are shaped by direct and indirect experience with these policies.

Strengths and Limitations

As a framework, the social construction of policy targets has wide-ranging uses and can be wielded as a tool for interrogating bias in policy. Further, it can help researchers understand the dynamics of policy change and can push studies beyond analyses of costs and benefits. It can also offer some understanding of the bidirectional nature of policy and political influence. Finally, social constructions are measurable, through survey methods, historical analysis, and textual analysis (Schneider & Ingram, 1993).

Some scholars have noted that a limitation of this framework is in the lack of research on *how* policy targets move from one category to another (e.g., how a certain group would move from "dependent" to "contender") (Pierce et al., 2014). In a response to this critique, Schneider and Ingram (2005) explained that shifts in the construction and perception of a target group could be a result of a change in the political attractiveness of the group, external events, new opportunities, or manipulations (Pierce et al., 2014).

Key Theorists: Anne Larason Schneider & Helen Ingram.

Examples of Use in Research: Hudson and Gonyea (2012); Maltby and Kreitzer (2023); Soss (2005).

References

Capano, G., & Howlett, M. (2020). The knowns and unknowns of policy instrument analysis: Policy tools and the current research agenda on policy mixes. *Sage Open, 10*(1). https://doi.org/10.1177/2158244019900568

Capano, G., Pritoni, A., & Vicentini, G. (2020). Do policy instruments matter? Governments' choice of policy mix and higher education performance in Western Europe. *Journal of Public Policy, 40*(3), 375–401.

Gormley, W. T. (1987). Bureau-Bashing: A framework for analysis. Presented at the annual meeting of the American Political Science Association, Chicago, IL.

Howlett, M. (2018). The criteria for effective policy design: Character and context in policy instrument choice. *Journal of Asian Public Policy, 11*(3), 245–266.

Hudson, R. B., & Gonyea, J. G. (2012). Baby Boomers and the shifting political construction of old age. *The Gerontologist, 52*(2), 272–282

Jaffe, A. B., & Stavins, R. N. (1995). Dynamic incentives of environmental regulations: The effects of alternative policy instruments on technology diffusion. *Journal of Environmental Economics and Management, 29*(3), S43–S63.

Kingdon, J. W. (2003). *Agendas, alternatives, and public policies.* Addison-Wesley Educational Publishers.

Kraft, M. E., & Furlong, S. R. (2018). *Public policy: Politics, analysis, and alternatives.* Cq Press.

Maltby, E., & Kreitzer, R. J. (2023). How racialized policy contact shapes the social constructions of policy targets. *Policy Studies Journal, 51*(1), 145–162.

McDonnell, L. M., & Elmore, R. F. (1987). Getting the job done: Alternative policy instruments. *Educational Evaluation and Policy Analysis, 9*(2), 133–152. 10.3102/01623737009002133

Pierce, J. J., Siddiki, S., Jones, M. D., Schumacher, K., Pattison, A., & Peterson, H. (2014). Social construction and policy design: A review of past applications. *Policy Studies Journal, 42*(1), 1–29.

Salamon, L. M. (1981). Rethinking public management: Third party government and the changing forms of government action. *Public Policy, 29*, 255–275.

Schneider, A., & Ingram, H. (1990). Behavioral assumptions of policy tools. *The Journal of Politics, 52*(2), 510–529.

Schneider, A., & Ingram, H. (1993). Social construction of target populations: Implications for politics and policy. *The American Political Science Review, 87*(2), 334–347. 10.2307/2939044

Schneider, A. L., & Ingram, H. M. (1997). *Policy design for democracy.* University of Kansas Press.

Schneider, A. L., & Ingram H. M. (2005). *Deserving and entitled: Social construction and public policy.* State University of New York Press.

Schneider, A., & Sidney, M. (2009). What is next for policy design and social construction theory? *Policy Studies Journal, 37*(1), 103–119.

Soss, J. (2005). Making clients and citizens: Welfare policy as a source of status, belief, and action. In A. L. Schneider & H. M. Ingram (Eds.), *Deserving and entitled: Social constructions and public policy* (pp. 291–328). State University of New York Press.

Taylor, C., Pollard, S., Rocks, S., & Angus, A. (2012). Selecting policy instruments for better environmental regulation: A critique and future research agenda. *Environmental Policy and Governance, 22*, 268–292.

Vedung, E. (1998). Policy instruments: Typologies and theories. *Carrots, Sticks, and Sermons: Policy Instruments and Their Evaluation, 5*, 21–58.

Veselý, A. (2021). Autonomy of policy instrument attitudes: Concept, theory and 'evidence'. *Policy Sciences, 54*(2), 441–455.

Williamson, B. (2016). Digital education governance: Data visualization, predictive analytics, and 'real-time' policy instruments. *Journal of Education Policy, 31*(2), 123–141.

9 Political Science

Marxism and Capitalism Theories

Definition and Overview

Marxism is generally seen as a philosophy developed in the 19th century by Karl Marx, that examines the interactions of economics, labor, and productivity, and the impact on the working class and society-at-large (Robinson, 2019). As a theory, Marxism posits that there is a continual struggle between the working class (referred to as the proletariat) and the upper class (referred to as the bourgeoisie) (Marx & Engels, 1932). According to Marxist principles, this struggle would lead to conflict and, eventually, to new structures where the proletariat controls both the means of production and the outputs of labor. This was a significant contribution to communist political thought throughout the 19th and 20th centuries (Smith, 2021).

    Capitalism, in contrast to Marxism, does not primarily focus on labor or the ownership of production, but rather on the unencumbered movement of goods and services between entities, where the individual or private sector is the driving force to provide supply for consumer demand (Kocka & Reimer, 2016). In a capitalism framework, the limitation (or elimination) of governmental interference or control is ideal, as the free market will help determine supply and demand of goods and the associated costs of final products and resources needed to make products (Sonenscher, 2022). In the capitalistic model, private ownership of property and capital is both essential and an end-goal for the individual (Hacker, 1957).

    As concepts, Marxism and capitalism are frequently seen to be two sides of a coin. However, although there are significant areas of direct contrast between them, Marxism and capitalism are not opposite frameworks (Briggs, 2019). Indeed, leveraging a Marxist/capitalistic framework in research is common and has been used in scholarship in nearly all academic disciplines, especially within the social sciences (Kumar, 2023; Kanth, 2015).

    The interplay between Marxism and capitalism has been explored and applied extensively in historical studies, examinations of economic success and collapse, and historical and contemporary political analysis. In the study of history, for example, historians frequently leverage a Marxist lens of historical materialism (the belief that all institutions are an outgrowth of economics and economic interactions) to provide insight into the development of societies and how labor and production align with the goals and outcomes (desired or real) of society (Hobsbawm, 1962; Habib, 2015). The examination of the relationships between labor and management, societal inequity, and the role of the working class provides the foundation of Marx's work, and has been revisited countless times since the publication of Das Kapital in 1867 (Simpson, 2021; Barkey, 2012). Part of

DOI: 10.4324/9781003261759-9

Marx's work was inspired by the philosophies of Georg Wilhelm Friedrich Hegel and his work *Phenomenology of Spirit* as they relate to self-consciousness and the mutual recognition of individuals and society.

Similar to Marxism, Capitalism also examines the interactions between parts of society, but in a narrower lens that primarily connects to economic systems (Kocka & Reimer, 2016). The foundation of capitalism is based on the exchange of goods and services between people, companies, governments, or numerous other entities (Cox, 1959). As a theory, capitalism emphasizes the use-value and exchange-value of goods and services. Scholars drawing on Marxist principles and ideas of capitalism in the development and application of other theories and frameworks (see CHAT in Chapter 6), have argued that a primary tension in a capitalist society is the contradiction between use-value and exchange-value (Engeström & Sannino, 2010).

Building upon the economic approach of capitalism, various political deviations have been developed that either supported the expansion of capitalism as a societal foundation or have looked to limit the free market in response to the needs of the general population (Baumol, 2002). Within this capitalistic model, governments and political systems emerged that provided varying degrees of oversight of the markets within their borders. While some nations eschewed the capitalistic approach for a more command-economy system where the free market is largely eliminated, other nations developed administrative systems that either supported the free market system or utilized a hybrid structure where some industries have little government interference and regulation and other industries have significant oversight by the government (Manish & Miller, 2020).

Marxism and Capitalism theories can each provide insight into the reasons governments, organizations, and people behave and interact in a particular way (Li & Maskin, 2021). While no one purely operates on a labor/production/market basis in their everyday lives, various historical events and current political and economic situations have a strong connection to both Marxist and capitalistic approaches. A study of political structures, for example, must consider the foundation upon which a government is based (Hoppe, 2017). In many cases, this may either be a capitalistic or a Marxist model.

Marxism and capitalism can be used as theoretical frameworks to better understand the nuances of societal-level views on labor, capital, and the exchange of goods and services for money. More specifically, Marxism could be used to understand public views and discourse on labor, markets, and capital, and to analyze issues of use-value and exchange-value at many levels. For researchers and scholars, the utilization of the Marxism/capitalism polarity can be helpful to understand the connections between human behavior and economics, and how society can be viewed by two opposite theories. Understanding the role of Marxism and capitalism in constructing and maintaining an organization, industry, civilization, or culture can and should be utilized in research that touches upon topics related to economics.

Background and Foundations

Communism and capitalistic theory are rooted in the work of Marx and Engles. Karl Marx was a German theorist whose work has been fundamental to studies of economics, political systems, history, sociology, and many more academic domains (Singer, 2018). His most famous writings remain the *Communist Manifesto* (1848) and *Capital* (1867). His ideas on the role of government, the proletariat, and the bourgeoisie introduced new concepts of governance, economics, and philosophy that continue to be refined in contemporary studies (Sdobnikov, 1973). Marx is widely considered to be both one of the most influential individuals in history and a major contributor to the foundations of the social sciences. Friedrich Engles, although most commonly associated as the co-author of the *Communist Manifesto* with Marx, also researched and published on issues related to 19th-century labor issues (*The Condition of the Working Class in England*, 1845) and the role of socialism in developing concepts of historical materialism as a basis for social and economic development (*Socialism: Utopian and Scientific*, 1880; Mayer, 1936).

In 1847, Marx and Engles produced *The Communist Manifesto* – a four-part narrative about the structure of the working class, the ruling class, and the governmental inter-actions between them (Sdobnikov, 1973). At the time, it received little notice, but became more widely read as the industrial revolution took hold throughout Europe, North America, and to a lesser degree, Asia (Padover, 1978). *The Communist Manifesto* is divided into four parts: An introduction, a section about the development of the two key classes (the bourgeoisie and the proletariat) within the contemporary labor system and a list of ten goals associated with an effective communist party, a third chapter which provides a critique of the bourgeoisie as well as a critical analysis of established social structures, and a final section that calls for action on the side of the proletariat to make changes for the betterment of society (Marx et al., 2021). In 1867, Marx built on ideas from *The Communist Manifesto* in *Capital*, which looks at the nuances related to capi-talistic production methods and is often seen as the foundational text for the emerging socialist movement of the late 19th and early 20th centuries (Marx & Engels, 1932).

Capitalism has a much longer history that spans back to the emergence of the initial civilizations in Mesopotamia, Egypt, and Greece (Lind, 1939). The concept of the ex-change of items of value between different parties is not new, nor is the process of production that leads to the items that can be bought and sold. Modern capitalism – the systems we see in our contemporary societies with multiple producers, banks, investors, and all the assorted elements of commerce – became solidified in the mid to late 19th century with the onset of the Industrial Revolution and the rapid growth of global pop-ulations (Stearns, 2020).

Perhaps the most famous economist related to capitalism is Adam Smith. His most famous 1776 work, *An Inquiry into the Nature and Causes of the Wealth of Nations*, continues to be utilized and studied in economics classrooms throughout the world. His contributions led to the evolution of contemporary economic thought and analysis throughout the 19th and 20th centuries (Phillipson, 2010). In his writings, Smith outlined the observed processes used in nations to distribute both wealth and power. Using a social scientist approach, instead of a theory more focused on religion and the role of God's will, Smith examined the balance between morality and the public good and individual financial and social betterment (Evensky, 2015). Smith's approach was unique at the time as it looked beyond accepted theological rationale for human and economic behavior and focused on the role of self-interest in the development and sustaining of a capitalistic system (Ross, 1995).

Key Terms and Concepts

The bourgeoisie refers to the individuals in a society that own and control the means of operation (Marx & Engels, 1932). Typically the non-working and wealthy class, the bourgeoisie was a smaller part of the overall population and had various levels of control over the general population, including the working class (the proletariat) (Sperber, 2022). The bourgeoisie can further be segmented into groups such as the petite bourgeoisie (the lower middle class), the moyenne bourgeoisie (the upper middle class), and the grande bourgeoisie (gentry and upper class) (Smith, 1981).

Capital is primarily associated with asset development and retention (Basu, 2021). While money to invest in a business can be seen as capital, so can the ownership of a factory that is used to produce a specific good (Cuyvers, 2017). Under capitalism, a key objective is to increase and expand the amount of capital one person (or group) possesses. The concept of capital has expanded over time to include human capital, social and cultural capital (see Chapter 4), and others.

Communism, according to Marx and Engels (1932), refers to an ideology that focuses on the overall good of the people or community resulting from the collective collaboration of the proletariat (Pons, 2010). While the term has taken on different connections to geopolitics and ideology throughout the 20th century, the core meaning centers on collective production and distribution of goods or resources to all individuals within the society or nation-state (Somerville, 1946). Taken to the extremes, a communist approach would lead to the elimination of currency, social classes, government, and all private property.

Free market directly contrasts with communism as it is dependent on private property and advocates for minimal, or no, interaction between commerce and government. Using a basis of supply and demand, free market scholars and economists can examine the role of limited supply, government interventions, and the interactions of labor within the market (Kates, 2014).

Historical materialism focuses on societal change and the development of societal classes as an outcome of human labor. It is tied to a Marxist perspective of history. Connected to the work of German philosopher Georg Hegel, historical materialism allows individuals to differentiate between different eras or epochs of time (Hegel & Fuss, 2019). There is also linkage between historical materialism and divergence, as the theory sees changes in production leading to social conflict (Croce, 1966). From this social conflict, new forms of production may emerge and add to the ongoing span of history through a historical materialism perspective.

The proletariat consists of the working class that must sell their labor to earn capital within a capitalistic system. Primarily a term used within a Marxist lens of analysis, the proletariat are often poor and do not own the means of production for their work (Lovell, 1988). The term proletariat differs from the concept of "working class" as the concepts of ownership, education, and the free movement of labor may not always apply within the use of the term proletariat (Naimark, 1979).

Socialism is used as either an economic or political term, depending on the context, and may sometimes incorporate elements of economics and politics in scholarship and practice (Linehan, 2012). Socialism features community or public ownership of the means of production, but within a democratic state. Ownership of industries, factories, or other means of production may be owned by the workers, a government entity, or any other group or individual (McMurtry, 1978). In contemporary usage, socialism is frequently divided between non-market, where the overall objectives of the means of production may focus on societal stability, economic planning, and resource allocation, and market socialism where production has a clear focus and connection to the profit motive above all other concerns (Arvidsson, 2017). The 20th century saw many nations move from a socialist state to a capitalistic model, with a few nations such as Portugal, India, and Tanzania still having references to socialism within their governmental structures.

Supply and demand, as a concept, is the foundation of most economic studies and analyses of capitalistic forms of economies (Grayson, 1965). The manipulation of the levers leading to the increase or decrease of supply and demand leads to a greater understanding of concepts such as the market equilibrium, elasticity of demand, substitute good theory, and a litany of other forms of economic analysis (Henderson, 1958). In its most basic form, supply and demand curves can outline market trends, pricing targets, and production levels. In a more complex analysis, supply and demand can provide insight into human behavior, commercial success and failure, governmental intervention strategies, and many other elements of economic interactions (Ariely, 2009).

In Research

Marxist approaches have been utilized in many different academic disciplines since its emergence in the mid-19th century. In educational studies, for example, Paulo Freire indirectly examines issues of power in education through a Marxist lens in his foundational work *Pedagogy of the Oppressed* (1968). In the history discipline, Marxism has been used in countless ways to illustrate specific actions such as anticolonialism (Rodney, 1972), nation-state history, and conflict studies (Gray, 1986). Many economists, including contemporary practitioners, connect to a Marxian approach (Laibman, 1992; Piore & Doeringer, 1971; Hudson, Miller & Feder, 1994) – as do numerous studies in sociology (Althusser, 1976; Bottomore, 1975). The counternarrative regarding Marxism is also present in numerous studies and essays. These critiques tend to focus on the impact on individual liberties (Chmielewska et al., 2021; Tismaneanu & Luber, 2021), the impact of global economic and political systems (Latif & Khan, 2011, Johnston, 2015), and the failure of nations, such as the Soviet Union, that were built on a Marxist framework (Paxton, 2021; Tikhonov, 2021).

The application of Marxist approaches is easily recognized, largely due to the utilization of words to describe classes, power dynamics, or societal institutions. For example, historian and social scientist Ifran Habib, when writing about the history of the emergence of Indian national identity, frequently refers to Marxism, the role of economics within society, and class divisions. In his 1975 work *Emergence of Nationalities*, he states "For India as a while, it would be true to stay that the loyalties to regional languages and cultures developed largely with the growth of the bourgeoisie in India during and after the second half of the 19th century" (Habib, 1975). In this example, his highlighting of the class divisions within historical India clearly indicates a Marxist approach with the utilization of the term "bourgeoisie."

There are studies across many disciplines that feature a capitalistic lens and/or approach, including geography (Castree, 1999; Herod, 2001; Dixon, 2011), criminology (Martin, 2009; Raymen & Smith, 2019; Cheng, 2012), and even food sciences (Jansen, 2015; Trewern et al., 2022). There is also a considerable amount of research that focuses on the interconnection of capitalism and politics (Beramendi et al., 2015; Friedman, 1962; Eden, 2016), as well as capitalism and economics (Wright, 1951; Baumol et al., 2007; Jacobs & Mazzucato, 2016). Critics of capitalism tend to focus on issues of economic disparity (Briggs, 1998; Lansley & Cambridge University Press, 2022), exploitation of labor (Breman, 2019; Jensen & Dyett, 2020), and the connection to power given to a limited number of people, corporations or organizations (Soederberg, 2010; Reich, 2015; Jenkins & Leroy, 2021).

Strengths and Limitations

In research, there are some benefits to examining issues or lines of inquiry with either a Marxist or capitalistic theory. The use of either of these two approaches allows the researcher to examine human behavior and historical development through a lens that connects to economics, politics, power, and a multitude of other academic disciplines (Sau, 2020). Through a Marxist lens, for example, a historian can view events using a proletariat/bourgeoisie dyadic (Blackledge, 2006). A psychologist can apply capitalism to connect the human approaches to consumerism and the impact of debt on the individual's mental state. There are limitless ways either of these two approaches can be used within academic research, which is partially why they are some of the most common research theories in use today (Figueroa, 2019).

Some of the challenges to using either a capitalistic or Marxist approach center on their specific limitations. While both can be, and are, used to examine larger groups of people or events that impact numerous individuals, neither approach works well when looking at the tendencies or behavior of individuals. This is especially apparent when exploring outlying individuals and any behavior that deviates significantly from the norm. In these cases, the societal-level lens Marxism and capitalism bring to an analysis is not effective.

Another challenge for both these approaches is their application to the 21st century. The application of classical Marxism to today's labor environment does not consider the proliferation of technology and instantaneous global communication (Bond et al., 2012). Capitalism, to perhaps a lesser degree, also faces some challenges when looking to integrate into the contemporary world. The role of non-governmental backed currency (i.e., cryptocurrency) requires modification to the capitalist lens, as does individual behavior models that do not result in monetary or other asset-based gains. In these circumstances, a shift away from these theories would be warranted (Meister, 2021).

Key Theorists: Karl Marx; Friederich Engles; Milton Friedman; Adam Smith.

Examples of Use in Research: Breman (2019); Cheng (2012); Clemens (2021); Dixon (2011); Martin (2009); Raymen and Smith (2019).

Libertarianism

Definition and Overview

Libertarianism emphasizes individual freedom and minimal government interference or intervention in the lives of the individual (MacBride, 1976). Based on this position, libertarians reject the intervention of governmental authority that would limit or constrain individual liberty and freedom. In the recent era, a connection to libertarianism and political platforms emerged, particularly as it related to economic constructs, and has focused on defining the government's role and impact on the individual, particularly in taxation (Boaz, 1997). This modern version, however, is a departure from the initial concept that first developed in the 18th century, where libertarianism was mainly focused on defending violations of liberty, especially in social structures (Boaz, 1997).

The concept of libertarianism differs from the concept of liberalism. Liberalism has a unique history, particularly in the United States, as it has been utilized as both complimentary and derogatory label in politics and individual viewpoints (Bell, 2014). As a concept, liberalism and those that support the liberal viewpoint are "interested in rights – human rights, bills of rights, and rights to do as one wishes" (Dixon, 1962, p. 137). While there may be overlap between the focus of liberalism and libertarianism, the two approaches vary dramatically regarding the role of government in society and with the individual. Where liberalism, in general, seeks government intervention to support all peoples (particularly those marginalized or oppressed; Delton, 2009), libertarianism would seek mitigation of oppression through other non-governmental interventions (Wendt, 2015).

There is a significant divide between the two primary classifications of libertarianism – strict libertarianism and classical libertarianism. Strict libertarians see the role of government and power structures as distanced and never impeding on individuals' rights (except perhaps to protect individuals from aggression of others). Classical libertarians understand the need for some government intervention (Murray, 1997). Classical libertarianism also views governmental actions through the lens of the impact on individual rights and freedoms. Classical libertarians may not be opposed to government intervention in all circumstances and may even see legitimate government intervention as extending "beyond the narrow functions of protecting individual rights and engage in other forms of socially beneficial activity" (Zwolinski & Ferguson, 2022, p. 2).

Libertarianism is particularly concerned with the individual right to own and control personal property, centering on the presumption that all individuals should be afforded the right to own property (Wolff, 1991). Any government intervention that deprives individuals of property is counter to the basic premise of libertarianism (Moller, 2019). Libertarianism is also characterized by the protection of individual freedoms and liberty, a distrust of governments and governmental intrusion on the individual's life, and free markets, but there are also many different perspectives of libertarian thought which have created unique branches in the theory such as populism and neo-libertarianism (Zwolinski & Ferguson, 2022, p. 2).

In the United States, libertarianism has been integrated within the rhetoric associated with national politics and elections (Lizzote & Warren, 2021). The approach of less government and enhanced individual freedoms and self-accountability has broad appeal to voters and, as such, has become a theme in local, state, and national campaigns (Niesse, 2022). And while the American Libertarian Party, which espouses limited governmental intervention, has never won a national election for President or Congress, the group did garner more than 4 million total votes in the 2016 presidential election (Devine & Kopko, 2021).

As a theoretical framework, libertarianism is particularly useful for examining the role of government in society, as well as the role of the individual. As such, libertarianism is primarily a societal-level theory, but it can also be applied to individual roles and perceptions. For example, as a theory, libertarianism could be used to understand how individual views and/or social discourse have framed government interventions in relation to individual rights and how that might have changed over time.

Background and Foundations

The focus on liberty and the role of the government in the daily life of individuals has been in existence since antiquity. In early Rome, liberty consisted of an individual's control of their "person, labor, and property" (Fantham, 2005). In the 18th century, the focus on liberty was apparent in areas where there was opposition to monarchical control, such as the United States (at the time, the British colonies in North America), and France. While the American approach to liberty focused on freedom for the individual and small, local government, the French interpretation of liberty centered on "collective democratic participation at the expense of dissent and individual expression" (Heuer, 2007). In the contemporary context, the role of the government and the ideal balance between government intervention and maintaining the social order are significant areas of study and research (Machan, 2021).

Several scholars have made contributions to the understanding and refining of concepts related to libertarianism. Robert Nozick wrote one of the more famous works related to libertarianism in 1974: *Anarchy, State, and Utopia*. His work focused on the societal impacts of minimal government. His insight into the relationship dynamics between individual, government, natural rights, and utility. Peter Vallentyne has also contributed to the modern concepts related to libertarianism. Currently the Florence G. Kline Chair in Philosophy at the University of Missouri, he has constructed significant resources regarding libertarianism and the various critiques of the libertarian approach. His edited volumes *Left-Libertarianism and its Critics: The Contemporary Debate* (Vallentyne & Steiner, 2000), and *The Origins of Left-Libertarianism: An Anthology of Historical Writings* (Vallentyne, 2000) provide significant insight into contemporary libertarianism.

As a theory, libertarianism centers on the economic aspects of governmental intervention in the market. Concepts such as laissez-faire economics, public choice theory, and free trade are commonly linked to libertarian approaches, particularly in strict libertarianism (Huebert, 2010). Yet, there are numerous other fields and areas of research that also draw on libertarian perspectives, including immigration, education, and anticolonialism – all of which focus on the rights of the individual and how it is balanced against the role of the state (Henderson, 2018).

Key Terms and Concepts

Classical libertarianism focuses on how the actions, or proposed actions of a government impact individual rights (Moller, 2019). If, for example, a government initiated new road construction, the classical libertarian approach would focus on individuals being displaced by the new road and how the governments' actions impacted those individuals' rights to property and liberty.

Strict libertarianism opposes any governmental intervention or impact on the individual. The role of government, according to strict libertarians, is only to provide protection against aggression that would impact the rights of the individual (Intropi, 2022). Under a strict libertarian interpretation, the government has very little role in individual lives and should never intervene in the economic marketplace.

Personal property consists of valued assets such as a house or a car, but can also refer to human labor and individual rights (MacInnis, 2011). The primary concern of libertarianism is generally the protection of personal property from use or seizure by a government or any entity in which the individual does not participate or (at least partially) control.

Governmental intrusion is resisted in a libertarian framework. Libertarianism opposes significant government intervention or intrusion on the individual and the rights belonging to that individual (Brennan, Van der Vossen, & Schmidtz, 2017), whether the intrusion is overt, such as mandatory military service, or less visible, such as when government limits competition or innovation.

In Research

Libertarianism is often applied to economics, social structures, or contemporary issues. For example, immigration and immigration reform are significant areas of study and commentary (Todea, 2010; Beltran, 2015; Hildalgo, 2017). The impact of taxes and movements to limit taxation on individuals is another area of focus (Fleischer, 2015; Svoboda, 2016; Vallentyne, 2012; Daskal, 2010), as is education (Brando, 2017; Currie-Knight, 2019).

Numerous examples of how libertarianism is applied in contemporary society exist in recent research. McMichael (2017), for example, examined the role of libertarian approaches and notes that "the most vocal proponents of the militarization thesis ... have been from the Libertarian Right." McMichael's discussion of contemporary policing and criminal justice ties into libertarian approaches and highlights the role of libertarian thought in the application of social constructs.

Libertarianism has also been applied to concepts such as marriage (Anonymous, 2015); social justice (Wendt, 2015; Vallentyne, 2007), and even pollution (Zwolinski, 2014; O'Driscoll, 1982). The commonality in these studies remains the emphasis on individual rights over any governmental power to intercede and impact the individual. This emphasis is also found in additional studies that examine libertarianism and the concept in studies related to "race, class, gender, and sexual orientation" (Babcock, 2012), as well as welfare and governmental assistance (Machan, 2002; Sterba, 2000).

Strengths and Limitations

The strength of libertarianism is its vast applicability as a theory. Through a libertarian lens, it is possible to examine many areas of contemporary society in a variety of geographic locations (Zafirovski, 2011). The core component of libertarianism – the protection of personal property from government intrusion – allows for application at multiple levels and disciplines beyond political science, including sociology, education, and public policy. Further, the concept of libertarianism has a strong connection to the histories of various nations around the world – whether it be related to colonialism or monarchical authority (Kruer, 2021). For example, a recent study on modern Nigeria examines the role of government in providing essential services against the protection of personal property, based on the failures of the government to provide for the Nigerian people (Alex, 2020). As part of the analysis, Alex (2020) draws on the libertarian perspective to advocate for abolishing the Nigerian government, due to unfair taxation and the governmental misappropriation of funds.

However, there are numerous and disparate branches that emerge from the foundation of anti-government intervention, which can be a challenge. Taken to an extreme, the border between libertarianism and anarchy becomes difficult to discern (Long, & Machan, 2016). Adding to the complexity is the adoption of language related to "libertarian" approaches in modern politics, particularly in the United States (Hazlett, 1992). The adoption of partial libertarian concepts and their utilization within a narrow political context only adds to the confusion about the basis and application of libertarianism (Epstein, 1998). The ideas and differences between strict and classical libertarianism are, for a sizeable part of any population, not well understood or studied by those involved in its political application.

Key Theorists Robert Nozick; Peter Vallentyne.

Examples of Use in Research: Brando (2017); Currie-Knight (2019); Petersen (2021); Wendt (2015); Zwolinski (2014).

Republicanism and Republican Democracy

Definition and Overview

Republicanism, as a concept, is broad, but can be loosely defined as a system of government where individual participation is required. In the republican model, individuals in a region or country (i.e., citizens) help form, organize, and maintain a specific form of government (Rowe, 1978). Relatedly, a republican democracy is defined as citizens selecting or electing representatives from their population to represent their interests in governmental operations (Fontana, 1994). This form differs from the concept of a direct democracy, where all citizens vote and have input on all governmental decisions. It is also important to note that the various frameworks associated with republicanism that are discussed here are not directly connected to the American Republican political party.

Republicanism and republican democracy are the most common forms of government in existence today (Tate, 2006). Even in the case of a country following a distinct economic model (e.g., a communistic model with a command economy), as long as individuals have some input into how the government operates, it is considered a republican democracy. Within the structure of republicanism, there are also numerous deviations and structures that can be employed as well. Neo-republicanism, for example, is a modern approach that can be used in contemporary political analysis and has both economic and political constructs (Mulvad, & Popp-Madsen, 2022).

In academic research and writing, republicanism can provide a foundation to explain governmental systems, the importance of citizen participation in governance, and challenges related to larger topics such as inequity and power distribution. Research related to the Arab Spring movements, for example, can build off the expressed desire and outcomes related to republicanism and republican democracy. In some instances, republicanism can also serve as a basis on which other frameworks can be built.

Background and Foundations

Republicanism stretches back to antiquity with both Greek and Roman governments based on a republican structure for specific periods of time. Plato's most famous work, *The Republic*, outlines the people's responsibility in civic engagement as a complement to individual contributions to society. In the ancient Roman context, republicanism ("res publica") was also connected to the public good and provided order for the public good (Wilkinson, 2012). The Roman concept of republicanism can also be expanded to include utopia-like states "in which historical and current political practices, institutions, and values become ideals designed to hold the commonwealth together" (Atkins, 2018, p. 3).

Numerous historical figures have been involved in developing the concept of republicanism and the implementation of republican democracies. Roman historian Polybius (200–118 BCE) is perhaps the oldest theorist who provided commentary and information about early republicanism. His five-volume history of ancient Rome, titled *The Histories*, is noted for its detail and first-person accounts of the rise of the Roman republic (McGing, 2010), and provides insight into the ancient definitions and operations of the concept of republicanism. Nearly 1800 years later, English philosopher and political theorist James Harrington (1611–1677) emerged as a key supporter of classical republicanism. Living through the English interregnum period, he produced one of the most influential works on republicanism (Hammersley, 2019). Harrington's most famous work, *The Commonwealth of Oceana* (1611), provided information about the contents of an ideal constitution and the consequential development of a utopian society, despite the publication being initially seized by the Cromwell government (Harrington, 1611).

Over time, the meaning and use of the word republicanism has changed, largely depending on the circumstance in which political transformations were taking place. During Oliver Cromwell's control of England as Lord Protector (1653–1658), for example, the term republicanism took on an anti-monarchy slant as scholars saw similarities in England and Rome and warned that a shift from "republican to monarchial government was a transition from freedom to slavery" (Gianoutsos, 2020, p. 187). By the American Revolution (1775–1781), the term had taken on an additional meaning related to the support for, or opposition to, the British monarchy and British rule. During that time period, many saw the term as being able to be used "both negatively and positively and in relation to the debates over colonial independence this was frequently exploited" (de Bolla, 2023, p. 67). In this sense, the link between republicanism and public virtue as defined in the late 1700s separated and took on its own definitions and connotations.

Perhaps the biggest shift in the concept of republicanism came in 1762 with Jean Jacque Rousseau's *The Social Contract*. The French term républicanisme became connected to Rousseau's belief in the use of a social contract to form and maintain an orderly society. Finding the balance between contributing to the social good and individual freedom was a centerpiece of Rousseau's theory as "each man, while uniting with all, nevertheless obeys only himself and remains as free as before" (Rousseau, 1762/1997, p. 72).

Modern republicanism has taken on yet another definition and context. While there are many different approaches to, and understandings of, what comprises modern republicanism, an initial definition should include that the concept of republicanism "offers a way of integrating social and political theory in that it emphasizes how political and social relations interact, most particularly through its emphasis on power and status" (Delanty & Turner, 2022, p. 172). While there remains a connection to processes that benefit both the social good and the individual, this new definition brings in other concepts such as power structures and societal order. These components are of interest in the contemporary era; however, they represent a clear departure from the meaning and application of republicanism in antiquity.

More recently, Phillip Pettit has contributed to the modern examination of republicanism. A political theorist and philosopher from Ireland, Pettit (1997) continues to examine the role of republicanism in the modern age and its impact on the concept of freedom, focusing on the interactions between individual freedom and republicanism. Ultimately, Pettit (1997) aspires to "show that this language of domination and freedom … connects with the long, republican tradition of thought that shaped many of the most important institutions and constitutions that we associate with democracy" (p. 4).

Key Terms and Concepts

Citizens are those who are obligated to participate in government for the good of society (Crook, 1967). Who is considered a citizen and who is not is specific to nation-states as well as to the broad history of republicanism. In general, citizenship was restricted to male landowners until the dawn of the 20th century, when the concept of citizen expanded to other populations, including women and non-land owners (Cott, 1998).

Democracy is a form of government, relying on the will of the citizens. Republicanism includes two primary forms of democracy: Direct democracy and republican democracy. Direct democracy has been used in limited historical examples; republican democracy, where individuals are selected to represent larger groups of citizens, is much more common in the world today (Lindsay, 1929).

Neo-republicanism focuses on the dualism of domination and individual freedom. Under this more current form of republicanism, scrutiny of the rights that may be available to individuals is paramount, as is the ability to utilize these rights. Neo-republicanism focuses not only on individuals' rights, but also on "whether there are forms of domination that affect individuals' ability to *use* their rights and *be* free" (Maxwell, 2019, p. 77).

Representative democracy refers to a form of government based on democracy and majority-rule, which engages a mechanism for assigning or electing individuals to represent the population (Altman, 2018). This form of government is utilized by many nations throughout the world in the 21st century (Tate, 2006).

Republics are formed when the power of government is distributed among selected or elected individuals who make decisions on behalf of a larger group of individuals or citizens (Beard, 1943). Many nations throughout the Americas and Europe utilize a republic structure as a mechanism that was intended to make government more effective and efficient (Tate, 2006).

In Research

As republicanism represents an overall application and direction of governance, the majority of research that uses a republicanism framework is found in the social sciences – particularly political science (Tucker, 2016; Zimmermann, 2019), history (Mahlberg & Wiemann, 2016; Nabors, 2017) and sociology (Hulliung, 2020; Brooks, 2017). Additionally, there is a plethora of works that center on the classic concepts of republicanism in both Greece and Rome (Hammer, 2015; Zetzel, 2022; Connolly, 2015; Wilkinson, 2012).

In contemporary research, republicanism can be applied to modern concerns and issues that impact citizens on a global scale. The newly established concept of global citizenship and its interplay with republicanism has provided interesting directions in understanding the future of nations and citizens around the world (Chapman et al., 2020). There is also ongoing research that seeks to clarify the role of citizenship within a larger geographic universe. Moving past the idea of local community-based citizenship toward a larger conceptualization of acceptance and inclusion of diverse populations (Stahl, 2020).

Strength and Limitations

A strength of republicanism as a framework is the broad application and usage of republican forms of government in the modern world (Honohan, 2005). There is significant opportunity to examine the shifts and modifications of the republican model across nations and cultures, as well as the ability to compare modern republicanism to its roots in antiquity, its impact on the Enlightenment era, and the present day (McGrane, 2011). For research centering on the Americas or Western Europe, the use of republicanism in research is extensive (Zeng, 2022).

As a foundation for research, however, republicanism does have some significant challenges. To begin, the concept of republicanism does not allow itself to be a standalone theory, but rather is utilized as a complementary method along with larger theories such as capitalism or libertarian approaches (Weinstock & Nadeau, 2004). Through the linkage of republicanism and a theory with a broader application, a strong foundation for research can be developed (Bohman, 2012).

Key Theorists: Polybius; James Harrington; Phillip Pettit.

Examples of Use in Research: Brooks (2017); Hulliung (2020); Zimmermann (2019).

Communitarianism

Definition and Overview

Communitarianism examines the connections between the individual and "community" – a term for which the meaning can vary depending on the context and actions. The interactions between individual and community provide the basis and foundation of communitarianism. Examining the connection between the individual and the community, and how one can influence the other, is a central focus of the concept. As an ethics-based theory, communitarianism can be defined as "the affirmation of the social context of one's existence, where both the individual and her community maintain separate moral standing, in an attached, interdependent relationship" (Foster, 1998, p. 134).

The key element of communitarian theory is that the communities' values supersede the individuals' values and that any issues or disputes that arise will be resolved using the best avenue for the community (Breslin, 2004). The community composition under communitarianism can take various forms – from the family community structure to more complex configurations such as schools and corporate workspaces (Oplatka, 2019). Proponents of communitarianism believe that communities become stronger through communitarianism and promote "social stability and cohesion" (Cowden & Singh, 2017).

Two current forms of communitarianism are emancipatory and responsive communitarianism. Emancipatory communitarianism focuses on finding the balance between the good of society and protecting individual rights (Prilleltensky, 1997). However, emancipatory communitarianism specifically focuses on supporting individuals who may be living in poverty or facing other disadvantages. Emancipatory communitarianism emphasizes social justice efforts to rectify these situations (Brubaker et al., 2010). Responsive communitarianism holds that every society has to accept and develop steps for the common good, as well as protect individual rights. Finding the balance between these two concepts is difficult and requires modifications to ensure that the balance is not tipped too far one way or the other (Etzioni, 2016).

Some of the primary objectives of communitarianism focus on positive rights that connect to enhancing the lives of individuals. Positive rights generally refer to those rights that produce benefits for the public good and which are created by a political mechanism in a society (Campbell, 2020). For example, building public parks can be considered a positive right as the larger community is receiving a benefit that can be used by all. Similarly, laws against pollution can also be seen as a positive right as they make a positive contribution to society. The challenge to the positive rights approach is the dissent of those who do not wish to have these positive elements forced upon them (Etzioni, 2001).

Within a research context, communitarianism has a strong connection to examinations of the role of community and the individual in contemporary society – particularly how the interplay of these two elements can provide solutions to existing social problems. For example, using a communitarian perspective to address issues of substance abuse provides insight into community-based organizations and the interaction with individuals within that community (Bermea et al., 2019). Communitarianism brings group goals – in this instance eliminating issues related to substance abuse – together with individual conditions (Ploeg et al., 2022).

Background and Foundations

While the origins of communitarianism stretch back to the 19th century, it was not until the 1980s, that communitarianism emerged as a counter approach to liberalism. The emerging communitarian community contradicted the perspectives of liberal scholars such as John Rawls, T.M Scanlon, and Robert Nozick to advocate for "common formulations of good rather than leaving it determined by each individual" (Etzioni, 2014, p. 242). While communitarians continued to focus on the impact of the community on the individual, liberal perspectives seemed "… wrong not by implying that human beings are capable of existing without strong and warm attachments to community but in misunderstanding the nature of attachment to community" (Reiner, 2011, p. 294).

In the 1990s, the theory of communitarianism gained new attention through the work of Amitai Etzioni, Phillip Selznick, and Robert Bellah (among others). The work of sociologist Amitai Etzioni, in particular, has focused on the basic tenets and application of communitarianism and how it can impact international relations and the application of law. Etzioni (1993) claims that the communitarian movement hoped to "bring about the changes in values, habits, and public policies that will allow us to do for society what the environmental movement seeks to do for nature: to safeguard and enhance our future" (p. 3).

Many communitarians place a greater emphasis on the role of community and how it shapes and influences the individual – so much so that social standing and identity come from the community and community interactions, as opposed to the individual (Ravitsky, 2016). This shift of focus away from the individual and toward the community gathered interest and support in the 21st century, with a greater focus on community and the role of community-based organizations in support of civic and community improvement (Tan et al., 2015).

In Research

Much of the research drawing on communitarianism focuses on ethics, morality, and the process of improving society. In the health sciences, for example, there are several instances where communitarian approaches help place public health issues in a larger context (Parker, 1999; Rauprich, 2008). Within the health care sector, finding the balance between approaches and interventions that support the comprehensive community as opposed to the individual has been studied in depth. There is also an emerging area of research that centers on communitarianism, particularly in regard to healthcare in a post-pandemic environment. Communitarianism research is also prevalent in governmental functions such as education (Ross et al., 2015; Weller, 2007); social work (Bermea et al., 2019); and criminal justice/studies of political extremism (Turner, 2016).

There is also a significant connection between communitarianism and various non-governmental societal structures and concepts. Both race (Taibi, 1992) and sexuality (Monro, 2003) have been explored through a communitarianism lens, as have welfare programs (Fyfe, 2005) and systems of support for marginalized individuals (Brubaker et al., 2010). In accordance with the focus of communitarianism, there are also studies in existence that look at the individual's role in civic engagement (Annette, 2011) and the obligation an individual has to his/her/their community (Bankoff, & Oven, 2019).

Strengths and Limitations

Communitarianism is based on logic and altruism. Developing a system where the individual contributes to the greater good, and where the government supports this action, has specific advantages in a society (Etzioni, 2014). Further, the linkage of communitarianism to larger issues such as ethics and morals provides a strong academic connection to multiple disciplines (Callahan, 2003). As a foundation for a research perspective, communitarianism provides a strong foundation to examine issues that impact larger groups and communities and the individuals within those groups. Building upon this foundational framework, it would be possible to conduct analysis related to best-choice theory, social justice theory, or a host of approaches that study larger populations with one or more commonalities.

There are various critiques of communitarianism, including its application in non-Western and distinct environments. For some, the concept is problematic as the terminology related to communitarianism is both vague and contradictory (Gray, 2005). Further, under communitarianism individuals are "not encouraged to act for the benefit of the community, it is assumed (implicitly) that they do so simply because they are part of it" (Dalacoura, 2002). Determining the motivations and factors impacting individual participation, particularly in a group setting can be difficult under communitarianism as the focus is on the larger construct or organization, not the individual. Lastly, communitarianism may not take into account dissenting voices that may not go along with perceived societal benefits through a communitarian approach (Pickett, 2001).

Key Theorists: Amitai Etzioni; Elizabeth Frazer.

Examples of Use in Research: Bermea et al. (2019); Ross et al. (2015); Turner (2016).

References

Alex, T. (2020). It belongs to me! A libertarian analysis of property rights in Nigeria. *Journal of libertarian Studies, 24*(2), 362–384.

Althusser L. (1976). *Essays in self-criticism.* Humanities Press.

Altman, D. (2018). *Citizenship and contemporary direct democracy.* Cambridge University Press. 10.1017/9781108634397

Annette, J. (2011). Faith communities, communitarianism, social capital and youth civic engagement. *Ethnicities, 11*(3), 383–397. 10.1177/1468796811407856

Anonymous (2015). Marriage, family, and government. *First Things,* (253), 6.

Ariely, D. (2009). *Predictably irrational: The hidden forces that shape our decisions.* Harper Collins Publishers.

Arvidsson, S. (2017). *The style and mythology of socialism: Socialist idealism, 1871–1914* (1st ed.). Routledge. 10.4324/9781315184814.

Atkins, J. W. (2018). *Roman political thought*. Cambridge University Press. 10.1017/978131622 7404

Babcock, G. (2012). Libertarianism, feminism, and nonviolent action: A synthesis. *Libertarian Papers*, *4*(16), S119.

Bankoff, G., & Oven, K. (2019). From nomadic communitarianism to civil socialism: Searching for the roots of civil society in rural Kazakhstan. *Journal of Civil Society*, *15*(4), 373–391. 10.1080/ 17448689.2019.1670386

Barkey, F. A., & Project Muse (2012). *Working class radicals: The socialist party in West Virginia, 1898–1920*. West Virginia University Press.

Basu, D., & Cambridge University Press (2021; 2022). *The logic of capital: An introduction to Marxist economic theory*. Cambridge University Press.

Baumol, W. J., Litan, R. E., & Schramm, C. J. (2007). *Good capitalism, bad capitalism, and the economics of growth and prosperity*. Yale University Press. 10.1604/9780300134797

Baumol, W. J., & Project Muse (2002). *The free-market innovation machine: Analyzing the growth miracle of capitalism*. Princeton University Press. 10.1515/9781400851638

Beard, C. A. (1943). *The republic: Conversations on fundamentals*. Viking Press.

Bell, D. (2014). What is liberalism? *Political Theory*, *42*(6), 682–715. http://www.jstor.org/stable/ 24571524

Bermea, A. M., Lardier, D. T., Forenza, B., Garcia-Reid, P., & Reid, R. J. (2019). Communitarianism and youth empowerment: Motivation for participation in a community-based substance abuse prevention coalition. *Journal of Community Psychology*, *47*(1), 49–62. 10.1002/jcop.22098

Beltran, E. C. (2015). Conservative Libertarianism and the Ethics of Borders. *Tópicos, Revista de Filosofía*, 227. 10.21555/top.v0i48.678

Beramendi, P., Häusermann, S., Kitschelt, H., Kriesi, H., & Cambridge University Press (2015). In P. Beramendi, S. Häusermann, H. Kitschelt, & H. Kriesi (Eds.), *The politics of advanced capitalism*. Cambridge University Press. 10.1017/CBO9781316163245

Blackledge, P., & Project Muse (2006). *Reflections on the Marxist theory of history*. Manchester University Press.

Boaz, D. (1997). *Libertarianism: A primer*. Free Press.

Bohman, J. (2012). Critical theory, republicanism, and the priority of injustice: Transnational republicanism as a nonideal theory: Critical theory, republicanism, and the priority of injustice. *Journal of Social Philosophy*, *43*(2), 97–112. 10.1111/j.1467-9833.2012.01554.x

Bond, P., Burawoy, M., Cock, J., Desai, A., Glaser, D., Jara, M., Luxton, M., Ngwane, T., Pillay, D., Satgar, V., Saul, J., Veriava, A., & Williams, M. (2018) In M. Williams, & V. Satgar (Eds.), *Marxisms in the 21st century: Crisis, critique & struggle*. Wits University Press. 10.18772/22 013127533

Bond, R. M., Fariss, Christopher J., Jones, Jason J., Kramer, Adam D. I., Marlow, Cameron, Settle, Jaime E., & Fowler, James H. (2012). A 61-million-person experiment in social influence and political mobilization. *Nature*, 489, 295–298 10.1038/nature11421.

Bottomore T.B. (1975). *Sociology as social criticism* (1st ed.). Pantheon Books.

Brando, N. (2017). Between equality and freedom of choice: Educational opportunities for the least advantaged. *International Journal of Educational Development*, 53, 71–79 10.1016/j.ije-dudev.2016.12.007.

Breman, J. (2019). Capitalism, labour bondage and the social question. *Capitalism, inequality and labour in India* (pp. 237–265). 10.1017/9781108687485.009

Breslin, B., & Project Muse (2004). *The communitarian constitution*. Johns Hopkins University Press.

Brennan, J., Van der Vossen, B., Schmidtz, D. (2017). *The Routledge Handbook of Libertarianism*. 10.4324/9781317486794

Briggs, V. M. (1998). American-style capitalism and income disparity: The challenge of social anarchy. *Journal of Economic Issues*, *XXXII*(2), 473–480.

Briggs, W. (2019). *Classical Marxism in an age of capitalist crisis: The past is prologue*. Routledge. 10.4324/9780429264993

Brooks, R. O. (2017). *Cicero and modern law*. Routledge. 10.4324/9781315095707

Brubaker, M. D., Garrett, M. T., Rivera, E. T., & Tate, K. A. (2010). Justice making in groups for homeless adults: The emancipatory communitarian way. *The Journal for Specialists in Group Work*, *35*(2), 124–133. 10.1080/01933921003705982

Callahan, D. (2003). Principlism and communitarianism. *Journal of Medical Ethics*, *29*(5), 287–291. 10.1136/jme.29.5.287

Campbel J. (2020). Natural rights, positive rights, and the right to keep and bear arms. *Law and contemporary problems*. *83*(3),31.

Chapman, D. D., Ruiz-Chapman, T., & Eglin, P. (2020). *The global citizenship nexus: Critical studies*. Routledge. 10.4324/9780429320668

Castree, N. (1999). 'Out there'? 'In here'? Domesticating critical geography. *Area*, 31, 81–86 10.1111/j.1475-4762.1999.tb00174.x.

Cheng, H. (2012). Cheap capitalism: A sociological study of food crime in China. *British Journal of Criminology*, *52*(2), 254–273. 10.1093/bjc/azr078

Chmielewska, K., Mrozik, A., & Wołowiec, G. (2021). In K. Chmielewska, A. Mrozik & G. Wołowiec (Eds.), *Reassessing communism: Concepts, culture, and society in Poland, 1944–1989*. Central European University Press. 10.7829/j.ctv1c3pdcf

Clemens, J. (2021). How do firms respond to minimum wage increases? Understanding the relevance of non-employment margins. *The Journal of Economic Perspectives*, *35*(1), 51–72. 10.1257/JEP.35.1.51

Connolly, J. (2015). *The life of Roman republicanism*. Princeton University Press. 10.1515/9781400852475

Cott, N. (1998). Marriage and Women's Citizenship in the United States, 1830-1934. *The American Historical Review*, 103, 1440 10.2307/2649963.

Cowden, S., & Singh, G. (2017). Community cohesion, communitarianism and neoliberalism. *Critical Social Policy*, *37*(2), 268–286. 10.1177/0261018316670252

Cox, O. C. (1959). *Foundations of capitalism*. Philosophical Library

Croce, B. (1966). *Historical materialism and the economics of Karl Marx*. Russell & Russell.

Crook, J.A. (1967). *Law and life of Rome*. Cornell University Press.

Currie-Knight, K. (2019). *Education in the marketplace: An intellectual history of pro-market libertarian visions for education in twentieth century America*. Palgrave Macmillan.

Cuyvers, L. (2017). *The economic ideas of Marx's capital: Steps towards post-Keynesian economics*. Routledge. 10.4324/9781315675329

Dalacoura, K. (2002). A critique of communitarianism with reference to post-revolutionary Iran. *Review of International Studies*, *28*(1), 75–92. 10.1017/S026021050200075X

Daskal, S., & Department of Philosophy, Florida State University (2010). Libertarianism left and right, the Lockean proviso, and the reformed welfare state. *Social Theory and Practice*, *36*(1), 21–43. 10.5840/soctheorpract20103612

de Bolla, P. (2023). "Republicanism": A grounding concept for the American revolution? *Intellectual History Review*, *33*(1), 57–81. 10.1080/17496977.2022.2152305

Delanty, G., & Turner, S. P. (2022). *Routledge international handbook of contemporary social and political theory*. Routledge. 10.4324/9781003111399

Delton, J. (2009). Conserving liberalism. *Salmagundi*, *162/163*, 3–24. http://www.jstor.org/stable/40550037

Devine, C. J., & Kopko, K. C. (2021). Did Gary Johnson and Jill Stein cost Hillary Clinton the presidency? A counterfactual analysis of minor party voting in the 2016 US presidential election. *The Forum: A Journal of Applied Research in Contemporary Politics*, *19*(2), 173–201. 10.1515/for-2021-0011

Dixon, A. (2011). Variegated capitalism and the geography of finance: Towards a common agenda. *Progress in Human Geography*, *35*(2), 193–210. 10.1177/0309132510372006

Dixon, M. (1962). Democracy and liberalism. *Social Studies*, *53*(4), 136.

Eden, D. (2016). *Autonomy: Capitalism, class and politics*. Routledge. 10.4324/9781315568508

Engeström, Y, & Sannino, A (2010). Studies of expansive learning: Foundations, findings and future challenges. *Educational Research Review*, 5, 1–24 10.1016/j.edurev.2009.12.002.

Epstein, R. A. (1998). Imitations of Libertarian Thought. *Social Philosophy and Policy*, 15, 412–436 10.1017/s0265052500002053.

Etzioni, A. (1993). Normative-Affective Choices. *Human Relations*, 46, 1053–1069 10.1177/001872679304600903.

Etzioni, A. (2001). Communitarianism, sociology of. *International encyclopedia of social & behavioral sciences* (pp. 2336–2339). Elsevier Ltd. 10.1016/B0-08-043076-7/01842-8

Etzioni, A. (2014). Communitarianism revisited. *Journal of Political Ideologies*, *19*(3), 241–260. 10.1080/13569317.2014.951142

Etzioni, A. (2016). Communitarianism. In S. Schechter,T. Vontz, T. Birkland, M. Graber, & J. Patrick (Eds.), *American Governance, vol. 1* (pp. 325–327). Gale Publishing.

Evensky, J., & Cambridge University Press (2015). *Adam smith's wealth of nations: A reader's guide*. Cambridge University Press. 10.1017/CBO9781107338296

Fantham, E. (2005). Liberty and the people in Republican Rome. *Transactions of the American Philological Association (1974-)*, *135*(2), 209–229. http://www.jstor.org/stable/20054131

Figueroa, A. (2019). *The quality of society: Essays on the unified theory of capitalism*. Palgrave MacMillan. 10.1007/9783030116569

Fleischer, M. P. (2015). Libertarianism and the charitable tax subsidies. *Boston College Law Review*, *56*(4), 1345.

Fontana, B. (1994). *The invention of the modern republic*. Cambridge University Press. 10.1017/CBO9780511558443

Foster, J. M. (1998). *The communitarian organization: Preserving cultural integrity in the transnational economy*. Garland Pub. 10.4324/9780203210550

Frazer, E., & Lacey, N. (1994). Blind alleys: Communitarianism. *Politics*, *14*(2), 75–81.

Friedman, M. (1962). *Capitalism and freedom*. University of Chicago Press.

Fyfe, N. R. (2005). Making space for "neo-communitarianism"? the third sector, state and civil society in the UK. *Antipode*, *37*(3), 536–557. 10.1111/j.0066-4812.2005.00510.x

Gianoutsos, J. A. (2020). *The rule of manhood: Tyranny, gender, and classical republicanism in England, 1603–1660*. University of Cambridge ESOL Examinations. 10.1017/9781108778916

Gray, C. S. (2005). Sandcastle of theory: A critique of Amitai Etzioni's communitarianism. *The American Behavioral Scientist*, *48*(12), 1607–1625. 10.1177/0002764205278080

Gray, J. (1986). Marxian Freedom, Individual Liberty, and the End of Alienation. *Social Philosophy and Policy*, 3, 160–187 10.1017/s0265052500000352.

Grayson, H. (1965). *Price theory in a changing economy*. Macmillan.

Habib, I. (2015). *A people's history of India, Vol. 1*. Tulika Books.

Habib, I. (1975). Emergence of nationalities. *Social Scientist (New Delhi)*, *4*(1), 14–20. 10.2307/3516387

Hacker, L. M. (1957). *American capitalism, its promise and accomplishment*. Van Nostrand.

Hammer, D. (2015; 2014). *A companion to Greek democracy and the Roman Republic*. Wiley Blackwell. 10.1002/9781118878347

Hammersley, R. (2019). *James Harrington: An intellectual biography*. Oxford University Press. 10.1093/oso/9780198809852.001.0001

Harrington, J. (1611–1677). *The commonwealth of Oceana: And a system of politics/James Harrington*; edited by J. G. A. Pocock. Cambridge University Press.

Hazlett, J. M. (1992). *The libertarian party and other minor political parties in the United States*. McFarland & Co.

Hegel, G. W. F., Fuss, P., & Dobbins, J. (2019). *The phenomenology of spirit*. University of Notre Dame Press.

Henderson, H. D. (1958). *Supply and demand*. University of Chicago Press.

Henderson, M. T., & Cambridge University Press (2018). In M. T. Henderson (Ed.), *The Cambridge handbook of classical liberal thought*. Cambridge University Press. 10.1017/9781108242226

Herod A. (2001). *Labor geographies: Workers and the landscapes of capitalism*. Guilford Press.

Heuer, J. (2007). Liberty and death: The French revolution. *History Compass, 5*(1), 175–200. 10.1111/j.1478-0542.2006.00362.x

Hildalgo, J. (2017). The libertarian case for open borders. In J. Brennan, B. Van der Vossen, & D. Schmidtz (Eds.), *The Routledge handbook of libertarianism*. Routledge. 10.4324/9781317486794

Hobsbawm, E. J. (1962). *The age of revolution, 1789–1848*. New American Library.

Honohan, I. (2005). Republicanism in the modern world. *Contemporary Political Theory, 4*(1), 90–92. 10.1057/palgrave.cpt.9300158

Hoppe, H. (2017). *Democracy, the god that failed: The economics and politics of monarchy, democracy and natural order*. Routledge, Taylor & Francis Group. 10.4324/9780203793572

Huebert, J. H. (2010). *Libertarianism today*. Praeger.

Hudson, M., Miller, G.J., & Feder, K. (1994). *A philosophy for a fair society*. Shepheard-Walwyn.

Hulliung, M. (2020). *From classical to modern republicanism: Reflections on England, Scotland, America, and France*. Routledge. 10.4324/9781003052043

Intropi, P. (2022). Reciprocal libertarianism. *European Journal of Political Theory*, 147488512210996. 10.1177/14748851221099659

Jacobs, M., & Mazzucato, M. (2016). *Rethinking capitalism: Economics and policy for sustainable and inclusive growth*. Wiley-Blackwell, in association with the Political Quarterly.

Jansen, K. (2015). Debate on food sovereignty theory: Agrarian capitalism, dispossession and agroecology. *The Journal of Peasant Studies, 42*(1), 213–232. 10.1080/03066150.2014.945166

Jenkins, D., & Leroy, J. (2021). *Histories of racial capitalism*. Columbia University Press. 10.7312/jenk19074

Jensen, N., & Dyett, J. (2020). Gendered exploitation under contemporary capitalism. *Perspectives on Global Development and Technology, 19*(1/2), 201. 10.1163/15691497-12341550

Johnston, L. (2015). *Marxism, class analysis, and socialist pluralism: A theoretical and political critique of Marxist conceptions of politics*. Routledge, Taylor & Francis Group. 10.4324/9781315714974

Kanth, R. K. (2015). *Capitalism and social theory: The science of black holes*. Routledge.

Kates, S. (2014). *Free market economics: An introduction for the general reader* (2nd ed.). Edward Elgar.

Kocka J., & Riemer J. (2016). *Capitalism: A short history*. Princeton University Press.

Kruer, M. (2021). *Time of anarchy: Indigenous power and the crisis of colonialism in early America*. Harvard University Press. 10.4159/9780674269545

Kumar, R. (2023). *Contemporary readings in Marxism: A critical introduction*. Routledge. 10.4324/9781003332084

Lansley, S., & Cambridge University Press (2022). *The richer, the poorer: How Britain enriched the few and failed the poor: A 200-year history*. Policy Press. 10.46692/9781447363231

Laibman D. (1992). Market and plan: The evolution of socialist social structures in history and theory. *Science & Society*. 56(1), 60-91.

Latif, M. I., & Khan, R. A. (2011). Marxism in twenty first century: A critical review. *Journal of Educational Research, 14*(2), 65.

Li, D. D., & Maskin, E. S. (2021). Government and economics: An emerging field of study. *Journal of Government and Economics, 1*. 10.1016/j.jge.2021.100005

Lind, L. R. (1939). Economic man in ancient Athens. *The Classical Journal (Classical Association of the Middle West and South), 35*(1), 27–38.

Lindsay, A. D. (1929). *The essentials of democracy*. University of Pennsylvania Press.

Linehan, T. P. (2012). *Modernism and British socialism*. Palgrave Macmillan. 10.1057/97811372 64794

Long, R. T., & Machan, T. R. (2016). *Anarchism/Minarchism: Is a government part of a free country?*. Routledge. 10.4324/9781315566955

Lovell, D. W. (1988). *Marx's proletariat: The making of a myth*. Routledge.

MacBride, R. L. (1976). *A new dawn for America: The libertarian challenge*. Green Hill Publishers.

Machan, T. R. (2002). What about the children? (Op-Ed). *Free Inquiry, 22*(2), 22.

Machan, T. R. (2021). *Libertarianism defended*. Routledge.

MacInnis, L. (2011). Libertarianism defended. *Contemporary Political Theory, 10*(1), 123–125. 10.1057/cpt.2009.29

Mahlberg, G., & Wiemann, D. (2016). *European contexts for English republicanism*. Routledge. 10.4324/9781315580869

Manish G.P. Miller S.C. (2020:2022) *Capitalism and inequality: The role of state and market*(1st ed.) Routledge, Taylor & Francis

Martin, G. (2009). Subculture, style, chavs and consumer capitalism: Towards a critical cultural criminology of youth. *Crime, Media, Culture, 5*(2), 123–145. 10.1177/1741659009335613

Marx, K., & Engels, F. (1932). *Das kapital: Kritik der politischen okonomie* (Volksausgabe. ed.). Verlag fur Literatur und Politik.

Marx, K., Engels, F., & Butler-Bowdon, T. (2021). *The communist manifesto: The political classic*. John Wiley & Sons, Incorporated.

Maxwell, L. (2019). Democratic dependency: A feminist critique of nondomination as Independence. In Y. Elazar & G. Rousselière (Eds.), *Republicanism and the future of democracy* (pp. 77–93). Cambridge University Press. doi:10.1017/9781108630153.005

Mayer, G. (1936). *Friedrich Engels: A biography*. Chapman & Hall.

McGing, B. C. (2010). *Polybius' histories*. Oxford University Press.

McGrane, D. (2011). From liberal multiculturalism to civic republicanism: An historical perspective on multiculturalism policy in Manitoba and Saskatchewan. *Canadian Ethnic Studies, 43*(1), 81–107. 10.1353/ces.2011.0019

McMichael, C. (2017). Pacification and police: A critique of the police militarization thesis. *Capital & Class, 41*(1), 115–132.

McMurtry, J., & Project Muse (1978). *The structure of Marx's world-view*. Princeton University Press.

Meister, R. (2021). Can capitalism short itself? *Justice is an option*. University of Chicago Press. 10.7208/chicago/9780226734514.003.0007

Moller, D. (2019). *Governing least: A New England libertarianism*. Oxford University Press. 10.1 093/oso/9780190863241.001.0001

Monro, S. (2003). Transgender politics in the UK. *Critical Social Policy, 23*(4), 433–452. 10.1177/ 02610183030234001

Mulvad, A. M., & Popp-Madsen, B. A. (2022). From neo-republicanism to socialist republicanism: Antonio Gramsci, the European council movements and the 'Second republican revival'. *Theoria (Pietermaritzburg), 69*(2), 97–118. 10.3167/th.2022.6917106

Murray, C. A. (1997). *What it means to be a libertarian: A personal interpretation* (1st ed.). Broadway Books.

Nabors, F. A., & Project Muse (2017). *From oligarchy to republicanism: The great task of reconstruction*. University of Missouri Press.

Naimark, N. M. (1979). *The history of the 'proletariat': The emergence of Marxism in the kingdom of Poland, 1870–1887*. East European Quarterly.

Niesse, M. (August 4, 2022). Libertarian appeal could push Ga. elections to runoffs: Third parties find tough road to run, but can be spoilers. *The Atlanta Journal-Constitution (2001)*, pp. A10.

Nozick, R. (1974). *Anarchy, state, and utopia*. Basic Books.

O'Driscoll, G. P. (1982). Pollution, libertarianism, and the law. *The Cato Journal, 2*(1), 45.

Oplatka, I. (2019). *Reforming education in developing countries: From neoliberalism to communitarianism*. Routledge. 10.4324/9781351234337

Padover, S. K. (1978). *Karl Marx: An intimate biography*. McGraw-Hill.

Parker, M. (1999). *Ethics and community in the health care professions*. Routledge. 10.4324/9780203010389

Paxton, S. (2021). *Unlearning Marx: Why the soviet failure was a triumph for Marx*. John Hunt Publishing.

Pettit, P. (1997). *Republicanism: A theory of freedom and government*. Oxford University Press. 10.1093/0198296428.001.0001

Phillipson, N. T. (2010). *Adam Smith: An enlightened life*. Yale University Press.

Pickett, B. L. (2001). Communitarian citizenship and civil disobedience. *Politics & Policy, 29*(2), 265–289. 10.1111/j.1747-1346.2001.tb00592.x

Ploeg, M., Knoben, J., & Vermeulen, P. (2022). We are in it together: Communitarianism and the performance-innovation relationship. *Research Policy, 51*(5), 104507. 10.1016/j.respol.2022.104507

Poire M., & Doeringer P. (1971). *Internal labor markets and manpower analysis*. Routledge.

Pons, S., Service, R., & Project Muse. (2010). *A dictionary of 20th-century communism*. Princeton University Press. 10.1515/9781400834525

Prilleltensky, I. (1997). Values, assumptions, and practices: Assessing the moral implications of psychological discourse and action. *American Psychologist, 52*, 517–535.

Rauprich, O. (2008). Utilitarianism or communitarianism as the foundation of public health ethics? *Bundesgesundheitsblatt, Gesundheitsforschung, Gesundheitsschutz, 51*(2), 137–150. 10.1007/s00103-008-0442-8

Ravitsky, V. (2016). Social paternalism in a communitarian context: Enhancing individuals' moral deliberation through a communal "moral voice". *American Journal of Bioethics, 16*(8), 20–22. 10.1080/15265161.2016.1187221

Raymen, T., & Smith, O. (2019). Deviant leisure: A critical criminological perspective for the twenty-first century. *Critical Criminology, 27*(1), 115–130. 10.1007/s10612-019-09435-x

Reich, R. B. (2015). *Saving capitalism: For the many, not the few*. Alfred A. Knopf.

Reiner, T. (2011). The sources of communitarianism on the American left: Pluralism, republicanism, and participatory democracy. *History of European Ideas, 37*(3), 293–303. 10.1016/j.histeuroideas.2010.10.008

Robinson, C. J., & Project Muse (2019). *An anthropology of Marxism* (2nd ed.). The University of North Carolina Press. 10.5149/9781469649931_robinson

Rodney, W. (1972). *How Europe underdeveloped Africa*. Black Classic Press.

Ross, A. J., Campbell, L. M., & MacGregor, R. G. (2015). It is time to balance communitarianism and individualism in South African medical education: Correspondence. *African Journal of Health Professions Education, 7*(2), 224–225. 10.7196/AJHPE.564

Ross, I. S. (1995). *The life of Adam Smith*. Clarendon Press. 10.1093/0198288212.001.0001

Rousseau, J. (1762/1997). *The social contract and other later political writings*. Edited and translated by V. Gourevitch. Cambridge University Press.

Rowe, G. S. (1978). *Thomas McKean: The shaping of an American republicanism*. Colorado Associated University Press.

Sau, A. (2020). *A Marxist theory of ideology: Praxis, thought and the social world*. Routledge. 10.4324/9780367810146

Sdobnikov, Y. (1973). *Karl Marx: A biography*. Progress.

Simpson, K. (2021). *Social haunting, education, and the working class: A critical Marxist ethnography in a former mining community*. Routledge. 10.4324/9781003099451

Singer, P. (2018). *Marx: A very short introduction* (2nd ed.). Oxford University Press.

Smith, B. G. (1981). *Ladies of the leisure class: The bourgeoisies of northern France in the 19th century*. Princeton University Press. 10.1515/9780691209487

Smith, K., & Cambridge University Press (2021). *Karl Marx's 'capital': A guide to volumes I-III* (2nd ed.). Anthem Press.

Soederberg, S. (2010). *Corporate power and ownership in contemporary capitalism: The politics of resistance and domination.* Routledge. 10.4324/9780203871690

Somerville, J. (1946). *Soviet philosophy: A study of theory and practice.* Philosophical Library.

Sonenscher, M., & Project Muse (2022). *Capitalism: The story behind the word.* Princeton University Press. 10.1515/9780691238876

Sperber J. (2022). *Age of interconnection: A global history of the second half of the twentieth century.* Oxford University Press

Stahl, K. A. (2020). Republican citizenship. *Local citizenship in a global age.* Cambridge University Press. 10.1017/9781316661352.013

Stearns, P. N. (2020). *The industrial revolution in world history* (5th ed.). Routledge. 10.4324/9781 003050186

Sterba, J. P. (2000). From liberty to welfare: An update. *Social Theory and Practice, 26*(3), 465–478. 10.5840/soctheorpract200026314

Svoboda, V. (2016). Libertarianism, slavery and just taxation. *Humanomics, 32*(1), 69–79. 10.11 08/H-05-2015-0031

Taibi, A. D. (1992). Race consciousness, communitarianism, and banking regulation. *University of Illinois Law Review, 1992*(4), 1103.

Tan, C., Chua, C. S. K., & Goh, O. (2015). Rethinking the framework for 21st-century education: Toward a communitarian conception. *The Educational Forum, 79*(3), 307–320. 10.1080/00131 725.2015.1037511

Tate, C. N., & Gale Group (2006; 2005). *Governments of the world: A global guide to citizens' rights and responsibilities.* Macmillan Reference USA.

Tikhonov, V. (2021). 'The soviet problem' in post-soviet Russian Marxism, or the afterlife of the USSR. *Historical Materialism: Research in Critical Marxist Theory, 29*(4), 153. 10.1163/15692 06X-12341986

Tismaneanu, V., & Luber, J. (2021). *One hundred years of communist experiments.* Central European University Press. 10.7829/j.ctv1c3pd9d

Todea, D. V. (2010). Libertarianism and immigration. *Libertarian Papers, 2*(30), 1–21.

Trewern, J., Chenoweth, J., & Christie, I. (2022). 'Does it change the nature of food and capitalism?' exploring expert perspectives on public policies for a transition to 'less and better' meat and dairy. *Environmental Science & Policy, 128*, 110–120. 10.1016/j.envsci.2021.11.018

Tucker, I. (2016). *A brief genealogy of Jewish republicanism: Parting ways with Judith Butler.* Punctum books. 10.21983/P3.0159.1.00

Turner, I. (2016). A communitarian justification for measures to prevent terrorism in the UK. *Perspectives on Terrorism, 10*(5), 68–82.

Vallentyne, P. (2012; 2011). Libertarianism and the justice of a basic income. *Basic Income Studies, 6*(2). 10.1515/1932-0183.1224

Vallentyne, P. (2007). Libertarianism and the state. *Social Philosophy & Policy, 24*(1), 187–205. 10.1017/S0265052507070082

Vallentyne, P. & Steiner, G. (2000). *Left libertarianism and its critics: The contemporary debate.* Palgrave.

Weinstock, D. M., & Nadeau, C. (2004). *Republicanism: History, theory and practice.* Frank Cass. 10.4324/9780203497548

Weller, S. (2007). *Teenagers' citizenship: Experiences and education.* Routledge. 10.4324/97802 03961384

Wendt, F. (2015). Justice and political authority in left-libertarianism. *Politics, Philosophy & Economics, 14*(3), 316–339. 10.1177/1470594×X14539698

Wilkinson, S. (2012). *Republicanism during the early Roman empire* (1st ed.). Continuum. 10.504 0/9781472540867

Wolff, J. (1991). *Robert Nozick: Property, justice, and the minimal state.* Stanford University Press.

Wright, D. M. (1951). *Capitalism*. McGraw-Hill.

Zafirovski, M. (2011). "Libertarianism" and the social ideal of liberty: Neo-conservatism's "libertarian" claims reconsidered. *Social Epistemology*, *25*(2), 183–209. 10.1080/0269172100374
9893

Zeng, E. Y. (2022). Empire and liberty in Adam Ferguson's republicanism. *History of European Ideas*, *48*(7), 909–929. 10.1080/01916599.2022.2040045

Zetzel, J. E. G. (2022). *The lost republic: Cicero's de oratore and de re publica*. Oxford University Press. 10.1093/oso/9780197626092.001.0001

Zimmermann, T. (2019). *European republicanism: Combining political theory with economic rationale*. Palgrave Macmillan. 10.1007/978-3-030-25935-8

Zwolinski, M. (2014). Libertarianism and pollution. *Philosophy & Public Policy Quarterly*, *32*(3/4), 9.

Zwolinski, M., & Ferguson, B. (2022). *The Routledge companion to libertarianism*. Routledge. 10.4324/9780367814243

10 Economics

Rational Choice Theory

Definition and Overview

Rational choice theory examines how individuals or organizations make decisions, particularly in relation to achieving specific objectives (Coleman & Fararo, 1992). Rational choice theory assumes that individuals typically (but not always) act in their own interest and tend to make decisions that they see as their best possible option. From a conceptual standpoint, rational choice theory links the structures seen within common economic structures, such as supply-demand curves, to the decisions made and actions taken by individuals within the marketplace (Wittek et al., 2013). Rational choice theory can be applied to matters of consumerism, governmental operations, social structures, and organizations, to understand how individuals and groups seek ways to promote the best possible outcomes as they perceive them (Peacock, 2020).

A foundational assumption of rational choice theory is that individuals will make decisions to increase or maintain their level of happiness or "utility" (Fischer et al., 2007). Rational choice theory also holds that individuals can or will have a preferential order or rank-order within a set of available options. This aspect of rational choice theory assumes that individuals can identify and process qualities that make something preferred and that the criteria for that rank-ordering are consistent over time (Ward, 2002). The formation of preferences, an essential initial step within rational choice theory, is less understood, but several recent studies have begun to examine the rationale undergirding individuals' preferences (Dietrich & List, 2013).

In the public sector, policy interventions are commonly associated with or informed by rational choice theory. Leaders in the public sector frequently must balance the best possible options for their constituents and citizens-at-large against their own self-interests, which commonly involves retaining their seat or elected position (Andeweg et al., 2011). To add to the complexity, determining the best option within public policy is also largely dependent on more general individual or group objectives which may be in direct support of, or opposition to, the goals and objectives of specific individuals and groups (Rutar, 2021). Still, in the development and implementation of policy and policy interventions, rational choice frameworks have become "the dominant yardstick against which to assess explanations of the policy process" (Griggs, 2006, p. 173).

One of the challenges in a rational choice framework is understanding individuals' motivations and practices when they select options that seemingly contradict their own best interests (Elster, 2016). For example, government policy interventions have sought to limit the use of tobacco-related products for the last forty years. Efforts have been made to

DOI: 10.4324/9781003261759-10

highlight the negative health effects of smoking for individuals, increase the cost of smoking to diminish consumer demand, and publicize the public health risks of smoking. Still, roughly 22% of adults worldwide continue to smoke (World Health Organization, 2022). Over the long term, this choice to smoke seems to contradict the rational choice theory, as smoking has negative consequences related to life expectancy and overall physical health. Yet, when we shift our focus from the long-term to the short-term, we get a better understanding of the individual choice in this example. For the individual smoker, the decision made may be in response to more immediate needs – the need to ingest nicotine in the short-term outweighs the long-term deleterious effects. In a rational choice framework, both the short-term and long-term desired outcomes must be examined to understand decisions made at the individual and organizational levels (Schuessler, 2000). Additional challenges to the rational choice framework emerge when individuals have weak preferences, particularly when it comes to consumer patterns and behavior (Panda, 2018).

What is seen as "rational" for one person, may not be understood as "rational" by someone else. As such, and similar to the challenges in understanding how policy and policy interventions influence individual behavior and decision-making, using a rational choice framework to understand the consumer marketplace is complicated by individual decisions that may go against the individual self-interest (Peacock, 2020). If, for example, a local grocery store is having a special on tomato sauce for brand X that dramatically lowers the cost per can for the consumer, shoppers may still eschew that option due to perceptions (real or imaginary) of inferior quality, or to use a coupon to purchase brand Z in an effort to maximize coupon usage. In both instances, rational choice theory is in effect as the individual consciously made the decision to evaluate the best option for their individual circumstances (Chaudhuri, 2006), even if it meant paying more for a can of tomato sauce.

On the whole, rational choice theory can help researchers understand the *typical* reactions of people and organizations when they are presented with options. Rational choice is the link between economics, psychology, and sociology that can help describe individual or organizational behavior (Blossfeld & Prein, 2019).

Background and Foundations

Rational choice theory was initially described by 18th-century economist Adam Smith. Smith characterized rational choice as an "invisible hand" guiding an individual to make decisions in their own best interest (Smith, 1776).

Many of the assumptions of rational choice theory form the foundation for ideas presented by political economist and sociologist Max Weber and sociologist George Homans. Both examined the role of people and the process of individual and group decision-making. Weber sought to understand and analyze the link between sociology and economics. Although he was primarily a political economist, one of his most important works was *The Protestant Ethic and the Spirit of Capitalism* (1905), in which he examined economic sociology, the sociology of religion, and the impact contemporary societal dynamics had on existing economic structures (Weber, & Zohn, 2017). To Weber, capitalism originated from the drive for individuals to own and run their own businesses or enterprises (Weber & Kalberg, 1905:2012). The effort required in establishing and maintaining these ventures was embraced and espoused by early Protestant leaders, particularly Martin Luther, who saw work and employment as providing benefits for society and the individual (Smith & Smith, 2011).

As a sociologist, Homans primarily explored human interactions. He examined exchange theory as well as rational choice theory and its application to group dynamics and operations (Homans, 2017). Primarily known for *The Human Group* (1950) and *Social Behavior: Its Elementary Forms* (1961), Homans set a foundation of choice within a logical expression of human self-interest and established five propositions to help explore human interactions (success proposition, value proposition, deprivation-satiation proposition, aggression-approval proposition, rationality proposition). Each proposition connects to both rational choice and social exchange approaches, particularly as each is linked to risk/reward dynamics between individuals and preexisting social structures (Treviqo & Tilly, 2016). Homans postulated that many interactions between individuals, particularly within a work environment, are based on a risk-reward system (Lawler & O'Toole, 2006). Asking for assistance on a school project, for instance, involves a certain element of risk for the individual asking for help. The rewards are seen through the assistance provided, the higher earned grade, and the strengthening of the relationships between the individuals involved in the exchange (Homans, 1951:2017).

Key Terms and Concepts

Optimal choice theory asserts that individuals will make specific choices to optimize their utility, or they will utilize scarce resources to provide the greatest benefit to their individual circumstances (Okasha, 2011).

Rationality is the basis of rational choice theory – that individuals will act rationally and in their own best interest (Thieme et al., 2022). Within a rational choice framework, individuals will be motivated by additional compensation, perceived superiority within the choice, and logical behavior within the marketplace.

Social exchange theory refers to the application of a cost-benefit analysis to social interactions that closely aligns with rational choice theory. Similar to cost-benefit analysis, social exchange theory parallels the positive/negative components within a social interaction that lead to the best possible option (Zhang & Jia, 2010).

Utility includes the degree of enjoyment or pleasure something provides to the individual. While this is difficult to measure, it is assumed that positive interactions through exchange tend to increase utility while negative interactions tend to decrease a person's overall utility (Giddings, 1891).

In Research

Rational choice theory is used across various disciplines, but is especially useful in sociology and economics. Contemporary research has focused largely on communal activities and processes such as voting and elections (Feddersen, 2004; Dehdari et al., 2021), criminal justice (Ming, 2016; Neissl et al., 2019; Matsueda et al., 2006), and media studies – including social media (Logan et al., 2018; Webster & Trevino, 1995). Each of these areas of study examines the organizational and societal implications of rational choice theory and can help provide additional clarity about the role of rational choice within larger social structures. For example, Logan et al. (2018) applied a rational choice framework alongside a Technology Acceptance Model (see Chapter 12) and User Technology Acceptance and Usage theory to understand individuals' social media use, finding that although people are more frequently experiencing social media fatigue, they continue to engage in social media because the perceived benefits outweigh the negative aspects of social media use.

Studies focused on the individual's decisions regarding rational choice have been more limited in contemporary studies. However, commentary on the usefulness of rational choice theory is plentiful and provides information on both the strengths and limitations of rational choice theory on the individual consumer (e.g., Jacoby, 2000; Chen et al., 2019; Bălău-Ariton, 2013).

Strengths and Limitations

Rational choice theory provides a baseline understanding of why individuals and organizations act the way they do within markets and other economic structures (Zafirovski, 2019). Once the basis of rational choice theory is understood, it is possible to examine those instances when rational choice is not apparent in the marketplace.

One limitation of rational choice theory lies in its foundation premise that individuals and collective organizations will typically act in a rational manner to maximize individual or organizational good (Heath, 1976). Of course, this is not always the case. Human history provides numerous examples where rationality was not the primary driver of interaction. Rational choice also does not incorporate the impact of various external influences within the structure of choice-making (Hayward, 2007). Constructs such as a religion, family experiences, and educational background can all have an influence on the individual's approach to rational choice, often with the movement away from choices that may be optimal for the individual or organization (Young, 2016).

Other limitations associated with rational choice include anomalies in consumer demand and decision-making (Wong, 2006). Branding, for instance, is a potential anomaly for rational choice as it shifts the perception of the good or service away from the actual product and into a larger sphere associated with concerns of external perception, internal self-gratification, and group-identification within a select group of consumers (Amaldoss & Jain, 2015). While rational choice has an impact on many daily activities and transactions, it does not neatly apply to instances of purchasing hysteria and substitute goods with increased status attached (Lenfant, 2006).

Key Theorists: George Homans; Adam Smith.

Examples of Use in Research: Feddersen (2004); Matsueda et al. (2006); Logan et al. (2018).

Signaling Theory

Definition and Overview

Signaling theory describes the process by which an individual or an organization provides indicators of qualities that other individuals or organizations may interpret as beneficial or useful (Lovenheim & Turner, 2018). These signals may be as subtle as the way a person sits in a chair during an interview, or as overt as a company proclaiming itself a "luxury brand" (Han et al., 2010). Not to be confused with signaling theory found in the natural sciences (e.g., biology), signaling theory in economics connects to human resource management, organizational management, and corporate finance, as all of these entities are reliant on specific signals for effective and efficient operations (Connelly et al., 2011).

From a human resources standpoint, educational attainment or degrees are primary signals indicating that the interviewee has the appropriate skills and background that will be needed by the hiring authority (Heisig, 2018). Signaling theory can be similarly applied in fields such as psychology and education – particularly industrial-organizational psychology (Raman & Pramod, 2022; Nyagadza et al., 2021). The use of signaling theory is widespread and can also impact decisions made regarding labor relations, foreign policy, and consumer patterns for both new and existing goods (Guest et al., 2021; Gugerty, 2009; Berger, 2019).

At the individual level, signaling theory can expand beyond the analysis of how individuals signal specific qualifications for a particular job and/or task to include the analysis of more subtle signals related to interpersonal communications, vocal tone and pitch, and nonverbal cues that indicate interest (or disinterest) (Xu & Ling, 2023; Wang et al., 2023). Signaling theory is largely dependent on both parties agreeing that specific signals have value (such as a university degree), but there may be instances where variations in the level of value of the signal may be different between two parties (Heisig, 2018).

At the organizational or institutional level, signaling theory is useful in corporate communications, brand marketing, and organizational and industrial relations (Cambier & Poncin, 2020; Utgard, 2018). The signals communicated to the buyer by the product or the company owning the product often lead to purchasing decisions (Bittar, 2018). In these circumstances, signals can offset an imbalance of information about competing products (a situation called information asymmetry) and lead the consumer or purchaser towards one brand or variety instead of another (Kim, 2021).

Signaling theory links to the concept of human capital (Hung & Ramsden, 2021). In this context, human capital refers to the skills and abilities a person develops that have some value in the labor market (Weinstein, 2022). Within the labor market, there are instances where circumstances change and, based on the perception of the value of the identified human capital, signaling theory adapts and reevaluates the perceived value and the importance of a specific skill or ability (Ge & Haller, 2018). This form of job market signaling is common and results in the ebbs and flows of the desired traits for employees as determined by those who hire them (Spence, 1973).

Another aspect of signaling theory is the concept of countersignaling. This refers to the idea that individuals at the highest levels of their profession do not have a need to express signals in regard to attaining a specific objective (Feltovich et al., 2002). For example, a musician such as Taylor Swift would not benefit from developing the signal associated with obtaining a graduate degree. The return on investment is minimal in this case, and the need for signaling is diminished due to the specialized skill set that Ms. Swift possesses (Araujo et al., 2007).

As a theoretical framework, signaling theory can support researchers in examining the value of education (Clark & Martorell, 2014), understanding the role that previous experience has in determining the value an individual brings to a job or career (Van Belle et al., 2020), and/or analyzing the level of governmental involvement within macroeconomic systems (Perri, 2019). In these examples, signals are utilized as messaging tools for external audiences. This communication then helps define and place a value on specific qualities held by the individual that can be leveraged into a job, a raise, or an intervention to modify monetary market (Shafi et al., 2018).

Background and Foundations

Signaling theory is an offshoot of contract theory and communications studies. The concept of signaling had been in existence for an extended time, but it was not until 1972 that it was fully described and defined. Economist Michael Spence initially developed the theory in his doctoral dissertation (Spence, 1972). Through his work on economic structures and signaling theory, he was awarded the Clark Medal from the American Economic Association in 1981 and the Nobel Prize in economic sciences in 2001. Spence's initial theory has been added to and refined throughout the 20th and 21st centuries and continues to have both macroeconomic (Rana Shahid Imdad et al., 2019) and microeconomic applications (Dilmé & Li, 2016). One of the more important augmentations to Spence's concept was the examination of information asymmetry by Joseph Stiglitz (Stiglitz, 2000). Understanding the challenges with signaling in an environment where the possession of information is not equal between the parties was a focal point for Stiglitz and complemented Spence's research within the discipline of economics (Edlin & Stiglitz, 1995).

Signaling theory builds on ideas from contract theory as well as various aspects of communication studies. Contract theory, in general, centers on the interaction between two entities and the results of that interaction, regardless if a formal contract was developed (Taneri & De Meyer, 2017). Economists have added components to contract theory, by expanding from general contract theory to more refined approaches such as social contract theory (Muldoon, 2016) and behavioral contract theory (Koszegi, 2014), and by including concepts such as property rights and incentives (Brousseau et al., 2002).

Key Terms and Concepts

Countersignaling – For those at the very highest levels of any profession or market, there is a lesser need to communicate signals to achieve an objective. For example, an established movie star does not need to add the signal of a college education to distinguish themselves from others in the labor market, as the return on investment in developing that signal would be minimal.

Human capital centers on the combination of employee skills, knowledge, or other characteristics that are valued in the labor market. These characteristics remain with the individual, are non-transferable to other people, persist with the individual as they move to new jobs and opportunities, and are frequently the focus of the motivations for additional training or education.

Information asymmetry refers to when the consumer or decision-maker does not have a balanced level of information about a person or product and utilizes various signals to help provide insight to reinforce or reconsider a decision. This is often seen this in the retail sector where consumers will select a product of which they are aware, instead of an unknown substitute product.

Job market signaling describes how the job or labor market(s) are modified based on a variety of signals. If the provided signals demonstrate that all applicants for a job possess similar signals, modifications to the job market may result in wage devaluation or the search for other distinguishing signals. These new distinguishing signals then have their own impact on the labor market as a new evaluation factor has been introduced. An example of this could be degree inflation, where jobs that previously only required bachelor's degrees move to requiring Master's degrees.

In Research

Signaling theory can be applied to understand a variety of interpersonal interactions. As such, the majority of the recent studies involving signaling theory have centered on business management, finance, and relationships within a business or corporate setting (Bergh et al.,

2014; Reuer et al., 2012; Rao et al., 2018). Emerging studies regarding entrepreneurism and the digital economy have also increasingly applied a signaling theory framework (e.g., Zhang et al., 2018; Alsos & Ljunggren, 2017; Gregory et al., 2013) as new modes of exchange and cyber-interaction have necessitated revisiting and reapplying the approaches first developed by Spence in the 1970s. There is also a segment of existing research that touches on the ethical and moral components of signaling theory and the potential for information asymmetry (Sun et al., 2020; Lee & Charles, 2021; Su et al., 2016).

Signaling theory has also been used to focus on the role of signals with various gender, ethnic, racial, and socioeconomic constructs. These areas of focus, particularly in regard to race (Kudashvili & Lergetporer, 2022; Sauer et al., 2010; Hipp, 2012) and gender (Nielsson & Steingrimsdottir, 2018; Kleinert & Mochkabadi, 2021), continue to be areas of emphasis for scholars in the 21st century. While the initial theory may not have been developed to specifically address these issues and concerns, it has been adapted in an effort to develop new knowledge about these modern societal issues and concerns.

Strengths and Limitations

One of the strengths of signaling theory as a theoretical framework is that it can represent a universal process that is seen in nearly all interactions and communications processes between people and groups (Connelly et al., 2011). These signals are especially relevant in human interactions involving commerce and economics as they form the framework for larger processes related to marketing, advertising, and consumer communications (Sharma & Romero, 2022). This theory also provides insight and tools to understand the role of gender, race, socioeconomic status (and other demographic indicators) and how the production of signals can impact the ability of specific individuals, or groups of individuals, to secure employment, housing, and equity within the criminal justice system (Cassidy et al., 2016.; Lee, 2017; Bagwell, & Bernheim, 1996).

Signaling theory can help researchers understand the role of communication, both intentional and unintentional, between individuals and groups and the outcomes associated with these interactions (Grecu et al., 2022). The broad application and suitability of this theory aligns well with research and studies related to the social sciences, particularly business-related disciplines making it a common foundation for studies that examine outcomes of human interactions (Steigenberger & Wilhelm, 2018; Zimmer et al., 2020).

One limitation of signaling theory is use of signals as a primary criterion to explain decisions. While there is clear evidence that signals do play a part in interactions such as hiring decisions or retail-consumer interactions, the utilization of signals within a digital environment or areas not related to commerce is much more difficult to discern and quantify (Al Adwan et al., 2022). The role of information asymmetry as a component of signaling theory is also difficult to measure as the intentions and mode of interactions between individuals and groups do vary when information is limited or purposefully held back from one party within the signaling process (Zhang et al., 2018).

There is also an inherent limitation in signaling theory that centers on the primary messages and indicators being signaled (Kharouf et al., 2020). The theory is dependent on the concept that provided signals are intentional and purposeful, as opposed to randomly developed or not processed by the receiver in the way they were intended (Kwon & Farndale, 2020). Unintended signals can lead to disparate outcomes that may not reflect the initial intention of the exchange. This effect can be compounded when barriers associated with language and cultural norms are also considered (Barker et al., 2019).

Key Theorists: Michael Spence (Originating author); George Akerlof; Joseph Stiglitz.

Examples of Use in Research: Boateng, S. L. (2019); Ernst et al. (2021); Luchtenberg et al. (2018).

Human Capital Theory

Definition and Overview

Human capital theory focuses on how individuals' specific knowledge and skills are valued and utilized in the labor market (Merriman, 2017). Within any labor pool, individuals vary in their experiences, qualifications, and relative value to the market – some with higher levels of education than others, and some with advanced skills when compared with other people in the labor pool (Kalleberg & Project Muse, 2011). As an example, if a job becomes available and it requires fluency in Arabic, then it is highly likely only those people with that particular skill will be considered for that job. This unique ability to speak Arabic is part of the successful job applicant's human capital – a combination of skills, abilities, education, and other preferred characteristics that differentiate individuals within a labor pool (Thomas et al., 2014). These skills can be clearly defined as explicit skills, more subtle behaviors, or implicit qualifications, but the value and extent of human capital differ for each individual (Ferran & Miravet, 2016).

As a theoretical lens, human capital categorizes degrees and diplomas, specialized training, cultural knowledge, communicative skills, and countless additional characteristics as elements of an individual's human capital (Shah & Steinberg, 2021). Economists see the individuals' decisions to invest in the expansion of their own human capital as an accepted strategy to obtain higher future earnings. As an example, many individuals invest time and money to obtain a university degree hoping that their investment will lead to increased financial compensation at some point in the future (Stark et al., 2011; Abel & Deitz, 2012).

A characteristic of human capital is that it lacks transferability. In other words, although people may possess similar knowledge, skills, qualifications, or characteristics that have value on the labor market, once individuals possess these things, they cannot be taken away or transferred to another person (Sturman et al., 2008). There are two aspects to this lack of transferability (Lovenheim & Turner, 2018). The first is that these skills are unable to be collateralized (Lambrecht & Pawlina, 2013). Once something has been learned, it is impossible for someone to seize or confiscate this knowledge even if money is owed as a result of the educational opportunity (Madsen et al., 2002). If one were to sit through a course on rainforest ecology (and presumably learn information in the process), this knowledge cannot be held, contained, or repossessed by an outside entity, even if the tuition or loans for tuition are never paid. The learning has been completed, and it is impossible for any individual or entity to revoke this information once obtained by the learner (Fonarova, Chernyak, National Mining University, & National Metallurgical Academy of Ukraine, 2017).

Another unique component of human capital theory is that the skills learned by the individual are not able to be transferred or owned by another person (except in historical instances involving slavery or indentured servitude; Fulmer & Ployhart, 2014). Human capital earned by the individual is an unpurchasable asset. It would not be possible, for example, for you to sell your newfound knowledge about rainforest ecology to another person within the labor market. The human capital developed by the individual can only be used by the individual, and a return on the investment for this human capital can only be made if the skills are utilized within the labor market (Pauleen & Gorman, 2011).

Educational endeavors, formal or informal, can increase an individual's human capital (Spring, 2015). Thus, researchers can use human capital theory to examine the structures associated with formal and informal schooling practices through a financial and economic lens (Bilkic et al., 2012). Using human capital theory, social scientists can evaluate an educational process or course of study based on the idea that the investment in the education should correlate with an increase in human capital (Hu et al., 2020). For instance, if spending eight years in medical school led to a job that paid less than a job that required only a secondary school diploma, then the investment in this individual's human capital did not lead to a positive return on investment (Carlson, 2021).

Human capital theory provides structure and a way to evaluate the value of skill acquisition, going to school, and the traits evident within the larger labor pool (Fraumeni & Fraumeni, 2021). Knowing that there is a way to define the benefit of obtaining new knowledge, and the limitations associated with non-transferability and individual ownership, assist in the understanding of the role and value of education and the various forms in which education is provided (Özdoğan Özbal, 2021).

Human capital theory can help researchers by providing a lens through which investment in education or other ways of acquiring knowledge and skills can be evaluated through a return-on-investment and overall cost analysis that incorporates concerns related to opportunity costs (Chakrabarti et al., 2023). Decisions about skills valued in the labor pool and the cost of acquiring these skills can be made by the individual within the parameters of a human capital framework. Human capital theory is useful for examining a number of overarching research topics such as education reform, equity studies, and power analysis (Wolhuter & Niemczyk, 2023; Iordan et al., 2022).

Background and Foundations

Personal skill development has been a humanistic process from antiquity (Goldin et al., 2011). As society developed and began to value specialized skills, the investment in human capital became standardized. It was not until the mid-20th century that the concept was further refined through the work of economist Gary Becker (Hershey, 2014). In his 1964 book *Human Capital*, Becker formalized and expanded on the concept of human capital and synthesized the utilization of human capital in contemporary society. He was the recipient of the Clark Medal for economics in 1967 and the Nobel Prize in Economics in 1992 (Glaeser & Shleifer, 2014).

Building upon Becker's work, Jacob Mincer developed a system to equate the connection between schooling and individual experiences and compensation levels (Grossbard & San Diego State University, 2006). The Mincerian Equation is frequently used in studies related to human capital to calculate the return on investment of formal and informal education (Mincer, 1989). He was awarded the ICA Prize in Labor Economics in 2002 and the Career Achievement Award from the Society of Labor Economists – now known as the Mincer Prize – in 2004.

The basis of human capital theory was established through formal and informal education processes and the various learning processes utilized by youth and adults (Goswami, 2011). Building upon the practices of cognitive development and ongoing brain development, the acquisition of specific and specialized talents is foundational to more applicable skills related to employment (Langlois, 2020). Accordingly, human capital requires the individual to learn basic skills and concepts (e.g., reading, math) before obtaining skills that are needed and desired within the job market (Tymon, 2013).

Key Terms and Concepts

Educational attainment refers to the completion of a degree or course of study that leads to a diploma, certificate, or some other signal of human capital enhancement (NCES, 2022). There are also instances, however, of educational attainment in non-traditional education settings that also contribute to an individual's human capital. Spending significant time in a foreign country or learning to cook from your parents are informal learning opportunities that can lead to educational attainment and an increase in individual human capital that can be utilized in the labor market (van Hoorn, 2019).

Opportunity costs are the costs incurred by the individual when they choose to participate in one activity over another (Leininger, 1977). For example, if an individual elects to go to university in the United States, total costs will not only include the expenses associated with tuition, fees, books, etc., but also the lost salary this person would have earned if they had been in the labor force during the time they were enrolled in university. These opportunity costs can be calculated in both the short term (e.g., not earning $40,000 a year while in school) and the long term (e.g., the long-term impact on compensation outcomes due to time not working while in school) (Watson, 2008).

Return on investment (ROI) is the value associated with adding to an individual's human capital (Blundell et al., 1999). Suppose it costs a worker $10,000 in tuition to secure a promotion at work that comes with a $5,000 increase in salary. We can quickly determine that the return on investment (ROI) for this investment in human capital would be a little over two years (when adjusting for inflation). There are instances, however, where an ROI on human capital investment is never fully realized. This is most often seen in occupations that require specific training, degrees, and credentials and offer lower salaries such as classroom teachers and social workers (Lobo & Burke-Smalley, 2018).

In Research

Human capital has a prominent position in labor studies as it focuses on the developed skills that differentiate people within the labor market (Becker, 1964; Mincer, 1974; Merriman, 2017; Wykstra, 1971). In practice, human capital can be used to inform and explore concepts related to skill acquisition and compensation, effectively measuring the costs of enhanced human capital against realized benefits (Slaughter & Ang, 2007).

In applying human capital theory, researchers have examined the direct connection to formal education structures (Fryer, 2018; Bilkic et al., 2012; Cappelli & Vasta, 2020), and the valuation of the acquisition of human capital for the individual (Marx & Turner, 2018; Cadena & Keys, 2015). There are also strong ties in examining the role of human capital in the fields of compensation (Chemmanur et al., 2013; Bagger et al., 2014; Autor & Handel, 2013). and income variations in a population (Sehrawat & Singh, 2019; Erosa et al., 2010).

Contemporary studies focusing on the acquisition of human capital have examined the role that human capital plays in issues of equity and access for marginalized people (Bedard, 2001, Perreira et al., 2006). Additional studies have clearly shown the link between limited human capital and poverty (Hong & Pandey, 2008; Purkayastha, 2006), and the correlations between human capital, ethnicity, and race (Benabou, 1996; Tomaskovic-Devy et al., 2005; Ressler, et al., 2020).

Strengths and Limitations

The strength of human capital theory centers on its wide application and connection to established global systems of education, and numerous labor pools across industries, locations, and environments (Zhao, 2008). This broad application has become even more relevant in our contemporary era where specific skill development, particularly in the continuously evolving technology industry has become highly specialized (Marvel & Lumpkin, 2007). Many institutions of higher education employ human capital theory in their operations as they seek to maximize their value by preparing graduates for in-demand careers that require specific skills (Perez-Vergara, 2019).

One of the primary limitations of human capital theory is its focus on the individual and their acquisition and incorporation of skills and knowledge within a labor pool or a specific job. The limited focus on the impact of human capital development on society-at-large is largely omitted in studies related to human capital attainment (McMahon & Project Muse, 2009). That a highly-educated citizenry can have other beneficial effects in a society, such as lower crime rates and higher rates of technological development, is frequently over-looked in studies with a traditional view of human capital (Sabates et al., 2021).

Another limitation centers on new forms of knowledge acquisition and how these skills and talents can be identified and recognized within the labor pool (Marginson, 2019). For example, technology requires individuals to be able to utilize a computer and a keyboard to access entry into the labor pool in many instances. The acquisition of these skills has been largely organic, as the individual is obtaining them through hours of interaction with technology (Fredriksen & Kagia, 2013). Identifying the point of acqui-sition of these skills can be difficult and the subtleties associated with technology skill acquisition may not be recognized as a differentiation within the labor markets. The basis of human capital theory is the utilization of skills within the labor pool. If the developed skills are not needed or utilized, the justification for expanding human capital becomes problematic (Moore & Daday, 2010).

Lastly, human capital theory critics see it as detracting from the humanistic element within education (Wigley & Akkoyunlu-Wigley, 2006). By identifying learning's primary goal as adding individual value within the labor pool, it takes away the concept of learning for individual betterment that is not associated with employment (Bottrill, 2022). The concept of "learning for learning's sake" is not a component of most studies related to human capital.

Key Theorist: Gary Becker.

Examples of Use in Research: Abel and Deitz (2012); Autor and Handel (2013); Bilkic et al., (2012); Sehrawat and Singh (2019).

References

Abel, J. R., & Deitz, R. (2012). Do colleges and universities increase their region's human capital? *Journal of Economic Geography, 12*(3), 667–691. 10.1093/jeg/lbr020

Al-Adwan, A. S., Alrousan, M. K., Yaseen, H., Alkufahy, A. M., & Alsoud, M. (2022). Boosting online purchase intention in high-uncertainty-avoidance societies: A signaling theory approach. *Journal of Open Innovation, 8*(3), 136. 10.3390/joitmc8030136

Alsos, G. A., & Ljunggren, E. (2017). The role of gender in entrepreneur–investor relationships: A signaling theory approach. *Entrepreneurship Theory and Practice, 41*(4), 567–590. 10.1111/etp.12226

Amaldoss, W., & Jain, S. (2015). Branding conspicuous goods: An analysis of the effects of social influence and competition. *Management Science, 61*(9), 2064–2079. 10.1287/mnsc.2014.2078

Andeweg, R. B., Winter, L. d., & Dumont, P. (2011). *Puzzles of government formation: Coalition theory and deviant cases*. Routledge. 10.4324/9780203007815

Araujo, A., Gottlieb, D., & Moreira, H. (2007). A model of mixed signals with applications to countersignalling. *The Rand Journal of Economics, 38*(4), 1020–1043. 10.1111/j.0741-6261. 2007.00124.x

Autor, D. H., & Handel, M. J. (2013). Putting tasks to the test: Human capital, job tasks, and wages. *Journal of Labor Economics, 31*(S1), S59–S96. 10.1086/669332

Bagger, J., Fontaine, F., Postel-Vinay, F., & Robin, J. (2014). Tenure, experience, human capital, and wages: A tractable equilibrium search model of wage dynamics. *The American Economic Review, 104*(6), 1551–1596. 10.1257/aer.104.6.1551

Bagwell, L. S., & Bernheim, B. D. (1996). Veblen effects in a theory of conspicuous consumption. *The American Economic Review, 86*(3), 349–373.

Bălău-Ariton, M. (2013). Rational choice, consumer vulnerability and empowerment: Diverging economic perspectives and issues for debate. *The International Conference 'the European Integration' – Realities and Perspectives, 8*(1), 166–172.

Barker, J. L., Power, E. A., Heap, S., Puurtinen, M., & Sosis, R. (2019). Content, cost, and context: A framework for understanding human signaling systems. *Evolutionary Anthropology, 28*(2), 86–99. 10.1002/evan.21768

Becker, G. S. (1964). *Human capital: A theoretical and empirical analysis, with special reference to education*. National Bureau of Economic Research; distributed by Columbia University Press.

Bedard, K. (2001). Human capital versus signaling models: University access and high school dropouts. *The Journal of Political Economy, 109*(4), 749–775. 10.1086/322089

Benabou, R. (1996). Equity and efficiency in human capital investment: The local connection. *The Review of Economic Studies, 63*(2), 237–264. 10.2307/2297851

Berger, J. (2019). Signaling can increase consumers' willingness to pay for green products. Theoretical model and experimental evidence. *Journal of Consumer Behaviour, 18*(3), 233–246. 10.1002/cb.1760

Bergh, D. D., Connelly, B. L., Ketchen Jr, D. J., & Shannon, L. M. (2014). Signalling theory and equilibrium in strategic management research: An assessment and a research agenda. *Journal of Management Studies, 51*(8), 1334–1360. 10.1111/joms.12097

Bilkic, N., Gries, T., & Pilichowski, M. (2012). Stay in school or start working? – the human capital investment decision under uncertainty and irreversibility. *Labour Economics, 19*(5), 706–717. 10.1016/j.labeco.2012.04.005

Bittar, A. d. V. (2018). Selling remanufactured products: Does consumer environmental consciousness matter? *Journal of Cleaner Production, 181*, 527–536. 10.1016/j.jclepro.2018.01.255

Blossfeld, H., & Prein, G. (2019). *Rational choice theory and large-scale data analysis*. Routledge. 10.4324/9780429303753

Blundell, R., Dearden, L., Meghir, C., & Sianesi, B. (1999). Human capital investment: The returns from education and training to the individual, the firm and the economy. *Fiscal Studies, 20*(1), 1–23. 10.1111/j.1475-5890.1999.tb00001.x

Boateng, S. L. (2019). Online relationship marketing and customer loyalty: A signaling theory perspective. *International Journal of Bank Marketing, 37*(1), 226–240. 10.1108/IJBM-01-2018-0009

Bottrill, C. (2022). Human capital futures: An educational perspective. *Journal of Tourism Futures, 8*(2), 254–258. 10.1108/JTF-04-2021-0101

Brousseau, E., Glachant, J., & Books, I. (2002). In E. Brousseau, & J. Glachant (Eds.), *The economics of contracts: Theories and applications*. Cambridge University Press. 10.1017/CBO9780511 613807

Cadena, B. C., & Keys, B. J. (2015). Human capital and the lifetime costs of impatience. *American Economic Journal: Economic Policy, 7*(3), 126–153. 10.1257/pol.20130081

Cambier, F., & Poncin, I. (2020). Inferring brand integrity from marketing communications: The effects of brand transparency signals in a consumer empowerment context. *Journal of Business Research, 109*, 260–270. 10.1016/j.jbusres.2019.11.060

Cappelli, G., & Vasta, M. (2020). Can school centralization foster human capital accumulation? A quasi-experiment from early twentieth-century Italy. *The Economic History Review, 73*(1), 159–184. 10.1111/ehr.12877

Carlson, S. (2021). What's a college degree worth? The imperfect science of measuring the return on investment of college. *The Chronicle of Higher Education, 68*(6), 26.

Cassidy, H., DeVaro, J., & Kauhanen, A. (2016). Promotion signaling, gender, and turnover: New theory and evidence. *Journal of Economic Behavior & Organization, 126*, A(June), 140–166. 10.1016/j.jebo.2016.03.016

Chakrabarti, R., Fos, V., Liberman, A., & Yannelis, C. (2023). Tuition, debt, and human capital. *The Review of Financial Studies.* 10.1093/rfs/hhac065

Chaudhuri, A. (2006). *Emotion and reason in consumer behavior.* Elsevier Butterworth-Heinemann. 10.4324/9780080461762

Chemmanur, T. J., Cheng, Y., & Zhang, T. (2013). Human capital, capital structure, and employee pay: An empirical analysis. *Journal of Financial Economics, 110*(2), 478–502. 10.1016/j.jfineco.2013.07.003

Chen, Q., Feng, Y., Liu, L., & Tian, X. (2019). Understanding consumers' reactance of online personalized advertising: A new scheme of rational choice from a perspective of negative effects. *International Journal of Information Management, 44*, 53–64 10.1016/j.ijinfomgt.2018.09.001

Clark, D., & Martorell, P. (2014). The signaling value of a high school diploma. *The Journal of Political Economy, 122*(2), 282–318. 10.1086/675238

Coleman, J. S., & Fararo, T. J. (1992). *Rational choice theory: Advocacy and critique.* Sage Publications.

Connelly, B. L., Certo, S. T., Ireland, R. D., & Reutzel, C. R. (2011). *Signaling theory: A review and assessment.* Sage Publications. 10.1177/0149206310388419

Dehdari, S. H., Meriläinen, J., & Oskarsson, S. (2021). Selective abstention in simultaneous elections: Understanding the turnout gap. *Electoral Studies, 71*, 102302. 10.1016/j.electstud.2021.102302

Dietrich, F., & List, C. (2013). A reason-based theory of rational choice. *Noûs, 47*(1), 104–134. 10.1111/j.1468-0068.2011.00840.x

Dilmé, F., & Li, F. (2016). Dynamic signaling with dropout risk. *American Economic Journal. Microeconomics, 8*(1), 57–82. 10.1257/mic.20120112

Edlin, A. S., & Stiglitz, J. E. (1995). Discouraging rivals: Managerial rent-seeking and economic inefficiencies. *The American Economic Review, 85*(5), 1301–1312

Elster, J., & Cambridge University Press (2016; 2017). *Sour grapes: Studies in the subversion of rationality.* Cambridge University Press. 10.1017/CBO9781316494172

Ernst, B. A., Banks, G. C., Loignon, A. C., Frear, K. A., Williams, C. E., Arciniega, L. M., Gupta, R. K., Kodydek, G., & Subramanian, D. (2021). Virtual charismatic leadership and signaling theory: A prospective meta-analysis in five countries. *The Leadership Quarterly.* 10.1016/j.leaqua.2021.101541

Erosa, A., Koreshkova, T., & Restuccia, D. (2010). How important is human capital?: A quantitative theory assessment of world income inequality. *The Review of Economic Studies, 77*(4), 1421–1449. 10.1111/j.1467-937X.2010.00610.x

Feddersen, T. J. (2004). Rational choice theory and the paradox of not voting. *The Journal of Economic Perspectives, 18*(1), 99–112. 10.1257/089533004773563458

Feltovich, N., Harbaugh, R., & To, T. (2002). Too cool for school? Signalling and countersignalling. *The Rand Journal of Economics, 33*(4), 630–649. 10.2307/3087478

Ferran, M., & Miravet, D. (2016). Using the job requirements approach and matched employer-employee data to investigate the content of individuals' human capital. *Journal for Labour Market Research, 49*(2), 133–155. 10.1007/s12651-016-0203-3

Fischer, F., Miller, G., & Sidney, M. S. (2007; 2006). *Handbook of public policy analysis: Theory, politics, and methods.* CRC/Taylor & Francis.

Fonarova, T., Chernyak, V., National Mining University, U., & National Metallurgical Academy of Ukraine, Ukraine. (2017). System basis for studying the interaction of national and individual human capital. *Baltic Journal of Economic Studies, 3*(4), 265–270. 10.30525/2256-0742/2017-3-4-265-270

Fraumeni, B., & Fraumeni, B. M. (2021). *Measuring human capital.* Elsevier Science & Technology. 10.1016/C2018-0-05171-3

Fredriksen, B., & Kagia, R. (2013). Attaining the 2050 vision for Africa: Breaking the human capital barrier. *Global Journal of Emerging Market Economies, 5*(3), 269–328. 10.1177/0974910113505794

Fryer, R. G. (2018). The 'pupil' factory: Specialization and the production of human capital in schools. *The American Economic Review, 108*(3), 616–656. 10.1257/aer.20161495

Fulmer, I. S., & Ployhart, R. E. (2014). Our most important asset: A multidisciplinary/multilevel review of human capital valuation for research and practice. *Journal of Management, 40*(1), 161–192. 10.1177/0149206313511271

Ge, S., & Haller, H. (2018). Job market signaling and returns to education. *Southern Economic Journal, 84*(3), 734–741. 10.1002/soej.12243

Giddings, F. H. (1891). The concepts of utility, value and cost. *Publications of the American Economic Association, 6*(1/2), 41–43.

Glaeser, E. L., & Shleifer, A. (2014). Retrospective: Gary Becker (1930–2014). *Science (American Association for the Advancement of Science), 344*(6189), 1233. 10.1126/science.1256540

Goldin, A. P., Pezzatti, L., Battro, A. M., & Sigman, M. (2011). From ancient Greece to modern education: Universality and lack of generalization of the Socratic dialogue. *Mind, Brain and Education, 5*(4), 180–185. 10.1111/j.1751-228X.2011.01126.x

Goswami, U. (2011). *The Wiley-Blackwell handbook of childhood cognitive development* (2nd ed.). Wiley.

Grecu, A., Sofka, W., Larsen, M. M., & Pedersen, T. (2022). Unintended signals: Why companies with a history of offshoring have to pay wage penalties for new hires. *Journal of International Business Studies, 53*(3), 534–549. 10.1057/s41267-021-00486-3

Gregory, C. K., Meade, A. W., & Thompson, L. F. (2013). Understanding internet recruitment via signaling theory and the elaboration likelihood model. *Computers in Human Behavior, 29*(5), 1949–1959. 10.1016/j.chb.2013.04.013

Griggs, S. (2006). Rational choice in public policy: The theory in critical perspective. In F. Fischer & G. Miller (Eds.), *Handbook of public policy analysis: Theory, politics, and methods.* CRC/Taylor & Francis.

Grossbard, S., & San Diego State University (2006). *Jacob Mincer: A pioneer of modern labor economics.* Springer Science.

Guest, D. E., Sanders, K., Rodrigues, R., & Oliveira, T. (2021). Signaling theory as a framework for analyzing human resource management processes and integrating human resource attribution theories: A conceptual analysis and empirical exploration. *Human Resource Management Journal, 31*(3), 796–818. 10.1111/1748-8583.12326

Gugerty, M. K. (2009). Signaling virtue: Voluntary accountability programs among nonprofit organizations. *Policy Sciences, 42*(3), 243–273. 10.1007/s11077-009-9085-3

Han, Y. J., Nunes, J. C., & Drèze, X. (2010). Signaling status with luxury goods: The role of brand prominence. *Journal of Marketing, 74*(4), 15–30. 10.1509/jmkg.74.4.15

Hayward, K. (2007). Situational crime prevention and its discontents: Rational choice theory versus the 'culture of now'. *Social Policy & Administration, 41*(3), 232–250. 10.1111/j.1467-9515.2007.00550.x

Heath, A. (1976). *Rational choice & social exchange: A critique of exchange theory.* Cambridge University Press.

Heisig, J. P. (2018). Measuring the signaling value of educational degrees: Secondary education systems and the internal homogeneity of educational groups. *Large-Scale Assessments in Education, 6*(1), 1–35. 10.1186/s40536-018-0062-1

Hershey, R. D. (May 5, 2014). Gary S. Becker, 83, Nobel winner who applied economics to everyday life: Obituary (obit); biography. *The New York Times.*

Hipp, J. R. (2012). Segregation through the lens of housing unit transition: What roles do the prior residents, the local micro-neighborhood, and the broader neighborhood play? *Demography, 49*(4), 1285–1306. 10.1007/s13524-012-0121-0

Homans, G. C. (1950). *The human group.* Harcourt, Brace.

Homans, G. C. (1961). *Social behavior.* Harcourt, Brace & World

Homans, G. C. (2017). *Coming to my senses: The autobiography of a sociologist.* Routledge. 10.4324/9781315080963

Hong, P. Y. P., & Pandey, S. (2008). Differential effects of human capital on the poor and near-poor: Evidence of social exclusion. *Journal of Poverty, 12*(4), 456–480. 10.1080/1087554 0802350138

Hu, X., Liu, X., He, C., & Dai, T. (2020). Education policies, pre-college human capital investment and educated unemployment. *Journal of Economics (Vienna, Austria), 129*(3), 241–270. 10.1 007/s00712-019-00676-6

Hung, J., & Ramsden, M. (2021). The application of human capital theory and educational signaling theory to explain parental influences on the Chinese population's social mobility opportunities. *Social Sciences (Basel), 10*(10), 362. 10.3390/socsci10100362

Iordan, M., Pelinescu, E., & Chilian, M. (2022). Human capital in the digital society. Some empirical evidence for the EU countries. *Holistic: Journal of Business and Public Administration, 13*(2), 25–40. 10.2478/hjbpa-2022-0013

Jacoby, J. (2000). Is it rational to assume consumer rationality? Some consumer psychological perspectives on rational choice theory. *Roger Williams University Law Review, 6*(1), 81.

Kalleberg, A. L., & Project Muse (2011). *Good jobs, bad jobs: The rise of polarized and precarious employment systems in the United States, 1970s to 2000s.* Russell Sage Foundation. 10.7758/ 9781610447478

Kharouf, H., Lund, D. J., Krallman, A., & Pullig, C. (2020). A signaling theory approach to relationship recovery. *European Journal of Marketing, 54*(9), 2139–2170. 10.1108/EJM-10-2019-0751

Kim, R. Y. (2021). When does online review matter to consumers? The effect of product quality information cues. *Electronic Commerce Research, 21*(4), 1011–1030. 10.1007/s10660-020-09398-0

Kleinert, S., & Mochkabadi, K. (2021). Gender stereotypes in equity crowdfunding: The effect of gender bias on the interpretation of quality signals. *The Journal of Technology Transfer.* 10.1007/ s10961-021-09892-z

Koszegi, B. (2014). Behavioral contract theory. *Journal of Economic Literature, 52*(4), 1075–1118. 10.1257/jel.52.4.1075

Kudashvili, N., & Lergetporer, P. (2022). Minorities' strategic response to discrimination: Experimental evidence. *Journal of Public Economics, 208.* 10.1016/j.jpubeco.2022.104630

Kwon, B., & Farndale, E. (2020). Employee voice viewed through a cross-cultural lens. *Human Resource Management Review, 30*(1), 100653. 10.1016/j.hrmr.2018.06.002

Lambrecht, B. M., & Pawlina, G. (2013). A theory of net debt and transferable human capital. *Review of Finance, 17*(1), 321–368. 10.1093/rof/rfs011

Langlois, A. (2020). The school enterprise challenge: Learning by doing. *Childhood Education, 96*(4), 22–33. 10.1080/00094056.2020.1796446

Lawler, E.E. & O'Toole, J. (2006). *America at work: Choices and challenges* (1st ed). Palgrave Macmillan. 10.1057/9781403983596.

Lee, L., & Charles, V. (2021). The impact of consumers' perceptions regarding the ethics of online retailers and promotional strategy on their repurchase intention. *International Journal of Information Management, 57*, 102264. 10.1016/j.ijinfomgt.2020.102264

Lee, Y. (2017). Costly signaling: Asian Americans and the role of ethnicity in the willingness to pay more for socially responsible products. *Journal of Promotion Management, 23*(2), 277–302. 10.1 080/10496491.2016.1267680

Leininger, W. E. (1977). Opportunity costs: Some definitions and examples. *The Accounting Review, 52*(1), 248–251.

Lenfant, J. (2006). Complementarity and demand theory: From the 1920s to the 1940s. *History of Political Economy, 38*(Suppl_1), 48–85. 10.1215/00182702-2005-017

Liao, Y. (2021). Gender and quality signals: How does gender influence the effectiveness of signals in crowdfunding? *Journal of Small Business Management, 59*(sup1), S153–S192. 10.1080/00472 778.2021.1966434

Lobo, B. J., & Burke-Smalley, L. A. (2018). An empirical investigation of the financial value of a college degree. *Education Economics, 26*(1/2), 78–92. 10.1080/09645292.2017.1332167

Logan, K., Bright, L. F., & Grau, S. L. (2018). 'Unfriend me, please!': Social media fatigue and the theory of rational choice. *Journal of Marketing Theory and Practice, 26*(4), 357–367. 10.1080/1 0696679.2018.1488219

Lovenheim, M., & Turner, S. E. (2018). *Economics of education.* Worth Publishers, Incorporated.

Luchtenberg, K. F., Seiler, M. J., & Sun, H. (2018; 2019). Listing agent signals: Does a picture paint a thousand words? *The Journal of Real Estate Finance and Economics, 59*(4), 617–648. 10.1007/ s11146-018-9674-z

Madsen, T. L., Mosakowski, E., & Zaheer, S. (2002). The dynamics of knowledge flows: Human capital mobility, knowledge retention and change. *Journal of Knowledge Management, 6*(2), 164–176. 10.1108/13673270210424684

Marginson, S. (2019). Limitations of human capital theory. *Studies in Higher Education, 44*(2), 287–301. 10.1080/03075079.2017.1359823

Marvel, M. R., & Lumpkin, G. T. (2007). Technology entrepreneurs' human capital and its effects on innovation radicalness. *Entrepreneurship Theory and Practice, 31*(6), 807–828. 10.1111/ j.1540-6520.2007.00209.x

Marx, B. M., & Turner, L. J. (2018). Borrowing trouble? human capital investment with opt-in costs and implications for the effectiveness of grant aid. *American Economic Journal. Applied Economics, 10*(2), 163–201. 10.1257/app.20160127

Matsueda, R. L., Kreager, D. A., & Huizinga, D. (2006). Deterring delinquents: A rational choice model of theft and violence. *American Sociological Review, 71*(1), 95–122. 10.1177/00031224 0607100105

McMahon, W. W., & Project Muse (2009). *Higher learning, greater good: The private and social benefits of higher education.* Johns Hopkins University Press.

Merriman, K. K. (2017). *Valuation of human capital: Quantifying the importance of an assembled workforce.* Springer International Publishing. 10.1007/978-3-319-58934-3

Mincer, J. (1974). *Schooling, experience, and earnings.* National Bureau of Economic Research; distributed by Columbia University Press.

Mincer, J. (1989). *Job training: Costs, returns, and wage profiles.* National Bureau of Economic Research. 10.3386/w3208

Ming, H. (2016). The resolution of social contradictions and attainment of societal governance through the justice system at the present stage-using the analytical framework of rational choice theory. *Social Sciences in China, 37*(2), 124–141. 10.1080/02529203.2016.1162014

Moore, M. D., & Daday, J. (2010). Barriers to human capital development: Case studies in Swaziland, Cameroon and Kenya. *Africa Education Review, 7,* 283–304 10.1080/18146627.2010.515418.

Muldoon R. (2016). *Social contract theory for a diverse word: Beyond tolerance.* Routledge-Taylor & Francis.

National Center for Education Statistics (2022). Educational Attainment of Young Adults. *Condition of Education.* U.S. Department of Education, Institute of Education Sciences. Retrieved June 23, 2022, from https://nces.ed.gov/programs/coe/indicator/caa

Neissl, K., Botchkovar, E. V., Antonaccio, O., & Hughes, L. A. (2019). Rational choice and the gender gap in crime: Establishing the generality of rational choice theory in Russia and Ukraine. *Justice Quarterly*, *36*(6), 1096–1121. 10.1080/07418825.2018.1543723

Nielsson, U., & Steingrimsdottir, H. (2018; 2017). The signalling value of education across genders. *Empirical Economics*, *54*(4), 1827–1854. 10.1007/s00181-017-1264-z

Nyagadza, B., Kadembo, E. M., & Makasi, A. (2021). When corporate brands tell stories: A signalling theory perspective. *Cogent Psychology*, *8*(1). 10.1080/23311908.2021.1897063

Okasha, S. (2011). Optimal choice in the face of risk: Decision theory meets evolution. *Philosophy of Science*, *78*(1), 83–104. 10.1086/658115

Özdoğan Özbal, E. (2021). Dynamic effects of higher education expenditures on human capital and economic growth: An evaluation of OECD countries. *Policy Reviews in Higher Education*, *5*(2), 174–196. 10.1080/23322969.2021.1893125

Panda, S. C. (2018). Rational choice with intransitive preferences. *Studies in Microeconomics*, *6*(1–2), 66–83. 10.1177/2321022218799001

Pauleen, D. J., & Gorman, G. E. (2011). *Personal knowledge management: Individual, organizational and social perspectives*. Gower. 10.4324/9781315600154

Peacock, M. S. (2020). *Amartya Sen and rational choice: The concept of commitment*. Routledge. 10.4324/9780429198946

Perez-Vergara, K. (2019). Higher education enrollment theories: Setting context for enrollment projections. *Strategic Enrollment Management Quarterly*, *7*(2), 13–33.

Perreira, K. M., Harris, K. M., & Lee, D. (2006). Making it in America: High school completion by immigrant and native youth. *Demography*, *43*(3), 511–536. 10.1353/dem.2006.0026

Perri, T. (2019). Signaling and optimal sorting. *Journal of Economics*, *126*(2), 135–151. 10.1007/s00712-018-0618-0

Purkayastha, D. (2006). Norms of reciprocity and human capital formation in a poor patriarchal household. *The Journal of Socio-Economics*, *35*(1), 72–82. 10.1016/j.socec.2005.12.005

Raman, R., & Pramod, D. (2022). The role of predictive analytics to explain the employability of management graduates. *Benchmarking: An International Journal*, *29*(8), 2378–2396. 10.1108/BIJ-08-2021-0444

Rana Shahid Imdad, A., Mahmood, I., & Hamid, K. (2019). The impact of financial signaling and information asymmetries of macroeconomic covariates and debt vs. equity. *Review of Economics and Development Studies (Online)*, *5*(4), 891. 10.26710/reads.v5i4.876

Rao, S., Lee, K. B., Connelly, B., & Iyengar, D. (2018). Return time leniency in online retail: A signaling theory perspective on buying outcomes. *Decision Sciences*, *49*(2), 275–305. 10.1111/deci.12275

Ressler, R. W., Ackert, E., Ansari, A., & Crosnoe, R. (2020). Race/ethnicity, human capital, and the selection of young children into early childhood education. *Social Science Research*, *85*, 102364. 10.1016/j.ssresearch.2019.102364

Reuer, J., Tong, T., & Wu, C. (2012). A signaling theory of acquisition premiums: Evidence from IPO targets. *Academy of Management Journal*, *55*(3), 667–683. 10.5465/amj.2010.0259

Rutar, T. (2021). *Rational choice and democratic government: A sociological approach*. Routledge. 10.4324/9781003172574

Sabates, R., Zhao, Y. V., Mitchell, R., & Ilie, S. (2021). Understanding the external social benefits of education in Ethiopia: A contextual analysis using young lives. *Journal of Education Finance*, *47*(1), 45–70.

Sauer, S. J., Thomas-Hunt, M. C., & Morris, P. A. (2010). Too good to be true?: The unintended signaling effects of educational prestige on external expectations of team performance. *Organization Science*, *21*(5), 1108–1120. 10.1287/orsc.1090.0523

Schuessler, A. A., & Project Muse. (2000). *A logic of expressive choice*. Princeton University Press. 10.1515/9780691222417

Sehrawat, M., & Singh, S. K. (2019). Human capital and income inequality in India: Is there a nonlinear and asymmetric relationship? *Applied Economics*, *51*(39), 4325–4336. 10.1080/00036846.2019.1591605

Shafi, K., Hameed, Z., Qadri, U., & Nawab, S. (2018). Exploration of global brand value announcements and market reaction. *Administrative Sciences, 8*(3), 49. 10.3390/admsci8030049

Shah, M., & Steinberg, B. M. (2021). Workfare and human capital investment: Evidence from India. *The Journal of Human Resources, 56*(2), 380–405. 10.3368/jhr.56.2.1117-9201R2

Sharma, N., & Romero, M. (2022). Brand implications of advertising products with their reflections. *The Journal of Product & Brand Management, 31*(2), 310–321. 10.1108/JPBM-04-2020-2834

Slaughter, S. A., & Ang, S. (2007). Firm-specific human capital and compensation-organizational tenure profiles: An archival analysis of salary data for IT professionals. *Human Resource Management, 46*(3), 373. 10.1002/hrm.20169

Smith, A. (1776). *An inquiry into the nature and causes of the wealth of nations: Representative selections*. W. Strahan and T. Cadell.

Smith, V. O., & Smith, Y. S. (2011). Bias, history, and the Protestant Work Ethic. *Journal of Management History, 17,* 282–298 10.1108/17511341111141369.

Spence, A.M. (1972). *Market Signaling* (Publication No. 0232151) [Doctoral dissertation, Harvard University]. ProQuest Dissertations & Theses Global.

Spence, A. M. (1973). Job market signaling. *The Quarterly Journal of Economics, 87*(3), 355–374. 10.2307/1882010

Spring, J. H. (2015). *Economization of education: Human capital, global corporations, skills-based schooling* (1st ed.). Routledge. 10.4324/9781315730233

Stark, E., Poppler, P. P., & Murnane, J. A. (2011). Looking for evidence of human capital (or the lack thereof) in College/University degrees held by managerial level employees. *Journal of Behavioral and Applied Management, 13*(1), 60. 10.21818/001c.17870

Steigenberger, M., & Wilhelm, H. (2018). Extending signaling theory to rhetorical signals: Evidence from crowdfunding. *Organization Science (Providence, R.I.), 29*(3), 529–546. 10.1287/orsc.2017.1195

Stiglitz, J. E. (1979). Equilibrium in product markets with imperfect information. *The American Economic Review, 69*(2), 339–345.

Stiglitz, J. E. (2000). The contributions of the economics of information to twentieth century economics. *The Quarterly Journal of Economics, 115*(4), 1441–1478. 10.1162/003355300555015

Sturman, M. C., Walsh, K., & Cheramie, R. A. (2008). The value of human capital specificity versus transferability. *Journal of Management, 34*(2), 290–316. 10.1177/0149206307312509

Su, W., Peng, M. W., Tan, W., & Cheung, Y. (2016; 2014). The signaling effect of corporate social responsibility in emerging economies. *Journal of Business Ethics, 134*(3), 479–491. 10.1007/s10551-014-2404-4

Sun, S., Johanis, M., & Rychtář, J. (2019; 2020). Costly signalling theory and dishonest signalling. *Theoretical Ecology, 13*(1), 85–92. 10.1007/s12080-019-0429-0

Taneri, N., & De Meyer, A. (2017). Contract theory: Impact on biopharmaceutical alliance structure and performance. *Manufacturing & Service Operations Management, 19*(3), 453–471. 10.1287/msom.2017.0617

Thieme, S., Richter, M., & Ammann, C. (2022). Economic rationalities and notions of 'good cure and care'. *Medical Anthropology, 41*(4), 460–473. 10.1080/01459740.2022.2037082

Thomas, H., Smith, R. R., Diez, F., & Books I. (2014). *Human capital and global business strategy*. Cambridge University Press. 10.1017/CBO9781139519380

Tomaskovic-Devy, D., Thomas, M. & Johnson, K. (2005). Race and the accumulation of human capital across the career: A theoretical model and fixed-effects application. *The American Journal of Sociology, 111*(1), 58–89. 10.1086/431779

Treviqo, A. J., & Tilly, C. (2016). *George C. Homans: History, theory, and method*. Routledge. 10.4324/9781315634524

Tymon, A. (2013). The student perspective on employability. *Studies in Higher Education, 38*(6), 841–856. 10.1080/03075079.2011.604408

Utgard, J. (2018). Retail chains' corporate social responsibility communication. *Journal of Business Ethics, 147*(2), 385–400. 10.1007/s10551-015-2952-2

Van Belle, E., Caers, R., Cuypers, L., De Couck, M., Neyt, B., Van Borm, H., & Baert, S. (2020). What do student jobs on graduate CVs signal to employers? *Economics of Education Review, 75,* 1–19. 10.1016/j.econedurev.2020.101979.

van Hoorn, A. (2019). Cultural determinants of human capital accumulation: Evidence from the European social survey. *Journal of Comparative Economics, 47*(2), 429–440. 10.1016/j.jce.2019.01.004

Wang, Y., Yang, Y., Wang, X., Zheng, Q., & Peng, R. (2023). How do voice characteristics affect tourism interpretation purchases? An empirical study based on voice mining. *Journal of Travel Research.* 4728752211510. 10.1177/00472875221151070

Ward, H. (2002). Rational choice theory. In D. Marsh & G. Stoker (Eds.), *Theory and methods in political science.* Palgrave Macmillan.

Watson, N. (2008). Opportunity cost. *Business Review, 15*(2), 32–34.

Weber, M., & Kalberg, S. (2012). *The protestant ethic and the spirit of capitalism.* Routledge. 10.4324/9781315063645

Weber, M., & Zohn, H. (2017). *Max Weber: A biography* (2nd ed.). Taylor and Francis. 10.4324/9780203786109

Webster, J., & Trevino, L. K. (1995). Rational and social theories as complementary explanations of communication media choices: Two policy-capturing studies. *Academy of Management Journal, 38*(6), 1544–1572. 10.2307/256843

Weinstein, R. (2022). Local labor markets and human capital investments. *The Journal of Human Resources, 57*(5), 1498–1525. 10.3368/jhr.58.1.1119-10566R2

Wigley, S., & Akkoyunlu-Wigley, A. (2006). Human capabilities versus human capital: Guaging the value of education in developing countries. *Social Indicators Research, 78*(2), 287–304. 10.1007/s11205-005-0209-7

Wittek, R., Snijders, T. A. B., & Nee, V. (2013). *The handbook of rational choice social research.* Stanford Social Sciences, an imprint of Stanford University Press.

Wolhuter, C. C., & Niemczyk, E. K. (2023). Reframing the concept of globalization and human capital in contemporary education. *International Journal of Educational Research, 118.* 10.1016/j.ijer.2023.102157

Wong, S. (2006). *The foundations of Paul Samuelson's revealed preference theory: A study by the method of rational reconstruction* (Rev. ed.). Routledge. 10.4324/9780203462430

World Health Organization (24 May, 2022). *Tobacco.* World Health Organization. Retrieved from: https://www.who.int/news-room/fact-sheets/detail/tobacco

Wykstra, R. A. (1971). *Education and the economics of human capital.* Collier-Macmillan.

Xu, Y., & Ling, I. (2023). Effects of face masks and photo tags on nonverbal communication in service encounters. *Journal of Retailing and Consumer Services, 73.* 10.1016/j.jretconser.2023.103322

Young, L. A. (2016). *Rational choice theory and religion: Summary and assessment.* Routledge.

Zafirovski, M. (2019). Always rational choice theory? Lessons from conventional economics and their relevance and potential benefits for contemporary sociologists. *The American Sociologist, 50*(4), 509–547. 10.1007/s12108-019-9412-

Zhang, Z., & Jia, M. (2010). Using social exchange theory to predict the effects of high-performance human resource practices on corporate entrepreneurship: Evidence from China. *Human Resource Management, 49*(4), 743–765. 10.1002/hrm.20378

Zhang, Z., Wen, J., Wang, X., & Zhao, C. (2018). A novel crowd evaluation method for security and trustworthiness of online social networks platforms based on signaling theory. *Journal of Computational Science, 26,* 468–477. 10.1016/j.jocs.2017.05.018

Zhao, S. (2008). Application of human capital theory in China in the context of the knowledge economy. *International Journal of Human Resource Management, 19*(5), 802–817. 10.1080/09585190801991145

Zimmer, M., Salonen, A., & v. Wangenheim, F. (2020). Business solutions as market signals that facilitate product sales. *Industrial Marketing Management, 91,* 30–40. 10.1016/j.indmarman.2020.07.014

11 Organizational Studies

Sensemaking Theory

Definition and Overview

Sensemaking theory provides a lens through which to analyze and understand meaning-making processes – specifically, how individuals interpret messages from their environments, why they interpret messages as they do, and how those interpretations shape and reshape the environment in which those individuals interact (Weick, 1995). The sensemaking process itself is where meaning is made – individual identities and organizational changes are shaped, reshaped, or constrained through the sensemaking process (Weick et al., 2005). The sensemaking process is iterative, wherein actors develop definitions, or "sense" over time (Weick, 1995). The process of sensemaking is thus simultaneously anticipatory and retrospective – an attempt to reconcile what is happening with what has happened, and with all that will happen in the future (Weick et al., 2005).

In his foundational work *Sensemaking in Organizations,* Weick (1995) identified seven critical properties of sensemaking, which included:

1 Identity construction, which is the idea that identity shapes how people make sense, and that the process of sensemaking in turn further shapes identity
2 Retrospection, which refers to the process of making meaning of something after it takes place, which then shapes future meaning-making
3 Enactment, which is the idea that people shape their environments as they respond to them
4 Social activity, which refers to the idea that sensemaking processes are not solely individual, but are collectively influenced by others
5 Ongoing, meaning that sensemaking is a never-ending process
6 Extracted cues, which are "simple, familiar structures that are seeds from which people develop a larger sense of what may be occurring" (Weick, 1995, p. 50)
7 The preference of plausibility over accuracy, which refers to the idea that sensemaking may be distorted by individuals' understanding of what is possible, not what is necessarily true (Weick, 1995; Nardon & Hari, 2022).

In order for sensemaking to occur, it must be "triggered" by something. Sensemaking triggers include situations or events, such as the process of change or reform, in which individuals experience disruptions, ambiguities, uncertainties, or turbulence in their environments (Duncan, 1972; Starbuck & Milliken, 1988; Weick, 1988; Weick, 1995). In the sensemaking process, individuals gather signals about how they should act in particular contexts and make meaning from situations and events in context. Sensemaking is an

DOI: 10.4324/9781003261759-11

ongoing, retrospective process of organizing perceived social constructs that results in a coordinated system of action (Weick et al., 2005).

Although there is a focus on individual interpretation in sensemaking theory, the sensemaking process is not a purely individual exercise (Weick et al., 2005). How actors make sense of a sensemaking trigger, change, or reform is also influenced by their interactions with others in the organization (Coburn, 2001; Spillane, 1999); the organizational environment and the institutional and organizational norms (Yanow, 1996); and how the reform is communicated, including depth (Coburn, 2005), specificity (Hill, 2001), and degree of voluntariness (Coburn, 2005). Organizational culture, structure, and routines develop from individuals' "micro-momentary actions," which refers to how actors interpret information from the environment, make meaning from that information, and then act on those interpretations (Porac et al., 1989; Weick, 1995). "Micro-mechanisms" – individuals' interpretations and actions – produce change over time (Weick et al., 2005).

Sensemaking is mediated by prior knowledge and existing beliefs (Spillane et al., 2002; Weick, 1995). Individuals rely on preexisting knowledge frames – referred to as schemas, "frames of reference," or "worldviews" (Porac et al., 1989; Weick, 1995) – to make sense of disruptive events or reforms. As such, experiences, values, and emotions can bias interpretations of changes or reform events (Schmidt & Datnow, 2005; Spillane et al., 2002). Schemas include explanations or theories about how the world operates and encode expectations about people and their behaviors and about social situations (Spillane et al., 2002). Individuals access their existing schemas to "fill-in-the-blanks" when faced with ambiguity or uncertainty. What individuals expect can lead them to pay particular attention to aspects of a situation or event that confirm rather than challenge their expectations.

Individuals often draw on their existing knowledge frames in such a way that it fortifies their current practices (Spillane, 1999; Jennings & Spillane, 1997), rather than leading to substantive or revolutionary change. According to Weick et al. (2005), for example, "When something needs to change or when there are disruptions, people will look first for reasons that allow them to continue the interrupted activity" (p. 409). This process is sometimes referred to as "assimilation." However, individuals can also draw on their existing knowledge frames to engage in incremental change (Coburn, 2001). In some cases, the sensemaking process can also lead to a reconstruction of existing knowledge frames, resulting in substantive individual and organizational changes, a process that can be referred to as "accommodation" (Spillane et al., 2002).

Sensemaking theory explains how actors in organizations or groups make sense of new initiatives, both individually and collectively, and how that sensemaking process helps or hinders the successful implementation of policies, reforms, or other changes. Sensemaking theory can help researchers identify and understand the process of change and how the interaction of individual interpretations and organizational characteristics can shape whether and how change happens.

Background and Foundations

Sensemaking theory is grounded in ideas from organizational theory, psychology, sociology, and public policy. Some of the foundational ideas for sensemaking were introduced in organizational studies in the 1960s by Karl E. Weick, an American organizational theorist. The development of sensemaking theory and its increasing use in a variety of disciplines demonstrated a shift in how scholars think about organizations – from a focus on how specific actions shape organizations to a focus on how individual and collective meaning-making shape organizational structure and practice (Weick, 1993). In later work, Weick (1995) developed sensemaking theory to specifically focus on the meaning-making processes that individuals engage in and which shape individuals and organizations. The core idea of sensemaking theory as described by Weick is that it represents the process through which people make sense of the past to predict the future (Weick, 1995).

Key Terms and Concepts

Schemas are knowledge structures or existing knowledge frames that connect related concepts to make sense of the world and to make predictions (Spillane et al., 2002).

Assimilation is the process whereby actors attempt to fit reforms into their existing frameworks – to make the unfamiliar, familiar (Spillane et al., 2002). Assimilation conserves existing knowledge structures.

Accommodation is the restructuring of existing knowledge frames (Piaget, 1972; Spillane et al., 2002), which can lead to substantive changes and schema reconstruction.

Sensegiving is a process through which individuals attempt to influence others' meaning-making toward a more preferred construction of reality (Gioia & Chittipeddie, 1991, p. 442).

In Research

Although sensemaking theory emerges from organizational studies, it has been used across disciplines to understand the process of change, at both the individual and organizational levels. In education, for example, sensemaking theory has been used extensively to examine policy implementation in schools and classrooms (see Bingham & Ogunbowo Dimandja, 2017; Burch & Spillane, 2003; Coburn, 2001; 2005). In other disciplines, including psychology, business, and management studies, sensemaking theory has been used to understand how people make decisions and how those decisions shape individual and organizational practices toward particular outcomes (see Jensen et al., 2009; Stein, 2004; Weick, 1993).

Studies using sensemaking have addressed regular processes of implementation as well as crises and disasters. Bingham & Ogunbowo Dimandja (2017) draw on sensemaking theory – and the concept of schemas in particular – to understand differences in how newer teachers interpreted and enacted a technology-based instructional reform and how more experienced teachers interpreted and enacted the same reform. Stein (2004), employing a psychology-based approach, explored people's sensemaking processes in response to disaster (Three Mile Island) or potential disaster (Apollo 13), in order to examine how sensemaking helped people survive in disaster situations and how it hindered survival. Similarly, in a study of the Mann Gulch fire disaster, Weick (1993) used sensemaking from an organizational perspective to understand how organizations unravel, and what leads to organizational resilience. Sensemaking theory can also be used with other compatible theories. Jensen et al. (2009), for example, used sensemaking theory in conjunction with institutional theory to understand information system implementation in healthcare.

Strengths and Limitations

A strength of sensemaking theory is that it can help researchers to better understand the process of individual interpretation and filtering in studies of implementation and organizational change. A sensemaking analysis can help to integrate issues of meaning-making and mind (particularly beliefs, identity, and emotion) into studies of organizations in flux. Researchers can apply sensemaking theory to analyze micro-processes of individual and collective interpretation and understanding. Sensemaking theory can also help researchers in attending to the roles of emotion, identity, and external messaging, and can provide a framework to analyze multiple levels of change over time, as it allows the researcher to zoom in on individual processes, while also keeping an eye on shifting context. This may provide a more nuanced understanding of individual and organizational change.

However, sensemaking theory does not necessarily address issues of power and organizational structure, which can limit, or render useless, collective understanding (Weick, 1995). As Weick (1995) notes, "Sense may be in the eye of the beholder, but beholders vote and the majority rules" (p. 6). Sensemaking theorists often discuss the process of sensemaking, using words like "construct," "enact," and "generate," but rarely discuss the sensemaking process in terms such as "react," or "comply with," which suggests that sensemaking may not consider that individuals internalize or adopt what is communicated to them in a larger context (Weick et al., 2005).

Another significant limitation of sensemaking is that it may exaggerate individual agency, and as a result, may do little to address institutional influences or the wider societal context (Spillane et al., 2002). Conceiving of sensemaking this way

> neglects evidence showing that organizational members are socialized (indoctrinated) into expected sensemaking activities and that firm behavior is shaped by broad cognitive, normative, and regulatory forces that derive from and are enforced by powerful actors such as mass media, governmental agencies, professions, and interest groups. (Weick et al., 2005, p. 417)

Some scholars have suggested integrating sensemaking theory with other theories that are more focused on contextual, environmental, cultural, or societal level factors, such as institutional theory (Jensen et al., 2009) or cultural-historical activity theory (Bingham, 2017).

Key Theorist: Karl Weick (originating author).

Examples of Use in Research: Bingham and Ogunbowo Dimandja (2017); Burch and Spillane (2003); Helpap and Bekmeier-Feuerhahn (2016); Weick (1993).

Organizational Ambidexterity

Definition and Overview

Organizational ambidexterity refers to an organization's ability to manage conflicting pressures by leveraging existing capabilities, working within existing limitations, and exploring innovative practices to increase efficiency and effectiveness. Organizational ambidexterity can be defined as an organization's capacity and ability to concurrently engage in "competing, strategic acts" (Simsek et al., 2009, p. 865). The two major facets of organizational ambidexterity are exploitation – the ability to draw on existing resources, skills, and knowledge, to maintain efficient and effective practices – and exploration – the ability to innovate and make larger, future-oriented changes (Bodwell & Chermack, 2010). As a theory, organizational ambidexterity is a framework for understanding organizations' capacities to innovate and explore new opportunities for improvement in the face of institutional pressures, while also making use of existing capabilities and maintaining effective practices and efficiency (Levinthal & March, 1993; March, 1991; Raisch et al., 2009).

An organization's ability to be ambidextrous can help the organization improve outcomes and promote sustainability in shifting institutional and policy climates (Simsek et al., 2009). Organizational ambidexterity can also help organizations adapt to changing institutional climates and manage the demands of both efficiency and exploration/innovation (O'Reilly & Tushman, 2004; Tushman & O'Reilly, 1996). The ability to manage these multiple demands is critical for organizations because pursuing one goal at the expense of the other can cause a variety of issues. Too much focus on efficiency and exploiting existing capabilities can lead to an organization becoming obsolete or outdated. However, pursuing exploration and innovation at the expense of organizational efficiency can lead to falling behind in current needs, and to underdeveloped ideas (March, 1991; Simsek et al., 2009).

The culture and community structure of an organization are fundamental to an organization's ability to be ambidextrous (Gibson & Birkinshaw, 2004). The organizational structure, and the community types developed and nurtured (Adler et al., 2015), the interdependence of and relationships between individuals in the organization (Raisch et al., 2009), and the extent of the organization's shared vision, social support, and trust (Ghoshal & Bartlett, 1997) can support or hinder ambidexterity. Indeed, different types of community have been linked with how an organization can manage conflicting pressures. Collaborative community, for example, is seen as ideal for an ambidexterity because it prioritizes collegiality, shared contributions, and intentional cooperation, instead of hierarchical leadership structures. Strong, internal community structures with high levels of trust have also been identified as being an important mechanism of ambidexterity because these kinds of communities are seen as being better able to make the decisions needed to increase ambidexterity (Raisch & Birkinshaw, 2008).

Like other theories discussed in this book, organizational ambidexterity can be used practically and theoretically. Organizational ambidexterity provides both a descriptive and a prescriptive analytical lens. In and of itself, organizational ambidexterity can be conceived of as a goal for any organization aiming to manage complex and/or conflicting pressures. This includes corporations and other organizations like schools or governmental organizations. The ability of an organization to be ambidextrous, and its capacity to engage in actions that have been shown to promote ambidexterity, can help support organizational change, improvement, and sustainability (Bingham & Burch, 2019). As a theoretical lens, organizational ambidexterity can support researchers in asking the right questions in their research on organizations, and in identifying practices that support ambidexterity as well as practices that may impede ambidexterity (Bingham & Burch, 2019). Drawing on organizational ambidexterity as a framework allows researchers to account for the complexity and agency involved in implementing changes or policies in a variety of organizations.

Organizational ambidexterity can also provide a framework for developing research questions, focusing the research, and classifying an organization's ambidextrous practices and structures. With organizational ambidexterity as a theoretical frame, individual-level and organizational-level actions could be categorized according to how they support or hinder experimentation with new practices and resources and efficient utilization of current practices and resources (Bingham & Burch, 2019). Bingham and Burch (2019) introduced a categorization matrix that can be used to situate organizational structures and practices and individual activities that support or thwart ambidexterity (see Figure 11.1).

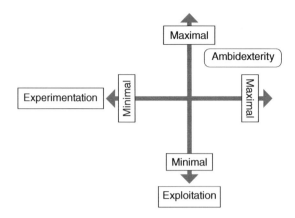

Figure 11.1 Organizational ambidexterity matrix. Adapted from Bingham & Burch (2019).

The bottom left quadrant indicates low levels of experimentation and efficient use of existing capabilities. The bottom right quadrant indicates high levels of experimentation, with low levels of efficiency. The top left quadrant represents high levels of efficiency with low levels of experimentation. Finally, the top right quadrant represents high levels of both experimentation *and* efficient use of existing resources and capabilities, indicating ambidexterity. Using this organizational ambidexterity matrix could help researchers identify areas of growth and action items for organizations and specify recommendations for practitioners and policymakers.

Background and Foundations

The term "organizational ambidexterity" was coined by Robert Duncan (1976). In the years since, scholars in organizational studies have argued that an organization's success and longevity depend on the capacity for ambidexterity (Levinthal & March, 1993; March, 1991). This has led to the use of organizational ambidexterity as a theory for understanding, explaining, and predicting organizational effectiveness and sustainability, as well as its use as a guiding framework of practical strategies for organizations to become ambidextrous.

Further fleshing out ideas about complex organizational environments managing conflicting pressures, March (1991) noted that a fundamental challenge facing organizations was the ability to use existing assets while also exploring new capabilities (O'Reilly & Tushman, 2013). March (1991) argued that honing existing knowledge and skills (termed "exploitation" in much of the work on ambidexterity) and experimenting with new knowledge and practices (termed "exploration") are two fundamentally distinct processes that can sometimes lead to tension or inefficiencies. Organizations have to be able to do both to perform well long-term (March, 1991). Building on Duncan (1976) and March (1991), Tushman and O'Reilly (1996) argued that ambidexterity was a requirement for the long-term success of an organization. Innovation can be time-consuming, with uncertain results, but without it, an organization can become stagnant. Pursuing the efficient use of existing resources and competencies coupled with the exploration of new practices – ambidexterity – is necessary and beneficial to long-term performance (Papachroni et al., 2015).

Key Terms and Concepts

Ambidexterity is an organization's ability to manage the pressures of using existing resources to maintain current levels of efficiency alongside processes of change, experimentation, and innovation (Raisch et al., 2009).

Differentiation is the degree of separation between exploitation and exploration into distinct organizational units (Raisch et al., 2009).

Exploitation, in an organizational ambidexterity framework, refers to an organization's orientation toward and ability to leverage existing competencies to create value and accomplish incremental change (Bodwell & Chermack, 2010).

Exploration refers to processes of innovation and risk-taking in an organization (Bodwell & Chermack, 2010).

Sequential Ambidexterity is when organizations are able to be ambidextrous due to shifting their structures over time.

Structural (Simultaneous) Ambidexterity is when organizations are able to be ambidextrous by having subunits dedicated to each goal (exploitation and exploration).

In Research

Organizational ambidexterity has been used extensively in organizational studies as a framework describing an ideal organizational state. As such, many researchers have used organizational ambidexterity to describe specific organizational structures and practices, understand the factors present in an organization that lead to an ambidextrous state, as well as to identify particular strategies for achieving ambidexterity. For example, Adler and colleagues (2013; 2015) focused on the kinds of community that can foster ambidexterity, finding that collaborative forms of community are most effective in becoming ambidextrous. Other researchers have identified strategies and practices like scenario planning as possible organizational components that can lead to ambidexterity (Bodwell & Chermack, 2010).

Organizational ambidexterity has also been used in other disciplines, to understand organizational effectiveness and structures that promote change. In education, for example, Bingham and Burch (2019) used an organizational ambidexterity framework to better understand how schools manage complex policy pressures. In their research, they found that schools that developed and supported a collaborative community structure over a more top-down, hierarchal organizational structure were better able to manage accountability pressures alongside innovation. Bingham and Burch also used this study to argue for the use of organizational ambidexterity as a framework for understanding policy implementation across disciplines.

Strengths and Limitations

One strength of organizational ambidexterity is that it supports researchers and organizational communities in understanding and embracing complexity (Bingham & Burch, 2019). Practically, because an organizational ambidexterity lens embraces complexity, while also offering prescriptive practices for how organizations can draw on participants' perspectives and knowledge, the concept of organizational ambidexterity can push organizations to distribute power and value the knowledge of its actors (Bingham & Burch, 2019; Tesar & Arndt, 2017). An organizational ambidexterity lens presses researchers to acknowledge and examine the tension between experimentation and efficiency, examine how organizational actors navigate this tension, and develop recommendations for ambidextrous practices so that organizations can successfully navigate this tension.

A limitation of an organizational ambidexterity framework is a lack of definitional clarity (O'Reilly & Tushman, 2013). There is some confusion in the literature around what ambidexterity means exactly, as well as what specifically the distinction is between exploitation and exploration (O'Reilly & Tushman, 2004; 2013). Broad application of the term ambidexterity has diluted its meaning. Further, it has not been used extensively in analyses of non-profit and governmental organizations (Bingham & Burch, 2019). Scholars have also argued that research drawing on organizational ambidexterity has yet to really flesh out the role of senior leadership in promoting ambidexterity (O'Reilly & Tushman, 2013).

Key Theorists: Robert Duncan; James March; Charles O'Reilly; Michael Tushman.

Examples of Use in Research: Adler et al. (2013); Bingham & Burch (2019).

Organizational Learning Theory

Definition and Overview

Organizational learning theory is focused on how organizations remain competitive in their given fields by adjusting organizational goals and actions, and on how they make those adjustments. The process of organizational learning involves making inferences from past behavior and historical organizational context, and using those inferences to guide current organizational behavior (Levitt & March, 1988). Ultimately, organizations learn by "encoding inferences from history into routines that guide behavior" (p. 320). Organizational learning theory argues that organizations change in response to direct experience, trial-and-error, and paradigm shifts.

Organizational learning occurs when an organization has the ability to recognize and correct errors, which implies that organizations must also know when they are *not* able to recognize and correct problems (Argyris, 1977). Argyris (1977; 1982) identifies two types of organizational learning, based on this assumption. First, there is single-loop learning, which Argyris (1982) describes as "designed to identify and correct errors so the job gets done and the action remains within stated policy guidelines" (p. 4). Most organizational learning is single-loop learning. Double-loop learning involves questioning the original goals of the organization and how those goals may need to be adjusted to correct errors (Argyris, 1982). Argyris argues that organizational structures and procedures often discourage double-loop learning. Double-loop learning requires changes in understanding and behavior – a paradigm reconstruction (Crossan et al., 1995). However, Huber (1991) has suggested that there is no practical difference between single- and double-loop learning. Organizational learning can further be classified as incremental or transformational (Crossan et al., 1995).

Organizational learning can result from a variety of internal and external practices, structures, and pressures. Cangelosi and Dill (1965) argued that organizational learning is a result of stress on the organization. They identified four phases of organizational learning, which included an initial phase, a searching phase, a comprehending phase, and a consolidating phase. They further argued that organizational learning is sporadic and occurs in steps, rather than being gradual and continuous. Further, organizational learning is related to success and failure, suggesting that failure leads to organizational change. Organizational learning theorists maintain that although learning can occur spontaneously and intuitively, systems can be developed that support better organizational learning (Daft & Huber, 1987, p. 31).

The concept of routines is critical to organizational learning and refers to rules, norms, procedures, and strategies present in an organization, alongside the belief structures, knowledge, and cultures that support or challenge any formal routines (Levitt & March, 1988). Routines are transmitted through "socialization, education, imitation, professionalization, personnel movement, mergers, and acquisitions" (p. 230). They are a part of the organization itself and are not just present in the individuals in the organization; thus, routines endure turnover. Routines change as a result of experience and learning in the organization.

Three assumptions of organizational behavior form the basis for organizational learning theory (Levitt & March, 1988). First, organizational behavior is based on routines. Similar to ideas in institutional theory (see Chapter 4), organizational learning holds that organizational decisions and behaviors reflect ideas of legitimacy and appropriateness in the field, rather than a logical assessment of consequences (DiMaggio & Powell, 1983, 1991; Levitt & March, 1988). Second, organizational actions are dependent on organizational history. Organizational routines are more informed by past actions than they are informed by anticipation of future needs. Organizational routines and behaviors change incrementally in response to feedback (Levitt & March, 1988, p. 320). Finally, organizational behavior is oriented to particular goals and targets and is shaped by organizational outcomes – the success or failure in achieving those targets (Levitt & March, 1988).

Organizational learning is useful for researchers who are interested in studying the mechanisms of learning and change at the organizational level, as well as how individual learning and actions at the individual level may impact changes in routines and practices at the organizational level. Organizational learning theory also provides clear categorizations of types and processes of organizational learning, including single- and double-loop learning, and the phases of organizational learning.

Background and Foundations

Organizational learning theory is grounded in cognitive and social psychology (Fauske & Raybould, 2005). The concept of organizational learning has been discussed in the organizational studies literature since the 1960s (Cangelosi & Dill, 1965). Organizational learning theory was developed to emphasize the roles of routines and ecological learning over theoretical models that focus solely on individual learning within organizations (Levitt & March, 1988). Organizational learning theory thus reflects a dualistic focus on both the structural and social cognitive systems of organizations. Recent strands of organizational learning theory have expanded to focus on organizational learning from experience, trial-and-error learning, and learning under ambiguous conditions (Levinthal & March, 1993; Levitt & March, 1988; Honig, 2008).

In early conceptions of organizational learning theory, organizational learning was defined as the capacity of an organization to correct errors (Argyris, 1977), but this definition has expanded somewhat to include the development and evolution of organizational knowledge and routines and the broader concept of organizational change (Duncan & Weiss, 1979; Crossan et al., 1995).

Organizational learning theory has reflected the varying views of organizational theorists, including those who have emphasized individual learning within organizations and those who see organizational learning as reflective of collective interpretations and actions (Crossan et al., 1995). Indeed, some scholars of organizational learning theory have focused on how individuals learn in organizations and the implications that have for organizational change (e.g., March & Olsen, 1975), while others have emphasized the role of collective learning and learning in groups (e.g., Daft & Huber, 1987). However, Crossan et al. (1995) argue that "research focusing solely on individual learning refers to learning within organizations as opposed to organizational learning" (p. 347). Ultimately, both individual and organizational learning are inextricably related. Angyris and Schön (1978) note that "there is no organizational learning without individual learning, and that individual learning is a necessary but insufficient condition for organizational learning" (p. 20).

Key Terms and Concepts

Organizational learning is the "process within the organization by which knowledge about action-outcome relationships and the effect of the environment of these relationships is developed" (Duncan & Weiss, 1979, p. 84). Organizational learning can also refer to an organization's ability to recognize and correct errors (Argyris, 1977), to improve organizational performance (Cangelosi & Dill, 1965), or to organizational change more generally.

Routines refer to "forms, rules, procedures, conventions, strategies, and technologies around which organizations are constructed and through which they operate" as well as the "structure of beliefs, frameworks, paradigms, codes, cultures, and knowledge that buttress, elaborate, and contradict the formal routines" (Levitt & March, 1988, p. 320).

In Research

Organizational learning theory has been used in the study of organizations ranging from schools to corporations to the military, in order to understand various characteristics of organizations and organizational outcomes. Joo and Park (2010), for example, used aspects of organizational learning theory to understand career satisfaction and turnover. Organizational learning theory has also been used extensively to understand innovation in organizational contexts and the relationship between aspects of organizational learning and the capacity to innovate. Jiménez-Jiménez and Sanz-Valle (2011), for example, used structural equation modeling to examine data from more than 400 Spanish firms and found that organizational learning influences innovation and that both organizational learning and innovation positively influence performance.

Organizational learning theory can also be used to understand specific ways in which organizational learning is achieved as well as to identify challenges in organizational learning and change. In education, for example, Fauske and Raybould (2005) drew on organizational learning theory to understand the implementation of instructional technology, and how that demonstrated a process of organizational learning. They found that organizational learning in an elementary school was influenced by "the priority of the learning in the organization, consistency and breadth of information distribution, unpredictability or uncertainty, the ease of learning new routines (how to) and the difficulty of learning new conceptual frameworks (why)" (Fauske & Raybould, 2005, p. 22). In another educational study, Honig (2008) drew on sociocultural learning theories and organizational learning theories to develop a framework for examining learning in school district central offices.

Strengths and Limitations

One of the key strengths of organizational learning theory is its broad applicability across disciplines and across many different types of organizations. Organizational learning theory is one of the more far-reaching theories because of its wide-ranging applicability, and because it can look at learning not only at the organizational level but also at the aggregate effects of individual learning.

Some of the identified limitations of organizational learning theory include inconsistent terminology and a lack of explicit assumptions (Crossan et al., 1995), as well as variations in the understanding of organizational learning across disciplines (Easterby-Smith, 1997). However, some researchers have argued that this ambiguity allows for greater applicability across disciplines (Easterby-Smith, 1997).

Key Theorists: Chris Argyris; Vincent E. Cangelosi & William R. Dill; Karl Weick.

Examples of Use in Research: Fauske and Raybould (2005), García-Morales et al. (2006); Honig (2008); Jiménez-Jiménez and Sanz-Valle (2011); Joo and Park (2010).

References

Adler, P. S., & Heckscher, C. (2013). Toward collaborative, ambidextrous enterprise. *Universia Business Review, 40*, 34–51.

Adler, P. S., Heckscher, C., & McCarthy, J. E. (2015). The mutations of professional responsibility: Toward collaborative community. In D. Mitchell & R. Ream (Eds.), *Professional responsibility* (pp. 309–326). Springer.

Argyris, C. (1977). Organizational learning and management information systems. *Accounting, Organizations and Society, 2*(2), 113–123.

Argyris, C. (1982). Organizational learning and management information systems. *ACM SIGMIS Database: The Database for Advances in Information Systems, 13*(2–3), 3–11.

Angyris, C., & Schön, D. A. (1978). *Organizational learning: A theory of action perspective.* Addison-Wesley.

Bingham, A. J. (2017). CHAT and sensemaking: An inclusive frame of analysis for investigating educational change. Paper presented in a featured session at the annual meeting of the American Educational Research Association (AERA).

Bingham, A. J., & Ogunbowo Dimandja, O. (2017). Staying on track: Examining teachers' experiences in a personalized learning model. *Journal of Ethnographic and Qualitative Research, 12*(2), 75–96.

Bingham, A. J., & Burch, P. (2019). Introducing organizational ambidexterity as a lens for policy research. *Policy Futures in Education, 17*(3), 402–420. 10.1177/1478210318813269

Bodwell, W., & Chermack, T. J. (2010). Organizational ambidexterity: Integrating deliberate and emergent strategy with scenario planning. *Technological Forecasting and Social Change, 77*(2), 193–202.

Burch, P., & Spillane, J. P. (2003). Elementary school leadership strategies and subject matter: Reforming mathematics and literacy instruction. *The Elementary School Journal, 103*, 519–535.

Cangelosi, V. E., & Dill, W. R. (1965). Organizational learning: Observations toward a theory. *Administrative Science Quarterly, 10*, 175–203.

Coburn, C. E. (2001). Collective sensemaking about reading: How teachers mediate reading policy in their professional communities. *Educational Evaluation and Policy Analysis, 23*(2), 145–170.

Coburn, C. (2005). Shaping teacher sensemaking: School leaders and the enactment of reading policy. *Educational Policy, 19*(3), 476–509.

Crossan, M. M., Lane, H. W., White, R. E., & Djurfeldt, L. (1995). Organizational learning: Dimensions for a theory. *The International Journal of Organizational Analysis, 3*(4), 337–360.

Daft, R. L., & Huber, G. P. (1987). How organizations learn: A communications framework. *Journal of Organizational Change Management, 5*, 1–36.

DiMaggio, P. J., & Powell, W. W. (1983). The Iron cage revisited: Institutional isomorphism and collective rationality in organizational fields. *American Sociological Review, 48*(2), 147. 10.23 07/2095101

DiMaggio, P. J., & Powell, W. W. (Eds.). (1991). *The new institutionalism in organizational analysis.* University of Chicago Press.

Dixon, N. M. (1992). Organizational learning: A review of the literature with implications for HRD professionals. *Human Resource Development Quarterly, 3*(1), 29–49.

Duncan, R. B. (1972). Characteristics of organizational environments and perceived environmental uncertainty. *Administrative Science Quarterly, 17*(3), 313–327.

Duncan, R. B. (1976). The ambidextrous organization: Designing dual structures for innovation. *The Management of Organization, 1*, 167–188.

Duncan, R. B., & Weiss, A. (1979). Organizational learning: Implications for organizational design. In B. Straw (Ed.), *Research in organizational behavior.* JAI Press.

Easterby-Smith, M. (1997). Disciplines of organizational learning: Contributions and critiques. *Human Relations, 50*(9), 1085–1113.

Fauske, J. R., & Raybould, R. (2005) Organizational learning theory in schools. *Journal of Educational Administration, 43*(1), 22–40.

García-Morales, V. J., Llorens-Montes, F. J., & Verdú-Jover, A. J. (2006). Antecedents and consequences of organizational innovation and organizational learning in entrepreneurship. *Industrial Management & Data Systems, 106*(1), 21–42.

Ghoshal, S., & Bartlett, C. A. (1997). *The individualized corporation.* Harper Collins.

Gibson, C. B., & Birkinshaw, J. (2004). The antecedents, consequences, and mediating role of organizational ambidexterity. *Academy of Management Journal, 47*(2), 209–226.

Gioia, D. A., & Chittipeddi, K. (1991). Sensemaking and sense giving in strategic change initiation. *Strategic Management Journal, 12*(6), 433–448.

Helpap, S., & Bekmeier-Feuerhahn, S. (2016). Employees' emotions in change: Advancing the sensemaking approach. *Journal of Organizational Change Management, 29*, 903–916.

Hill, H. C. (2001). Policy is not enough: Language and the interpretation of state standards. *American Educational Research Journal, 38*(2), 289–318.

Hogan, S. J., & Coote, L. V. (2014). Organizational culture, innovation, and performance: A test of Schein's model. *Journal of Business Research, 67*(8), 1609–1621.

Honig, M. I. (2008). District central offices as learning organizations: How sociocultural and organizational learning theories elaborate district central office administrators' participation in teaching and learning improvement efforts. *American Journal of Education, 114*(4), 627–664.

Huber, G. P. (1991). Organizational learning: The contributing processes and the literatures. *Organization Science, 2*(1), 88–115.

Jennings, N., & Spillane, J. (1997). Aligned instructional policy and ambitious pedagogy: Exploring instructional reform from the classroom perspective. *Teachers College Record, 98*(3), 449–479.

Jensen, T. B., Kjærgaard, A., & Svejvig, P. (2009). Using institutional theory with sensemaking theory: A case study of information system implementation in healthcare. *Journal of Information Technology, 24*(4), 343–353.

Jiménez-Jiménez, D., & Sanz-Valle, R. (2011). Innovation, organizational learning, and performance. *Journal of Business Research, 64*(4), 408–417.

Joo, B. K., & Park, S. (2010). Career satisfaction, organizational commitment, and turnover intention: The effects of goal orientation, organizational learning culture and developmental feedback. *Leadership & Organization Development Journal, 31*(6), 482–500.

Levinthal, D. A., & March, J. G. (1993). The myopia of learning. *Strategic Management Journal, 14*(S2), 95–112.

Levitt, B., & March, J. G. (1988). Organizational learning. *Annual Review of Sociology, 14*(1), 319–338.

Magala, S. J. (1997). Karl E. Weick: Sensemaking in organizations. *Organization Studies, 18*(2), 317–338. 10.1177/017084069701800206

March, J. G., & Olsen, J. P. (1975). The uncertainty of the past: Organizational learning under ambiguity. *European Journal of Political Research, 3*(2), 147–171.

Maitlis, S., Vogus, T. J., & Lawrence, T. B. (2013). Sensemaking and emotion in organizations. *Organizational Psychology Review, 3*(3), 222–247. 10.1177/2041386613489062

March, J. G. (1991). Exploration and exploitation in organizational learning. *Organization Science, 2*(1), 71–87.

Nardon, L., & Hari, A. (2022). The sensemaking perspective. In *Making sense of immigrant work integration: An organizing framework* (pp. 15–30). Springer International Publishing.

O'Reilly, C. A., & Tushman, M. L. (2004). The ambidextrous organization. *Harvard Business Review, 82*(4), 74.

O'Reilly, C. A., & Tushman, M. L. (2013). Organizational ambidexterity: Past, present, and future. *Academy of Management Perspectives, 27*(4), 324–338.

Odden, T. O. B., & Russ, R. S. (2019). Defining sensemaking: Bringing clarity to a fragmented theoretical construct. *Science Education, 103*(1), 187–205. 10.1002/sce.21452

Papachroni, A., Heracleous, L., & Paroutis, S. (2015). Organizational ambidexterity through the lens of paradox theory building a novel research agenda. *The Journal of Applied Behavioral Science, 51*(1), 71–93.

Piaget, J. (1972). *The psychology of the child*. Basic Books.

Porac, J. F., Thomas, H., & Baden-Fuller, C. (1989). Competitive groups as cognitive communities: The case of Scottish knitwear manufacturers. *Journal of Management Studies, 26*(4), 397–416.

Raisch, S., & Birkinshaw, J. (2008). Organizational ambidexterity: Antecedents, outcomes, and moderators. *Journal of Management, 34*, 375–409.

Raisch, S., Birkinshaw, J., Probst, G., & Tushman, M. L. (2009). Organizational ambidexterity: Balancing exploitation and exploration for sustained performance. *Organization Science, 20*(4), 685–695.

Schein, E. H. (1992). *Organizational culture and leadership*. Jossey-Bass.

Schein, E. H. (1996). Culture: The missing concept in organization studies. *Administrative Science Quarterly, 41*, 229–240.

Schein, E. H. (2010). *Organizational culture and leadership*. John Wiley & Sons.

Schmidt, M., & Datnow, A. (2005). Teachers' sense-making about comprehensive school reform: The influence of emotions. *Teaching and Teacher Education, 21*(8), 949–965.

Schwandt, D., & Marquardt, M. J. (1999). *Organizational learning*. CRC Press.

Simsek, Z., Heavey, C., Veiga, J. F., & Souder, D. (2009). A typology for aligning organizational ambidexterity's conceptualizations, antecedents, and outcomes. *Journal of Management Studies, 46*(5), 864–894.

Spillane, J. P. (1999). External reform initiatives and teachers' efforts to reconstruct their practice: The mediating role of teachers' zones of enactment. *Journal of Curriculum Studies, 31*(2), 143–175.

Spillane, J. P. (2000). Cognition and policy implementation: District policymakers and the reform of mathematics education. *Cognition and Instruction, 18*(2), 141–179.

Spillane, J. P., Reiser, B. J., & Reimer, T. (2002). Policy implementation and cognition: Reframing and refocusing implementation research. *Review of Educational Research, 72*(3), 387–431. 10.3102/00346543072003387

Starbuck, W. H., & Milliken, F. J. (1988). Executives' perceptual filters: What they notice and how they make sense. In D. C. Hambrick (Ed.), *The executive effect: Concepts and methods for studying top managers* (pp. 35–65). JAI.

Stein, M. (2004). The critical period of disasters: Insights from sense-making and psychoanalytic theory. *Human Relations, 57*(10), 1243–1261.

Tesar, M., & Arndt, S. (2017). Cross-cultural complexities of educational policies. *Policy Futures in Education, 15*, 665–669.

Tushman, M. L., & O'Reilly, C. A. (1996). The ambidextrous organization: Managing evolutionary and revolutionary change. *California Management Review, 38*, 1–23.

Weick, K. E. (1969). *The psychology of organizing* (1st ed.). Addison-Wesley Pub. Co.

Weick, K. E. (1979). *The psychology of organizing* (2nd ed.). McGraw-Hill.

Weick, K. E. (1988). Enacted sensemaking in crisis situations. *Journal of Management Studies, 25*(4), 305–317.

Weick, K. E. (1993). The collapse of sensemaking in organizations: The Mann Gulch disaster. *Administrative Science Quarterly, 4*(38), 628–652.

Weick, K. E. (1995). *Sensemaking in organizations*. Sage.

Weick, K. E., Sutcliffe, K. M., & Obstfeld, D. (2005). Organizing and the process of sensemaking. *Organization Science, 16*(4), 409–421. 10.1287/orsc.1050.0133

Yanow, D. (1996). *How does a policy mean?: Interpreting policy and organizational actions*. Georgetown University Press.

12 Business

Stakeholder Theory

Definition and Overview

Stakeholder Theory (ST) focuses on how individuals in organizations, particularly managers, make decisions to drive economic value creation and manage the expectations of all stakeholders (Friedman & Miles, 2002; Amis et al., 2020). Stakeholders in a corporate context include not only shareholders (providing capital), but also employees, suppliers (providing goods and services), customers, and communities. Stakeholder theory holds that incentives and discipline should be deployed across stakeholders to achieve successful outcomes or goals for the corporation or organization (Freeman et al., 2018).

ST is concerned with organizational management and corporate governance (Freeman, 1984; Phillips et al., 2003; Fassin, 2011) and is most recently associated with the Corporate Social Responsibility movement, which encourages corporations to prioritize more than profitability, adding an element of moral responsibility and other non-economic values (Mitchell et al., 1997). While commonly associated with business firms, ST also applies to other organizations, such as non-profits and government agencies (Phillips et al., 2003; Freeman et al., 2018). Stakeholder Theory was developed to answer three questions:

1 How can corporations create value?
2 How can we understand ethics in capitalism?
3 What should we be teaching in business schools?

ST provides clear definitions for stakeholders and their interests, categorizes types of stakeholders, and delineates the differences between stakeholder and shareholder. Employees, shareholders, surrounding communities, suppliers, and customers make up the primary stakeholder group. While shareholder's interests often lie in economic return on investments, stakeholder's interests go beyond corporate financial success to interests that may be non-economic (Amis et al., 2020). For example, employees might focus on career development and work-life balance. For the communities in which organizations are situated, their interests might be related to consistent employment and manufacturing decisions that do not negatively impact the environment in which they live. Customer interest might be in the purchase of safe and value-rich products or services. Lastly, supplier interests may lie in a reciprocal, stable, and long-term relationship with the corporation that creates win-win situations for both parties (Amis et al., 2020).

Primary stakeholders can be categorized as dormant or definitive, depending on the situation. For example, shareholders may be dormant until there is a crisis which significantly

DOI: 10.4324/9781003261759-12

reduces the value of their investment. Then they may move from dormant to definitive by adding an element of attention, accountability, noise, and urgency, occasionally in partnership with other parties such as the government and media (Mitchell et al., 1997).

Beyond the primary stakeholder group, there are secondary stakeholders that are more influential than value-add to the corporation (Mitchell et al., 1997). This group includes the media, special interest groups, advocate groups, governments, and competitors. Secondary stakeholders have the potential to significantly impact the corporation and can be categorized as dangerous, inactive, or dormant, depending on their salience. A dangerous stakeholder is one who can exercise a strong coercive action that could inflict damage on a company. Examples could be employees sabotaging a company or activists protesting with work-stalling strikes (Mitchell et al., 1997). A dormant stakeholder has the power to significantly impact the firm, but is not currently directly active in influencing the firm. An example might be a group of laid off employees who file a class action lawsuit that could result in high financial damages and bad press (Mitchell et al., 1997).

Stakeholder Theory has evolved into three distinct types: Descriptive, normative, and instrumental (Donaldson & Preston, 1995; Fassin, 2011). Descriptive ST applies to real-life situations to describe what *is*, or reality. Normative ST describes the application as it *should be*, or the ideal. Instrumental ST focuses on how managers "attend to the needs of the stakeholders *as a means to achieving* other organizational goals such as profit or shareholder wealth" (Phillips et al., 2003, p. 479). Instrumental ST is about the practical application – using ST as a means to an end.

Beyond stakeholders, there are also stakewatchers, stakekeepers, and stakeseekers (Holzer, 2008; Fassin, 2009). Stakewatchers are advocates representing employees (i.e., unions) or consumers (e.g., Consumer Reports) (Fassin, 2009). Stakekeepers are regulatory agencies who are typically dormant until there are concerns, such as the SEC or the media (Holzer, 2008). And finally, stakeseekers are those who desire to impose influence on a corporation, but who do not have an official relationship or role (Fassin, 2011).

Stakeholder Theory can support researchers in identifying, classifying, and better understanding the various interests and influences of stakeholders in organizational contexts, particularly corporate and other business organizations. ST can help researchers make sense of and analyze the relationships and interconnectedness among those with the highest (primary) stakes in the business or organization as well as their value contribution or creation (Freeman et al., 2020).

Background and Foundations

Stakeholder Theory grew out of investment capitalism, which put forth the idea that "the one and only obligation of business is to maximize its profits while engaging in open and free competition without deception or fraud" (Friedman, 1962, p. 133). However, power, incentives, and the prioritization of shareholder returns can result in unethical and illegal actions, decisions, and activities within corporate America. As society became sensitive to the moral behavior and environmental impact of businesses, a new theory evolved to better understand how businesses organize and create value: Conscious Capitalism, also known as Stakeholder Capitalism (Freeman et al., 2007; Freeman et al., 2018).

Stakeholder Theory (ST) was originally coined by Edward Freeman in 1984 in his text *Strategic Management: A Stakeholder Approach*. ST is rooted in Agency Theory, which holds that there are two parties in a cooperative agreement, a principal and an agent, where one (the agent) represents the other (principal) in common everyday work (Amis et al., 2020). Agency Theory is typically about the two parties of corporations and shareholders, or those providing capital in support of the business in the hope that there will be a value-added return on investment. ST extends Agency Theory by recognizing the many stakeholders affected by and involved in creating value by working in cooperation with each other. ST broadens corporate value creation beyond shareholder return, suggesting that the world of business is more complex than profitability (Freeman et al., 2018).

Key Terms and Concepts

A **stake** goes beyond ownership and can be a moral, legal, or other claim on the corporation or organization (Mitchell et al., 1997).

Stakeholder can mean "any group or individual who can affect or is affected by the achievement of the organization's objectives" (Freeman, 1984, p. 46), or, more simply, "groups to whom the corporation is responsible" (Alkhafaji, 1989, p. 36). There are two layers, also known as primary and secondary stakeholders (see Figure 12.1).

A **claimant** is any person or organization that stakes a concrete claim, interest, or right in the corporation (Freeman, 1984); often claimants are primary stakeholders such as shareholders, suppliers, employees, customers, and the community.

An **influencer** is any person or organization that can influence or be influenced by the corporation (Freeman, 1984). Influencers do not have a direct stake in creating value for the firm (Freeman et al., 2018). This is a list of groups "twice-removed" from the corporation and secondary stakeholders, like the media, special interest groups (e.g., Greenpeace), advocate organizations (e.g., unions), governments, and competitors (Fassin, 2011; Freeman et al., 2018).

Stakekeepers are advocates, regulators, or gatekeepers, who do not generally have a direct stake or impact (Fassin, 2011; Holzer, 2008). An example is the Securities and Exchange Commission (SEC) in the United States, which is a stakekeeper for shareholders, and to some degree, employees and customers. This group is capable of placing

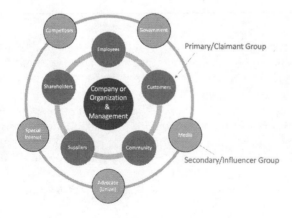

Figure 12.1 Example of stakeholder theory layers. Adapted from Freeman (2010).

constraints on the corporation or organization. The media can also be a stakekeeper by holding corporations accountable.

Stakewatchers are influencers who often serve as advocates for the claimants, such as unions or consumer watch groups (Fassin, 2009). Stakewatchers monitor their constituent stakes with care, guarding the interests of those with a direct stake (Fassin, 2011). The firm has no official responsibility to the stakewatchers, however, stakewatchers can do significant harm to a corporation's reputation and business.

Stakeseekers are those who wish to achieve stakeholder status, or wish to have voice in influencing the corporation (Holzer, 2008). These are also known as "stake imposters" (Fassin, 2011, p. 41).

In Research

Researchers in the social sciences, as well as in business and economics research have used ST to consider how corporations manage the relationships between the stakeholders (e.g., Bridoux & Stoelhorst, 2014) as well as how the characteristics of CEOs may impact corporate social responsibility and irresponsibility (Tang et al., 2015). Researchers have also studied particular stakeholders to better understand the relationships among different types of stakeholders and their influence on particular initiatives. For example, Ring (2021) conducted a multi-case study examining the relationships among corporations, their communities, and sustainability initiatives. Recommendations for future research with ST include examining how to support the primary stakeholder of community – the most controversial of the primary stakeholders (Phillips et al., 2003).

Strengths and Limitations

Stakeholder theory is "one of the most prominent and well-known theories of business management" (Stieb, 2009, p. 402). It is unique in its attention to ethics and values as a primary focus for organizational management. ST's strength in research is in its "conceptual breadth;" however, this has yielded different definitions and has made ST subject to varied interpretations (Phillips et al., 2003, p. 479).

Stakeholder Theory's strength in practical application at corporations and organizations is in how the approach and philosophy encourage management to take a more holistic view of their organizations' impact – to look beyond economics to the broader society (Freeman et al., 2018). Additionally, ST focuses on critical qualities like ethics, integrity, generosity, openness, respect, alignment, and work to the benefit of as many stakeholders as possible.

As with many theories, definitional clarity remains a limitation of ST. Miles (2011) discovered that in 493 ST articles, there were 453 definitions of the theory indicating a level of conceptual breadth that may not be useful (Phillips et al., 2003, p. 479), and which could create a consistency problem in research, and a significant problem in empirical analysis (Miles, 2011). Further, there exist many distortions (e.g., stakeholders must be treated equally) and misinterpretations (e.g., ST requires changes to laws or is equivalent to socialism) (Phillips et al., 2003).

Practical application of ST has its limitations as well. Some have argued that focusing on any stakeholder not designed to increase revenue and profitability (e.g., the community), is a waste of time in corporations (Freeman et al., 2018). Another limitation of ST in practice is that if the "primary purpose of a firm is to create value for the stakeholders," it can be difficult to measure value-creation in terms other than economics (Freeman et al., 2018, p. 27). Others have argued that ST emphasizes the redistribution of power, decision-making, and reward across more than the investors, or shareholders (Stieb, 2009), which could have the downstream effect of less investment, which ultimately hurts the ability of the business to grow, and possibly to survive long term.

Key Theorists: Edward Freeman (Originating author); Thomas Donaldson; Yves Fassin; Robert Phillips.

Examples of Use in Research: Bridoux and Stoelhorst (2014); Ring (2021); Tang et al. (2015).

Resource-Based View

Definition and Overview

Resource-based View (RBV) provides a framework to examine why one firm or entity outperforms another and assumes that success comes from possessing or having access to necessary strategic resources (D'Oria et al., 2021). Resources are considered strategic when they support firms in attaining "sustained competitive advantage" (D'Oria et al., 2021, p. 1384). What a firm does with its resources is as important to performance as having resources (Haas & Hansen, 2005).

In an RBV framework, strategic resources are categorized into four types: Valuable, rare, inimitable, and non-substitutable. These four strategic resource types are useful for "empirical indicators" in research and are commonly referred to by the acronym VRIN (Barney, 1991, p. 99). For corporations, examples of these resources include innovations, equipment, real estate, and culture, as well as intangible or invisible assets such as reputation, labor skills, or knowledge. Strategic use of these kinds of resources can help a business gain or maintain competitive advantage. A strategy is considered a sustained or persistent competitive advantage if competitors cannot duplicate it to achieve the same ends.

RBV was originally developed to understand why one firm might out-perform another – a central question for strategic management, economic and organizational research, and for the purpose of improving organizational performance (Grant, 1996; Peteraf & Barney, 2003). RBV is an important and influential driver in understanding high-performance corporations (D'Oria et al., 2021).

RBV is considered a firm-focused theory. Firm-focused theories form a large branch of economics research and are designed to "explain or predict their [a firm's] structure and behaviors" and how they are related to a firm's goals or aims (Marshall, 1920; Grant, 1996, p. 109; Rutherford, 2012). See Figure 12.2 for examples of firm-focused theories.

RBV is intended to explain the connection between a business's key resources and its success or advantage amongst a field of peer competitors (Barney, 1991). Given this, RBV can be used to examine the connection between any number of resources or routines and potential corresponding outcomes. RBV can be applied to examine financial elements such as revenue, profitability, and share value as well. As a theoretical framework, RBV can be applied in many situations where organizations have resources, the capabilities to use them, and competition such as schools, governments, churches, sporting teams, and even individuals.

Theory of the firm	Theorist (Year)	Focus Summary
Neoclassical	Ricardo (1817)	Analyzing and predicting purchase and supply decisions by firms (Grant, 1996). In other words, how markets determine goods and services quantity and pricing for sale, assuming perfect and accurate information (Barney, 2001).
Behavioral, see also Bounded Rationality	Simon (1955) Cyert & March (1963) Loasby (1976) Bandura (1986)	The study of human and firm decision-making and behavior (Rutherford, 2012). *Bounded rationality* can be described as prudent decisions based on the practicality that there exists human limitations of knowledge, information, and skill in calculation (Cyert & March, 1962)
Evolutionary	Penrose (1959) Nelson & Winter (1982)	The analysis of the long-term collective knowledge, routines, and skills that are acquired and integrated by the firm and driving its direction, while its members come and go over time (Rutherford, 2012). Unique to Nelson and Winter (1982) is the idea that routines vary, are selected appropriate to the situation and times, and retains as their value persists (Barney, 2001).
Knowledge-based	Grant (1996) Nickerson & Zenger (2004)	Considered an extension of RBV (Pitelis, 2007). Focuses on knowledge as the key resource for the firm's successful performance (Grant, 1996)
Dynamic Capabilities	Teece et al., (1997)	Considered an extension of RBV (Pitelis, 2007). Focuses on the need for a firm and its managers to possess the ability to adapt and change with the industry, innovations, and competition (Teece et al., 1997)
Agency	Jensen & Meckling (1976)	Focuses on the relationship and cooperation between various parties within the organization such as the shareholders and managers of a firm (Rutherford, 2012)
Growth	Penrose (1959) Marris (1964)	Focuses on the firm's and manager's efforts to maximize its cumulative growth, including the impact of mergers and acquisitions (Rutherford, 2012).

Figure 12.2 Theories of the firm examples.

Background and Foundations

Resource-Based View is rooted in Edith Penrose's book *The Theory of the Growth of the Firm* (1959). Penrose was one of the first economists to discuss firm resources and the necessary, appropriate, and strategic use of those resources by management to drive successful outcomes, firm growth, and competitive advantage (Penrose, 1959; Barney et al., 2011; D'Oria et al., 2021). Economist Birger Wernerfelt (1984) coined the phrase, "resource-based view" and built on Penrose's work to develop Resource-based Theory (RBT) (Barney et al., 2011). Wernerfelt's RBT theory focused on the *internal* resources that gave a firm a competitive advantage, as opposed to a firm's products or other external forces on which most research was focused at that time (Wernerfelt, 1984; Barney et al., 2011;

D'Oria et al., 2021). RBT also emphasized resources or actions that competitors could not mimic in action or develop in skills.

Barney (1991) formalized RBV as a theory, building on Wernerfelt's RBT (Barney, 1991; D'Oria et al., 2021). Barney defined strategic resources as those controlled by the firm and in one of three primary categories: Human, physical, and organizational (Barney, 1991). Resources that are rare, valuable, inimitable, and non-substitutable are strategic and allow a firm sustained competitive advantage and high performance. RBV (resource-based view) and RBT (resource-based theory) are often used interchangeably in literature to represent the same concept, even by Barney himself (see Barney et al., 2011).

Additional theories have emerged and evolved from RBV, contributing to new understandings of firms' use of resources. For example, Teece and colleagues (1997) developed a theory of Dynamic Capability, which refers to how organizations adjust over time as the business and competitive landscape evolve (Teece et al., 1997). Dynamic Capability Theory explains how businesses manage the need to integrate change into their processes and how they use particular resources to adapt. The Knowledge-Based Theory of the Firm (Grant, 1996), which focuses on the role knowledge acquisition and use have on a firm's value (D'Oria et al., 2021), also evolved from RBV.

As RBV evolved, research drawing on RBV came to focus on the *use* of the resources, or how a firm and/or its managers make use of any assets that are rare, valuable, and/or non-substitutable to give that firm a competitive advantage. This latter clarification is referred to as *resource orchestration* (D'Oria et al., 2021). Resource orchestration includes different types of usage such as bundling, leveraging, and structuring. Bundling is merging multiple resources to create new capabilities, while leveraging is taking advantage of existing resources for use in new ways that benefit the company (D'Oria et al., 2021). Structuring is the careful management of resources; adding and removing them as necessary to create a competitive advantage.

Resources, actions, and outcomes or performance create what is known as the Strategic Resource-Action-Performance pathway (see Figure 12.3). In this framework, resources and actions interact to drive outcomes for firms.

Key Terms and Concepts

An **asset** is a tangible item or intangible idea, capability, process, or knowledge that has value and is able to earn income or increase performance and competitive advantage (Barney, 2001; Rutherford, 2012).

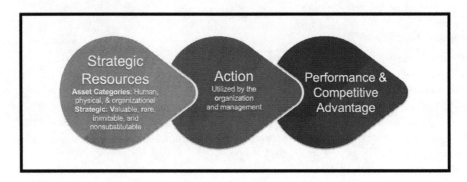

Figure 12.3 Strategic resource-action-performance pathway. Adapted from Barney (1991).

Capability is a firm's ability to manipulate or use resources to achieve performance goals (D'Oria et al., 2021).

Competitive advantage is when a firm is implementing a successful strategy that peers in the industry are not or cannot (Barney, 1991; Nothnagel, 2008).

Resources refer to all attributes and assets the firm controls and can access easily and regularly. Resources are used to drive competitive advantages, as well as positive stock and financial performance (Barney, 2001; D'Oria et al., 2021).

A resource has **value** when it can enable the improvement of a firm's efficiency or effectiveness rendering the firm to have increased competitive advantages (Barney, 1991; Nothnagel, 2008).

A resource has **rarity** when it is unique or scarce (Nothnagel, 2008).

In Research

RBV has primarily been applied in research on strategic management, economics, and business; however, RBV could be useful in any context in which there exists an entity, resources, action utilizing those resources, desired successful outcomes, and competitors for comparison. Alternate contexts could include non-profits, individuals, sports teams, education, churches, and governments. In RBV research, the focus is generally on measuring an entity's attributes, examining how they adapt and/or evolve over time, and exploring the impact of resources and strategic use on performance, competitive advantage, and successful outcomes (Barney, 2001).

As a business theory, RBV has been used to examine whether and how organizational culture (Barney, 1986) or other aspects of an organization, like identity (Fiol, 1991), corporate social responsibility (Mackey et al., 2007), CEO's (Castanias & Helfat, 1991), and projects (Ghapanchi et al., 2014), contribute to competitive advantage.

Strengths and Limitations

A notable strength of RBV is its testability (Barney & Mackey, 2005). Each of the resource types (human, physical, and organizational) and qualities (value, rarity, inimitability, and non-substitutability) is measurable against various aspects of firm performance, including financials, stock prices, and patents.

However, RBV has its critics. Crook et al. (2008) validated the direct link between strategic resources and performance but found that having strategic resources is not enough for successful outcomes. Kraaijenbrink et al. (2010) argued that RBV alone was static and unable to provide explanatory results. Priem and Butler (2001) note that the definition of resource value is tautological, or that the theoretical logic was flawed – specifically, the RBV argument that a resource is valuable and can lead to a competitive advantage, is saying the same thing two different ways. Still, Barney (2001) points out that research has demonstrated that a resource may have value (e.g., it is able to be monetized) but still may *not* provide a competitive advantage. Finally, there is also debate over whether RBV is a theory with verifiable predictions, or simply a view (Miller & Shamsie, 1996; Nothnagel, 2008).

Key Theorists: Edith Penrose (Theory foundation); Birger Wernerfelt (Originating author for RBV); Jay Barney (Originating author for RBT); Robert Grant; David Teece.

Examples of Use in Research: Ghapanchi et al. (2014); McWilliams and Siegel (2011); Miller and Shamsie (1996); Shan et al. (2019).

Technology Acceptance Model

Definition and Overview

Technology Acceptance Model (TAM) aims to explain and predict the perceptions and beliefs that feed a user's *intentions* to use, *actual* use, and *acceptance* of technology such as software, computers, and eventually phones, the cloud, and automobiles (Davis, 1986; Davis, 1989; Yousafzai et al., 2007). TAM was developed for the Information Systems or Information Technology (IS or IT) domain. As a theoretical perspective, TAM looks at how individuals' beliefs about technology use and user personality relate to and/or explain technology adoption intention (Girod et al., 2017; Gimpel et al., 2020). Additionally, TAM holds that technology acceptance is mediated by culture (Schepers & Wetzels, 2007).

The four primary constructs within TAM are perceived use (PU), perceived ease of use (PEOU), intention, and attitude. The focus of TAM research is on *use*, and a user's attitude and beliefs about *use*, rather than the attitude and beliefs about the technology itself. A user's PU of the technology and their PEOU are the two antecedents to technology acceptance in a TAM framework. PEOU naturally impacts PU (Davis, 1986; Davis, 1989; Yousafzai et al., 2007). For example, if a technology is difficult to use, it may be useful, but PU would decrease because of lower PEOU. PU was initially defined as the "subjective probability that using a specific application system will increase [a person's] job performance within an organizational context" (Davis, 1986. p. 985). However, as TAM began to be used as a framework to look at the broader acceptance of technology, PU has been redefined to encompass the expected impact of technology to improve the general quality of life (Dönmez-Turan & Kır, 2019).

TAM is useful for researchers interested in better understanding the adoption and use of technology (e.g., artificial intelligence, communication devices, social media, educational technology, etc.). Originally, TAM was intended to apply to a work setting (Davis, 1986). However, over time TAM has come to cover all technology use, such as communicating with others, online shopping, gaming, telemedicine, remote work and learning, or driving to work (Yousafzai et al., 2007; Tao et al., 2020; Feng et al., 2021). On the whole, TAM is a widely used, empirically supported model that can be used to study any type of technology adoption (Davis, 1989; Hu et al., 1999; Feng et al., 2021).

Background and Foundations

Fred Davis (1986) developed TAM to examine the adoption of word processing technology in his dissertation research at MIT (Massachusetts Institute of Technology). It was adapted from two popular psychology theoretical frameworks related to intention of use: Theory of Reasoned Action (TRA) (Fishbein & Ajzen, 1975) and Theory of Planned Behavior (TPB) (Ajzen, 1991; Yousafzai et al., 2007). Both TRA and TPB seek to explain how beliefs impact behavior (Gimpel et al., 2020). TRA explains the determinants of behavior (King & He, 2006), while TPB links attitudes, norms, and perceived control in behavior with intention and actual use. However, TAM differs from TRA and TBP in its focus on technology, and particularly its application in the field of computing and IS/IT.

TAM has evolved since its original development. Davis (1989) conducted additional research to verify the connection between beliefs and attitudes on intention to

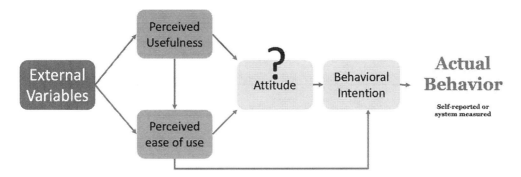

Figure 12.4 Original TAM model. Adapted from Davis (1989).

use, and ultimately removed attitude from the equation due to the "weak direct link" between PU and attitude, as opposed to the strong link between PU and intentions (Davis, 1989, p. 997) Indeed, TAM was found to be more parsimonious without the attitude mediator (Yousafzai et al., 2007). Arguably, in certain settings, technology usage is mandatory, so attitude may be irrelevant (Taylor & Todd, 1995). However, as technology use in daily life evolves, attitude may become more important as a behavior variable. PEOU, conversely, had minor impact on intentions. Therefore, as TAM developed further, the focus became the trade-off between PU and PEOU and understanding the influence of external variables on these two important determinants when it came to technology adoption, see Figure 12.4 (Yousafzai et al., 2007).

In the years since TAM was developed, other researchers have developed variants and extended versions, referred to as TAM2 and TAM3 (Feng et al., 2021). TAM2 was proposed by Davis and Venkatesh, another key researcher in the field of technology acceptance (Feng et al., 2021). They separated out attitude as a mediator and added in experience and voluntariness. TAM3, developed by Venkatesh and Bala (2008) added PEOU determinants of self-efficacy and facilitating conditions. Moving beyond TAM2 and TAM3, Venkatesh developed the Unified Theory of Acceptance and Use of Technology (UTAUT) through the merging of eight related models. See Figure 12.5 for further details on the development of TAM variation (Feng et al., 2021).

Key Terms and Concepts

Perceived Usefulness (PU) is the expected impact of technology to improve the quality of life (Dönmez-Turan & Kır, 2019). PU is also sometimes known as performance expectancy, or PE (Yang et al., 2022).

Perceived Ease of Use (PEOU) refers to the "degree to which the user expects the target system to be free of effort" (Davis, 1986. p. 985). PEOU is considered a critical factor in determining intentions to use technology (Yang et al., 2022).

Effort Expectancy (EE) is the amount of work involved to use technology, or how difficult it is to use (Yang et al., 2022).

Social Influence (SI): The level with which important friends, coaches, family, or co-workers are pressuring someone to use technology. This can also involve concern for one's image (Yang et al., 2022).

Researchers	Model	Variables & Factors
Davis (1986)	TAM – Technology Acceptance Model	PU, PEOU, Attitude, Intentions
Venkatesh & Davis (2000)	TAM2 - Technology Acceptance Model, version 2	PU, PEOU, Intentions, and Subjective Norm. No use of the attitude variable.
Venkatesh, Morris, Davis & Davis (2003)	UTAUT - Unified Theory of Acceptance and Use of Technology *Criticized for complexity and not factoring in personal characteristics, meta-UTAUT was developed to do so by Dwivedi et al., in 2019. Meta-UTAUT is considered to be simpler, yet more comprehensive to use (Yang et al., 2022)	The combination of eight models: TRA, TAM, a motivational model, TPB, a merged model of TAM+TPB, PC utilization, innovation diffusion theory, and social cognitive theory (SCT). This model adds the consideration of social influences, effort and performance expectancy, and facilitating conditions. No use of the attitude variable. Four determining factors: Performance expectancy, effort expectancy, social influence, and facilitating conditions – or infrastructure support (Yang et al., 2022)
Venkatesh & Bala (2008)	TAM3 Technology Acceptance Model, version 3	TAM2, plus determinants of PEOU such as self-efficacy and facilitating conditions. No use of the attitude variable.
Venkatesh, Thong & Xu (2012)	UTAUT2 - Unified Theory of Acceptance and Use of Technology, version 2	UTAUT, plus "hedonic motivations, price value, and habits" (Feng et al., 2021, p. 86)

Figure 12.5 Evolution of TAM. Adapted from Feng et al., 2021.

Attitude (AT) refers to individuals' positive or negative attitudes, or feelings, toward the use of technology in their specific context (Fishbein & Ajzen, 1975; Yang et al., 2022). As technology gained usage outside the workforce, attitude has become a more important factor in adoption.

Facilitating Conditions refers to the beliefs someone has about the infrastructure supporting their use of technology. Examples include IT support or a technology savvy family member (Gimpel et al., 2020).

In Research

Technology Acceptance Model has been widely used as a model to understand what causes user adoption of technology (Yousafzai et al., 2007). As TAM is comprised of many variables, researchers have often focused on a specific variable (or two) for a research study. It is rare for a study to deploy all of the variables (Yousafzai et al., 2007). TAM can be used to understand consumer and user behavior across many user populations (Davis, 1989), and has been used to explore a variety of technologies, ranging from Davis's (1989) original topic of word processors; to cell phones, email, databases, and spreadsheets; to more recent developments such as chatbots, telemedicine android robots, gaming, and OpenAI's ChatGPT (Chau & Hu, 2001; Yousafzai et al., 2007; Feng et al., 2021).

Strengths and Limitations

TAM is regarded as a "robust, parsimonious, and powerful model for predicting users' acceptance of technology," and as such, it remains a popular model in use today in the domain of technology adoption (Yousafzai et al., 2007, p. 251; Venkatesh, 2000; King & He, 2006). Scholars have argued that TAM has clear generalizability across time, cultures, and settings (Cook & Campbell, 1979; Yousafzai et al., 2007). Additionally, TAM also has a mature arsenal of psychometric instruments, which can be useful for researchers (Yousafzai et al., 2007).

One limitation of TAM is that there is scant research that examines all of the TAM factors together: External variables, PU, PEOU, intention to use, and actual use. Furthermore, not all relationships are validated in all studies – producing conflicting and inconsistent results (King & He, 2006). Additionally, TAM research is often self-reported by users, as opposed to objective reporting from systems recording actual usage. In a meta-analysis performed by Yousafzai et al. in 2006, only 9% of 145 TAM studies tested *actual* usage (2007). This can lead to weaker discriminant validity (Yousafzai et al., 2007). Research suggests that both reported and actual usage be measured. Finally, a major limitation of TAM is the complexity of extensions; so many as to render it chaotic. Bagozzi (2007), who was a coauthor with Davis (1989), has claimed that the model is at the precipice of crisis (Feng et al., 2021).

Key Theorists: Fred Davis (Originating author); Richard Bagozzi; Yogesh Dwivedi; Viswanath Venkatesh.

Examples of Use in Research: Cengiz and Bakırtaş (2020); Kamal et al. (2020); Scherer et al. (2019); Yang et al. (2022).

Uncanny Valley Theory

Definition and Overview

Uncanny Valley Theory, hereafter UV, posits that humans experience an affinity dip, or a feeling of eeriness as a robot or artificial intelligence character comes close to, but is not perfectly aligned with human features (Mori, 1970; Mori et al., 2012; Spassova, 2021). Further, the dip and peak are more extreme with movement involved, as opposed to still life (Mori et al., 2012). On the continuum of human likeness, from industrial robots to human-shaped robots (humanoids) to robots designed to copy humans as closely as possible (androids), UV is primarily related to android development (Groom et al., 2009; Ho & MacDorman, 2010). See Figure 12.6 for a hypothetical graphic depiction of this continuum.

Over time, UV has evolved into a theory of the more generic negative human reaction when perceiving something to be near human, but not quite (Burleigh et al., 2013). This can also apply to virtual agents, such as chatbots (Mimoun et al., 2012).

Uncanny Valley Theory relies on the mathematical concept of a *monotonically increasing function* (Mori et al., 2012). This function describes a relationship where "$y = f(x)$ increases continuously with the variable x" (Mori et al., 2012, p. 98). A simple example of a monotonically increasing function is car speed increasing as the pedal is pressed. Although the name may not be broadly used, this function is a widely understood phenomenon (Mori, 1970; Mori et al., 2012).

Building robots that closely approximate, if not look, feel, and behave exactly like humans, has long been a goal in the field of robotics (Mori et al., 2012). With each new

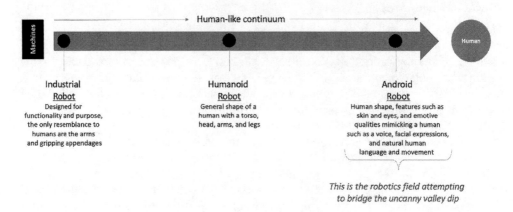

Figure 12.6 Human-like continuum. Adapted from Kageki (2012).

generation of robots, the field makes gains toward achieving this goal. Applying the common assumption based on the *monotonically increasing function,* one would expect that as a robot came to look more and more like a human, our affinity toward that robot *should* increase (Mori et al., 2012). However, there is an area on that upward curve, just before perfect mimicry of a healthy human, where affinity dips dramatically and changes to a feeling of eeriness or even revulsion (Mori, 1970). In other words, when a robot or android gets too close to looking or behaving like a human, our brains sense something is amiss, and we experience an adverse reaction. This affinity dip is known as the *uncanny valley.*

Mori also speculated that *movement* would further enhance the dip in affinity (Mori, 1970; Mori et al., 2012). As an illustration, imagine walking through a manufacturing floor filled with android robots. This might elicit feelings of uneasiness. However, if one of them *moves,* that uneasiness quickly intensifies into a sense of horror, panic, or revulsion (Mori et al., 2012). Interestingly, Mori suggests that roboticists do not attempt to scale the second peak to achieve high affinity. Instead, designers should purposefully build in a distancing effect to stop robot development after achieving the first peak and should not try to accurately mimic humans (Spassova, 2021). Mori postulates that people are more likely to be comfortable with near-humanlike appearance and behavior, but not too near (Mori, 1970).

Mori did not articulate why the UV effect occurred, he only observed that it occurs (Burleigh et al., 2013). While Mori initially put this theory out as a hypothetical, UV has been researched widely in the 50 years since, and has been proven empirically in various fields, including psychology, neurology, robotics, and animation, achieving "dogmatic status" (Burleigh et al., 2013, p. 759).

UV has been applied in fields where automation or animation is attempting to mimic the look and feel of a human (or an animal), such as movies, chatbots, prosthetics, toys, and video game design (Mori et al., 2012; Burleigh et al., 2013). Two basic trends have evolved in attempts to overcome UV in robotics, automation, and animation development (Spassova, 2021). The first trend is the attempt to achieve the affinity peak associated with human comfort with another healthy human. The second trend is to purposefully avoid trying to achieve perfect anthropomorphic creations (Mori et al., 2012; Spassova, 2021).

Uncanny Valley Theory is useful for researchers examining how individuals or groups of individuals react to and relate to automation and Artificial Intelligence (AI) in their contexts and in society.

Background and Foundations

UV was originally an intuitive observation made in an essay written by Japanese roboticist Masahiro Mori in 1970 (Mori, 1970; Mori et al., 2012). A professor from the Tokyo Institute of Technology, Mori was not stating an empirically-based conclusion founded in years of research, but was explaining something he had observed – a phenomenon Mori hypothesized would be more evident as the field of robotics developed.

UV was perfectly timed with the advent of robotics development, particularly robots designed to mimic humans physically and visually. Mori's article did not receive widespread attention until it was republished in a European art magazine (Reichardt, 1978). After the development of UV, researchers, psychologists, neurologists, and product designers have tried to prove, disprove, understand, and overcome the effects of UV associated with robots, animation, video game design, and chatbots (Schindler et al., 2017; Ciechanowski et al., 2019; Kim et al., 2022).

Since the advent of UV, others have developed benchmarks measuring qualities of embodied agents such as eeriness, likeability, anthropomorphism, social affect, warmth, familiarity, and rapport (Ho & MacDorman, 2010). The Godspeed indices measure five areas including animacy, perceived intelligence, anthropomorphism, perceived safety, and likeability (Bartneck et al., 2009; Ho & MacDorman, 2010). Each of these indices comprises sub-descriptions, or adjectives. Descriptors under the UV have evolved into sub-theories and variations, such as Embodied Agent Realism, on the theme of "digital, visual representations of an interface, often taking on human form" (Diel & MacDorman, 2021; Groom et al., 2009, p. 842).

Other sub-theories include Realism Maximization hypothesis, Social Threshold Model of Influence, Ethopoiea Theory, and Consistency hypothesis. Additionally, UV is also closely related to other robotics and computer acceptance theories (Groom et al., 2009; Mimoun et al., 2012). Technology Acceptance Model (TAM) and its iterations are one example (Davis, 1986). Additionally, TAM's evolution to UTAUT (unified theory of acceptance and use of technology) is a closely related theory (Venkatesh et al., 2003). See Figure 12.7 for details on additional UV sub-theories (Diel & MacDorman, 2021).

Key Terms and Concepts

Monotonically increasing function: A mathematical term describing a common phenomenon whereby $y = f(x)$ increases continuously with the variable x. For example, heat increases accordingly as the gas burner is turned up. This mathematical principle describes such a common occurrence that people assume it to be true in all circumstances, even when it is not (Mori, 1970; Mori et al., 2012). It may be that running burns calories and running faster might burn more calories, however, running faster might instead result in a fall or heart attack. Sometimes pausing, stopping, or retreating is the better course of action.

Theory	Description
Configural processing	UV is caused by perceived deviations in expected patterns associated with healthy humans (Chattopadhyay & MacDorman, 2016).
Atypicality	UV is caused by an atypical feature or quality that deviates from expectation (Katsyri et al., 2015).
Perceptual mismatch	UV is caused by characteristics or qualities of one category appearing in another category, such as a robot with a perfect human voice. (Meah & Moore, 2014)
Category uncertainty	UV is caused by uncertainty in an ambiguous entity, perhaps due to an entity straddling distinct categories such as the living and the dead (MacDorman & Ishiguro, 2006).
Novelty avoidance	UV is due to a human inclination to avoid what we do not know or understand (Sakasi et al., 2017).
Mate selection	Predicts UV by a human evolutionary mechanism utilized for determining mate selection (MacDorman & Ishiguro, 2006)
Psychopathy avoidance	Predicts UV by the perception of inauthentic cues in an effort to appropriately evaluate other humans (Tinwell et al., 2013).
Empathy	UV results in reaction to an empathy response, yet knowing the entity is not real or human (MacDorman & Entezari, 2015).
Threat avoidance	UV results as a perceived threat of danger and the need to avoid the entity (MacDorman & Ishiguro, 2006).

Figure 12.7 Uncanny valley: Nine sub-theories.

In Research

The use of UV in research has spread beyond the field of robotics. It is useful in analyzing anything that is attempting to mimic life, including animals. UV has also been used in neuroscience research, or why our brains experience this affinity dip phenomenon. For example, Schindler et al. (2017) studied the effect of artificial faces on the brain (See also Diel & MacDorman, 2021). Additionally, UV research in the field of psychology has aimed to understand "what makes us human" and what triggers eeriness and comfort (Mori et al., 2012, p. 100). Research can be divided into two groups: 1). Trying to validate or prove that UV exists; or 2). Trying to understand *why* UV exists – to better understand the mechanisms behind human behavior in order to better understand humans. This information feeds into the design and development of robotics and human-computer interactions (Diel & MacDorman, 2021).

Strengths and Limitations

A major strength of UV is its widespread understanding and acceptance in the field of computers, as well as its empirically-based support after 50 years of research (Diel & MacDorman, 2021). Due to the common and frequent use within media such as movies, even non-researchers or non-robotics experts have heard of the phrase "uncanny valley."

A significant criticism of UV is that "almost like" a human is hard to define (Spassova,

2021, p. 24). Individuals may have different tolerances for a robot's human-like behaviors depending on their morphology. It is unclear at what point a robot passes "too humanlike" and it would be challenging to define for the larger, global population because it is a subjective concept. For example, in Japan, hotels are deploying humanoid robots as front-desk concierges (Shin & Jeong, 2020), yet no matter how human-like a robot appeared, guests preferred an actual human due to the desire for authentic and sincere exchanges. Kim et al. (2022) demonstrated two different UVs, one for humanoid robots and another separate UV for non-humanoid robots. It might be necessary to distinguish between humanoid and non-humanoid robots (e.g., chatbots with a cartoonish versus a human face) when using UV as a framework.

Further, Kim et al. (2022) argued that *uncanny* might not be the best term to describe the negative emotions generated when humans are around robots. For example, creepy, scary, and eerie might better describe the responses from people. The term uncanny is generally considered a neutral term and therefore, the theory title itself might cause confusion in research or with research participants (Kim et al., 2022).

Key Theorists: Masahiro Mori (Originating author); Hiroshi Ishiguro; Karl MacDorman.

Examples of Use in Research: Ben Mimoun et al. (2012); Ciechanowski et al. (2019); Prakash and Rogers (2015); Shin and Jeong (2020).

Phronetic Theory

Definition and Overview

Phronetic theory is rooted in the Greek term *phronesis*, meaning knowledge based on practical wisdom as opposed to book or experiential knowledge (Flyvbjerg, 2001). Critical to the concept of phronesis is acting on knowledge in a way that benefits humankind or the greater good (Rowley & Gibbs, 2008). Phronetic theory also emphasizes the influence of power, ethics, and values on the application of practical wisdom and outcomes (Flyvbjerg, 2004; Delmar, 2006; Flyvbjerg, 2013). The application of phronetic theory or research methods is asking the question, "How was practical wisdom understood and applied in a challenging situation to drive for the best outcome for all parties?" (Flyvbjerg, 2001).

Modern organizations are highly dynamic, and decisions must be made even when uncertainty exists, which can increase risk. It is in these environments that practical judgment and insights are necessary to make decisions that are beneficial to the organization, as well as to all stakeholders. In other words, governments, societies, and businesses should not only consider the data, but should also apply wisdom in decision-making with positive intention. This overlay of applying wisdom with positive intent in decisions is the foundation of phronetic theory (Rowley & Gibbs, 2014).

Under the umbrella of phronetic theory, there is also qualitative phronetic methodology, where knowledge is sought for the purpose of practical application in the world in order to better communities and society. Research with a phronetic, or practical style, leans toward inclusion of stakeholders in determining research questions, collecting data, determining conclusions and positive outcomes. For example, a phronetic methodology in a study on employee benefits would include the employees, aim to understand the historical context of the situation, and seek to have a positive outcome for all parties.

Phronetic theory is particularly useful in research exploring elements of power, problems of ethics and values, and in which the context is critical (Delmar, 2006).

Phronetic theory can support researchers in conducting highly-contextualized research, and in ensuring issues of power are emphasized in research, while also "analyzing values, praxis and knowledge" (Tissaw, 2003, p. 279). Phronetic theory focused on the practical, real, and rational issues (Flyvbjerg, 2002); therefore, the highly-contextualized nature of case studies aligns particularly well with this framework. Examples from real-life are more effective at communicating knowledge than theories and methods (Flyvbjerg, 2004). Phronetic theory extends the concept of power and value in understanding decision-making, and also the concept of applying common sense, along with empirical input and craftmanship in the production of a physical product (Farthing, n.d.).

Phronesis can be expressed in social science research through conclusions that are not universally true, but contextually dependent (Spicker, 2011). Conclusions do not offer causal explanations, are non-universal, and are not naturally self-evident (Fitzpatrick, 2011). An example of a phronetic proposition from research is that while low-income individuals are likely to need the most healthcare, they are also the least likely to receive it (Spicker, 2011). Another example is that policies impacting society will likely fail to meet the constituents they were intended to reach.

Background and Foundations

Phronetic Theory is based on the Greek philosophical concept of *phronesis* as developed by Plato (427–347 BC) and Aristotle (384–322 BC). Phronesis invokes and applies practical wisdom and considers both what is good and bad for people (Aristotle, 2000). It is the application of common sense, practice judgment, or prudence (Flyvbjerg, 2004). Phronesis can also be described with an emphasis on ethics, or "ethical judgment that unfolds in practice" (Delmar, 2006, p. 22).

To understand phronetic theory, one must first understand the three intellectual virtues of the philosopher Aristotle – episteme, techne, and phronesis – as described in *The Nicomachean Ethics* (Delmar, 2006). Phronetic knowledge is based on experience, knowledge, and situational understanding that allows one to act and make decisions in a positive way for a given circumstance (Delmar, 2006). There is no current, modern equivalent for the Greek word *phronesis*, like there is for *episteme* (e.g., epistemology) and *techne* (e.g., technology), therefore, the term "phronetic" is used to describe research focusing on common sense founded in value-rationality.

While Aristotle may have used the term phronesis in his writings, Flyvbjerg (2001) introduced it into social science research intending to influence research conversations toward thoughtful analysis and consideration of society, rather than simply empirical research for research's sake (Tissaw, 2003). As Flyvbjerg explained, "the goal of phronetic research is to produce input to the ongoing social dialogue and praxis in a society, rather than to generate ultimate, unequivocally verified knowledge" (2001, p. 139).

Key Terms and Concepts

Episteme refers to scientific, empirical, analytical yet theoretical knowledge concerning context-free universals (Spicker, 2011). Epistemic knowledge remains true outside of location and time (Delmar, 2006; Flyvbjerg, 2004). During the Enlightenment, this type of knowledge became the ideal. Epistemic research is focused on revealing universal laws and truths and is based on analytical rationality – the "know why" (Delmar, 2006; Kirkeby, 2011).

Techne refers to intellectual know-how, craft, skill, or the art of judgment focused on application and production (Flyvbjerg, 2002; Kirkeby, 2011; Spicker, 2011). Techne is context-dependent; the application of knowledge toward something practical (Flyvbjerg, 2004). Where the field of chemistry might be considered epistemic, chemical engineering, or the application of chemistry, is considered technical (Spicker, 2011).

Phronesis refers to practical wisdom, ethics, and skill, common sense, or prudence. Phronesis balances scientific and instrumental rationality with value-rationality (Flyvbjerg, 2002; 2004). Phronetic knowledge comes from experience that builds tacit skills, ethics, and expertise based on values and context, where one becomes a virtuoso (Flyvbjerg, 2004; Kirkeby, 2011). Phronesis is concerned with applying knowledge in making the right choices (Spicker, 2011).

In Research

Flyvbjerg developed Phronetic Theory for application in urban planning research (Farthing, n.d.). As such, phronetic theory has been used in studies of aspects of urban planning, including transit, sustainability, and food planning within communities; real estate planning; and social sustainability. However, while originally used in urban planning, PT has expanded into other disciplines such as business, political science, and economics (Farthing, n.d.).

Phronetic theory is commonly applied in health-based research, as well as business and management, social policy, and political science research along with urban planning and architecture fields (Kirkeby, 2011). Anywhere there are elements of power, values, and an ethic of care, phronetic research can be applied (Briassoulis, 2022; Delmar, 2006). Flyvbjerg (2002) proposes four value-based questions as foundational in phronetic research planning: 1). Where are we going (e.g., with planning or design)? 2). Who gains and loses, and by which mechanisms of power? 3). Is this development desirable? 4). What, if anything, should we do about it? (Kirkeby, 2011; Briassoulis, 2022).

Examples of the use of phronetic theory or methodology in research include Hemmestad et al.'s (2010) research on sports coaching. Using the phronetic theory concepts of morality and power, complexity, and flexibility in actions of social contexts, their research sought to understand the activity of coaching and how to practically produce better experiences and outcomes. Dillard and Vinnari (2017) utilized phronetic theory in accounting research and explored its impact on society, and communities, particularly disadvantaged communities. Using a phronetic theory approach in a meta-analysis of 353 articles, Dillard and Vinnari (2017) searched for social, economic, and environmental injustices and how they might have been perpetuated by critical accounting practices.

A similar research methodology to Flyvberg's phronetic methodology is Rowley and Gibbs's pillars of a practically wise organization (Kuljak, 2014). The seven pillars include "understanding dynamic complexity; developing personal wisdom competency; deliberating toward ethical models; refreshing shared sustainable vision; group wisdom dynamics; deliberated praxis; and embodied learning" (Rowley & Gibbs, 2008, p. 85).

Strengths and Limitations

One of the notable strengths of phronetic theory is its ability to fill in the gap left by Kuhnian scientific and epistemic research in the natural sciences (Kuljak, 2014). Social science and the study of human behavior and interactions cannot always be reduced to predictive and measurable universals. Phronetic theory considers the ethics, values, power, care, and the right thing to do, "searching for answers practical, prudent, and capable of changing reality" (Kuljak, 2014, p. 79). Phronetic theory is useful for social understanding for the purpose of positive change.

A limitation of phronetic research is its lack of common understanding and use. While the terms are explainable, their application in research is more challenging to explain and understand. Further, phronetic theoretical conclusions or generalizations can be hard to validate due to differences in interpretation (Spicker, 2011). Additionally, Flyvbjerg has been criticized for placing too much emphasis on situational and pragmatic conclusions (Fitzpatrick, 2011). This heavy reliance on the context makes it difficult for future researchers to test and critique conclusions.

Key Theorists: Bent Flyvbjerg (Originating author); Stewart Clegg.

Examples of Use in Research: Delmar (2006); Dillard and Vinnari (2017); Hargreaves (2012); Hemmestad et al. (2010).

References

Ajzen, I. (1991). The theory of planned behavior. *Organizational Behavior and Human Decision Processes, 50*(2), 179–211. 10.1016/0749-5978(91)90020-T

Alkhafaji, A. F. (1989). *A stakeholder approach to corporate governance. Managing in a dynamic environment.* Quorum Books.

Amis, J., Barney, J., Mahoney, J. T., & Wang, H. (2020). Why we need a theory of stakeholder governance—and why this is a hard problem. *The Academy of Management Review, 45*(3), 499–503. 10.5465/amr.2020.0181

Aristotle. (2000). *Nicomachean ethics* (R. Crisp (Ed.)). Cambridge University Press.

Bagozzi, R. P. (2007). The legacy of the technology acceptance model and a proposal for a paradigm shift. *Journal of the Association for Information Systems, 8*(4), Article 12. https://aisel.aisnet.org/jais/vol8/iss4/12

Barney, J. B. (1986). Strategic factor markets: Expectations, luck, and business strategy. *Management Science, 32*(10), 1231–1241. 10.1287/mnsc.32.10.1231

Barney, J. B. (1991). Firm resources and sustained competitive advantage. *Journal of Management, 17*(1), 99–120. 10.1177/014920639101700108

Barney, J. B. (2001). Resource-based theories of competitive advantage: A ten-year retrospective on the resource-based view. *Journal of Management, 27*(6), 643–650. 10.1016/S0149-2063(01)00115-5

Barney, J. B., Ketchen, D. J., & Wright, M. (2011). The future of resource-based theory: Revitalization or decline? *Journal of Management, 37*(5), 1299–1315. 10.1177/0149206310391805

Barney, J. B., & Mackey, T. B. (2005). Testing resource-based theory. In Ketchen, Bergh & Dhanaraj (Eds.), *Research methodology in strategy and management* (pp. 1–13). Emerald. 10.1016/S1479-8387(05)02001-1

Bartneck, C., Kulic, D., Croft, E., & Zoghbi, S. (2009). Measurement instruments for the anthropomorphism, animacy, likeability, perceived intelligence, and perceived safety of robots. *International Journal of Social Robotics, 1*(1), 71–81. 10.1007/s12369-008-0001-3

Ben Mimoun, M. S., Poncin, I., & Garnier, M. (2012). Case study—Embodied virtual agents: An analysis on reasons for failure. *Journal of Retailing and Consumer Services, 19*(6), 605–612. 10.1016/j.jretconser.2012.07.006

Briassoulis, H. (2022). The making of good public plans phronesis, phronetic planning research and assemblage thinking. *Planning Theory*, 147309522211025. 10.1177/14730952221102533

Bridoux, F., & Stoelhorst, J. W. (2014). Microfoundations for stakeholder theory: Managing stakeholders with heterogeneous motives. *Strategic Management Journal*, 35(1), 107–125. http://www.jstor.org/stable/24037212

Burleigh, T. J., Schoenherr, J. R., & Lacroix, G. L. (2013). Does the uncanny valley exist? An empirical test of the relationship between eeriness and the human likeness of digitally created faces. *Computers in Human Behavior*, 29(3), 759–771. 10.1016/j.chb.2012.11.021

Castanias, R. P., & Helfat, C. E. (1991). Managerial resources and rents. *Journal of Management*, 17(1), 155–171. 10.1177/014920639101700110

Cengiz, E., & Bakırtaş, H. (2020). Technology acceptance model 3 in understanding employee's cloud computing technology. *Global Business Review*, 97215092095717. 10.1177/097215092 0957173

Chau, P. Y. K., & Hu, P. J. (2001). Information technology acceptance by individual professionals: A model comparison approach. *Decision Sciences*, 32(4), 699–719. 10.1111/j.1540-5915.2001. tb00978.x

Ciechanowski, L., Przegalinska, A., Magnuski, M., & Gloor, P. (2019). In the shades of the uncanny valley: An experimental study of human–chatbot interaction. *Future Generation Computer Systems*, 92, 539–548. 10.1016/j.future.2018.01.055

Clegg, S. (2008). Bent Flyvbjerg: Power and project management – an appreciation. *International Journal of Managing Projects in Business*, 1(3), 428–431. 10.1108/17538370810883855

Clegg, S., Flyvbjerg, B., & Haugaard, M. (2014). Reflections on phronetic social science: A dialogue between Stewart Clegg, Bent Flyvbjerg and Mark Haugaard. *Journal of Political Power*, 7(2), 275–306. 10.1080/2158379X.2014.929259

Cook, T. D., & Campbell, D. T. (1979). *Quasi-experimentation: Design & analysis issues for field settings*. Houghton Mifflin.

Crook, T. R., Ketchen Jr, D. J., Combs, J. G., & Todd, S. Y. (2008). Strategic resources and performance: A meta-analysis. *Strategic Management Journal*, 29(11), 1141–1154. 10.1002/smj.703

Cyert, R. M., & March, J. G. (1963). *A behavioral theory of the firm* (2nd ed.). Prentice Hall.

Davis, F. (1986). *A technology acceptance model for empirically testing new end-user information systems: Theory and results* (Doctoral dissertation). MIT Sloan School of Management.

Davis, F. (1989). Perceived usefulness, perceived ease of use, and user acceptance of information technology. *MIS Quarterly*, 13(3), 319–340. 10.2307/249008

Davis, F. D., Bagozzi, R. P., & Warshaw, P. R. (1989). User acceptance of computer technology: A comparison of two theoretical models. *Management Science*, 35(8), 982–1003. 10.1287/mnsc.35. 8.982

Davis, F. D., & Venkatesh, V. (1996). A critical assessment of potential measurement biases in the technology acceptance model: Three experiments. *International Journal of Human-Computer Studies*, 45(1), 19–45. 10.1006/ijhc.1996.0040

Delmar, C. (2006). Caring-ethical phronetic research: Epistemological considerations. *International Journal for Human Caring*, 10(1), 22–27. 10.20467/1091-5710.10.1.22

Diel, A., & MacDorman, K. F. (2021). Creepy cats and strange high houses: Support for configural processing in testing predictions of nine uncanny valley theories. *Journal of Vision*, 21(4), 1. 10.1167/jov.21.4.1

Diel, A., Weigelt, S., & MacDorman, K. F. (2022). A meta-analysis of the uncanny valley's independent and dependent variables. *ACM Transactions on Human-Robotic Interaction*, 11(1), 1–33. 10.1145/3470742

Dillard, J., & Vinnari, E. (2017). A case study of critique: Critical perspectives on critical accounting. *Critical Perspectives on Accounting*, 43, 88–109. 10.1016/j.cpa.2016.09.004

Donaldson, T., & Preston, L. (1995). The stakeholder theory of the corporation—concepts, evidence, and implications. *The Academy of Management Review*, 20(1), 65–91. 10.5465/AMR. 1995.9503271992

Dönmez-Turan, A., & Kır, M. (2019). User anxiety as an external variable of technology acceptance model: A meta-analytic study. *Procedia Computer Science, 158*, 715–724. 10.1016/j.procs.2019.09.107

D'Oria, L., Crook, T. R., Ketchen, D. J., Sirmon, D. G., & Wright, M. (2021). The evolution of resource-based inquiry: A review and meta-analytic integration of the strategic resources–actions–performance pathway. *Journal of Management, 47*(6), 1383–1429. 10.1177/0149206321994182

Dwivedi, Y. K., Rana, N. P., Jeyaraj, A., Clement, M., & Williams, M. D. (2019). Re-examining the unified theory of acceptance and use of technology (UTAUT): Towards a revised theoretical model. *Information Systems Frontiers, 21*, 719–734. 10.1007/s10796-017-9774-y

Farthing, S. (n.d.). Phronetic planning research: So what? [Abstract]. https://www.gla.ac.uk/media/Media_35731_smxx.pdf.

Fassin, Y. (2009). The stakeholder model refined. *Journal of Business Ethics, 84*(1), 113–135. 10.1007/s10551-008-9677-4

Fassin, Y. (2011). A dynamic perspective in Freeman's stakeholder model. *Journal of Business Ethics, 96*(Suppl 1), 39–49. 10.1007/s10551-011-0942-6

Feng, G. C., Su, X., Lin, Z., He, Y., Luo, N., & Zhang, Y. (2021). Determinants of technology acceptance: Two model-based meta-analytic reviews. *Journalism & Mass Communication Quarterly, 98*(1), 83–104. 10.1177/1077699020952400

Fiol, C. M. (1991). Managing culture as a competitive resource: An identity-based view of sustainable competitive advantage. *Journal of Management, 17*(1), 191–211. 10.1177/014920639101700112

Fishbein, M., & Ajzen, I. (1975). *Belief, attitude, intention, and behavior: An introduction to theory and research*. Addison-Wesley.

Fishbein, M., & Ajzen, I. (2010). *Predicting and changing behavior: The reasoned action approach*. Psychology Press.

Fitzpatrick, T. (2011). Response 2: Social science as phronesis? The potential contradictions of a phronetic social policy. *Journal of Social Policy, 40*(1), 31–39. 10.1017/S0047279410000346

Flyvbjerg, B. (2001). *Making social science matter: Why social inquiry fails and how it can succeed again*. Cambridge University Press.

Flyvbjerg, B. (2002). Bringing power to planning research: One researcher's praxis story. *Journal of Planning Education and Research, 21*(4), 353–366. 10.1177/07356X021004002

Flyvbjerg, B. (2004). Phronetic planning research: Theoretical and methodological reflections. *Planning Theory & Practice, 5*(3), 283–306. 10.1080/1464935042000250195

Flyvbjerg, B. (2013). Five misunderstandings about case-study research. In P. Atkinson & S. Delamont (Eds.), *Qualitative inquiry* (pp. 219–245). Sage. 10.1177/1077800405284363

Freeman, R. E. (1984). *Stakeholder management: Framework and philosophy*. Pitman.

Freeman, R. E. (1999). Divergent stakeholder theory. *The Academy of Management Review, 24*(2), 233–236. 10.5465/amr.1999.1893932

Freeman, R. E. (2010). *Stakeholder theory*. Cambridge University Press.

Freeman, R. E., Dmytriyev, S. D., & Phillips, R. A. (2021). Stakeholder theory and the resource-based view of the firm. *Journal of Management, 47*(7), 1757–1770. 10.1177/0149206321993576

Freeman, R., Harrison, J., & Zyglidopoulos, S. (2018). Stakeholder theory: Concepts and strategies. In *Elements in organization theory*. Cambridge University Press. 10.1017/9781108539500

Freeman, R. E., Martin, K., & Parmar, B. (2007). Stakeholder capitalism. *Journal of Business Ethics, 74*(4), 303–314. 10.1007/s10551-007-9517-y

Freeman, R. E., Phillips, R., & Sisodia, R. (2020). Tensions in stakeholder theory. *Business & Society, 59*(2), 213–231. 10.1177/0007650318773750

Friedman, M. (1962). *Capitalism and freedom*. University of Chicago Press.

Friedman, A. L., & Miles, S. (2002). Developing stakeholder theory. *Journal of Management Studies, 39*(1), 1–21. 10.1111/1467-6486.00280

Ghapanchi, A. H., Wohlin, C., & Aurum, A. (2014). Resources contributing to gaining competitive advantage for open source software projects: An application of resource-based theory. *International Journal of Project Management, 32*(1), 139–152. 10.1016/j.ijproman.2013.03.002

Gimpel, H., Graf, V., & Graf-Drasch, V. (2020). A comprehensive model for individuals' acceptance of smart energy technology – A meta-analysis. *Energy Policy, 138*, 1–11. 10.1016/j.enpol.2019.111196

Girod, B., Mayer, S., & Naegele, F. (2017). Economic versus belief-based models: Shedding light on the adoption of novel green technologies. *Energy Policy, 101*, 415–426. 10.1016/j.enpol.2016.09.065

Grant, R. M. (1996). Toward a knowledge-based theory of the firm. *Strategic Management Journal, 17*(S2), 109–122. 10.1002/smj.4250171110

Groom, V., Nass, C., Chen, T., Nielsen, A., Scarborough, J. K., & Robles, E. (2009). Evaluating the effects of behavioral realism in embodied agents. *International Journal of Human-Computer Studies, 67*(10), 842–849. 10.1016/j.ijhcs.2009.07.001

Haas, M. R., & Hansen, M. T. (2005). When using knowledge can hurt performance: The value of organizational capabilities in a management consulting company. *Strategic Management Journal, 26*(1), 1–24. 10.1002/smj.429

Hargreaves, T. (2012). Questioning the virtues of pro-environmental behaviour research: Towards a phronetic approach. *Geoforum, 43*(2), 315–324. 10.1016/j.geoforum.2011.09.006

Hemmestad, L. B., Jones, R. L., & Standal, Ø. F. (2010). Phronetic social science: A means of better researching and analysing coaching? *Sport, Education and Society, 15*(4), 447–459. 10.1080/13573322.2010.514745

Ho, C., & MacDorman, K. F. (2017). Measuring the uncanny valley effect. *International Journal of Social Robotics, 9*(1), 129–139. 10.1007/s12369-016-0380-9

Ho, C., & MacDorman, K. F. (2010). Revisiting the uncanny valley theory: Developing and validating an alternative to the Godspeed indices. *Computers in Human Behavior, 26*(6), 1508–1518. 10.1016/j.chb.2010.05.015

Holzer, B. (2008). Turning stakeseekers into stakeholders: A political coalition perspective on the politics of stakeholder influence. *Business & Society, 47*(1), 50–67. 10.1177/0007650307306341

Hu, P. J., Chau, P. Y. K., Sheng, O. R. L., & Tam, K. Y. (1999). Examining the technology acceptance model using physician acceptance of telemedicine technology. *Journal of Management Information Systems, 16*(2), 91–112. 10.1080/07421222.1999.11518247

Jensen, M. C., & Meckling, W. H. (1976). Theory of the firm: Managerial behavior, agency costs and ownership structure. *Journal of Financial Economics, 3*(4), 305–360. 10.1016/0304-405X(76)90026-X

Jones, T. M., & Wicks, A. C. (1999). Convergent stakeholder theory. *The Academy of Management Review, 24*(2), 206–221. 10.5465/amr.1999.1893929

Kageki, N. (2012). An uncanny mind: Masahiro Mori on the uncanny valley and beyond: An interview with the Japanese professor who came up with the uncanny valley of robotics. IEEE Spectrum. https://spectrum.ieee.org/an-uncanny-mind-masahiro-mori-on-the-uncanny-valley

Kamal, S. A., Shafiq, M., & Kakria, P. (2020). Investigating acceptance of telemedicine services through an extended technology acceptance model (TAM). *Technology in Society, 60*, 101212. 10.1016/j.techsoc.2019.101212

Katsyri, J., Forger, K., Makarainen, M., & Takala, T. (2015). A review of empirical evidence on different uncanny valley hypotheses: Support for perceptual mismatch as one road to the valley of eeriness. *Frontiers in Psychology, 6*, 390, 10.3389/fpsyg.2015.00390

Kim, B., de Visser, E., & Phillips, E. (2022). Two uncanny valleys: Re-evaluating the uncanny valley across the full spectrum of real-world human-like robots. *Computers in Human Behavior, 135*, 107340. 10.1016/j.chb.2022.107340

King, W. R., & He, J. (2006). A meta-analysis of the technology acceptance model. *Information & Management, 43*(6), 740–755. 10.1016/j.im.2006.05.003

Kirkeby, I. M. (2011). Transferable knowledge: An interview with Bent Flyvbjerg. *Arq, 15*(1), 9–14. 10.1017/S1359135511000315

Kraaijenbrink, J., Spender, J. C., & Groen, A. J. (2010). The resource-based view: A review and assessment of its critiques. *Journal of Management, 1*(36), 349–372. 10.1177/0149206309350775

Kuljak, M. (2014). Phronetic research—methodology that matters to corporate governance research. *Montenegrin Journal of Economics, 10*(2), 79. http://www.repec.mnje.com/mje/2014/v10-n02/mje_2014_v10-n02-a17.pdf

Loasby, B. J. (1976). *Choice, complexity, and ignorance: An enquiry into economic theory and the practice of decision-making.* Cambridge University Press.

MacDorman, K. F., & Ishiguro, H. (2006). The uncanny advantage of using androids in social and cognitive science research. *Interaction Studies, 7*(3), 297–337, 10.1075/is.7.3.03mac

MacDorman, K. F., & Entezari, S. (2015). Individual differences predict sensitivity to the uncanny valley. *Interaction Studies, 16*(2), 141–172, 10.1075/is.16.2.01mac

MacDorman, K. F., & Chattopadhyay, D. (2016). Reducing consistency in human realism increases the uncanny valley effect; increasing category uncertainty does not. *Cognition, 146,* 190–205, 10.1016/j.cognition.2015

Mackey, A., Mackey, T. B., & Barney, J. B. (2007). Corporate social responsibility and firm performance: Investor preferences and corporate strategies. *The Academy of Management Review, 32*(3), 817–835. 10.5465/AMR.2007.25275676

Marshall, A. (1920). *Principles of economics* (8th ed.) Macmillan.

McWilliams, A., & Siegel, D. S. (2011). Creating and capturing value: Strategic corporate social responsibility, resource-based theory, and sustainable competitive advantage. *Journal of Management, 37*(5), 1480–1495. 10.1177/0149206310385696

Miles, S. (2011). Stakeholder: Essentially contested or just confused? *Journal of Business Ethics, 108*(3), 285–298. 10.1007/s10551-011-1090-8

Miller, D., & Shamsie, J. (1996). The resource-based view of the firm in two environments: The Hollywood film studios from 1936 to 1965. *Academy of Management Journal, 39*(3), 519–543. 10.2307/256654

Mitchell, R., Agle, B., & Wood, D. (1997). Toward a theory of stakeholder identification and salience: Defining the principle of who and what really counts. *Academy of Management Review, 22*(4), 853–888. 10.2307/259247

Mori, M. (1970). The uncanny valley. *Energy, 7*(4), 33–35. http://ieeexplore.ieee.org/xpl/tocresult.jsp?isnumber=6213218&punumber=100

Mori, M. (2005). On the uncanny valley. In *Proc. Humanoids 2005 Workshop: Views of the Uncanny Valley,* Tsukuba, Japan, December 2005. http://www.androidscience.com/theuncannyvalley/proceedings2005/MoriMasahiro22August2005.html

Mori, M., MacDorman, K. F., & Kageki, N. (2012). The uncanny valley [from the field]. *IEEE Robotics & Automation Magazine, 19*(2), 98–100. 10.1109/MRA.2012.2192811

Nelson, R. R., & Winter, S. G. (1982). *An evolutionary theory of economic change.* Harvard University Press.

Nickerson, J. A., & Zenger, T. R. (2004). A knowledge-based theory of the firm – the problem-solving perspective. *Organization Science, 15*(6), 617–632. 10.1287/orsc.1040.0093

Nothnagel, K. (2008). *Empirical research within resource-based theory: A meta-analysis of the central propositions* (1st ed.). Gabler. 10.1007/978-3-8349-9830-9

Penrose, E. (1959). *The theory of the growth of the firm.* Oxford University Press.

Peteraf, M. A., & Barney, J. B. (2003). Unraveling the resource-based tangle. *Managerial and Decision Economics, 24*(4), 309–323. 10.1002/mde.1126

Phillips, R. (2003). *Stakeholder theory and organizational ethics.* Berrett-Koehler.

Phillips, R., Freeman, R. E., & Wicks, A. C. (2003). What stakeholder theory is not. *Business Ethics Quarterly, 13*(4), 479–502. 10.5840/beq200313434

"Phronesis." (2018). *The Oxford Review Encyclopaedia of Terms*. Retrieved from https://www.oxford-review.com/oxford-review-encyclopaedia-terms/phronesis-definition-meaning/

Pitelis, C. N. (2007). A behavioral resource-based view of the firm: The synergy of Cyert and March (1963) and Penrose (1959). *Organization Science*, 18(3), 478–490. 10.1287/orsc.1060.0244

Prakash, A., & Rogers, W. A. (2015). Why some humanoid faces are perceived more positively than others: Effects of human-likeness and task. *International Journal of Social Robotics*, 7(2), 309–331. 10.1007/s12369-014-0269-4

Priem, R., & Butler, J. (2001). Tautology in the resource-based view and the implications of externally determined resource value: Further comments. *The Academy of Management Review*, 26(1), 57–66. 10.2307/259394

Reichardt, J. (1978). *Robots: Fact, fiction, and prediction*. Viking.

Ricardo, D. (1817). *Principles of political economy and taxation*. J. Murray.

Ring, J. E. (2021). Operationalizing sustainable development, stakeholder theory, corporate social responsibility to improve community engagement outcomes. *Journal of Sustainable Development*, 15(1), 1. 10.5539/jsd.v15n1p1

Rowley, J., & Gibbs, P. (2008). From learning organization to practically wise organization. *The Learning Organization*, 15(5), 356–372. 10.1108/09696470810898357

Rutherford, D. (2012). *Routledge dictionary of economics*. Routledge.

Sasaki, K., Ihaya, K., & Yamada, Y. (2017). Avoidance of novelty contributes to the uncanny valley. *Frontiers in Psychology*, 8, 1792. 10.3389/fpsyg.2017.01792

Savage, G. T., Nix, T. W., Whitehead, C. J., & Blair, J. D. (1991). Strategies for assessing and managing organizational stakeholders. *Executive (Ada, Ohio)*, 5(2), 61–75. http://www.jstor.org/stable/4165008

Schepers, J., & Wetzels, M. (2007). A meta-analysis of the technology acceptance model: Investigating subjective norm and moderation effects. *Information & Management*, 44(1), 90–103. 10.1016/j.im.2006.10.007

Scherer, R., Siddiq, F., & Tondeur, J. (2019). The technology acceptance model (TAM): A meta-analytic structural equation modeling approach to explaining teachers' adoption of digital technology in education. *Computers and Education*, 128, 13–35. 10.1016/j.compedu.2018.09.009

Schindler, S., Zell, E., Botsch, M., & Kissler, J. (2017). Differential effects of face-realism and emotion on event-related brain potentials and their implications for the uncanny valley theory. *Scientific Reports*, 7(1), 45003-45003, 10.1038/srep45003

Schwab, K. (2021). *Stakeholder capitalism: A global economy that works for progress, people and planet*. John Wiley & Sons, Inc.

Shan, S., Luo, Y., Zhou, Y., & Wei, Y. (2019). Big data analysis adaptation and enterprises' competitive advantages: The perspective of dynamic capability and resource-based theories. *Technology Analysis & Strategic Management*, 31(4), 406–420. 10.1080/09537325.2018.1516866

Shin, H. H. & Jeong, M. (2020). Guests' perceptions of robot concierge and their adoption intentions. *International Journal of Contemporary Hospitality Management*, 32(8), 2613–2633. 10.1108/IJCHM-09-2019-0798

Simon, H. A. (1955). A behavioral model of rational choice. *The Quarterly Journal of Economics*, 69(1), 99–118. 10.2307/1884852

Spassova, K. (2021). Mimetic machines in the uncanny valley. *Identities*, 18(1–2), 22–33. 10.51151/identities.v18i1-2.482

Spicker, P. (2011). Generalisation and phronesis: Rethinking the methodology of social policy. *Journal of Social Policy*, 40(1), 1–19. 10.1017/S0047279410000334

Stieb, J. A. (2009). Assessing Freeman's stakeholder theory. *Journal of Business Ethics*, 87(3), 401–414. 10.1007/s10551-008-9928-4

Tang, Y., Qian, C., Chen, G., & Shen, R. (2015). How CEO hubris affects corporate social (ir)responsibility. *Strategic Management Journal*, 36(9), 1338–1357. 10.1002/smj.2286

Tao, D., Wang, T., Wang, T., Zhang, T., Zhang, X., & Qu, X. (2020). A systematic review and meta-analysis of user acceptance of consumer-oriented health information technologies. *Computers in Human Behavior, 104*, 106147. 10.1016/j.chb.2019.09.023

Taylor, S., & Todd, P. A. (1995). Understanding information technology usage: A test of competing models. *Information Systems Research, 6*(2), 144–176. 10.1287/isre.6.2.144

Teece, D. J. (1986). Profiting from technological innovation: Implications for integration, collaboration, licensing and public policy. *Research Policy, 15*(6), 285–305. 10.1016/0048-7333(86)90027-2

Teece, D. J., Pisano, G., & Shuen, A. (1997). Dynamic capabilities and strategic management. *Strategic Management Journal, 18*(7), 509–533. 10.1002/(SICI)1097-0266(199708)18:7<509::AID-SMJ882>3.0.CO;2-Z

Tinwell, A., Nabi, D. A., & Charlton, J. P. (2013). Perception of psychopathy and the uncanny valley in virtual characters. *Computers in Human Behavior, 29*(4), 1617–1625, 10.1016/j.chb.2013.01.008

Tissaw, M. (2003). Emancipative social science: Theory and method, reflexivity and power, values and foundations. *Theory & Psychology, 13*(2), 275–284. 10.1177/0959354303013002007

Venkatesh, V. (2000). Determinants of perceived ease of use: Integrating control, intrinsic motivation, and emotion into the technology acceptance model. *Information Systems Research, 11*(4), 342–365. 10.1287/isre.11.4.342.11872

Venkatesh, V., & Bala, H. (2008). Technology acceptance model 3 and a research agenda on interventions. *Decision Sciences, 39*(2), 273–315. 10.1111/j.1540-5915.2008.00192.x

Venkatesh, V., & Davis, F. D. (2000). A theoretical extension of the technology acceptance model: Four longitudinal field studies. *Management Science, 46*(2), 186–204. 10.1287/mnsc.46.2.186.11926

Venkatesh, V., Morris, M. G., Davis, G. B., & Davis, F. D. (2003). User acceptance of information technology: Toward a unified view. *MIS Quarterly, 27*(3), 425–478. 10.2307/30036540

Venkatesh, V., Thong, J. Y., & Xu, X. (2012). Consumer acceptance and use of information technology: Extending the unified theory of acceptance and use of technology. *MIS Quarterly, 36*(1), 157–178. 10.2307/41410412

Wernerfelt, B. (1984). A resource-based view of the firm. *Strategic Management Journal, 5*(2), 171–180. 10.1002/smj.4250050207

Wernerfelt, B. (1989). From critical resources to corporate strategy. *Journal of General Management, 14*(3), 4–12. 10.1177/030630708901400301

Wernerfelt, B. (2016). *Adaptation, specialization, and the theory of the firm: Foundations of the resource-based view*. Cambridge University Press. 10.1017/CBO9781316466872

Yang, C., Li, C., Yeh, T., & Chang, Y. (2022). Assessing older adults' intentions to use a smartphone: Using the meta-unified theory of the acceptance and use of technology. *International Journal of Environmental Research and Public Health, 19*(9), 5403. 10.3390/ijerph19095403

Yousafzai, S. Y., Foxall, G. R., & Pallister, J. G. (2007). Technology acceptance: A meta-analysis of the TAM: Part 1. *Journal of Modelling in Management, 2*(3), 251–280. 10.1108/17465660710834453

Index

Note: Page numbers in *italic* indicate figures

Abel, J.R. 160, 163
Abes, E.S. 38, 39, 40
Abisuga, A.O. 107–110
Acker, J. 35
Adebayo, C.T. 29–30
Adler, P.A. 55, 56
Adler, P.S. 94–95, 176, 179
Ahlfinger, N.R. 79
Ainsworth, M. 65–67
Ajzen, I. 194, 196
Akerlof, G. 160
Akkoyunlu-Wigley, A. 163
Aksom, H. 53
Al Adwan, A.S. 159
Alex, T. 138
Alford, R. 2–3, 5
Alkhafaji, A.F. 188
Alsos, G.A. 159
Althusser, L. 134
Altman, D. 141
Alvarez Cáccamo, C. 74
Amaldoss, W. 156
American Psychological Association 76
Amis, J. 186, 188
Andersen, J.A. 115, 117
Anderson, K.L. 35
Anderson, L. 95, 97
Anderson, M.L. 95, 98
Anderton, C.L. 62, 64
Andreweg, R.B. 153
Anfara, V.A. 15
Ang, S. 162
Anicich, E.M. 71
Annette, J. 144
Anonymous 138
Anthony S.B. 34
Anyon, Y. 29, 30
Araujo, A. 157
Argyris, C. 179–182
Ariely, D. 134
Aristotle 202

Arndt, S. 178
Arnold, K.D. 88
Arvidsson, S. 134
Atkins, J.W. 139
attachment theory 64–67; attachment-related
    anxiety 64, 65; attachment-related
    avoidance 64, 65–66; foundations of 65;
    four stages of 64; human attachment 66;
    research within 66; strengths and
    limitations 66
Autor, D.H. 162, 163
Avolio, B.J. 107, 111, 114, 116–117

Babcock, G. 138
Bagger, J. 162
Bagozzi, R.P. 197
Bagwell, L.S. 159
Bakermans-Kranenburg, M.J. 64
Bakirtas, H. 197
Bala, H. 195
Bălău-Ariton, M. 156
Bandura, A. 87, 115
Bankoff, G. 144
Barber, S.J. 76
Barker, J.L. 159
Barkey, F.A. 130
Barney, J.B. 190–193
Bartholomew, K. 64–65
Bartlett, C.A. 176
Bartneck, C. 199
Barrow, J. 107, 108
Bass, B.M. 107, 114, 116–117
Basu, D. 133
Baumol, W.J. 131, 134
Beard, C.A. 141
Beck, L. 66–67
Becker, G. 161–162
Beckert, J. 52–53
Bedard, K. 162
Beechey, V. 35
Bekmeier-Feuerhahn, S. 175

Made in the USA
Las Vegas, NV
10 February 2024

85474350R00129